ZIONISM AND THE ROADS NOT TAKEN

THE MODERN JEWISH EXPERIENCE
Paula Hyman and Deborah Dash Moore, editors

Zionism and the Roads Not Taken

―――――

Rawidowicz, Kaplan, Kohn

―――――

NOAM PIANKO

INDIANA UNIVERSITY PRESS

Bloomington and Indianapolis

This book is a publication of

Indiana University Press
601 North Morton Street
Bloomington, Indiana 47404-3797 USA

www.iupress.indiana.edu

Telephone orders 800-842-6796
Fax orders 812-855-7931
Orders by e-mail iuporder@indiana.edu

∞ The paper used in this publication meets the minimum requirements of the American National Standard for Information Sciences—Permanence of Paper for Printed Library Materials, ANSI Z39.48-1992.

Manufactured in the United States of America

LIBRARY OF CONGRESS CATALOGING-IN-PUBLICATION DATA

Pianko, Noam.
   Zionism and the roads not taken : Rawidowicz, Kaplan, Kohn / Noam Pianko.
      p.   cm. — (The modern Jewish experience)
   Includes bibliographical references and index.
   ISBN 978-0-253-35455-6 (cl : alk. paper) — ISBN 978-0-253-22184-1 (pb : alk. paper)
   1. Jews—Identity—History—20th century. 2. Jews—Intellectual life—20th century. 3. Zionism and Judaism. 4. Kaplan, Mordecai Menahem, 1881–1983. 5. Kohn, Hans, 1891–1971. 6. Rawidowicz, Simon, 1897–1957. I. Title.
   DS143.P566 2010
   320.54095694092'2—dc22   2009051590

1 2 3 4 5   15 14 13 12 11 10

CONTENTS

ACKNOWLEDGMENTS

Growing up, I spent a tremendous amount of time under a huge mural entitled "The Old and the New Palestine" in the social hall of my family's synagogue. The picture of muscular, sun-tanned young men and women building up the Land of Israel had been commissioned decades earlier by the founding rabbi of the community, Mordecai Kaplan. Even during my childhood, the placement of this image piqued my curiosity and raised questions in my mind about the relationship between Zionism, Israel, and American Judaism. What relevance did this foreign vision of Jews picking fruit in Palestine have for me, an afternoon Hebrew school student struggling to vocalize ancient Hebrew liturgical passages and completely oblivious to anything more agricultural than watching the trees bloom in Central Park? This book represents many years of grappling with these questions, first on a personal level and later in a variety of academic settings.

I am indebted to many teachers and colleagues for nourishing and sharpening my intellectual passions along the way. When I was an undergraduate at Brown University, an incredibly accessible group of faculty members in the History and Religious Studies Departments, especially Wendell Dietrich, Mary Gluck, and Harold Roth, introduced me to the critical methodologies of research and academic scholarship and inspired me to continue pursuing these interests at the graduate level.

Paula Hyman, my dissertation adviser at Yale University, generously shared her wisdom and innovative approaches to Jewish history. She has far surpassed any expectations I had about the role my dissertation supervisor would play in mentoring me and shaping my career in academia. I am deeply grateful for her ongoing support. As members of my dissertation committee, Jon Butler and Frank Turner pushed me to situate my research within the larger context of modern intellectual history and religion in America. Arnold Eisen welcomed me during the year I spent as a visiting student at Stanford University. His approach to modern Jewish thought added an important layer to my research, and he has remained a friend and an important sounding board for my ideas throughout the years. I feel so fortunate to have studied with a group of individuals who I admire so much as both scholars and as people.

The University of Washington's Jackson School of International Studies has been an ideal place to work and teach since 2004. I have enjoyed fruitful collaborations with my colleagues here: in the classroom, in my scholarship, and within my departmental setting. Working with the Jackson School's interdisciplinary faculty has encouraged me to view the study of Jews and Judaism as a lens for addressing pressing global political, economic, and cultural issues. Anand Yang, Director of the Jackson School, and Paul Burstein and Gad Barzilai, chairs of the Samuel and Althea Stroum Jewish Studies program during the last five years, all worked tirelessly to facilitate my transition to the university and to make sure that I have had the resources and support necessary to succeed here.

My participation in the UW Jewish Studies program has enabled me to meet superb colleagues from across the university, including Richard Block, Susan Glenn, Kathie Friedman, Martin Jaffee, Scott Noegel, Naomi Sokoloff, and Robert Stacey. I have also benefited from working closely with Joel Migdal, who has provided thoughtful feedback on my project and professional advice. The process of organizing a conference on Jewish political thought with Michael Rosenthal gave me a chance to hone my approach to the topic. Until last year, I was fortunate enough to have Sarah Abrevaya Stein as a colleague and neighbor. It was her advice that encouraged me to find my own voice during the process of revising this manuscript. Finally, it has been a pleasure to get to know Althea Stroum who, along with her late husband Samuel, had a great vision for Jewish Studies at UW and around the country; it is an honor to occupy the chair that bears their names.

This book has also benefited from the feedback of a number of talented senior scholars at other universities who have gone out of their way to share their thoughts about this project. The imprint of my discussions with David Myers about the history of Jewish nationalism and Zionism appears throughout the following pages. I am thankful to have found in him such a sharp and intellectually demanding conversation partner; he has been instrumental in both refining and affirming the theoretical framework of this book. For many years, Deborah Dash Moore has taken the time to share her expertise and guidance. She encouraged me not to shy away from making bold statements, and in particular pushed me to use the language of Zionism more explicitly as the link between the subjects of this work. Derek Penslar offered his insightful feedback on several chapters of the manuscript at an early stage in the process. I have also benefited from exchanges about this material at conferences and in other settings with Michael Alexander, David Biale, Eric Goldstein, Tony Michels, Riv-Ellen Prell, Jonathan Sarna, Mel Scult, and Steven Zipperstein. Special thanks to Steven Ascheim, Yfaat Weiss, and Christian Wiese for inviting me to participate in a conference on Hans Kohn at the Hebrew University, where feedback from both the organizers and participants honed my own understanding of Kohn's life and thought. I am doubly appreciative to Benjamin Ravid, the son of Simon Rawidowicz. Ben warmly welcomed me to his house and permitted me access to his father's archival material. In addition, he read the book's chapter on Rawidowicz with great attention to detail, confirming biographical details and the timeline of his father's publications.

My participation in several writing groups over the years has put me in conversation with a talented group of young scholars and helped me improve my work in a supportive peer community. Deena Aranoff, Mara Benjamin, Lila Corwin Berman, Rebecca Kobrin, James Loeffler, Avinoam Patt, and Daniel Schwartz read through countless drafts of this material during my graduate school years, offering both encouragement and suggestions on my dissertation project. Since arriving at the University of Washington, I have met regularly with several colleagues in the history department to exchange work and ideas, including Purnima Dhavan, Elena Campbell, Florian Schwarz, David Spafford, and Adam Warren. Members of the University of Washington History Reading Group have also imparted their collective wisdom regarding several chapters. It goes without saying that I take full responsibility for what has emerged as the final product of years of discussions with all these individuals.

Wiebke Light, Hannah Pressman, and Or Rogovin were kind enough to review some of my German and Hebrew translations, and Amy Smith Bell lent her keen editorial eye to the manuscript. Collecting the primary source material for this book required the help of talented archivists from around the globe: Ellen Kastel of the Jewish Theological Seminary in New York, Fred Krome of the American Jewish Archives in Cincinnati, Michael Simonson and Molly Hazelton of the Leo Baeck Institute in New York, Colin Harris at the New Bodleian Library in Oxford, and numerous staff members at the Central Zionist Archives and the National and University Archives, both in Jerusalem.

A number of institutions and foundations made this project possible through their financial largess. A stipend from the Wexner Graduate Fellowship supported my graduate studies. Moreover, the professional staff of the Wexner Foundation during my tenure as a fellow—especially Elka Abrahamson, Bob Chazan, Cindy Chazan, and Larry Moses—provided invaluable professional support, inspiration, and mentorship. A fellowship from the Center for Jewish History in New York enabled me to take full advantage of their archival holdings. More recently, the Royalty Research Fund at the University of Washington facilitated the completion of this book by providing teaching release time while I worked to complete the writing process. The Samuel and Althea Stroum Jewish Studies program at the University of Washington has furnished travel grants for research trips and, along with the Jackson School of International Studies, dedicated subvention funds toward the book's publication.

I am honored that this book is included in the Modern Jewish Experience series at Indiana University Press. Janet Rabinowitch, the director of the press, has had great faith in this project and has impressed me with her professionalism, attention to detail, and efficiency. Thanks to Joyce Rappaport for skillfully copyediting the manuscript and to Managing Editor Miki Bird for pushing the publication process through in a timely fashion.

My family has had more influence on this project than they probably realize. The experiences of my parents, Rina and Howard Pianko, as Jewish immigrants in the United States with close family ties to Eastern Europe and Israel, put the realities of twentieth-century Jewish history and the dilemmas of Jewish peoplehood front and center in our home. My brothers Daniel and Gideon, my sister-in-law Melissa, and my in-laws Alan and Neda Nussbaum have lived through many years of hearing me talk about this project and always encouraged me to push forward. My daughter, Yona, born during the final stages of my work on this manuscript, will, I hope, have no recollection that one of her first sentences was "Daddy working." I will certainly remember watching her hop past my home-office door quizzically asking, "What doing?" Such moments put the stress of completing a book manuscript in its proper perspective. My wife, Rachel Nussbaum, has been my strongest supporter, intellectual partner, and emotional guide as I have navigated the personal and professional journey leading to the publication of this book. I cannot thank her enough for the hours she has spent helping me generate new ideas, reading my work, and, most important, believing in my abilities as a scholar and teacher. It is to her that I dedicate this book.

ZIONISM AND THE ROADS NOT TAKEN

Breaking the Sovereign Mold

Nation beyond State
in Modern Jewish Thought

"What will become of the Jewish people?" Israeli novelist and Zionist provocateur A. B. Yehoshua's answer to this question stunned a crowd of American Jewish leaders who had gathered at a major conference of the American Jewish Committee in 2006. Yehoshua argued that he saw quite a limited future for Jews in the diaspora. Even more infuriating to his audience, however, was his insistence that he "would not cry" if Jews were to disappear from the diaspora.[1] Although framed in a particularly insensitive fashion, Yehoshua's comments reflected a logic based on classic principles of Zionist ideology and its understanding of Jewish nationalism. They echoed an ideology of Zionism associated with "statism" that had been popularized by Prime Minister David Ben Gurion after the founding of the state.[2] Ben Gurion believed that only political independence would rescue Jews from their perverse existence as a religious community in exile, ensure their normalization as a modern people, and restore their place as active participants in the world.

Like Ben Gurion, Yehoshua believed that complete membership in the nation of Israel required participation in the various aspects of life as a citizen of the state of Israel. As he put it: "[Being Israeli] is in my skin; it's not in my jacket."[3] Without living in a Jewish state, he felt, and sharing the political, economic, and social concerns of citizenship, one cannot live a full Jewish life. The voluntary, religious bonds created by Jewishness in the diaspora remain inferior to the political ties forged as citizens in the homeland. Participation in Jewish self-government thus constitutes the realization of Jewish nationalism and the basic criterion for complete expression of national solidarity.

This narrative of Jewish nationalism elevated the state to the highest expression of Jewish national life and the culmination of Jewish history. After thousands of years, the collective group known since biblical times as *Am Yisrael* (the people of Israel), named after the patriarch Jacob or Israel, would revive its original political, social, and cultural boundaries of solidarity through territorial sovereignty and self-determination. Or, to put it more succinctly, the historical nation of Israel would return to the Land of Israel and establish the State of Israel. As a result of this transformation, the Jewish people would finally resolve their exceptional status by embodying the doctrine of national sovereignty—the belief that nationhood is equivalent to statehood. Conversely, statism implied that Jews in the diaspora would concede the possibility of creating national culture and define themselves primarily in relationship to the state.

The most interesting part of Yehoshua's speech, as historian David Myers has pointed out, however, was not *what* he said—his belief that authentic Jewish national life was only possible in the state was a theme he had harped on for decades.[4] Far more interesting was the *reaction* to his speech. His statement sparked dozens of angry responses from Jewish leaders within Israel and throughout the United States. The outcry against Yehoshua's negation of the diaspora language was so ardent that the organizers of the symposium collected the reactions in a publication called *The A. B. Yehoshua Controversy.* The responses indicate that a new generation of American and even Israeli audiences have become increasingly uncomfortable with the underlying hierarchical assumption of the state as the primary address of national solidarity and the center of Jewish peoplehood (Yehoshua himself acknowledged that he was surprised that his oft-repeated claims garnered such a vociferous outcry). This change in attitude reflects the fact that political and communal leaders have begun to replace the center-periphery model of diaspora–Israel relations with a vision of partnership and mutual engagement.

Nevertheless, the perceived equivalence of the State of Israel with the nation of Israel remains deeply embedded in popular consciousness and Jewish studies. Indeed, the possibility of articulating Jewish nationhood as anything but statehood seems quite puzzling. Moreover, new models of Zionism calibrated to reflect today's political and social trends—especially the diminishing correlation between nation and state triggered by communication advances, demographic mobility, and the promotion of cultural diversity—have been slow to arise. Zionism, and with it the question of Jewish nationhood, remains stuck between a nation-state paradigm, which valued ethnonational homogeneity, and a future concept of Jewish nationalism that reflects the realities of identity formation in a global era.[5]

What would an alternative to Yehoshua's vision look like? New interpretations of Zionism would have to address unresolved questions about Jewish collective identity given today's realities of unprecedented interconnectedness and transnational ties. What is Zionism and how does it relate to Jewish collective or national identity? Does Zionism have relevance outside the homeland for Jews and Jewish communities, beyond galvanizing political and financial support? How can a Jewish state serve as a center for Jews living in vastly different political, cultural, and social contexts? Can one definition of Israel encompass Jews living both as sovereign citizens committed to preserving a particular ethnonational tradition in the state and as a minority group heavily invested in diversity and equal rights in the diaspora? What is the role of Judaism within the Jewish state? Does the Jewish experience of solidarity mirror other models of nationality, sovereignty, and difference developing in the twenty-first century? Addressing these underlying issues requires that American Jewish and Israeli leaders reopen questions that they have for decades tacitly agreed to defer.

One untapped resource for addressing these questions anew and expanding conceptual possibilities for Zionism and Jewish peoplehood today can be found in the rich diversity of interwar Zionism. Before the creation of the State of Israel in 1948, the questions just raised, as well as other, far more general questions about the relationship between nation and state, were openly debated within Zionist ideology and Western political thought. This book explores roads not taken in the intellectual history of Zionism that conceptualized nation beyond state as the central teaching of Jewish nationalism and the future organizing principle of international relations and world politics.[6]

Contrary to one Zionist narrative, key Jewish intellectuals asserted Zionism's mission as modeling an alternative to nation-state nationalism that would reconfigure the relationship between nationality, sovereignty, and international politics. Zionism, they contended, outlined the blueprint for a conception of national identity equally relevant for homeland and diaspora populations, compatible with particular and human allegiances, and distinct from patriotism or political citizenship. As the embodiment of the Jewish political tradition, Zionism testified to the limits of national self-determination on both moral and pragmatic grounds. It also exemplified the universal benefits of cultivating national ties across spatial and political boundaries. For these Zionists, however, the rejection of statehood as the primary criterion of nationhood was not associated with undermining the importance of a national homeland for Jews in Palestine. The established categories for thinking about twentieth-century Jewish nationalism—diaspora autonomy and (statist) Zionism—fail to capture the complex synthesis of diaspora and Zionism in the positions they endorsed.

Three individuals shed light on these roads not taken in the intellectual history of Zionism and twentieth-century nationalism more generally—the Hebraist Simon Rawidowicz, the American Jewish thinker Mordecai Kaplan, and the scholar of nationalism Hans Kohn. These thinkers are well known to specialized audiences in distinct fields and disciplines for specific accomplishments—for example, Rawidowicz's pathbreaking analysis of modern Jewish intellectual history, Kaplan's reconstruction of American Judaism, and Kohn's highly influential studies of the history of nationalism. Yet they have been largely ignored as Jewish political theorists who viewed Zionism as a platform for negotiating the fundamental categories and assumptions of modern political thought. To capture the divergent approaches to Zionism and its significance for diaspora Jewish life expressed by Rawidowicz, Kaplan, and Kohn, I call their formulations respectively "global Hebraism," "national civilization," and "cultural humanism." At the same time, juxtaposing their formulations recovers more than the anomalous visions of outlying thinkers. Rawidowicz, Kaplan, and Kohn highlight overlapping strategies for theorizing Jewish identity that eschewed the binary choices—such as homeland versus diaspora, political autonomy versus individual assimilation, and ties based on consent versus descent—imposed by the logic of nation-state nationalism and Western liberalism. The patterns evident in their programs are shared, to varying degrees, by a wide range of thinkers rarely studied as intellectuals grappling with a similar set of Jewish concerns or adapting parallel strategies for contesting modern political thought.

The narrative arc of this book bridges time and space to trace the ways in which Rawidowicz, Kaplan, and Kohn joined Jewish and non-Jewish thinkers committed to reimagining the fundamental categories of nationality during the period between World War I and the establishment of the State of Israel in 1948. Placing their thought in its proper historical context indicates that the evolution of the meaning of nationalism did not follow the smooth trajectory from imperial subject to national citizen mapped onto the first half of the twentieth century. Moreover, Zionist thinkers actively participated in contesting this course. They negotiated emerging categories of national identity and attempted to reconfigure its relationship to changing concepts of collective solidarity such as race, ethnicity, and religion.

The acceptance of self-determination as the primary right of national movements and the realization of Jewish statehood marginalized these voices. Ultimately, Rawidowicz, Kaplan, and Kohn were unable to shape Zionism according to their understanding of Jewish nationalism. During their careers, the three moved from the center of Zionist thought and activism to being ideological outliers. Precisely because of their failed efforts to create a lasting counternarrative in Zionist thought, however, Rawidowicz, Kaplan, and Kohn provide a perspective from which to critically assess Zionism's meaning and relevance, past, present, and future.

These forsaken figures offer a cautionary tale about equating contingent historical expressions of Zionism and nationalism with those concepts understood today as normative. Rawidowicz, Kaplan, and Kohn saw themselves as navigating a constant course while the discourse of Zionism radically changed around them. They did not leave Zionism; rather, Zionism left them outside its evolving ideological parameters. In order to reintegrate these roads not taken into the historical narrative of Zionism, this book deliberately stretches contemporary notions of nationalism and Zionism to include expressions no longer considered within the definition of the term. Recovering their struggles to theorize outside the crystallizing nation-state paradigm underscores the knotty issues faced by Jewish intellectuals in the interwar period and chronicles the innovative approaches devised to address them.

One would think that the fascination of more recent scholarship with transnational associations, minority rights, and the moral limits of sovereignty should have sparked increased interest in Jewish conceptions of nationalism. Jewish communities have exemplified the possibility of creating cultural, religious, and legal ties across territorial and geographic borders. In the premodern period, for example, Jews had a rich tradition of self-government, civil autonomy (including taxation and a separate legal system), and political organizations that spanned feudal realms. In the modern period the Jews represented the classic other within European nationalism. This position led Jewish intellectuals and leaders to pioneer strategies for parrying the demands of national integration and for conceptualizing new categories of identity. Since the late 1940s, Jews have grappled with being a global population increasingly split between multiple diaspora centers and a state in the national homeland.

In reality, however, Jews have remained largely invisible in the writings of scholars who have engaged this growing discourse. Jewish political thought has been perceived by many as, paradoxically, too integrationist and too statist to merit serious engagement. On the one hand, the diaspora Jewish community is viewed as a religious group happily integrated into its host societies. Conversations within the field of ethnic studies, for instance, rarely consider the Jewish case because Jews' "whiteness" combined with their economic success calls into question their status as a minority group. On the other hand, the State of Israel, and its ideology of Zionism, is perceived by both its defenders and its critics as being committed to national sovereignty.[7] As a result of these conflicting assumptions, few scholars have considered the history of Zionism in tracing the evolution of political critiques of national sovereignty or in locating the early and influential expressions of collective solidarity within and across political boundaries.[8]

I conclude that interwar Zionism has tremendous contemporary relevance for those interested in considering the nature of group cohesion today. The themes addressed by interwar Zionists—balancing patriotism and particularism, reconciling liberalism and nationalism, and challenging the analytical distinctions between religion, ethnicity, and race—have shifted to mainstream concerns. Zionism's roads not taken thus illuminate the breaks and, more important, the surprising continuities between early twentieth-century efforts to conceptualize the boundaries of the Jewish nation as distinct from political sovereignty and twenty-first century debates about identity in an era increasingly characterized by multiculturalism, transnational solidarity, and minority rights. The same estrangement experienced between the Jew and the nation-state, felt so palpably as the "Jewish question" at the dawn of the twentieth century, now is felt by a far wider swath of the world population.

The remainder of this chapter prepares the groundwork for rehabilitating these neglected expressions of Zionist thought. I introduce the book's three main protagonists, their formulations, and the ways in which the historical lens for thinking about nationalism, both Jewish and general, needs to be reconfigured to fully appreciate the scope of pre-state Zionism and its contributions to political thought.

Three (Exceptional?) Roads Not Taken

The assumption that Zionism exemplifies the paradigm of the nation-state and its attendant negation of diaspora communities was not the inevitable outcome of Zionist ideology during the first half of the twentieth century.[9] As the discourse of European nationalism and Zionism evolved after World War I, some Jewish intellectuals saw Zionism as an opportunity to redefine national membership, both Jewish and, more generally, beyond the concrete borders of homeland and state. Before the establishment of the State of Israel in 1948, and even during the decade immediately after independence, Zionism was pregnant with possibilities that are now considered far outside its ideological parameters, past and present. As Western political theory and many Zionist intellectuals embraced the principles of self-determination, other influential Jewish thinkers explored the complicated and ambiguous theoretical terrain left unresolved by the still widely accepted claim that the globe could (and should) be divided into discrete political units with homogeneous ethnonational populations.

Against this backdrop, it is far less surprising that Rawidowicz, Kaplan, and Kohn considered their formulations of Jewish nationalism within the interwar ideological parameters of Zionism. This book employs a capacious definition of "Zionism" to capture a more accurate picture of the term in its specific historical context. These three figures were disillusioned to varying degrees during their careers with the Zionist movement; they were even attacked by critics as "anti-Zionist."[10] Thus I have deliberately maintained the language as it was used by mid-century intellectuals, even though the theories depart from conventional readings. Employing a more expansive definition of Zionism casts light on a set of debates and conversations that have long been overlooked.

My first goal in assessing Rawidowicz's, Kaplan's, and Kohn's concepts of nationality side by side is to amplify a counternarrative of Zionism that challenged the increasingly dominant paradigm of national sovereignty between World War I and the period immediately following establishment of the State of Israel in 1948. Born between 1881 and 1896, Rawidowicz, Kaplan, and Kohn lived in suspended animation between the post–World War I moment (when radical reorganization of global political structures seemed possible) and post–World War II (when the nation-state paradigm became dominant). The three protagonists have been forgotten as Zionist political theorists because their ideas deviated from the normative path of nationalism as understood both by Zionists and modern political thought more broadly.[11]

Rawidowicz, Kaplan, and Kohn each began their personal and intellectual journeys rooted within the diverse ideological parameters of pre–World War I Zionism. Rawidowicz, born in northeastern Poland, moved to Berlin, where he joined a circle of leading Hebrew authors and publishers (including Israel's future national poet, Haim Nahman Bialik). He went on to create the first international association of Hebrew speakers, open a Hebrew publishing house, and publish his articles on Jewish nationalism in the leading Zionist journal, *Ha'olam*. Born in Prague, Kohn became a disciple of the philosopher and Zionist Martin Buber and his writings on Jewish nationalism as a member of the Bar Kochba circle of young Zionists. Kohn served as an executive in the Zionist Organization, published regular articles in the *yishuv's* (prestate settlement) leading newspapers, and helped found Brit Shalom, a prominent prestate organization in Palestine that promoted a binational state. One of the first supporters of Zionism at the Jewish Theological Seminary, Kaplan worked with leaders of the Zionist Organization in the United States and hailed Zionism as an integral part of the reconstruction of American Jewish life in his writings.

Although their views on key issues (such as the Arab question, the importance of diaspora communities, and opposition to national sovereignty) differed from others in the Zionist movement, Kaplan, Rawidowicz, and Kohn were not marginal or even exceptional figures. They wrote for mainstream Zionist journals, worked for the movement, and dedicated their intellectual energy toward advocating for Zionism and Jewish national renaissance. All three viewed settlement in Palestine as central to their project. On a personal level, they each left the diaspora to put their ideologies temporarily into practice in the great laboratory of Palestine.

Rawidowicz, Kaplan, and Kohn developed their own understandings of Zionism immediately after World War I—a moment in which national normalcy was not necessarily tantamount to national sovereignty. Indeed, the decades after the Versailles peace conference represented a period of rapid political, economic, and cultural change during which concepts of nation and state were debated across a wide spectrum of revolutionary ideologies. Chapter 2 of this book illustrates the dynamic cross-pollination of various transatlantic ideological networks that employed Zionism as a theoretical tool to promote states of nations rather than nation-states as the most stable structure for international relations. Zionism would shape the postwar reconstruction in conjunction with programs advocating for internationalism based on multinational commonwealths and even a world-state.

The chapter contextualizes Rawidowicz's, Kaplan's, and Kohn's approaches to Zionism by exploring shared intellectual influences and affinities with their mentors (specifically the cultural Zionist Ahad Ha'am and the historian Simon Dubnow) as well as a number of their contemporaries and conversation partners (such as the American Zionist Horace Kallen, the Jewish Theological Seminary professor Israel Friedlaender, the Zionist activist Judah Magnes, and the British internationalist Sir Alfred Zimmern).[12]

Across diverse ideological and geographic terrain, thinkers associated with Zionism defined Jewish political thought in opposition to the concept I refer to as the "sovereign mold." This idea refers to a loosely defined collection of expectations, including (1) that territorial boundaries correlate with particular national populations, (2) that national groups have a right to political independence, and (3) that substatist loyalties—such as ethnic, religious, racial, or other special interest groups—must remain secondary to a primary allegiance to the state. Rawidowicz, Kaplan, and Kohn inveighed against the state's authority to demand ethnonational conformity among its citizenry. Decoupling the link between nation and state was viewed as a program for strengthening expressions of nationality and promoting diversity within nation-states on both sides of the Atlantic.

Despite their overlapping criticism of the sovereign mold, Rawidowicz, Kaplan, and Kohn did not see themselves as, nor did they represent, a particular school of Zionist thought. My second goal in juxtaposing these particular figures is to explore three distinct and idiosyncratic visions for Zionism as a framework for theorizing nation beyond state. (They did know of one another during their lifetimes—a reflection of their overlapping interests and shared networks around Zionist publications, intellectual circles, and cultural activities. Kaplan and Kohn met at least once in 1931 at a lecture on Zionism. Kaplan indicated his admiration for Rawidowicz's work in a handwritten note that he sent to Rawidowicz along with a signed copy of his magnum opus, *Judaism as a Civilization*. Rawidowicz included respectful critiques of Kaplan's essays in his own writings. Kohn reviewed an essay by Rawidowicz in 1929.)[13]

Each thinker formulated concepts of Zionism that reflected his engagement with different intellectual traditions, his experiences living in different cities around the world, his interest in writing for different audiences, his personal journeys, and especially his relationship to Jews and Judaism. Their visions of the basis of national solidarity range from language and textual interpretation, to religious folkways, to universal civic ideals. So, too, did they disagree on the ideal level of national preservation in the diaspora—from Rawidowicz's communitarian emphasis on diverse cultural groups to Kohn's concept of nationalism as the historical force engendering human integration.

Rawidowicz's global Hebraism, the subject of chapter 3, introduced the most highly developed twentieth-century expression of deterritorialized and decentralized Jewish nationalism. Not until recently, however, have scholars assessed Rawidowicz's significance, beyond his contributions to the Hebrew Renaissance during the 1920s in Weimar Germany and the scholarship he produced as an exiled professor in Great Britain and the United States during the 1940s and 1950s.[14] Rawidowicz's symbolic insistence on writing in Hebrew for a diaspora audience certainly contributed to the neglect of his scholarship. Global Hebraism rejected the primacy of Palestine and instead envisioned national life flourishing irrespective of locale or political context. According to this model, the Hebrew language and the culture of textual interpretation would generate fluid boundaries, creating a dynamic equilibrium between integration and autonomy far more consistent with centuries of Jewish life than state-framed definitions of Jewish nationality.

Despite the classic Hebrew sources and traditional references embedded in his writings, Rawidowicz developed a theory of collective solidarity that anticipated modern theories of language as shaping collective boundaries, developed in the context of hermeneutics and poststructuralism. His reliance on traditional Jewish sources, classical rabbinic Hebrew, and an explicit rejection of secular terminology (language he refers to as *lo'az*, the rabbinic term for non-Jewish influence) suggests at best a disinterest (more likely, an aversion) to engaging with European political thought. The form he selected to convey his reading of Jewish identity and history, however, belies a thoughtful reading of rabbinic Judaism's concept of deferred messianism and its intellectual centers in both Jerusalem and Babylon as a sharp critique of what he considered the messianic impulse in German and Zionist political thought. As Rawidowicz moved westward, from Germany to England and then to the United States, he expanded his critique of the nation-state to apply to liberal democracies as well. Although he implicitly dealt with general questions, he remained focused on writing for a Jewish audience and within the language (both literally and figuratively) of traditional sources.

The theory of national civilization, laid out most extensively in Kaplan's *Judaism as a Civilization* (1934), defined membership on the grounds of shared social associations, religious practices, cultural engagements, and connection to a homeland. Chapter 4 explores the ways in which Kaplan's political thought sought to blur the emerging boundaries between religion, nationality, and race by constructing a new political category of nationality, called "civilization," as a model for Jews in both the United States and Palestine. Kaplan articulated a moral argument that viewed particular attachments as the most effective path toward guaranteeing individual rights and creating harmony between different groups. Thus he turned the meaning of progress on its head by linking civilization with national diversity, not ethnocultural uniformity.

Kaplan's national civilization not only attempted to reconstruct Judaism, but more important, to reconstruct American democracy to make space for minority national groups. The chapter challenges Kaplan's legacy as arguably the most influential American Jewish thinker because of his ability to transpose Judaism into an American key.[15] This conventional reading overlooks Kaplan's notion of civilization as contributing to a transatlantic conversation about nationality intended to transform Zionism and American nationalism.

Chapter 5 argues that Kohn, considered one of the "founding fathers of academic studies of nationalism," transformed key principles of nationalism first outlined in Zionist tracts, such as the German-language *Die Politische Idee des Judentum* (The political idea of Judaism; 1924) and the two-volume Hebrew book, *Perakim letoldot hara'ayon hatzioni* (A history of Zionist thought; 1929), into dozens of influential scholarly books such as his *Idea of Nationalism* (1944) and *American Nationalism* (1957).[16] Highlighting continuities between Kohn's seemingly disconnected careers as a German Zionist and an American scholar complicates the very oppositional dichotomy between civic and ethnic concepts that he is credited with popularizing. The civic-versus-ethnic contrast, still referred to as the "Kohn dichotomy," erases the tension between Western liberalism and romantic nationalism in Kohn's personal experiences and historical analysis. His theory of nationalism is more accurately remembered as cultural humanism—a term that closely captures his enduring debt to the Zionist ideology that shaped his worldview. In particular, Kohn retained an appreciation for the moral and pragmatic value of preserving groupness, and even national diversity, within the state as the path toward human integration and universal equality. Exploring his German Zionism suggests the importance of rereading one of the most important theories of American nationalism.

Rethinking the Meaning, Function, and Scope of Nationality

These three expressions forged within the rich ideological firmament of interwar Zionism—Rawidowicz's global Hebraism, Kaplan's national civilization, and Kohn's cultural humanism—never reached fruition. Indeed, their failure to influence Zionism was so great that it is hard to imagine that thinkers engaged in questions of defining nationality outside of statehood began their careers as self-defined Zionists. What factors limit our ability to integrate figures such as Rawidowicz, Kaplan, and Kohn into the historical narrative of Zionism?

The victory of the very conceptual vocabulary of Zionism, and nationalism more generally, which Rawidowicz, Kaplan, and Kohn sought to replace, impedes the recovery of Zionisms opposed to the sovereign mold and an understanding of its relationship to larger trends in political thought. A singular idea of Zionism, based on a conception of Jewish normalization through self-government and territorial sovereignty, emerged that over-shadowed the diverse possibilities that had characterized the movement. As a result of this process, historians and theorists have been largely cut off from Zionism's heterogeneity and pioneering engagement with the dilemmas of nationality and sovereignty.

Considering Rawidowicz, Kaplan, and Kohn within the proper historical context also requires a working definition of nationality that expands the term's contemporary meaning, function, and geographic scope. Rawidowicz's, Kaplan's, and Kohn's itinerant lives—constantly shifting between geographies, ideologies, and intellectual networks—mirror their intellectual dislocation and illuminate the anxieties that accompany eschewing the dominant currents of their times. I thus interpret formulations of nationality as a revealing window that sheds light on personal and theoretical attempts to reconcile solidifying categories of modern Jewish life and the construction of political ideologies. Moreover, considering theories of nationality within their local and global contexts demonstrates that theories of nationality are not complete, consistent, and systematic programs. Rather, they have evolved as an ongoing project that reflects the equivocal conclusions and conflicting pulls felt by individual theorists. The inner contradictions and semantic parameters, best captured through intellectual biography, created an intellectual bricolage that belies a consistent trajectory within each thinker.[17]

The working definition of nationality employed throughout this book amplifies three dimensions of Jewish political thought that have been eclipsed by nation-state narratives—the theoretical ambiguity of formulating nationality outside the sovereign mold, the role of Jewish political thinkers as active agents in the development of Western political thought, and the transnational and interdisciplinary conversation that links theorists from disparate geographic and intellectual milieus.

Including Counterstate Paradigms in the Study of Zionism

A nation, the historian Hugh Seton-Watson wrote in 1977, is a "community of people, whose members are bound together by a sense of solidarity, a common culture, a national consciousness." Seton-Watson explains the term "state," in direct contrast, as "a legal and political organization, with the power to require obedience and loyalty from its citizens."[18] These definitions differentiate between collective ties based on historical, cultural, ethnic, or religious bonds and connections forged by the political rights of the sovereign power over its citizens. Seton-Watson's position on the importance of retaining an analytical distinction between nation and state, however, is a minority one among scholars of nationalism. Theories of nationalism that assume a congruence between the two terms overshadow efforts by scholars committed to disarticulating notions of nation and state.

The historian Ernst Gellner has exemplified this tendency with his claim that nationalism "[is] primarily a political principle, which holds that the political and the national unit should be congruent."[19] Although scholarship on nationalism has spawned diverse ways of thinking about the nature of nationality, the literature tends to share Gellner's basic assumption—namely, that statehood remains an essential component of national identity, either as the spark leading to the construction of national culture or as the reflection of national aspirations. Indeed, his claims reflect a basic assumption of the modernist paradigm in the study of nationalism: nationalists, motivated by various economic, political, and social forces linked to the modern state, "invented" the nation where it did not previously exist.[20] In the words of the historian Anthony Smith, one of the most vocal opponents of this approach, this "became the standard orthodoxy by the 1960s."[21]

The frequent slippage in terminology between "nation" and "state" is implicitly reinforced in such key terms as "the United Nations," "transnational," "international relations," and even with the hyphen in the term "nation-state" itself. The very language used for discussing these concepts in today's political vernacular reflects the enduring premise that homogeneous ethnonational populations correspond directly to sovereign territories. Expressions of nationality that contested this dominant trend have been sidelined from the mainstream narrative of political thought.[22] Formulations of nation as distinct from state, when they are addressed, are often viewed as organic, familial, or ethnic—as opposed to rational or civic—and thus as potentially morally problematic because of the emphasis on national partiality over individual rights.[23]

An enduring bias in theories of Western liberalism and modernization nourishes this presumed clash. In the late nineteenth century, the philosopher and economist John Stuart Mill argued that "boundaries of government should coincide in the main with those of nationalities."[24] For Mill, only a homogeneous national culture would ensure the equality of all citizens and create the shared sense of membership necessary to establish a successful state. The inclination toward applying a nation-state paradigm as a lens to explain the historical development and to define the guidelines of nationalism also has deep roots in a perceived opposition between individual rights and ethnonational diversity. National memberships based on political ties to the state are more inclined to preserve individual rights, human values, voluntary associations, and toleration of ethnocultural differences. Ethnic nationalism, on the other hand, remains associated with tribal attachments rooted in descent, coercion, or territory. As a result, liberal scholars remain suspicious of affirmations of national solidarity outside of statehood.

The close association of nation and state in scholarship on both nationalism and liberalism makes it difficult to imagine a liberal nationalism compatible with particular solidarity across territorial and political boundaries—precisely the theoretical space within which Rawidowicz, Kaplan, and Kohn placed their conceptions of Zionism. Fortunately, increasing numbers of scholars have begun to question the practical or moral efficacy of limiting concepts of nationalism to the congruence criteria outlined by Gellner and other key shapers of the field. Singling out the yearning for political self-determination as the primary historical or normative criterion for defining nationality fails to capture the historical diversity, psychological reality, and social networks that characterize national ties.

Approaching the study of nationalism from multiple disciplines and perspectives, such commentators as the philosopher Charles Taylor, the legal theorist Chaim Gans, the political theorist Aviel Roshwald, and the multicultural advocate Will Kymlicka have dramatically expanded the definition of nationality to include nonstatist expressions.[25] The overlapping interest in broadening the analytical tools for thinking about nationality reflects a greater appreciation for the failure of the nation-state model to explain the perseverance of national bonds in the face of contemporary developments. These interventions provide a methodological framework for my own more inclusive definition of national identity. In particular, subsequent chapters adapt the terms suggested by the historian Rogers Brubaker. Brubaker distinguishes between "state-framed" and "counterstate" typologies. While the first category includes national movements primarily focused on achieving territorial sovereignty, he explains the latter as formulations that are "distinct from or in opposition to an existing state."[26]

Integrating counterstate models into the study of Zionism points the way toward rethinking historical approaches to Jewish political thought. Jewish studies have lagged behind other fields in considering the diverse scope and functions of twentieth-century conceptions of nationality. This does not mean that Jewish studies scholars have been insensitive to modern Jewish political thought as a variegated phenomenon. Rather, the ideological and practical expressions of Jewish nationality have been largely interpreted within categories derived primarily from state-seeking, rather than counterstate, expressions. As a result, the master narrative of modern Jewish political thought tends to be recast through the prism of two avenues for normalizing Jewish identity in the modern world—the nationalists committed to achieving national sovereignty in the homeland and the integrationists dedicated to affirming Jews' patriotic attachment to their country of citizenship. Yet these opposing narratives trace their genealogy to the same process of translating the ambiguous contours of the people of Israel into the either/or categories compatible with the world's political organization into discrete political, territorial units with homogeneous national populations.[27] Either demands statehood as the rightful expression of nationality or rejects the vocabulary of nationality and instead claims more acceptable categories for minority identity, such as religious creed or ethnicity.[28]

This binary rubric accurately outlines the broad map of twentieth-century mainstream political movements and explains the ultimate shift toward two distinct modes of Jewish life as a nationality in Israel and a religious community in America today. It also enables scholars to organize the tremendous diversity of modern Jewish politics, trace the schools that galvanized mass movements during the twentieth century, and document the increasing ideological polarization of a revolutionary era. However, a teleological reading of the evolution of modern Jewish politics as leading inevitably toward the establishment of the State of Israel and the dominance of American Jewry following the Holocaust obscures the fluid possibilities and elastic contours of interwar political ideologies that characterized the first half of the twentieth century.

Expanding the construct of Zionism to include counterstate expressions provides a more inclusive approach that integrates formulations excluded from studies of Zionism particularly and discussions of nationalism more generally. State-framed assumptions anachronistically assume that there was widespread consensus in the interwar period that a sovereign state was the fundamental criterion of Zionism. Yet it was not until the 1940s that statehood became the official policy of the Zionist movement. Nevertheless, the central dichotomies that shape the categorization of Zionism versus diaspora nationalism in the first half of the twentieth century assume a great deal of clarity around the issue of Zionism's interwar objectives, specifically around the goal of creating a Jewish state and the role of the diaspora.

Analytical distinctions between political ideologies based on advocating for autonomy versus integration, here versus there, and nationality versus religion fail to fully capture the ambiguities that characterize global Hebraism, national civilization, and cultural humanism.[29] Rawidowicz, Kaplan, and Kohn fiercely resisted the urge to be swept up in either of the two competing political theories that had solidified by the mid-twentieth century:

(1) Zionism's definition of Jewish national identity as equivalent to citizenship in the homeland, and (2) a diasporist approach that emphasized social and cultural integration for a religious minority. Instead, they positioned their theories of Jewish nationalism as opposed to both the homogenizing demands of nation-state nationalism for ethnoreligious conformity and the Zionists' vision of implementing precisely such a vision in Palestine.

Taken together, Rawidowicz, Kaplan, and Kohn shed light on a gray area in prestate ideologies that blur boundaries between Zionism and diaspora nationalism.[30] Although there were certainly vocal figures who defined the ideological poles, there was also a continuum of positions that regularly crossed what would now be viewed as ideologically incompatible positions. These formulations of Jewish nationalism did not necessarily seek the systematic synthesis or theoretical consistency expected by subsequent scholars.

Rawidowicz, Kaplan, and Kohn illustrate this phenomenon by incorporating positions and allegiances in their personal lives and theoretical ruminations that are now perceived as oppositional, even oxymoronic. Applying a counterstate category to interwar Jewish nationalism exposes a shared set of historical predicaments, strategic solutions, and intellectual networks far more difficult to recover when such thinkers as Rawidowicz, Kaplan, and Kohn are placed in clear ideological camps.[31] Focusing the lens of historical scholarship on figures perceived as exceptional for muddled positions that clash with the clarity of a state-seeking typology documents the conflicting yearnings, irresolvable dilemmas, and opposing objectives that characterized a wide swath of interwar Jewish politics.

There is another somewhat misleading distinction in categorizing streams of Zionist thought that can be avoided by adapting the terminology of counterstate nationalism. Here I speak of the distinction between political versus cultural or spiritual Zionism. Political Zionists sought political autonomy in Palestine and believed that Zionism needed to convince the vast majority of Jews to leave the diaspora for the homeland. Only by settling in Palestine could Zionism succeed in protecting Jews from their precarious situation in the diaspora. Cultural Zionism, most notably associated with Ahad Ha'am and Martin Buber, focused on the problem of Jewish national culture. These nationalists conceived of Palestine as the center for the renewal of Jewish life. From the homeland center, Jewish national culture would radiate to the majority of Jews who would remain in the diaspora. The Zionist protagonists in this book adapted many of Ahad Ha'am's (and in the case of Kohn, Martin Buber's as well) conceptions of cultural Zionism.[32] They could thus be (and Kaplan has in fact been) characterized as cultural Zionists.[33]

Yet there is a potential problem with referring to them as cultural, as opposed to political, Zionists: the misconception that they are not political thinkers. The association of national politics with the apparatus of the state and its government presumes that concepts of Zionism that prioritized cultural, spiritual, or religious revival had little relevance for political questions. But this is not the way in which many of Ahad Ha'am's disciples understood his theory of nationalism. As I discuss further in chapter 2, Kohn was not alone when he commented on Ahad Ha'am's influence on his thought: "Under the influence of Ahad Ha'am, we were cultural rather than political Zionists. This corresponded to my general attitude, which made me doubt the wisdom of augmenting the number of nation-states and proud sovereignties, and to my distrust of reliance on numbers and power."[34]

Although Kohn himself used the category of cultural Zionism, he understood the term as a direct challenge to the state-seeking paradigm. Whether or not Ahad Ha'am himself supported the ultimate creation of a Jewish state, many of his disciples saw him as introducing the theoretical foundation for Zionism's challenge to state-seeking nationalism. Cultural Zionism thus had a far wider significance: first, in its direct influence on Zionist thinkers who understood their mentor as a political theorist advocating for undermining the relationship between nation and state; and second, in its largely unmapped dissemination into scholarly theories of nationalism through the work of academics inspired by Ahad Ha'am (Sir Alfred Zimmern, Horace Kallen, and Hans Kohn represent prime examples of this phenomenon).

Brubaker's discussion of his own motivations for thinking about nationalism through state-seeking versus counterstate paradigms adds another dimension to the historiographical value of adopting his counterstate terminology. Reorienting the study of nationality around two legitimate paths—one state-framed and one counterstate—neutralizes the moral hierarchy implied by the civic–ethnic distinction. Brubaker argues that the division negates the binary distinction between civic nationalism's voluntary, liberal, and cosmopolitan principles versus ethnic nationalism's coercive, ascriptive, and intolerant tendencies.

The interwar theories of Zionism analyzed throughout this book anticipated efforts by Brubaker to construct alternate conceptual paradigms of nationality as a way of contesting the false dichotomies encoded within the division between civic and ethnic typologies. For the Zionists whom we explore here, neither civic nor ethnic typologies, the two emerging possibilities for defining national identity, constituted a viable basis for Jewish collective solidarity. Their understanding of nationalism was too oriented toward particular solidarity to meet the criteria of a civic nationalism and too concerned with individual rights to fit into the ethnic, or cultural, criteria. Neither assuaged their anxiety about the plight of Jews after World War I nor their personal sensitivity to the exclusive nature of both types of nationalism. Jews, their sensibilities warned them, had little place in the dominant typologies of nationalism. As a result, Jewish intellectuals had a vested interest in contesting, even while deeply rooted within, state-seeking models of national identity.

The Strategic Function of Zionism

Considering counterstate streams of Zionist ideology sheds light on a process difficult to record from within a historical framework shaped by the doctrine of national sovereignty: the efforts of Jewish intellectuals to reformulate general conceptual definitions of nationality and sovereignty at a moment when these terms were very much still open for debate. Cognizant of a range of theoretical possibilities—including both ethnic nationalism and civic nationalism, multinational imperialism, and socialist internationalism—Jewish thinkers creatively read and misread the dominant theories of nationalism, internationalism, and liberalism to negotiate the discourse of citizenship and sovereignty. Moreover, when juxtaposed, a thematic thread emerges through the work of these intellectuals. They attempted to create a trajectory of modernity that valued difference as the step beyond unity. Their shared interest in recasting the telos of progress can be seen in the promulgation of such key terms as "ethical," "civilization," and "progress" throughout these theories. Jewish nationality therefore served as a corrective not only to the sovereign mold, but also to the basic philosophical orientation of modernity.

In recognition of this fundamental dimension of the theories of Zionism discussed throughout the book, the working definition of "nationality" includes the term's mediating function at the crossroads of conflicting intellectual and political forces.[35] Studying Jewish political thought primarily as an internal consideration of the ties that bind Jews to one another, or the imitation of externally imposed categories, disregards a counterintuitive dimension of this discourse: the construction of Jewish nationality as a prescription for non-Jewish theorists calibrated to negotiate and contest the terms of Jewish social and political integration into the state and the international order.

By adopting the very categories of identity they sought to undermine, Jewish intellectuals engaged in a subtle dialogue with their surroundings in a struggle to integrate those aspects of nationalist discourse beneficial to their objectives and to transform connotations that they felt undermined the continuity of Jews and Judaism.[36] The discourse of Jewish nationalism served as a rhetorical tool to neutralize states' claims to cultural uniformity by proposing theories of citizenship that eschewed ethnonational assimilation and tolerated, even promoted, the social and cultural autonomy of minority groups.[37] Considering Jewish nationality as an important site of political engagement, negotiation, and resistance in the contest for the meaning of national identity significantly expands the ways in which this term was deployed. Jewish nationality not only emulated but also subverted dominant paradigms of Western political thought.

Reading theories of nationality as the record of grappling with Jewish concerns and external political realities captures pioneering efforts to address an enduring problem in modern politics. I am referring to the challenge of articulating a conceptual language for preserving the status of stateless nations. The antipathy toward recognizing "otherness" in modern politics and philosophy remained rooted in the bedrock of foundational assumptions connecting unity and uniformity. Only by highlighting the particular claims concealed by the cosmopolitan rhetoric of the Enlightenment, and inverting their conclusions by inserting diversity as the sine qua non of universal harmony, could Jewish nationalists justify their demands for collective recognition. Whether consciously or unconsciously, these thinkers recognized the zero-sum game of identity construction.

This dilemma put Rawidowicz, Kaplan, and Kohn into a fascinating bind. On the one hand, they could not address their concerns by passively adapting the conceptual vocabulary of Western political thought. Existing models of liberalism and nationalism lacked the conceptual framework for integrating the other and separating nationalism from patriotism.[38] Justifying greater degrees of collective recognition as minority groups thus required redefining existing categories or creating alternative categories of otherness. On the other hand, however, nationalists committed to challenging the sovereign mold consciously recognized the need to frame their revisions within the existing categories of identity (this despite claims that their vision of Jewish political theory emerged from Jewish sources, not the various streams of Western political thought clearly shaping their notions of nationality). They intended their arguments about Jewish collective cohesion—with its distinct confluence of religion, race, history, and homelessness—to serve as a universal model for a broad audience of Jews and non-Jews. Only by tweaking non-Jewish assumptions would new categories of Jewish identity gain currency. To sum up this aspect of the function of nationalism more succinctly: Jewish nationalists were "ethnopolitical entrepreneurs" who viewed Zionism as an effective avenue for contesting the forces of nationalism that threatened individual and collective rights in the homeland and the diaspora.[39]

Although modern national groups all had to invent national boundaries from heterogeneous populations, the Jewish case offered unique challenges. Demographically, Jewish communities spread across multiple geographical areas. The proposed homeland had a small fraction of the total world Jewish population, and the vast majority of the Jewish nation was far more interested in moving to the United States than to the ancient homeland. Furthermore, the Jews' connection to Palestine was based on a two-millennia-old historical attachment, rather than an enduring tie to actually living on the land. Finally, the ambiguous position of Judaism as a religious and ethnic community confounded the pattern of other secular nationalist movements that did not have to rely on religious sources to construct a national narrative.

One Zionist response to the Jewish question was to erase these abnormalities by shaping Judaism in the mold of national sovereignty. Rawidowicz, Kaplan, and Kohn had a fundamentally different approach toward Jewish normalization than that generally attributed to Zionist solutions to the Jewish question. This approach transposed the particular challenges of constructing definitions of Jewish nationalism into a universal model for other national groups to emulate. They strove to normalize Jews by "Judaizing" Western political thought. Zionism, they optimistically believed, could catalyze a transformation to make stateless people the norm by exemplifying the ethical and pragmatic attributes of Jewish national cohesion.

Global and Interdisciplinary Perspective

One of the questions raised is, how did Rawidowicz, Kaplan, and Kohn translate the concepts of European Zionism into models of American democracy and Jewish communal life? For historians ever more interested in tracing the global intellectual and social networks that linked people and ideas outside the boundaries of the nation-state, these case studies provide fruitful models for consideration. The émigré journeys of the protagonists and the transatlantic nature of their conversations provide intellectual biographies that span diverse geographical and ideological milieus. Indeed, global Hebraism, national civilization, and cultural humanism demonstrate a variety of ways in which Zionism served as a conduit between European political thought and the evolution of what it means to be an American.

Moreover, their interest in reconceptualizing Jewish nationality outside of territorial and political boundaries led these Jewish thinkers to imagine notions of collective identity that crossed nation-state lines. As a result, their theoretical formulations, and historical interpretations, were sensitive to the relevance of transnational bonds in shaping historical forces and processes. Yet Jewish political history, especially within the context of the United States, like the study of political thought more generally, is often related within the framework of discrete geographical units. This regional approach diminishes the role of the immigrant experience, ethnic concerns, and transnational ties in the construction of political thought, both Jewish and American.[40] Scholars have tended to assume that Jews have little political history within the United States. In the words of Naomi Cohen, a leading chronicler of American Zionism, "The Americans rejected the European-held philosophy of diaspora nationalism, or the idea that the Jews constituted a political group in countries outside Palestine."[41] Based on this understanding, American Jewish intellectuals and leaders are interpreted as charting a different path: the construction of a religioethnic identity that would culminate in a harmonious American Jewish synthesis. This synthesis rejected nationalist claims (even American Zionists downplayed Jewish nationalism as little more than American patriotism) and instead embraced an identity based on religious confession and the state's recognition of Jews as individual citizens.

This narrative reflects important distinctions between Jewish experiences on both sides of the Atlantic. The political contexts of Jews in the United States and in Europe diverged significantly during the second half of the twentieth century. The European political environment, particularly in Eastern Europe, where many Jews were never granted citizenship, was radically different from the American context. As a result, the revolutionary politics of both the nationalist and the socialist variety that characterized this period fizzled rapidly in the United States. Mass movements and nationalist political parties did not develop in the United States as they had emerged during the same period throughout Central and Eastern Europe. National minority rights clashed with the view of America as a place of integration that eschewed nationalist claims. Furthermore, Jews in the United States did not face the same levels of persecution that had galvanized the demand for collective protection elsewhere. The United States promised unprecedented political, social, and religious opportunities based on liberal individualism.

Yet the chasm separating these two political contexts implied by the mainstream narrative of American exceptionality was far less clear to intellectuals in their own lifetimes than it has become to historians chronicling their experiences.[42] Despite important sociopolitical differences, the historical record indicates that Jewish intellectuals on both sides of the Atlantic saw the United States as a potential promised land for implementing theories of nationality, redefining sovereignty, and nurturing Jewish collective consciousness. Theories of Zionism as models for diaspora life extended to the United States as well. The two lands—Europe and America—shared political realities and criticisms of nationalism that transcended the Atlantic barrier that has often been projected onto chronicles of early-twentieth-century intellectual history.[43] Although Jewish nationalism has been used in the past to underscore regional differences, this book analyzes the discourse of nationality and Zionism as an integral part of twentieth-century Jewish Atlantic history.

Studying figures committed to Zionism in the diaspora as a language for transforming America into a nation of nationalities complicates the notion that American Zionism was completely sanitized of its European anti-integrationist position. It raises questions about whether or not American Jewish historians have largely ignored this possibility. Perhaps in order to narrate a history of integration and harmonious synthesis between Americanism and Judaism, American Jewish historians rejected the notion that they could be part of a nation or that Zionism could mean something distinct from national sovereignty or a strategy for U.S. acculturation. Underscoring transatlantic continuities replaces a trajectory of progressively increasing rootedness with one that highlights dislocation by characterizing Jewish immigrants as unrooted wanderers grappling with multiple national, intellectual, and social allegiances.[44]

This approach is particularly crucial in studying émigré intellectuals, whose intellectual biographies are too often bifurcated between their European and American stages. Further compounding the problem, disciplinary boundaries cause scholars to differentiate the contributions of Jewish thinkers from key public intellectuals who happen to be Jewish. The distinct legacies of Rawidowicz, Kaplan, and Kohn formulated conventionally as diaspora Hebraist, religious thinker, and scholar of nationalism reflect this artificial categorization of Jewish thinkers along geographic lines (Europe versus America), disciplinary boundaries (history, religious thought, and political theory), choices in modern Jewish politics (diasporist and Zionist), and academic fields (Jewish studies and general thought). That their work transcended these arbitrary boundaries demonstrates the importance of considering Jewish history, in general, and conversations about Jewish political thought among exiled and highly mobile intellectual wanderers, in particular, as inherently global and interdisciplinary in nature.

My adoption of this lens is not meant to diminish the recognition that political thought develops within specific spatial and temporal coordinates.[45] Rather, mapping theories of nationality across geographical regions reveals disjunctures and variations that reflect a particular mix of intellectual, social, and political forces.[46] Conscious of the importance of tracing the evolution of each theory of nationality within historical circumstances, I have organized this book around individual biographies. The chapters exploit the tools of intellectual history to gain a more nuanced appreciation for the interpenetration that took place between Jewish thinkers and their specific milieu. I have attempted to synthesize intellectual history's attention to space and time with modern Jewish thought's appreciation for considering general philosophical dilemmas and close textual analysis.

Jews, Zionism, and Contemporary Politics of Difference

Now, well into the twenty-first century, it is a particularly important time to rehabilitate and revive these dissenting streams of Zionist thought that offer models of Jewish nationality as distinct from, and even defined in opposition to, the nation-state model. That this rich, yet overlooked, history merits consideration today may not be immediately obvious, however. Alternative theories of Zionism failed to challenge the dominant course of twentieth-century Jewish thought or history. The division between two typologies of Jewish life they eschewed—religion in the diaspora and nationality in the homeland—has only solidified since 1948. The vast majority of the world's Jewish populations now live as citizens in the state of Israel or as a religioethnic minority group in the United States. The thinkers' visions of Arab–Jewish coexistence in Palestine, cultural and linguistic bonds uniting Jewish populations in the diaspora, and visions of a stateless national group as the model for a new international order were impractical in their own lifetimes and even less feasible decades later. It is thus easy to dismiss the formulators of grand theories of interwar nationality as naïve dreamers and insignificant historical actors.

Chapter 6 considers the relevance of these historical formulations for Jewish thought and political thought more generally. As the quotation at the start of the chapter demonstrated, Yehoshua contends that one can only live an authentically Jewish life as a Hebrew-speaking citizen and resident of the state of Israel. I argue that rebutting Yehoshua should focus not on his negation of the diaspora, but instead on a far more complex project— identifying the ways in which Zionist logic continues to limit possibilities for Jewish peoplehood, reopening conversations long ago frozen as taboo topics, and debating foundations of Jewish peoplehood that escape the logic of the sovereign mold. Rehabilitating the tradition of Zionists committed to breaking the sovereign mold thus supplies a road map for redefining Israel in the twenty-first century. In particular, the theories of Zionism unearthed through this book provide a foundation for addressing what has unfortunately become a highly charged space in public discussions of Jewish politics between activists denouncing Zionism and Jewish statehood as "anachronistic" and the persisting unwillingess among Israel advocates to question the centrality of the state in defining Jewish nationalism today. Evaluating the meaning and relevance of Zionism through an Israel versus anti-Israel lens only diverts attention from far more pressing problems— namely, addressing the attenuated sense of collective consciousness among Jews in the United States and articulating a compelling definition of Jewish peoplehood with two divergent demographic centers. The path toward building a stronger sense of collective solidarity and closer ties between diaspora and homeland communities demands reconsidering the centrality of the Jewish state and reengaging the rich political tradition of nation beyond state in Zionist thought.

Recovering the diversity of interwar Zionist thought also has broader appeal beyond debates about the State of Israel and the morality of Zionism. The forces of globalization and political shifts engendered by the end of the Cold War have rendered the sovereign mold far less effective as an analytical tool for explaining the growing realities of collective attachment and transnational loyalties. Contrary to theories of modernization, however, globalization has actually fueled the preservation of particular allegiances within and across state boundaries. Large diaspora communities thrive and cultivate enduring bonds to their homelands and other populations dispersed around the world.[47] From Muslim immigrants in Europe to Latino populations in the United States to Kurdish citizens of northern Iraq, global diaspora communities maintain a sense of shared solidarity. Such communities often demand increasing levels of collective recognition and group rights despite state-building efforts to assimilate them into the dominant national culture.[48] These opposing tendencies—the process of universal integration and the rise of particular global networks—expose fissures in the correlation between nationhood and statehood. The failure of the sovereign mold's vision of the world divided into units of overlapping ethnonational and political identities to match emerging patterns of solidarity has fueled scholarly and popular interest in reconsidering fundamental assumptions reinforced by the sovereign mold.

Recognizing the urgency of these questions, a variety of political philosophers, social scientists, and cultural theorists have sought a number of alternative approaches, including redefining the discourse of nationality by adding conceptual qualifiers ("liberal nationalism" and "long-distance nationalism"), introducing new philosophical and political vocabulary ("multicultural citizenship" and "rooted cosmopolitism"), and even forging novel fields of study (diaspora and transnational studies).[49] Although these approaches differ significantly from one another, they share a renewed interest in understanding the ties that bind individuals in an increasingly transnational era and expand the expectations of citizenship to promote particular allegiances within the nation-state.

The paradigms of interwar Zionism developed by Rawidowicz, Kaplan, and Kohn anticipated the contemporary tension between the forces of unity and diversity and the stubborn refusal of religious and national groups to conform. Concepts of diaspora, liberal nationalism, and multicultural citizenship are conceptually grounded in, and owe a significant debt to, the theorists of these conceptions of Zionism. Indeed, their work addresses key questions that have re-emerged around the world today as correlation between nation and state diminishes: How should liberal theories of nationalism balance a commitment to individual equality with demands by minority groups for collective rights? What does nationalism mean when disconnected from political membership in a state? What are possibilities of collective identification beyond racial dichotomies and class categorizations? What psychological bonds exist and motivate national membership, despite the constructed, fluid, and nonessential nature of national identity? What role does religion play in national solidarity? How do homeland and diaspora communities interact with one another? Zionism's roads not taken are uniquely suited to consider these questions and to contribute to the expanding literature grappling with these issues today.

— 2 —

"Sovereignty Is International Anarchy"

Jews, World War I, and the Future of Nationalism

"Sovereignty is international anarchy" is not a claim one might expect to hear from an American Zionist writing a book about the post–World War I political order in 1918. Yet, one year after the Balfour Declaration promised a "national home for the Jewish people," public intellectual and Zionist Horace Kallen vehemently objected to the premise of national self-determination (the official policy of the United States at the Paris Peace Conference).[1] Moreover, Kallen traced his opposition to national sovereignty to the teachings of the Jewish political tradition. As heir to this tradition, Zionism represented the hope for a new stage in the evolution of nationalism that challenged the doctrine of national sovereignty without eroding the legitimacy of national identity. The Jewish people, past and present, exemplified the ethical benefits and pragmatic necessity of promoting the coexistence of diverse national groups within a single polity as the future of nationalism.

The association of a Zionist thinker with the rejection of the principle of national sovereignty is baffling from a post-1948 perspective. Zionism has come to stand precisely for the right of the Jewish people to have a state in the national homeland. In fact, those most critical of Zionism and the state of Israel tend to frame their negative assessment of the state in language that echoes Kallen's censure of national sovereignty. But the relationship between Zionism, nationalism, and sovereignty appeared quite differently to Kallen during the first two decades of the twentieth century. Although his counterstate conception of Zionism would certainly be considered marginal today, it was not atypical at the time for American or European Jewish thinkers.[2] The intellectual and political milieu created a moment of possibility for an alternate logic of Zionism that viewed the solution to the Jewish question in rejecting the division of the globe into distinct units with homogeneous populations rather than establishing precisely such a place for the Jewish people.

Probing this phenomenon of counterstate Jewish nationalism in the early twentieth century raises two questions. First, what shared concerns, historical forces, and political ideologies made the concept of nation beyond state so appealing at the time for Jewish intellectuals in general and to Zionists in particular? Second, what strategies did Jewish thinkers develop to address the dilemmas of articulating collective boundaries outside of territorial sovereignty? Addressing these questions sets the historical and intellectual backdrop for the subsequent chapters' investigation of three of the most sophisticated expressions of interwar, counterstate Zionism: Rawidowicz's global Hebraism, Kaplan's national civilization, and Kohn's cultural humanism. These expressions developed within a fruitful and manifold context of Jewish and non-Jewish debates about nationalism and the international order.

Examining this moment without a historical lens molded by events that occurred midcentury—the Holocaust, the creation of the State of Israel, and the emergence of the nation-state as the organizing principle of international relations—sheds light on the rationale for rejecting, rather than emulating, the nation-state model as the most promising solution to the Jewish question. From this historical vantage point, the dominance of national sovereignty as the organizing principle of world politics, and the possibility of establishing a Jewish state, were far from certain outcomes. Instead, with the national question very much open for debate in Western political thought, the possibility that a new set of guiding principles that would recognize Jewish national identity across territorial and political boundaries (including Palestine) was quite a logical path to explore. Moreover, the prevalence of potential ideological partners committed to replacing nation-state nationalism with other paradigms created an incubator for radical experimentation and innovation, especially around conceptions of Jewish nationalism and Zionism.

My intention is not to provide an exhaustive overview of the diverse spectrum between counterstate and state-seeking Jewish nationalisms that thrived in this period. Instead, this chapter aims to identify and explore a shared theoretical predicament catalyzing Jewish interest in theories of nationalism—namely, the totalizing logic of nation-state nationalism and its implications for preserving Jews' individual and collective rights. I also introduce the overlapping strategies developed for contesting this logic. Jewish thinkers molded conceptions of nationalism that consciously disputed the either/or logic of the nation-state template by underscoring the compatibility of national autonomy and civic integration, particular solidarity and human allegiances, and categories of identity intended for homeland and diaspora settings. The both/and logic of counterstate Jewish nationalism advocated for a liberal, inclusive, and depoliticized theory of collective identity.

To emphasize the concurrent theoretical trends across spatial boundaries and ideological categories, the examples selected in this chapter focus on a few zones of contact that demonstrate the interconnectedness between Jewish and non-Jewish efforts to reject self-determination as the template for nationalism. These sites of interpenetration generated theoretical syntheses between Jewish political thought and formulations of a multinational state in late imperial Russia, national cultural autonomy within the Austro-Hungarian Empire, British internationalism, and American cultural pluralism. Focusing on several Jewish thinkers, including historian Simon Dubnow, international relations professor Alfred Zimmern, cultural Zionist Ahad Ha'am, scholar Israel Friedlaender, and American pluralist Horace Kallen reinforces important regional differences, but also facilitates a global and comparative analysis of this particular moment in Jewish thought and political thought in general.

Categorizing these multidimensional figures as "Zionist" or "diasporist," "Jewish thinkers" or "political theorists of Jewish descent," and "European" or "American" overlays anachronistic geographic and disciplinary boundaries that cloud common concerns and a shared discourse across what have become distinct fields of study. Rather than presenting ideological or regional clarity, the historical record demonstrates anxiety, hazy boundaries, and ambiguous formulations during this moment of radical social, political, and intellectual transition. Probing the often unsystematic conceptions of Jewish nationalism, and its strategic engagement with the nation-state paradigm, reveals a nuanced and complex process of exploring paths of particular preservation and individual rights before many of the assumptions about national identity, minority rights, and citizenship had crystallized by the middle of the century.

World War I and the Question of Nationality

The historian Jonathan Frankel argued that Jewish political thinkers responded in a paradoxical fashion to the unparalleled (at least in the modern period) destruction, dislocation, and persecution sparked by World

War I.[3] Wartime political and military upheavals generated a large number of unwanted refugees, kindled waves of anti-Semitism, and contributed to increased brutality against Jewish populations. The vulnerability of Jews as a stateless community was even more pronounced because so many Jewish population centers stood in contested zones between the great powers. The war thus underscored Jews' political weakness as a dispersed community. Their individual and collective security in Europe remained precarious in the war's aftermath.

Despite the hostilities and the uncertain status of many Jewish communities, however, Frankel highlighted the cautious optimism that characterized the war's effect on Jewish intellectuals. "Many Jews—movements, groups, individuals—came to the conclusion that the moment of emancipation or autoemancipation had arrived," Frankel wrote. "The Jewish people had it within their grasp at last to solve the Jewish question."[4] The belief in the dawn of a new era, with the potential to readdress fundamental questions about Jewish identity, generated tremendous ideological creativity, theoretical experimentation, and historical opportunities.

Frankel's reminder to analyze interwar Jewish politics as a distinct moment of promise, rather than as a prelude to the Holocaust, helps avoid a teleological reading of Zionism as inevitably leading to statehood. Situated against the backdrop of the twentieth-century narrative of European destruction, state-seeking Zionism emerges as the most obvious response for Jewish nationalists seeking emancipation following the cataclysm of the war. From a post-Holocaust vantage point, the events of World War I could easily be interpreted as marking the first convulsion of an unavoidable process that would lead to the destruction of European Jewry fewer than thirty years later. The effects of Jews' marginal position as outsiders during the war underscored Theodor Herzl's analysis of the failure of Jewish integration within Europe and bolstered his claim that Jewish normalization demanded a Jewish state. Herzl had presented Zionists with one potential solution—the creation of a Jewish state. This approach operated under the premise that the normalization and acceptance of Jews in the international order rested in Jews' adopting the logic of nation-state nationalism. The clearest path to emancipation was to exploit President Woodrow Wilson's articulation of the principle of national self-determination, promulgated at the Paris Peace Conference, and the Balfour Declaration to press for a Jewish homeland—and eventually, a state.

Yet the possibility of shifting a large percentage of the global Jewish population to the national homeland, let alone establishing a sovereign territory, was by no means the only (or the most likely) solution for early-twentieth-century Zionists. Frankel's description of the period, especially the sanguine hopes for radically overhauling the relationship between Jews and the state, suggests that postwar Jewish nationalists, including those strongly in favor of Zionism and settlement in Palestine, identified other options they considered more viable paths toward securing national preservation and individual freedom. The disintegration of imperial rule and the gradual process of decolonialization created a brief window during which theorists and activists advocated various alternate possibilities for envisioning the future of nationalities and the global political order. Such key concepts as nationality, sovereignty, and international relations were in flux. Changing borders, refugees, and demographic shifts exacerbated the disconnect between states and their ethnonational population and national identity. These historical conditions created the perception among political theorists of a tabula rasa of political possibilities.

As a result, programs that advocated for states of many nationalities, rather than for national states, and to separate ethnic or cultural identity from political citizenship, abounded. The postwar transition sparked calls for concepts ranging from minority national rights, federated international bodies, and even options for a world government. Although the details of these plans differed, and many of them never developed past the stage of abstract formulations that lacked specific details, they shared a basic assumption that nation-state nationalism was the primary cause of the war and would need to be replaced by alternate notions in order to build a peaceful postwar order. The prevalence of such notions was apparent at the Paris Peace Conference, which included numerous proposals for minority protection schemes. Also apparent was the support such critiques of nation-state nationalism had among world Jewry. The historian Carole Fink, one of the few scholars to look closely at the Jewish minority rights movement, has argued that Jewish leaders took a leading role in advocating for the recognition of national rights.[5] For Jews and non-Jews alike, distinguishing "nation," "state," and "territory" was not a marginal concept in the early decades of the twentieth century.

The Logic of Nationalism: A Transatlantic Concern

A significant number of geographically diverse Jewish nationalists aligned their work with intellectual currents and political movements dedicated to formulating concepts of nations as distinct from states. This phenomenon represents a shared concern with the totalizing demands of nation-state nationalism. Liberal strains of nationalism articulated during the nineteenth century viewed the nation-state as a particular political unit dedicated to spreading civic right and Enlightenment values. Such formulations of nationalism promised integration and individual rights for Jews. However, they also introduced a binary logic that made national identity an exclusive allegiance that demands complete loyalty. Each individual belonged to one primary ethnocultural community. One could not be German and French, for instance.

Conflating nation and state raised the stakes of this either/or logic even further by confusing patriotism and nationalism.[6] Full acceptance as a citizen derived from national membership. The legal standing of citizens, based on a social contract with the nation-state, could be altered by the sovereign national power depending on each individual's national status. Even if rights were not formally linked to membership in the nation, those perceived as non-nationals could face social and political discrimination. Thus, the retention of multiple group loyalties (especially across nation-state boundaries) was problematic and had the potential to undermine the rights granted by the state to its citizenry.

At the same time, nationalism severely restricted acceptable categories of difference within the polity to subordinate categories of identity (such as religion) that reinforced the primacy of national solidarity over other collective ties. The philosopher Charles Taylor has analyzed the relationship between nationalism and modernity, describing this force as intimately linked to the rationale of the nation-state paradigm. He identifies the "homogenization of identity and allegiance that it [the state] must nourish for survival."[7] In order for the state to achieve its economic, social, and political objectives, it must reinforce some degree of national conformity. The emerging choice between conformity for insiders and marginalization for outsiders left Jewish thinkers unable to express difference without further undermining their claims for equality and citizenship, increasingly based on their degree of national conformity. The shift in the rhetoric of nationalism toward more conservative, ethnic tendencies at the start of the twentieth century exacerbated the implications of the logic of linking people, territory, and state. This trajectory placed a greater emphasis on ethnonational uniformity, and in some cases raised the bar for integration by underscoring descent as the primary criterion for national membership. As a result, confidence in the nation-state as the guarantor of individual rights eroded.

It is important to avoid the tendency to focus primarily on how so-called romantic, cultural, or völkisch varieties of nationalism undermined individual rights and collective legitimacy. Historians of nationalism tend to divide its expressions in the modern period into two categories—civic and ethnic variations.[8] As general categories, civic and ethnic paradigms outline fundamentally different claims about the nature of national cohesion, the central objectives of membership, and the relationship between nation and state. Ethnic nationalism is a tradition linked to the German Romantic tradition, beginning with Johann Gottfried von Herder in the eighteenth century and developing through Johann Gottlieb Fichte and Georg Wilhelm Friedrich Hegel in the nineteenth. These figures developed the concept that authentic nationality reflects organic ties rooted in blood, spirit, and land. On the other side of the spectrum are theories of nationality that view the voluntary commitment to universal civic principles (such as individual rights, free choice, and equality) as the basis for national cohesion. Civic nationality, at least in theory, eschews innate characteristics such as race, language, or culture advocated by ethnic nationalists as the primary grounds for national unity.

Yet this typological distinction does not reflect the ways in which many Jewish intellectuals viewed the logic of nation-state nationalism. (Indeed, the popularizer of this concept was Hans Kohn, whose intellectual journey from German Zionism to American nationalism is the subject of chapter 5. Tracing the development of the civic–ethnic dichotomy in Kohn's thought historicizes its evolution and demonstrates his own ambiguous relationship to the rigid dichotomy attributed to his scholarship.) Clearly, the threats posed by states committed to a particular community based on organic, familial categories are more easily discernible. Associating national membership with unchanging biological or cultural characteristics severely restricted the possibility of being considered a conational, with its attendant rights of citizenship.

From the perspective of the counterstate nationalists explored in this book, however, liberal nationalisms associated with the rhetoric of universal principles demanded conformity and promoted intolerance as much as exclusivist, or ethnic, conceptions. More recent scholars of nationalism have helped explain the limited relevance of this distinction for minority groups. The political theorist Bernard Yack, for instance, exposes what he has called the "myth of civic nationalism."[9] Yack contends that the discourse of equality at the heart of civic conceptions masks particular concerns within universal rhetoric. Both civic nationalism and ethnic nationalism implicitly undermined efforts to preserve corporate identity, and at their logical extremes they defined difference as antithetical to their fundamental projects.[10] Conceptions of national sovereignty were thus simultaneously too particularistic and too universalistic for securing Jewish integration and preserving Jewish solidarity.

One particularly important ramification of the perceived difference between the exclusivist, unwelcoming nationalism in Central and Eastern Europe and a liberal, integration-compatible nationalism in Western Europe and the United States was its tendency to reinforce the existence of a qualitative difference between the American Jewish and European Jewish experiences of nationalism. Although the success of the American–Jewish synthesis is not often told explicitly through the language of civic nationalism, the concepts help delineate why the experience of Jews in the United States differed so markedly from those in Europe. The United States represents the exemplar of civic nationalism. A state that unites its citizenry around shared principles of equality and freedom welcomed Jews, as opposed to the European experience, which excluded Jews because of their inability to integrate into the tribal bonds that had served as the cohesive basis of Central and East European nationalisms.

Historicizing the civic–ethnic dichotomy challenges the narrative of a harmonious synthesis between American Jewish thinkers and the state. Notable variations in theories of nationalism and Jewish responses to these conceptions of the national identity exist. The realities of Jewish integration in the United States were significantly different than those in Europe. The corporate status of Jewish communal life, which characterized most of European Jewry until the nineteenth century, never existed in North America. Jewish immigrants found themselves in a country that welcomed them as full citizens (with some early restrictions on Jews serving as elected officials), provided unprecedented opportunities for acculturation, and viewed religious association as completely voluntary.[11] These characteristics underscore unique aspects of the American Jewish experience.

Despite these important historical and theoretical differences, however, American Jewish intellectuals viewed the dangers of nation-state nationalism and the promise of separating nation from state as a problem germane not only to their European brethren, but also to their own political milieu. The work of recent American historians, such as Gary Gerstle, has situated early-twentieth-century Jewish intellectuals within a broader context that disputes the exceptional status of nationalism in the United States. Gerstle has illuminated the intertwined streams of civic and ethnoracial conceptions of American identity that characterized U.S. history. His analysis suggests that rhetoric rooted in exclusivist theories based on ethnoracial characteristics and liberal civic theories dedicated to individual rights contributed to nativism and pressure for immigrants to conform.[12]

The most obvious parallel for American Jews was the rise of nativism and racialized concepts of American identity that manifested themselves in new immigration regulations as well as popular publications. A series of immigration acts in the late 1910s and early 1920s exhibited the tremendous currency nativism and racial nationalism had achieved. The acts severely curtailed immigration from Eastern and Southern Europe, a move that was aimed primarily at Jewish and Italian immigrants. In fact, the U.S. Congress justified this last series of stringent immigration acts by citing "the menace that eastern and southern Europeans, especially Jews and Italians posed to the United States."[13] The racial and biological language that was used to justify the act reflected the considerable increase in discussions of scientific racism and eugenics. The proliferation of racial science relegated all non-Anglo-Saxons, including "Hebrews," to inferior status.[14] For the American Jewish community living through this explosion in anti-immigrant fervor and racial categorization, who obviously lacked the foreknowledge of what the twentieth century would bring, these theories must have augured perniciously.

It was not only streams of American racial and ethnic nationalism that posed a threat to Jews' individual and collective rights. Pressure for Jews to conform to certain national characteristics and to exclude Jews from full acceptance also emerged from proponents of integration, progressive liberalism, and a religious Social Gospel Movement. If one trend in theories of Americanization was the exclusionary language of racial nationalism, the second trend was civic nationalism. This theory of American identity was often linked with the notion of the melting pot, which had a long history in U.S. political discourse. The French-born essayist Hector St. John de Crèvecoeur helped to coin this phrase in 1782, when he wrote in *Letters from an American Farmer*: "What then is the American, this new man? Here individuals of all nations are melted into a race of men."[15]

Israel Zangwell's 1908 play *The Melting Pot* vitalized this vision of U.S. identity and ushered it into the foreground of twentieth-century identity discussions. The melting-pot concept allowed for a number of possible interpretations, particularly regarding two fundamental questions. First, which of the many "flavors" would become dominant in the new national identity? And second, what would be the level of political, cultural, and social conformity demanded from each member of the nation? Notions of melting pots never guaranteed neutral unbiased territory for creating an equal mixture that embraced all of its constituent members. As the theorist Werner Sollors has commented, Pauline tropes of universal identity integrally linked with critiques of Jewish particularism profoundly prejudiced Zangwell's and Crèvecoeur's notions of the melting pot.[16] This etymology of the term in Christian thought suggests that although the reformers encouraged the integration of new Americans into their "new national-ism," they demanded a high price of national, religious, and linguistic conformity.

Even many of the reforms that gave the period the name the "Progressive Era" further defined a unified, organic American identity as the ultimate end of the melting-pot process by promoting a shift from individualism to corporate identity. Unlike racial nationalists, Progressives rejected the erection of racial boundaries to safeguard American biological purity; in its place, they developed a monolithic vision of American nationality that eliminated a large section of the political, cultural, and social spaces previously available to minority communities. The tone of the new nationalism constricted the separation in liberal societies between political citizenship and national character. American identity now was seen to connote a commitment to a national mission that entailed not only political membership, but also certain cultural and religious assumptions.

Unlike classic liberalism, which stressed the autonomy of the individual as the primary political actor, Progressive thought developed a political philosophy that emphasized the national corporate group.[17] As the political scientist Rogers M. Smith has explained, in classic liberalism individuals were considered members or foreigners depending only on their status of citizenship and not on their decision to join voluntary religious, political, or social organizations.[18] The Progressive concept of citizenship maintained certain standards that made cultural, religious, and political demands on individual citizens. In opposition to the notion that the individual political actor was responsible for only his own actions, many Progressive thinkers constructed ideas of citizenship "that stipulated that the possession of social knowledge entailed the duty of reflecting on and articulating ideas of national public good unmediated by party, interest, region or sectarian religion."[19] This major shift in U.S. political culture had a significant impact on discussions of "otherness" and American identity. The expansion of the definition of American identity to include a range of characteristics therefore challenged the possibility of alternative communal affiliations.

The Progressive conflation of patriotism and nationalism in U.S. politics spread into political practice through the contributions of such writers as Walter Croly, the editor of *The New Republic*. Croly's highly influential 1909 work, *The Promise of American Life* (which Theodore Roosevelt used as the basis of his New Nationalism campaign in 1912), decried the moral and social ills brought about by American individualism. To fulfill the "promise of American life," Croly advocated the restoration of American "solidarity." By conferring more power on the government's ability to promote the national public interest, he hoped to eradicate the economic and social troubles of big business. American democracy, Croly claimed, had failed because "the national interest has not been consistently asserted as against special and local interests."[20]

The stress on placing national considerations over individual or group rights during this period manifested itself in both Theodore Roosevelt's and Woodrow Wilson's calls as president for minority Americans to fully embrace their U.S. identity—without other markers of identity. According to the historian John Higham, Roosevelt considered the hyphenated identity a menace to society. His militant nationalism propelled him on a crusade against the notion of dual identities, and he stood out "as the standard-bearer and personification of 'unhyphenated Americanism.'"[21] Wilson, provoked by the xenophobia of the war years, continued the Americanization thrust with his "100 percent America" campaign. This movement burgeoned to such a degree that "by the time of the Armistice the 100 percent spirit . . . reigned supreme. Where the liberal American-izers had looked to the government for aid in the immigrant education program, 100 percenters now pressed to enlist the state's authority for purposes of repression and exclusion."[22]

The slippage between nation and state in the American context even expanded to include religious intellectuals preaching an explicit variation of the message. Liberal Protestantism, and particularly the social gospel movement, which had reached its apogee in the first two decades of the twentieth century, embraced Progressive politics as a vehicle for Christianizing America and thus ensuring the social salvation of the entire nation.[23] Through this syncretic fusion of social gospel and Progressive thought, these adherents hoped to "realize the nineteenth-century dream of a Protestant nation. . . . It was the old concept of Christendom, refurbished to fit the realties of voluntaristic, pluralistic, liberty-loving Protestantism."[24] The eruption of religious, racial, and national expectations of American citizenship in the years surrounding the Great War severely restricted options for articulating the meaning of Jewish identity and its relationship to the state. The extensive vocabulary that would develop in the second half of the twentieth century to include Jews as an ethnic group, or as one of the three core religions of American nationalism, did not yet exist. As the American historian David Hollinger has explained, "American political ideology and constitutional doctrine so emphasized individuality that the pluralists of the early twentieth century were endowed with very few tools for talking about the claims of groups."[25] Jewish intellectuals faced the challenge of inventing new conceptual vocabulary that would both counter the claims of American nationalism and promote an alternate category to define "oth-erness" in the American context.

Projecting the existence of a categorical distinction between American civic and European ethnic nationalisms in the early interwar period over-shadows the existence of shared concerns and Jewish responses across the Atlantic. Nationalism's totalizing logic—exacerbated by the tendency to merge civic, religious, racial, and ethnic conceptions of collective identi-ty—manifested itself on both sides of the Atlantic. So did the dilemmas it raised for Jewish thinkers grappling with ways to express otherness within the state without accepting the poles of assimilation or alienation. As long as the concepts of nation and state remained intertwined, theoretical and practical opportunities for creating an equilibrium between Jews and the state that recognized both the right to integration and to the preservation of particular collective were quite restricted. In response to this realiza-tion, Jewish thinkers identified potential allies in mainstream programs and movements dedicated to reconsidering the logic of nationalism.

From Nation-States to States of Nations

The scholar and American Zionist Israel Friedlaender wrote in 1905: "Therefore we must clearly distinguish between state and nationality, as has long been done with regard to state and religion."[26] This comment exem-plifies the first objective for Jewish thinkers interested in fragmenting the totalizing claims of national sovereignty: developing a theoretical distinc-tion between the organic bonds of national solidarity and the patriotic ties of citizens to the state. The intellectual sources of Friedlaender's concept of separating nation and state reflect the overlapping currents of Jewish and Western political thought grappling with the nation-state model in Europe and the United States. This section of the chapter traces the broad reach of Jewish and non-Jewish theories and programs that advocated for categori-cal distinctions between national allegiance and political citizenship.

Even before the conclusion of World War I brought questions about the relationship between nation and state to the forefront of public debates in Western Europe and the United States, the possibilities of formally creating multinational polities evolved in Central and Eastern Europe. The demo-graphic patchwork of ethnic groups created tremendous ethnonational rifts within heterogeneous populations. Political theorists and politicians con-ceived of various models for mitigating hostility by recognizing collective rights within the framework of the state. For instance, political reforms in late imperial Russia provided a brief period in which the Kadet Party aspired toward creating a multinational state that would support the cultural autonomy of minority populations as well as their rights as individual citizens.[27]

The Jewish historian Simon Dubnow saw these developments as potentially well suited for the implementation of his comprehensive theory of Jewish nationalism, which he called "autonomism" or "diaspora nationalism."[28] In the years leading up to and immediately following the Russian Revolution of 1905, Dubnow outlined a program of Jewish nationalism that sought cultural, social, and educational autonomy, along with a complete guarantee of civic equality. In 1906, he created a political party called the Folkspartei to translate his theoretical program into political action, and by 1915 he had established a monthly journal dedicated to advocating for extraterritorial autonomy.[29] Dubnow viewed his activism and writings on Jewish nationalism as a forum for addressing the central problem of modern political thought: "Contemporary legal philosophers and political scientists frequently confuse the terms 'nation' and 'state'. . . . For them, the typical nation is the uni-national state."[30]

Negating the tendency to confuse nation and state in Western political thought was an issue of central concern that Dubnow chose to address in a rather indirect fashion—through a series of essays exploring Jewish nationalism.[31] Jewish nationalism introduced a more ethical alternative to the nation-state model that celebrated the Jews' ability to thrive without sovereignty. The shared culture and language linking the Jewish people exemplified the most progressive grounds for collective solidarity. Dubnow's attempt to partner with the liberal Kadet Party failed—he remained frustrated by the high degree of Russification and conformity that they demanded from minority groups. Moreover, the entire project of liberal reforms in Russia became increasingly unlikely after the failed revolution of 1905. Yet Dubnow's belief that a political entity that rejected the uni-national state provided a path toward Jewish national and individual rights underscores a shared predicament for subsequent Jewish nationalists writing in different milieus.

Dubnow's analysis of the threat of merging the concepts of nation and state, his vision of Jewish political thought as the highest level in the development of nationalism, and his belief that a multinational state represented the best hope for normalizing Jewish life has significant parallels with a number of the Zionist intellectuals explored in this chapter and throughout this book. Indeed, Friedlaender, a Zionist who opposed Dubnow's rejection of Palestine as a territorial center, called for the separation of nation and state in a review essay of Dubnow's theory of nationalism. In the case of Friedlaender and Dubnow, Zionism and diasporism differed on the role of Palestine. However, the two theorists agreed on a far more basic assumption about Jewish political thought: namely, that Jews, the pariah of the nation-state era, would emerge as the normative model for the post-nation-state moment. Streams of Zionism and diasporism had a common theoretical agenda of outlining a Jewish mission of unlinking nation from state as the template for twentieth-century nationalism. The Russian context, with Dubnow the most influential example, did not present the only theoretical or geographical context for grappling with these relationships in Jewish thought. The collapsing Austro-Hungarian Empire, which included a number of Jewish population centers, also served as a fertile backdrop for promoting the categorical distinction between nation and state. As the historian Malachi Hacohen has explained, "the ambiguity of Austrian nationality gave Jews an opportunity missing elsewhere for negotiating Jewish and national identity."[32]

Jewish intellectuals thinking within this milieu also had the support of mainstream intellectuals and political leaders formulating nonstatist, deterritorialized definitions of nationality. In order to address the tremendous national tensions, the Austrian Marxist theorist Karl Renner, who served as chancellor of Austria from 1918 to 1920, developed a model of national cultural autonomy in such key works as *State and Nation* (1899) and the *Struggles of the Austrian Nations over the State* (1902).[33] In these works, Renner critiques the "territorial principle" that underlies the concept of national sovereignty. This principle, Renner contends, assumes that "if you live in my territory you are subjected to my domination, my law and my language."[34] Such a claim, he concludes, "is the expression of domination, not of equal rights."[35] Given heterogeneous population, demographic shifts, and economic interchange, any attempt to align a specific land with a people would disenfranchise those groups not part of the ethnonational elite. Renner proposes an alternate definition of a nation as a "cultural community."[36] Adopting a cultural rather than territorial basis of identity created the possibility of a multinational state sensitive to collective loyalties and individual rights.

Another influential scholar, Friedrich Meinecke, the founder of German political intellectual history, further contributed to the active debates about the relationship between nationhood and statehood. His book, *The Idea of Reasons of State* (1925), traced the historical development of the relationship between ethics and realpolitik from Machiavelli through World War I.[37] In his conclusion, Meinecke critiqued the notion of the "power state" and denounced the "false idealization of power politics."[38] Both Meinecke's power state and Renner's territorial principle laid the groundwork for a moral critique of blurring the organic ties of national solidarity and the political apparatus of the state and its demands of citizenship. As the historian Yfaat Weiss has underscored, these distinctions shaped the Zionism of a number of Central European Jewish thinkers, including Hans Kohn and his teacher, the philosopher Martin Buber.[39] Zionism promised to create a laboratory for implementing moral principles that demanded a multinational state to avoid the potential problem of fusing political power and national solidarity.[40]

Efforts to break the sovereign mold took root in the Western European context as well. British internationalists insisted that the doctrine of national sovereignty presented the most destabilizing threat to postwar government and international relations. Liberal internationalists disagreed with the doctrine's fundamental premise—that each ethnonational community had the right to self-determination and territorial sovereignty—on both practical and normative grounds. This equation of national collectivity with a sovereign polity would fuel enduring strife between nation-states committed to their particular concerns. From an ethical perspective, remapping the globe in accordance with nation-state boundaries would impede progress toward the spread of universal justice and equality by erecting boundaries rather than promoting integration through education, social interaction, and economic cooperation. The antidote to the militarism and belligerent nationalism engendered by national sovereignty, liberal internationalists contended, was the creation of a "federation of nationalities" or the establishment of a "commonwealth."

A brief, albeit significant and overlooked, synthesis developed between internationalism, with its vision of a commonwealth of nationalities, and Zionism during the first third of the twentieth century. A disproportionate number of leaders in colonial government, Zionism, and the creation of the field of international studies were of Jewish descent.[41] An enduring British Empire held great hope for many Jews as an ideal political structure to mitigate their alien status as a stateless community. One of the architects and propagators of the synthesis was Sir Alfred Zimmern. During the war years, Zimmern had been a central figure in the Round Table group, a society of British intellectuals that promoted internationalism. In addition, he had served as a member of the Political Intelligence Department in the British Foreign Office (1918–1919), where he focused on postwar reconstruction plans. Shortly after the war he was appointed the world's first professor of international relations in 1919 at the University College of Wales and later the Montague Burton Professor of International Relations at Oxford University (from 1930 to 1944).[42] From 1905 until the 1920s, Zimmern, whose Jewish father had converted to Christianity before marrying his mother, was a strong supporter of Zionism and was engaged in theorizing Jewish nationalism.

Zimmern's vision of nationality and internationalism developed as he explored his own Jewish identity and Zionism beginning around 1905, and continuing for about two decades. Zimmern publicly attributed his understanding of nationality as cultural, rather than political, to his experience as a man of Jewish heritage: "I learnt to value Nationality, not from reading Mazzini's essays . . . nor from sympathizing with European Nationalist movements . . . but from realizing, as I grew to manhood, that I was not an Englishman, and from my sense of the debt I owe to the heritage with which I am connected by blood and tradition."[43] Over the next two decades, the idea of nationality he developed in his writings in the Round Table and used as the basis for the British draft proposal for the peace treaty reflected his devotion. Like Dubnow, Zimmern promulgated the notion that the Jews represented the nation that had best learned "to eschew the misleading confusion of nationality and statehood and to avoid the pitfall of considering the nation-state as the normal and final unit of government."[44]

Although Zimmern has been largely ignored by Jewish historians, his interwar writings had a tremendous effect on his contemporaries, including a number of American Jewish thinkers.[45] Chapter 4 in this book tells the story of Mordecai Kaplan, one of the most influential American Jewish thinkers, who integrated Zimmern's theory of nationalism and internationalism into his own concept of "Judaism as a civilization." The American Jewish theorist responsible for introducing Zimmern, and the synthesis between Zionism and internationalism he championed, to Kaplan and other Jewish intellectuals was Horace Kallen, whose declaration that sovereignty was "international anarchy" was discussed earlier.[46] Kallen developed a close friendship with Zimmern during the British internationalist's visit to the United States in 1912.[47] Their intellectual exchange is clearly evident in Kallen's evolving understanding of Zionism's role in promoting internationalism. "Zionism and the Struggle towards Democracy," which Kallen published in the Nation magazine in 1915, contends that "Zionism reasserted the prophetic idea of internationalism as a democratic and cooperative federation of nationalities."[48]

Placing Kallen within this transatlantic context offers new perspectives on his seminal conception of American pluralism. Kallen is remembered primarily as the architect of an American conception of cultural pluralism and not as an advocate of a stream of Zionism and internationalism that challenged the nation-state paradigm. Yet "Democracy versus the Melting-Pot," the essay considered the blueprint for the concept of cultural pluralism, does not mention the term "cultural pluralism" even once.[49] Instead, Kallen uses vocabulary such as nationality, federation of nationalities, and commonwealth that had very specific connotations for his contemporaries regarding the ethical and practical need to contest the spread of self-determination as the principle of nationalism. Kallen's reputation as a pluralist blunts the extent to which his most important contributions to American thought, such as "Democracy versus the Melting-Pot," framed the debate as part of a much larger question of nationality and its relationship to the American state. Referring to Kallen as a pluralist (a term he only associated with "Democracy versus the Melting-Pot" when it was reprinted in 1924) rather than a nationalist links the American Jewish thinker to a uniquely American discourse of difference that had little relationship to, and thus avoided the pitfalls of, European nationalism. Although Kallen contributed theoretical building blocks for what would later become American concepts of ethnicity and multiculturalism, they emerged from within the capacious parameters of Zionism and its emerging strategies for negotiating the demands of European nationalism.

American Jewish historians would also not be predisposed to link Kallen's interest in Zionism with a nationalist orientation. The "Americanization of Zionism" thesis, a central historiographical narrative in American Jewish history, diminishes the full scope of Zionism's impact in the United States.[50] According to this account, the American experience transformed European Zionism to meet the unique political opportunities available to Jews in the United States. The separatist claims and political analysis of European Jewish nationalism had little relevance in the United States.[51] As opposed to the persecution and political instability that galvanized early-twentieth-century European Jews to develop and embrace Jewish nationalism, the United States promised a harmonious balance between Judaism and Americanism.[52]

The oft-repeated episodes from Kallen's intellectual biography—specifically the rejection of his father's traditional Judaism and his introduction to Zionism through the lectures of his professors at Harvard University—fit the contours of embracing Zionism as a path away from the "old" European context and assimilating the expectations of Americanism. Until recently, few scholars have analyzed Kallen's own claims about the role that his personal sense of discrimination and proud associations with Judaism and Zionism played in staking out his vision of integration without assimilation.[53] Kallen's legacy provides an instructive example of how the history of American Zionism downplays Zionist ideology's active opposition to homogenizing and exclusivist trends in American nationalism.[54]

Kallen did not write "Democracy versus the Melting-Pot" at the post–World War II moment when the American–Jewish synthesis crystallized and the idea of cultural pluralism gained popular currency. Instead, he engaged American nationalism at a time of tremendous insecurity for Jews, both in the United States and around the world. From the perspective of several leading American Jewish thinkers, such as Kallen, American and European nationalism were not qualitatively different. Kallen penned "Democracy versus the Melting-Pot" shortly after reading a pamphlet in which his colleague at the University of Wisconsin, the sociologist Edward Alsworth Ross, had concluded that the immigration of such groups as "Eastern European Hebrews" will lead to "the rise of a Jewish question here, perhaps riots and anti-Jewish legislation."[55] The anxiety that Jews would remain permanent outsiders reminded Kallen of the tremendous stakes involved in disputing the demands of the American state and nationalism more generally. Constructing a counterstate paradigm of Jewish nationalism emerged as one strategy for addressing this anxiety and eliminating it by undermining the theoretical basis of its perceived root causes.

Reconfiguring the Basis and Boundaries of National Membership

Jewish thinkers' engagement with multinationalism, internationalism, and cultural pluralism shed light on a global phenomenon of synthesizing Jewish political thought with theories of nationalism opposed to national sovereignty. Establishing a distinction between nation and state, however, was only the first step in validating the collective status of stateless populations. The next step involved defining alternate boundaries of national identity. The doctrine of national sovereignty set concrete boundaries—such as citizenship, border controls, education systems, cultural policies, and language requirements—that constitute the basis of national membership. Identifying grounds for national cohesion beyond the material characteristics typically underscored by the doctrine of national sovereignty compels theorists to identify alternate criteria.

In formulating counterstatist national ties, Jewish thinkers grappled with a catch-22. To an external audience, the primary function of formulating Jewish nationalism was to provide a template that would neutralize the state's monopoly on national identity and promote integration. To an internal audience, however, the Jewish nationalist had the opposite concern—to locate sustainable grounds for solidarity, cohesion, and particular preservation. Theorizing national boundaries thus functioned to promote discordant objectives: integration and differentiation. Counterstate nationalists sought a logic of nationalism that walked a fine line between affirming the particular aspects of Jewish national identity and highlighting permeable boundaries between Jews and non-Jews. This section of the chapter explores the emergence of a Jewish logic of nationalism that mitigated this tension by replacing an either/or logic of nationalism with a more inclusive both/and approach. In particular, Jewish theorists constructed formulations of Jewish nationalism that rejected three specific choices encoded within the nation-state paradigm—assimilation or autonomy, nationalism or humanism, diaspora or homeland—as false dichotomies.

One common strategy for developing a conceptual language for collective identity between the poles of assimilation and autonomy was the adoption, and reinterpretation, of terms associated with German Romanticism—such as "idea," "spirit," and "culture"—to describe the ties that bind Jews to one another. The nineteenth- and early-twentieth-century roots of these concepts in German Romanticism and Idealism provided rich possibilities for justifying the national status, despite their stateless condition and demographic dispersion. By emphasizing that each national group shared a particular living essence reflected in a set of characteristics shared by members of the group, these theories downplayed the importance of territory and self-determination. Moreover, the terminology enabled Jewish thinkers to propose a diverse (and often, even within the same thinker, inconsistent) range of constituent elements, including language, history, connection to a homeland, and even religion, to highlight various grounds of membership.[56]

Yet adapting this conceptual language as the basis for national boundaries had a significant disadvantage. The essentialist rhetoric of terms such as spirit was associated with the very theories of nationalism whose emphasis on descent and blood prevented the possibility of integration for minority populations. Why would Jewish thinkers employ concepts associated with ascriptive characteristics as a tool for articulating the compatibility of national autonomy and integration as citizens? Understanding the choice of this terminology, and the process of transvaluing its connotations, in the theories of Dubnow, Kallen, and Zimmern, highlights the challenge of developing a conceptual vocabulary to articulate notions of national collectivity that eschewed the polar possibilities of assimilation or autonomy.

Dubnow viewed the concept of spirit as a crucial basis in his search to legitimate a stateless, deterritorialized national identity as the most advanced stage in political thought. Yet he remained deeply aware that organic notions of solidarity ran the risk of creating rigid boundaries and tribal exclusivity. As a result, Dubnow adapted the term and repudiated some of its connotations. He defined the spirit of Judaism as the discovery that "there is no single definite idea which runs through all periods like a silk thread. There are various ideas, which increase cultural creativity and deep yearning for social progress in every generation."[57] This argument makes two counterintuitive claims: first, the unique spirit of the Jewish political tradition is the appreciation of diversity; and second, the core characteristic that differentiates Jews from other national groups is their enduring commitment to progress and evolution. Dubnow remained consciously aware of both, and used the terminology he attributed to Fichte, the author of the nationalist tract "Addresses to the German Nation," and undermined its emphasis on fixed biological characteristics at the same time. Dubnow's spirit embodies the competing ideals of unity and multiplicity, fixed essence and dynamic evolution. Juxtaposing conflicting principles thus helps explain the notable lack of detail provided by Dubnow (and other thinkers adopting the same ambiguous terminology) about the specific grounds of national identity. Underscoring fixed attributes would undermine the delicate attempt to establish an intentionally vague relationship between unchanging characteristics and permeable borders.

The theories of nationalism, both Jewish and general, developed by Kallen and Zimmern indicate the existence of a parallel strategy among self-identified Zionist intellectuals for defining the essence of Judaism as the process of change. Zimmern's spiritual principle of nationalism and Kallen's conception of Hebraism as a living spirit serve primarily to underscore Jewish political thought's historical ability to maintain an evolving equilibrium between national autonomy and international integration.[58] Neither thinker linked his notions of spirit to Dubnow, the most obvious source for altering concepts of the national spirit to meet integrationist objectives. Instead, both theorists traced the intellectual genealogy for their understanding of the Jewish spirit to the Zionist ideology of Ahad Ha'am.

For Zimmern and Kallen, Ahad Ha'am represented "the best exponent of nationalist theory in modern times"; he was the thinker most closely associated with the Jewish political tradition as espoused by the prophets from Amos to Job.[59] Why would highly acculturated Western intellectuals place Ahad Ha'am, a man committed to a romantic, linguistic articulation of nationalism, in such an esteemed position in demonstrating the compatibility of the Jewish spirit with integration and pluralism? For Zimmern and Kallen, Ahad Ha'am set the groundwork for shifting the meaning of national spirit from its genesis in organic, familiar, and essentialist ties to a purposefully imprecise phrase promoting the dynamic interaction between national groups.

Ahad Ha'am's conviction that the diaspora was an enduring fact of Jewish life propelled him to consider the relationship between various national groups living within shared territorial and political boundaries.[60] He developed a concept of "imitation" to address this reality. Imitation promoted a middle path between the twofold dangers of self-effacing assimilation, on the one hand, and radical national separation on the other. Preserving discrete national groups (often dispersed across political boundaries) and promoting the interactions of diverse nationalities within a single polity ignite conversations that propel both groups toward greater degrees of cooperation and cosmopolitan aspirations. Indeed, Ahad Ha'am had already paved the way for the fusion of Jewish nationalism and internationalism by concluding that the process of imitation "widens its [the nation's] scope, and becomes intersocial or international."[61] No wonder Zimmern insisted in 1905, shortly after reading the cultural Zionists' essays for the first time, "Ahad Ha'am should be commended to British Internationalists."[62]

Kallen's discussion of the Hebrew spirit, which he referred to as "Hebraism," as the glue connecting Jews past and present, also reflects the influence of Ahad Ha'am. Kallen defines Hebraism as "the name for this living spirit which demands righteousness, expressed in all the different interests in which Jews, as Jews, have a share—in art, science, philosophy, and social organization and in religion."[63] In adopting this term, Kallen both nods to Ahad Ha'am's language and further distinguishes himself from the cultural Zionist. The primary function of Hebraism was not to establish a set of particular beliefs, practices, or allegiances. Despite the similarity with linguistic or völkisch categories of nationality, Kallen clearly stresses the evolving and multifaceted aspects of Jewish national culture. The conscious shift from static content to dynamic process at the heart of Jewish national cohesion makes this theory of collectivity completely compatible with the model of imitation. The specific details of Hebraism were far less important than its historical ability to maintain an evolving equilibrium between particular allegiances and cosmopolitan aspirations, national autonomy and international integration.

A variation of Kallen's modified interpretation of Ahad Ha'am's concept of spirit emerges as an underlying argument in "Democracy versus the Melting-Pot." The essay's promotion of dissimilation, rather than assimilation, upholds the paradoxical contention that perpetuating national boundaries stimulates the intermingling of distinct communities. Kallen wrote: "Although it [Jewish nationality] is far more in tune than the other quarters, it is also far more autonomous in spirit and self-conscious in culture."[64] The Jewish spirit stands out for its distinct ability to embody two poles: the dynamic engagement with other national groups and the passionate affirmation of its individuality.

A noteworthy difference distinguishing Kallen's Hebraism from Ahad Ha'am's conception of national spirit is the omission of the centrality of the Hebrew language. Utilizing a theory of linguistic nationalism while jettisoning the particular national language undermines the internal consistency of Ahad Ha'am's cultural Zionism. Kallen's reliance on Hebrew sources, specifically the prophetic writings, as the primary source of Jewish national culture was a poor substitute for the reemergence of Hebrew as a living language that would bridge ancient sources and modern culture. At the same time, however, the decision reconfigured Hebraism to an American milieu by underscoring the process of integration as the defining characteristic of the Hebrew spirit and eliminated the most concrete border: the need for American Jews to actually know or learn the Hebrew language. As a result, Kallen's Zionism went even further than diasporist Dubnow in identifying nationality with integration. Writing in a multilinguistic context, Dubnow (like his friend Simon Rawidowicz, the subject of chapter 3) retained language as a primary marker of difference. Zimmern and Kallen (paralleling Hans Kohn's interpretation of cultural Zionism) took the logic of the spirit of progress to its essence—a catalyst for mutual understanding and accelerated cultural amalgamation.

This function of the language of spirit in Kallen's writings has been completely overshadowed by another, far more famous, quotation from "Democracy versus the Melting-Pot." The essay concludes: "men may change their clothes . . . they cannot change their grandfathers."[65] For recent interpreters of the history of American pluralism, such as Werner Sollors and David Hollinger, this emphasis on descent demonstrates Kallen's adoption of the biological criteria of group identity negatively associated with the term spirit.[66] This distorts the conscious effort Kallen made through his writings during the early decades of the twentieth century to find a language of collectivity that supported both permeable and fixed boundaries of identity.

These readings fail to appreciate Kallen's attempt to dissolve the tension between national autonomy and integration. Kallen grappled with national boundaries that would fall "between race and more external forms of associative unity."[67] For Kallen, "the mythology of race" did not contradict the claim that men "cannot change their grandfather." This balancing act between what scholars today might contrast as essentialism and hybridity reflects conflicting yearnings to limit the exclusivist claims of nationalism to make space for Jews as a distinct, and equal, minority community and to legitimate the national boundaries of the Jewish people.

Jewish thinkers revised concepts of national spirit and culture as tools for navigating these contrasting objectives. The primary strategic benefit of deploying these terms was what they were *not*—concepts of nationality based on territorial or political ties. One could identify with both a particular national spirit and a patriotic allegiance to the host country. In addition, concepts of spirit and culture appealed because their semantic elasticity allowed them to do double-duty as terms reflecting Jewish political thought's commitment to facilitating both acculturation and differentiation. Such an essentialized definition created a clear boundary between Jews and other groups that transcended territory or sovereignty. Yet the terms could be adjusted to blur the dichotomy between the choices of fixed identity and a complete rejection of the enduring ties created by family loyalties, sociological attachments, and intellectual curiosity. Addressing this dilemma, however, left Jewish nationalists such as Kallen and Zimmern open to two potential criticisms: their notions of collectivity are too amorphous for those interested in national autonomy and too impermeable for integrationists.

Nationalism, Liberalism, and Humanism

One of the noteworthy patterns that emerged in counterstate expressions of Jewish nationalism was its association with universal principles connected to modernity, progress, and morality. A number of thinkers unequivocally equated Jewish nationalism (generally in opposition to the nation-state variety) with such key terms as civilization, progress, liberalism, and ethical. The juxtaposition of Jewish particularity with universal allegiances reflects a second area in which Jewish nationalists sought to alter the logic of nationalism. They argued for a symbiotic, rather than divergent, relationship between national and human loyalties. Nurturing collective national ties within political boundaries promised equal rights, peaceful coexistence, and human progress.

Dubnow's concept of "ethical nationalism" provides a starting point for interrogating the strategy of fusing human and national objectives. "If some artificial language would coin a new word for our ethical nationalism," Dubnow wrote, "we would gladly leave to you the old disreputable and hollow term. As long as such a word is still lacking, however, it is our duty to establish by exact definition how the existing term should be used."[68] What does he mean by ethical nationalism? For Dubnow, the ethical idea was intimately linked to the recognition of national diversity as the most effective path toward promoting human allegiances. He justifies his normative claims about the human value of difference by contrasting two terms: cosmopolitanism and universalism. From Dubnow's *Nationalism and History*:

> [Cosmopolitanism] rejects the psychological and ethical foundations of nationalism and does not recognize any intermediate links between the

individual and humanity. Universalism, on the other hand, recognizes that each individual is a member of a people, and that each people is a member of the family of nations or of mankind, and demands therefore that the same brotherhood prevail between the peoples of the community of mankind as exists between individuals in each people.[69]

This idea challenges classic liberalism's assumption that sameness or uniformity provides the most effective path toward ensuring equality. Human freedom and progress, Dubnow posits, require a clear distinction between conformity-seeking cosmopolitanism and diversity-tolerant universalism.[70] Introducing this dichotomy demonstrates Dubnow's sensitivity to the promise and perils of liberalism. The liberal tradition provided the primary theoretical engine for Jewish emancipation and acceptance. While liberalism secured individual rights—a coveted assumption for Jewish intellectuals—it also linked the preservation of such rights to erasing collective allegiances. This placed Dubnow in a bind. On the one hand, he viewed thinkers such as the British liberal John Stuart Mill and the French thinker Ernst Renan as laying the basis for applying civil rights to all citizens of the state.[71]

Yet Dubnow's attitude toward Mill was complicated by Mill's claim that "free institutions are next to impossible in a country made of different nationalities"[72] (Zimmern also pointed to Mill's writings as "fundamentally wrong" on this count).[73] For Mill, the dissolution of cultural and ethnic differences would prevent intergroup strife from undermining the principles of individual equality. As a result, liberalism pressured conformity, prevented state or public recognition of different minority communities, and generated antipathy toward religious traditions that did not conform with liberal values. The individual freedom sought by liberalism created a double-edged sword: hiding beneath the cloak of universal individuality is a compassionate theory of elimination. The political theorist Steven Smith has called this the "unspoken premise of liberalism."[74] As he explains, "Jews were to be welcomed into the liberal polity so long as they ceased to be distinctively or recognizably Jewish."[75]

Given this assumption, how could Jewish theorists retain the promise of liberal integration without the bedrock assumption of uniformity? Only by highlighting the particular claims concealed by the cosmopolitan rhetoric of the Enlightenment, and inverting their conclusions by inserting diversity as the sine qua non of universal harmony, could Jewish nationalists justify their demands for individual rights and collective recognition. To make this argument, Dubnow suggests that an integral part of human freedom is the recognition of allegiances to cultural, historical, or ethnic communities.

Human beings do not make choices as autonomous individuals without ties to particular communal contexts. The larger horizon within which individuals make decisions constitutes a critical aspect of human freedom.[76] One of Dubnow's conversation partners, Simon Rawidowicz, identified this as the "right to be different." A more capacious (and ethical) definition of liberalism would recognize both individual equality and collective attachments.

A second dimension to the argument that ethical nationalism (modeled by the Jewish case) and humanism are compatible relied on another assumption about the national essence of Judaism. Earlier, the chapter discussed Dubnow's emphasis on evolution and progress as core characteristics of Jewish nationality. Another aspect distinguishing Judaism's conception of collective solidarity was the dedication to promoting equality and tolerance. The national mission of the Jewish people was rooted in the shared commitment to individual rights, universal equality, and free choice of associations. This instrumental definition resolved potential tension between particular and universal allegiances by equating the ultimate objective of both loyalties. Yet addressing this friction intended to justify Jewish preservation through liberal categories severely weakens the claims counterstate Jewish nationalism can make regarding the nature of membership. As an ethical nationalism, the grounds of Jewish collective identity eschew coercion, reject any special position relative to other national groups, and discard illiberal cultural, religious, or political practices. Thus, the challenge to liberalism remains fixed in its universalistic logic. Particular bonds exist primarily for the sake of promoting universal brotherhood.

Formulations synthesizing Zionism and internationalism included parallel attempts to negotiate the relationship between nationalism and liberalism. Zimmern's collection of essays, *Nationality and Government,* echoed (even at times with the same terminology) Dubnow's normative rejection of cosmopolitanism. The failure to preserve distinct cultures and social networks thus engenders "moral degradation," "drab cosmopolitanism," and "spiritual atrophy."[77] Assimilation may result in great material profit but will certainly eviscerate man's "strength to keep his own soul alive." For Zimmern, the "Boston Jew from a Russian ghetto" who "apes the manners and customs of New England" represented the problematic by-product of the nation-state's policy of cultural homogeneity.[78]

To emphasize the moral value of national diversity, Zimmern advanced a dichotomy between two typologies of nationalism. He included Zionism and British nationalism in a category he called "civilization nationalism." This model contrasted directly with Prussian *Kultur.* Prussian Kultur, he concluded, represented the epitome of a modern state that erased collective identities and associations to preserve the national character of the state. The alternate model, British civilization, stood "for something moral and social and political."[79] This concept renounced cultural homogeneity and ensured the right to practice separate national customs, speak different languages, and preserve religious practices. Zimmern's definition of civilization can be summarized as progress toward the establishment of multinational commonwealths or composite states. The path of progress and civilization therefore demanded not only individual rights for citizens but also the recognition of distinct national groups.

Variations of Jewish civilization nationalism and Zionism, as opposed to Prussian Kultur, appeared in Kallen's essays written for both Jewish and non-Jewish audiences (the contrasting nationalisms was the main theme in a 1919 *New Republic* article).[80] In the *Menorah Journal*, Kallen underscored Zionism's "service to civilization" as a check against conformity, which he associated with nation-state nationalism and imperialism. Kallen's most famous dichotomy, the distinction between democracy and the melting pot, does not explicitly use the civilization–Kultur dichotomy (adopting Zimmern's specific examples of British civilization and Prussian Kultur while the United States remained a neutral party during the war was not an option). Yet Kallen's concept of American democracy mirrors Zimmern's civilization concept as the basis for creating a commonwealth or federation of nationalities. Likewise, the detrimental alternative for the United States, the melting pot, shares the associations Zimmern linked to Prussian Kultur, specifically the demand for national uniformity and resistance to diversity within the polis.[81]

Making theoretical distinctions between universalism and cosmopolitanism, civilization and Kultur, and democracy and the melting pot contributed a rubric for classifying nationalisms that differed in important ways from the civic–ethnic dichotomy described earlier in the chapter. The distinction is not between those theories of nationalism that cling to national partiality versus those that espouse universal principles. Instead, the bifurcation separates nationalisms that promote tolerance and diversity from those dedicated to homogenization and ethnic conformity. Nationalism, compatible with the ideals of civilization and progress, must recognize the right to be different. Juxtaposing universal and particular terminology had a twofold objective: to demonstrate that liberalism should incorporate particularism as a crucial dimension for preserving and promoting individual rights; and to establish that nationalism could only contribute to human progress by renouncing the tendency toward intolerance, exclusion, and coercive demands for homogeneity.

Precisely this blending of Western liberal and Romantic typologies of nationalism characteristic of Jewish thinkers in the early twentieth century exemplifies a problematic synthesis for some scholars. The political scientist Jeanne Morefield, for instance, has criticized Zimmern as a "liberal in a muddle." According to Morefield, "Zimmern also brought together two seemingly contradictory notions of nationhood: the liberal understanding of nationhood as something one enters into by choice, and the more German idea of Volk nationalism based on a shared ethnic parentage. In this manner, Zimmern transformed nationhood into both a voluntary and natural—liberal and organic—phenomenon."[82] Zimmern's espousal of universal human rights clashes, she argues, with his embrace of "organic" metaphors (including the concept of a national "spirit" discussed earlier) to describe solidarity. For Morefield, Zimmern fuses aspects of what scholars now perceive as mutually exclusive categories of civic nationalism and ethnic nationalism. This assumption demonstrates a general suspicion among liberal theorists about the problem of recognizing particular group loyalties.[83] Particular loyalties may demand coercive criteria of membership that undermine an individual's autonomy and freedom. Moreover, commitment to a specific group potentially erodes an individual's allegiance to all of humankind and the equal treatment of fellow citizens.

But the choice between national and human allegiances created two untenable choices for some Jewish political thinkers: complete integration or national autonomy. To escape this either/or logic, Jewish nationalists had little choice but to seek a middle-ground approach now deemed muddled and contradictory. Zimmern's civilization, Dubnow's ethical nationalism, and Kallen's democracy consciously adapted terminology associated with liberal progress, modernity, and integration. Yet they emphasized terms of integration that delineated the retention of national diversity as the means for achieving progress and coexistence. Their strategy was to formulate an intentionally ambiguous position that negotiated liberalism's guarantee of individual rights with nationalism's organic grounds of membership (especially romantic and völkisch expressions) that transcended territory and statehood. Reading the failure to reconcile Jewish nationalism with either civic or ethnic conceptions as a muddled position shifts the attention of intellectual historians away from documenting the very process of negotiating the meaning and moral parameters of national identity that characterized the interwar period.

Morefield's analysis of Zimmern raises an additional concern about the juxtaposition of liberal and organic concepts. She underscores efforts among colonial elites to obfuscate power differentials in the name of liberal progress. The liberal principles espoused by British supporters of internationalism masked an integral part of their self-interest in distinguishing nation from state: an attempt to preserve the British sphere of imperial influence and to address anticolonial nationalism's demands for autonomy and intendance. Guaranteeing limited cultural autonomy and universal rights deflected calls for self-determination among colonialized populations. Zimmern's repudiation of national sovereignty on the grounds of promoting liberal ideals serves as an apologetic for his agenda of preserving the British Empire.

Morefield's warning about the ulterior motives engendering the fusion of liberalism and nationalism in early-twentieth-century thought adds important dimensions to this book's analysis of the phenomena within counterstate Zionism. Morefield sensitizes readers to the full implications of the adoption of key terms, such as civilization and progress, to define Jewish nationalism. Jewish intellectuals also integrated the problematic set of assumptions encoded within the logic of these terms. Placing Jews in the category of civilization reconfigured their position without challenging the legitimacy of hierarchies based on racial, geographic, or religious considerations. The project of civilizing Jews was completely compatible with (and most likely engendered) the placement of other groups in inferior positions. Zimmern was particularly guilty of this tendency. Morefield notes that "the majority of his [Zimmern's] prewar writings on commonwealth and empire reveal an almost insouciant assumption that full citizenship rights be denied to nonwhite 'dependencies' based on their well-understood immaturity."[84]

Kallen explicitly shared the sense of noblesse oblige that shaped the attitude of British internationalists toward nonwhite, indigenous populations. Indeed, he proudly declared noblesse oblige as the "motto of the Jew."[85] Jews deserve this motto because they, like the British, have a civilizing mission to accomplish among the primitive Arab population of Palestine. Kallen explained: "The fellah of Palestine is a case of the arrested development and enforced degradation typical of the whole Arabic-speaking and Mohammedan world. The cultural level on which he has found stability is barbarous. His rise above it is restricted by the accumulations of immemorial precepts, prescriptions, and taboos which even in the Bible appear in already vestigial form."[86]

Kallen's specific reference to the Bible's rejection of primitive behaviors characterized by the Arab population reflects the need to draw a clear dichotomy between progressive Jews and uncivilized Arabs. The establishment of this hierarchy, and the resulting self-proclaimed duty of raising the standards of this population, sets the logical foundation for deferring (for an unspecified period) the individual and collective rights of the majority Arab population. In a 1915 essay outlining the "constitutional foundation of the new Zion," Kallen suggested that democracy be delayed for a long period—"perhaps a generation" of "transition and preparation."[87] Kallen turned a deaf ear to the collective claims of the Arab population by arguing that they will opt (voluntarily, Kallen assured his readers) to fully "absorb Jewish standards of life, labour, and thought."[88]

Comparing the programs for Palestine with American democracy reveals that Kallen did not apply his theories uniformly.[89] The two defining principles of American democracy as developed in "Democracy versus the Melting-Pot"—the protection of individual rights, such as the right to vote, and the recognition of the enduring value of national solidarity—do not apply to the situation in Palestine. To be consistent with these principles, Kallen would have advocated for a federation of Arab and Jewish nationalities coexisting within Palestine. The two semiautonomous groups would preserve their unique cultures and cooperate with the sovereign political power in the region. Instead, however, Kallen's concept of the relationship between Jews and Arabs in Palestine has a lot in common with the melting pot, a notion he rejected vociferously as the antithesis of American democracy. He dismissed Arab national claims, and wrote, rather, that Palestine would become "a unity established through a meeting of minds, an interchange of intellectual culture, a cooperation in the public enterprises . . . and the progressive enrichment of the daily life of the two people."[90] Deeply transformed by the "the example of Jewish success and prosperity before his eyes," the Arab majority would willingly embrace the immigrants' culture.[91]

Kallen failed to see a double standard in advocating for the melting of the Arab population into a Jewish one in Palestine and the fragmentation of a monolithic American national identity in the United States. His inability to note any contradictions reflects the inner logic of the worldview he shared with British internationalists. The elevation of Jewish nationality to the pinnacle of civilization, and the corollary demotion of the Arabs in Palestine, prevented Kallen from even considering that the indigenous population might contest full integration within a Jewish polity. Kallen noted that this process "must be accomplished not by coercion but by contagion [which] is, of course, obvious."[92] Kallen's self-understanding of raising the quality of life among the indigenous population enables him to frame the establishment of Jewish standards in Palestine in the liberal rhetoric of free choice and autonomy.

The application of British internationalism, specifically the association of Judaism and civilization, thus had another advantage for Zionist intellectuals committed to building a Jewish homeland in Palestine and sensitive to the enduring plight of Jewish minority groups scattered around the globe. Internationalism provided a clear justification for the inconsistent application of the universal principles of individual and collective rights. The assumptions of British internationalism supported contradictory objectives: the rights to individual and collective claims in the diaspora would be granted immediately while Arab demands for national recognition and democratic representation in Palestine could be deferred indefinitely. Internationalism insulated liberal Zionists from claims of disenfranchising the Arab population in Palestine. Kallen's description of Judaism as an "anti-imperial" political tradition masked the immersion of his own conceptualization of Jewish political thought within an intellectual tradition deeply influenced by British imperialism.

The attention to power dynamics and the particular demands of universal rhetoric highlighted by Morefield and other critical theorists complicates the motivations attracting counterstate Zionists to theories of internationalism and to key terms such as civilization to define Jewish collective identity. Yet by ignoring the Jewish concerns and experiences of such figures as Kallen and Zimmern, historians of political thought fail to situate the uncertain position of Jewish and Zionist theorists.[93] Just as Jewish collectivity was often considered outside of nation-state nationalism, it was also excluded from formulations of counterstate national identity.[94] Jewish intellectuals struggled to align Judaism with such concepts as civilization, humanism, and progress at precisely the moment in which questions about their qualifications for integrating were being challenged by alien acts, nativism, and discrimination in the United States and Europe.

As both insiders and outsiders, Jewish nationalists navigated between white and black, colonial authority and colonialized oppressed, elite intellectual circles and discriminated minority group. Anxiety about the perceived inferior status of Jews necessitated a polemical effort to demonstrate the Jewish traditions and exemplification of the characteristics deemed necessary for acceptance and integration. Underscoring these particular attributes of Jewish nationalism was also calculated to remind non-Jewish nationalisms to respect the individual rights of Jewish citizens. These additional factors meant that Jewish intellectuals had their own motivations for aligning themselves with the ideological movements that they viewed as potential partners. Jewish nationalists adopted a conceptual vocabulary that reinforced hierarchies between various groups and were, at the same time, victims of such exclusionary categories.

Between Homeland and Diaspora

Identifying Jewish nationalism as the harbinger of a new stage in the evolution of nationalism and sovereignty challenged a third assumption generated by the binary logic of nation-state nationalism—the distinction between diaspora and homeland. The doctrine of national sovereignty links membership in the national group to living in the homeland, a territory connected by history, demography, and national consciousness to a particular people. Individuals living outside the established homeland had an uncertain status that undermined the rationale of territorial self-determination. State-seeking Zionist thinkers responded to the central role that land played in establishing the boundaries of national membership by evolving a categorical distinction between Jewish life in the diaspora and the homeland.[95] Following the logic of the nation-state model, individuals could choose between mutually exclusive options of vanishing in the diaspora (either by persecution or assimilation) or creating a vibrant national identity in the homeland.

Counterstate Zionists, I argue throughout this book, viewed the relationship between diaspora and homeland through quite a different lens that reflected their larger project of replacing the either/or logic of the nation-state paradigm with an integrated approach to theorizing Jewish national life. They envisioned one definition of Jewish national identity applicable to Jews around the globe. As a result, their writings illuminate an important moment of ideological fluidity before the rigid distinction between here and there emerged as a definitive crossroads separating paths in modern Jewish nationalism. Zionism was understood as a unifying principle relevant for Jews living in two distinct contexts: as minority communities living outside Palestine and as a semiautonomous community in the homeland.

How could Zionism offer a uniform theory of nationalism for addressing the Jewish question in both homeland and diaspora settings? Part of the appeal of internationalism for Kallen and Zimmern was its legitimization of the same national status for Jews scattered around the world. Jews' position as a minority national group within a commonwealth in the United States or Europe would not be categorically different from their status in Palestine. This did not necessarily mean that the geographic distinction between homeland and diaspora had no relevance. Indeed, counterstate Zionists developed a variety of stratagems for recognizing the distinct and unique aspects of settlement in Palestine without elevating living in the homeland to the sine qua non of national membership.

Cultural Zionism's concept of the Land of Israel as a spiritual center provided one such possibility. Ahad Ha'am believed that a territorial homeland would invigorate Jewish national culture for the remainder of the Jewish population scattered around the world. The center-periphery model he outlined became an essential part of the definition Zimmern integrated as his own concept of nationality. Zimmern wrote: "Nationality is a spiritual principle of peculiar force and dignity, springing from the intimate life of the soul, and embodied in a distinctive corporate mode of life and related to a particular homeland."[96]

Kallen harnessed Ahad Ha'am's center-periphery paradigm to equate the ties that bind Jews across homeland and diaspora to those that link Englishmen across the British Empire. Kallen insisted: "[A]s a matter of fact, the 'diaspora' is only a partial thing; it is like the diaspora of the English in the British Empire. The Jews always had a center of reference, a spiritual capital to look to."[97] The center-periphery metaphor served to strengthen the argument that Zionism and British internationalism shared a common basis for thinking about the relationship between national identity and territory. The homeland remained central as an organizing principle of collective solidarity, but not as the physical address for all members of the national community. The existence of a spiritual center would ensure the preservation of minority national communities around the world. Palestine, Zimmern contended, was not intended "to get rid of the Jews from the west," but instead to "deepen and dignify their corporate life."[98] The centripetal pull of a cultural center provided grounds for collective identity that avoided the coercive language of blood and descent as the organizing principle of national membership.[99] This basis for shared solidarity fit in particularly well with the argument linking Jewish nationalism and humanism.

Theorizing Palestine as a homeland center, but not a sovereign state or the place for all Jews to live, thus enabled Zimmern and Kallen to turn what state-seeking Zionists viewed as the great liability of Jews' stateless status into the ideal model of nationality in a post-nation-state era. Internationalism provided a strategy for theoretical hedging at a moment in which Jewish confidence in nation-state nationalism faced new challenges. Internationalism, augmented by Judaism's status as a civilization, supported the simultaneous pursuit of two unlikely possibilities that could potentially secure Jewish individual and collective security: the creation of a Jewish homeland with semiautonomous status in Palestine and the recognition of minority rights for Jews in the diaspora. As discussed earlier, their fusion was also based on a series of assumptions about the role of European Jews in Arab lands. The prevalence of these assumptions, and the fact that only a small number of Jewish settlers had actually arrived in Palestine, enabled

Zimmern and Kallen to ignore the potential tension between articulating one definition of Jewish nationality that resisted the claims to homogeneity and conformity of European and American host countries and encouraged the acceptance of precisely such an ethnonational character in a territory populated by a resisting Arab-majority population. They failed to fully come to terms with how the same pluralistic, integrationist, humanistic, and even deterritorialized concepts of Jewish national identity calibrated to create space for Jewish citizens in Europe and the United States could also apply to creating a Jewish homeland in Palestine.

As the interwar period progressed, however, this quandary became increasingly difficult to neglect, for two reasons. First, the situation in Palestine changed. Arab voices began to challenge Jewish immigration and to assert their own demands for national recognition. The possibility of ignoring the tension between Jewish nationalism as a force toward integration and pluralism clashed with the emerging realities of ethnonational strife on the ground. Second, the eclipse of new visions of international organization by the spread of the nation-state paradigm as the template for nationalism lessened the possibility that stateless nationalities would become the norm in the postwar era. The growth of national self-determination left Jewish proponents of counterstate nationalism with fewer ideological allies or realistic political possibilities.

As a result of these shifts, Rawidowicz, Kaplan, and Kohn grappled far more directly with the increasingly difficult task of harmonizing their views of Jewish political thought as the peaceful alternative to nation-state nationalism with an emerging national conflict in Palestine. Each thinker grew increasingly disillusioned with Zionism and, at the same time, Zionist ideology grew less open to counterstate visions of nationalism perceived as untenable options, given the violence and tension in Palestine. The marginalization of counterstate Zionism in the years leading up to 1948 did not resolve the main tension it highlighted, however. Indeed, the Jewish people, today almost equally split between homeland and diaspora settings, continue to struggle with the issue of squaring two different perspectives on Jewish collective identity—one underscoring Judaism's commitment to universal equality grounded in the separation of nation and state, and the other seeking a Jewish state linked to preserving a particular ethnoreligious tradition.

In 1934, Kaplan wrote in *Judaism as a Civilization*, "Nationalism is not a political, but a cultural concept. Its fundamental purpose is to humanize and civilize."[100] His explication of nationality as a cultural concept whose primary function is to "humanize and civilize" confounds contemporary assumptions about nationalism and Zionism. Kaplan disengages national identity from citizenship and aligns the concept with the realization of human values and progress. This juxtaposition demonstrates the same "seemingly contradictory notions of nationhood" described earlier by Morefield in her critique of Alfred Zimmern. Yet this chapter demonstrates that Kaplan's formulation of Zionism as cultural or spiritual bonds dedicated to humanize and to civilize was not an exceptional claim in early-twentieth-century Jewish or Western political thought.

Kaplan, as had Rawidowicz and Kohn, encountered concepts of Jewish nationalism and Zionism in his formative years (specifically, but not exclusively, through the work of such figures as Kallen, Zimmern, and Dubnow) that conceived of Jewish political thought in direct opposition to nation-state nationalism. Their formulations exhibit a number of patterns and themes that reflect the dilemmas and possibilities of establishing counterstate nationalism as a universal applicable model. National identity promoted a language of difference fully compatible with citizenship, liberalism, and geographic dispersion. By working within the framework of a larger critique of the nation-state in the early twentieth century, Jewish nationalists saw an opportunity to shift the logic of nationalism from fostering particularism, exclusion, and mutually exclusive loyalties to humanism, inclusion, and multiple allegiances.

Challenging the premise of national sovereignty and formulating counterstate concepts of nationalism offered an alternative to state-seeking Zionism's strategy for solving the Jewish question—normalization by emulating the nation-state model. Contesting the meaning of nationalism offered another possibility: the normalization of the unique Jewish case by transforming the general definition of nationality to match the Jews' stateless status. Subsequent developments in Europe and Palestine (as well as the rise of conflict) make the belief that national identity could be harnessed to promote diversity, tolerance, and peaceful coexistence rather than division appear naïve and idealistic. Indeed, counterstate Zionists severely underestimated the enduring force of nation-state nationalism in Europe. In retrospect, 1917 represented a turning point that made self-determination the basic blueprint for nationalism and international relations for the twentieth century.

At the same time, however, Jewish thinkers identified persisting weaknesses in the doctrine of national sovereignty—a limited framework for recognizing and understanding the experiences of individuals attached to multiple identities, including ties that bind stateless, diaspora, or transnational populations. We now turn to three Zionists who dedicated their considerable intellectual talents to grappling with this undertheorized space in modern political thought.

Portrait of Simon Rawidowicz, probably in Berlin, 1920.
Courtesy of Simon Rawidowicz Archives.

3

Text, Not Territory

Simon Rawidowicz, Global Hebraism, and the Centering of Decentered National Life

In 1954, Simon Rawidowicz exchanged a series of confrontational letters with Prime Minister David Ben Gurion about his decision to name the state "Israel." Rawidowicz exclaimed, "'Israel' cannot be reserved exclusively for the State and shared by the State and outside the State alike. . . . As long as the State of Israel and the Diasporas of Israel have not clarified this matter for themselves and the world, the confusion becomes more serious from day to day. [I am annoyed by the] speed with which some of the best of our people in the State have hastened to remove Israel outside the State from the totality of Israel."[1] The designated name Israel, Rawidowicz continued, "cannot but lead to the conclusion that Israel, as such, does not relate to the concept Jewish in any sense. Israel becomes nothing but a geographical-political term, devoid of Jewish identity."[2] Eretz Yisrael (the Land of Israel), Rawidowicz suggested, was a far better alternative because it prevented any terminological confusion between the citizens of the state and the entirety of the Jewish people. After reading Rawidowicz's comments, a strongly opposed Ben Gurion, the man primarily responsible for the choice of Israel, responded with an emphatic repudiation: "The name 'Israel' applies since 14 May 1948 only to the Jewish state."[3]

Ben Gurion and Rawidowicz's dispute was not merely over semantics. At stake in this exchange was the struggle to define the meaning of the traditional Hebrew term that refers to the Jewish people—Am Yisrael—and with it, the nature of Jewish collective self-definition in a new era of sovereignty. Ben Gurion's position—that "only the citizens of the Jewish state are Israel"—followed logically from his ideology of *mamlakhtiyut*, or statism.[4] The Zionist leader believed that only political independence would rescue

Jews from their perverse existence as a religious community in exile, ensure their normalization as a modern people, and restore their place as active participants in world history. Because the state represented the future for Jews and Judaism, Ben Gurion believed, it inherited the legacy of the term used throughout the textual tradition to refer to the entire people. Jews living outside the political boundaries—that is, in the diaspora—would not be worthy of the title Israel.

Whether Ben Gurion was aware of it, there was another level to his insistence on keeping the name Israel. Following the expectations of European nationalism meant that normalization required linking sovereignty, territory, and people. The term Israel symbolically conflated these various characteristics. Adopting Rawidowicz's proposed name, the Land of Israel, would have only exacerbated one of the greatest challenges of fitting the Jewish people into the sovereign mold: the demographic reality that the vast majority of the national population lived outside the geographic homeland.

Rawidowicz's letter to Ben Gurion did not come out of the blue. Rawidowicz's position reflected an argument he had been waging among his Zionist and Hebraist friends and polemical opponents for almost two decades. Rawidowicz inveighed against this effort of casting various geographic, political, and cultural expressions of Jewish national life into a nation-state paradigm. The decision to call the state Israel solidified the suppression of Rawidowicz's position by symbolically equating the nation of Israel with the State of Israel. For Rawidowicz, Ben Gurion's normalization was actually a distortion of the category Israel. The term had always referred to Jews living in multiple centers, without an implied hierarchy between homeland and diaspora. Naming the state Israel, Rawidowicz believed, thus created a split in the global Jewish community by legitimating a set of binary characteristics that he had spent a lifetime trying to blur: diaspora versus homeland, religious versus secular, exile versus redemption, and dependent subjects versus independent sovereigns. Israel, Rawidowicz argued in his Hebrew writings, represented a very different type of nation. Unlike modern nation-states, the Jewish nation was united by language and texts rather than by territory and citizenship. The debate over whether to employ the term Israel or the Land of Israel was really a disagreement about whether Jewish nationality should emulate nation-state nationalism or model paradigms of global nationality dedicated to breaking the sovereign mold linking nation and state.

Who was this largely forgotten voice who boldly challenged Ben Gurion's decision about the name of the state, a decision that few, then or now, would even think to question?[5] Simon Rawidowicz was an erudite scholar of Jewish intellectual history, a prolific Hebrew writer and publisher, and one of the twentieth century's most creative Jewish political theorists. Throughout his lifetime, Rawidowicz was both a self-affirming Zionist and a critic of state-seeking Zionism who advocated for building Jewish national centers in the diaspora as well as in Palestine.

Rawidowicz developed this understanding of Jewish nationalism by proposing the concepts of Babylon and Jerusalem as a symbolic alternative to constructing national myth around a territorial nation-state. Although state-seeking Zionist ideology and historiography underscored the Land of Israel as the territorial center of the people of Israel, Rawidowicz emphasized the place that Babylon played in the development of the Jewish textual tradition. After the destruction of the Second Temple, the center of rabbinic learning gradually shifted from Palestine to Babylon. The legal code that developed in exile—the Babylonian Talmud—would become the authoritative legal, religious, and literary document in the Jewish canon (the Palestinian Talmud largely disappeared after this).

Rawidowicz used this narrative to find key terms from within the tradition to comprehend the relationship between space and national boundaries. In his view, Babylon becomes a symbolic counterpoint to Jerusalem, upon which he erects a counterstate Zionist conception of the people of Israel. Rawidowicz's writings refer to Israel as a synonym for the Jewish people—not the name of the state, which he contended should be called something other than the term traditionally applied to the entire people of Israel. But he does not embark on this alternative path by rejecting the existence of the state, represented in his dyad by Jerusalem, or the centrality of the Land of Israel. This is why he is such a refreshing figure to reconsider. His work invites a conversation about the meaning of nationality when it is disconnected from the state but not necessarily *without* a state.

Rawidowicz certainly did not select the ideal moment to articulate this theory of Jewish nationality that pushed for Babylon as one of its centers. He formulated his theory between the 1930s and the 1950s—decades that witnessed the complete eradication of the modern Babylons of Europe as well as the reestablishment of Jerusalem with the founding of a political state. Despite (or perhaps partially because of) his erudition, fecund pen, and prescient insights, Rawidowicz's attempts to write against the trajectory of Zionist thought in the first half of the twentieth century have left him a neglected figure. Thanks to the recent passionate interest of a number of scholars, especially the Jewish historian David Myers, Rawidowicz's fascinating intellectual and personal journey between Zionism and diasporism has begun to gain the attention it deserves.

This chapter contributes to this rehabilitation of Rawidowicz's work by focusing on his unique vision of national cohesion linked by *textual* interpretation rather than *territory*—a theory of Zionism I call global Hebraism. Heavily influenced by East European diaspora Jewish nationalism, Rawidowicz envisioned text as defining the collective boundaries of the Jewish people. His emphasis on Hebrew language in the diaspora, his criticisms of the State of Israel's attitude toward the Arab minority in the state, and his esoteric rabbinic writing style marginalized his iconoclastic message, however. Proposing a fundamentally new interpretation of Rawidowicz's historical relevance, I argue that his views prefigured strategies for advocating distinct group boundaries while remaining cognizant of multiple loyalties, fluid identity formation, and antiessentialist critiques of collective consciousness.

In recovering Rawidowicz's theories, I pay special attention to what I see as the three pillars of global Hebraism: a decentered geography, a permeable hermeneutic community, and an appreciation of the cohesive power of Judaism's deferred messianic yearning that preserved a clear boundary between religious myth and political aspirations. I have deduced these tenets from Rawidowicz's rather speculative and unsystematic treatment of Jewish political thought. Particularly interesting are his efforts to mine Jewish sources for terms, symbols, and even words that would neutralize the diaspora–homeland dichotomy and support nonspatial boundaries for Jewish collective life. Rawidowicz developed a series of metaphors—such as an ellipse with two centers or a rabbinic concept called *eruvin*—to theorize the flow of national culture and the decentered evolution of organic relationships. One of the primary ties that bind members in Rawidowicz's vision is Hebrew language. He viewed language not as an end in itself, but as a medium for enabling the construction of communities of interpretation.

Rawidowicz's penetrating and deeply insightful work is best appreciated years after its publication. His questioning the role of the state in defining Israel maps the fissures in narratives of Jewish nationalism. By raising unresolved dilemmas, many of which have become taboo topics in Jewish political thought, his work shows fault lines that continue to destabilize a sense of shared peoplehood connecting Jews in the diaspora with those in the homeland. Moreover, global Hebraism introduces a vision of Zionism with potential lessons for theorizing nation beyond state today. Few typologies of nationalism or diasporaism posit the existence of multiple centers with equal roles in nourishing the ties that bind dispersed populations. Rawidowicz's work explores the theoretical and practical difficulties of constructing one narrative of nationality robust enough to reflect the experiences of individuals living as part of a majority population in a homeland as minority citizens dispersed around the world.

Rawidowicz: An Intellectual Biography

Before delving into the analysis of the various components of global Hebraism, let us begin with a brief look at Rawidowicz himself. This biographical component is crucial in appreciating Rawidowicz's lifelong effort to preserve an organic sense of national membership, nourished by lived experiences and permeable boundaries, against forces of ideological clarity, pure national characteristics, and rigid boundary markers. The either/or logic of the sovereign mold paradigm—which forced dichotomies between homeland and diaspora, subject and sovereign, secular and religious, national members and alien outsiders—failed to match Rawidowicz's personal experiences or his understanding of how Judaism had functioned for centuries. Rather than the either/or logic, the conjunction *and* better reflects his approach to blurring the ideological polarity that characterized his own lifetime. This appreciation for the fluidity, diversity, and decentralized nature of Israel's historical experience led Rawidowicz to the surprisingly radical claim that stands at the conclusion of his landmark *Babylon and Jerusalem:* "May the name of the people of Babylon be as the name of the people of Jerusalem: Israel."[6]

Summarizing Rawidowicz's intellectual biography is beyond the scope of this chapter, but I offer some key reference points.[7] Rawidowicz made significant contributions to multiple fields—including philosophy (both German and Jewish), literary analysis, Hebrew publishing, and historical scholarship—over a lifetime that spanned living in Russia-Poland at the fin de siècle, Weimar Berlin in the 1920s and early 1930s, Great Britain during World War II, and the United States of the early Cold War.[8] His many contributions, specifically his engagement with influential intellectual circles at each of these moments in twentieth-century history, merit in-depth analysis. My objective here, however, is to amplify a unifying thread in Rawidowicz's oeuvre that is potentially obscured by his multiple areas of interest. Rawidowicz's scholarly and popular writing reinforced the claim that "the people of Israel have an inherent national status, with a state or without."[9] In grounding this claim, Rawidowicz focused primarily on reading Jewish sources and historical precedents that challenged their compatibility with the logic of the sovereign mold.

Like other figures developing counterstate theories of Zionism during this period, Rawidowicz viewed Jewish nationalism as a vehicle for challenging emerging assumptions about the relationship between nation and state in Western political thought. His interpretation of Judaism, while couched in very traditional language and terminology, reveals (as I explore in detail below) both a deep grounding in and a philosophical critique of the non-Jewish intellectual milieu. This aspect of his thought is easily obscured by his passion for rabbinic commentaries, use of Hebrew wordplay, and his intentional understatement of the role of external influences on Jewish thought. Yet Rawidowicz does acknowledge political philosophy, and specifically the engagement with non-Jewish thought, as a crucial part of his work. Jewish political philosophy, he wrote,

> does not, unfortunately, receive the attention it deserves. The Jewish scholar or theologian frequently refuses, *a priori,* to pay attention to it, either out of fear of being mixed up with "politics" or because he dislikes it. . . . For in this field lie burning problems of the Jewish present and future, questions which concern the very essence of Jewry as a national or political community . . . and their correlation with other political communities and present systems of thought.[10]

An appreciation of this political prism, specifically the attempt to define an alternative conception of Israel and to reconfigure the appropriate equilibrium between Jews and gentiles, guides this intellectual biography. In taking this approach, I am conscious of the tension between Rawidowicz's fascination with external political developments and his explicit claims to analyze current events through traditional religious categories and rabbinic constructs. Despite these latter claims, his work does not represent the ruminations of a philosophical idealist uninterested in engaging the political realities of his century. Key insights about Rawidowicz, and the function of global Hebraism, emerge only by challenging his emphasis on the internal development of Jewish thought. Contrasting the theories of the medieval Jewish philosopher Moses Maimonides with those of Prime Minister David Ben Gurion or the ideas of the biblical commentator Rashi with those of the American Jewish Committee indicates Rawidowicz's keen interest in using traditional sources to address contemporary political questions. Between the lines of his rabbinic metaphors and classical Hebrew, he searched primarily for a political philosophy to gird Judaism's survival.

The apparently conflicting relationship between the form (classic Hebrew, esoteric language games, and Talmudic references that demand a thorough grounding in Jewish textual tradition) and the content (engagement with early-twentieth-century philosophical and political thought) of Rawidowicz's writings on nationalism prompts an interesting question.

Why raise a universal set of questions about identity formation through such a particular lens? An understanding of the tension and intimate link between form and content, a central theme in this chapter and a defining feature of global Hebraism, begins with Rawidowicz's formative years.

As mentioned earlier, Rawidowicz's biography bridges radically different moments in modern Jewish history and engages multiple ideological streams. Several important dimensions of his life story—including his immersion within Jewish sources as a yeshiva student in Eastern Europe, his leadership role in the Hebrew renaissance in Weimar, and his scholarly research into nineteenth- and twentieth-century philosophy (both Jewish and general)—helped shape Rawidowicz's iconoclastic views. Before taking a more in-depth look at how these strands are woven together into the theory of global Hebraism, let us contextualize these dimensions.

One can best categorize Rawidowicz as part of the last generation of Eastern European *maskilim* (followers of the Haskalah or Jewish Enlightenment). Born in 1896 in Grayewo, a town in northeastern Poland, his early education consisted heavily of rabbinic sources. After studying Talmud daily with his father as a boy, Rawidowicz went off at age fourteen to learn the traditional canon of Jewish religious life at the Lida Yeshiva. The language and hermeneutic approach he mastered as a child continued to serve as the basic expression of his Jewish identity, even though his level of observance waned. Growing up within the polyglot milieu of Eastern Europe shaped the association in his thought between national movements and linguistic and social autonomy.

In a number of key ways, this integral link between language and national status resembled the autonomism of his friend and mentor Simon Dubnow (discussed in chapter 2). The two thinkers became close friends while living in Berlin. Rawidowicz published the first volume dedicated to the memory of the great Jewish historian, who was killed by the Nazis in 1941.[11] Rawidowicz's comments about the dearth of Jewish thinkers engaged in political thought actually appeared in the context of extolling Dubnow in the introduction to this memorial volume. Rawidowicz's sensitivity to the relationship between Jews and non-Jews, specifically as it applied to the possibility of minority nationalism and the centrality of language in constructing such diasporic boundaries, emerged from his formative years living within the same multinational Russian imperial context that nourished Dubnow's program of autonomism. Despite these similarities with Dubnow, however, it would be wrong to pigeonhole Rawidowicz as a direct heir to the diaspora nationalist and thus as an anti-Zionist. Three crucial differences demonstrate that Rawidowicz straddled key ideological positions separating the developing diaspora–Zionist divide—a passion for Hebrew rather than Yiddish as the national tongue, the belief that national culture could thrive both inside and outside of Palestine, and the rejection of diaspora political autonomy.

Rawidowicz's commitment to Hebrew developed in relationship to the concurrent revival of Hebrew literature, a major influence on his life. Despite his highly regarded command of spoken and written Yiddish, Rawidowicz took the position of supporting Hebrew as the national tongue and the key to Jewish cultural survival. Arriving in Berlin in 1919, he quickly took a leading role in the renaissance of Hebrew literature in Weimar Germany. He taught Hebrew classes, created Ayanot (the Hebrew publishing house dedicated to promulgating post-rabbinic Hebrew sources), and founded the Brit Ivrit Olamit (the Hebrew World Union).[12] His abilities as a writer and publisher were so impressive that Haim Nahman Bialik, the future national poet of Israel and leader of the Hebrew revival in Weimar Berlin, begged him to consider working as an editor in chief for his journal *Dvir*.[13] In addition to these activities, the East European immigrant quickly made a name for himself as an important scholar of medieval and modern Jewish philosophy.

By the late 1920s, however, Rawidowicz's position began to more clearly diverge from that of other Hebraists who had shifted their energy away from Europe and toward Palestine. The role of the diaspora, both ideologically and practically, as the center of Hebrew literature and language was beginning to rapidly diminish.[14] Like many of his contemporary Hebraists, Rawidowicz also seriously considered moving to Palestine and appreciated its significance for Hebrew cultural production. Rawidowicz's father and several of his siblings, including his favorite brother, Abraham, settled in Palestine in the mid-1920s. "All people of Israel like us," he wrote to his brother in 1930, "need to take it upon themselves to live in Palestine, even if it is a land of Arabs."[15] Rawidowicz made two visits to Palestine, in 1925 and 1933, to explore the possibility of joining these family members and to actively pursue a position in Jewish philosophy at the Hebrew University.[16] The decision to remain in the diaspora was certainly not ideological. Economic and professional hurdles prevented Rawidowicz from fulfilling his desire to live closer to his family and among a cohort of like-minded Hebraists and scholars.[17] Despite his personal efforts to relocate to Palestine, Rawidowicz disagreed with the emerging negation of the potential for Hebrew culture in the diaspora.[18] Rawidowicz embarked on a campaign in a number of leading Zionist and Hebrew journals, including *Ha'olam, Dvir,* and *Moznayim,* to affirm the endurance of Hebrew culture in the diaspora. Even more controversially, he argued that the diaspora played an integral part in the preservation of Hebrew national culture.[19] Over the following three decades, this remained a central theme in his oeuvre.

Rawidowicz considered his own position on the equal centrality of diaspora and homeland as fully within the parameters of Zionism. As Myers has reported, Rawidowicz continued to affirm his Zionist bona fides, and explained to an audience gathered to discuss Hebrew language in the diaspora that "my Zionism is no less than those who discharge their obligations by 'negating the Diaspora' or reciting 'Kaddish' [the mourner's prayer] for Diaspora Jewry."[20] Rawidowicz's literary circle, including Bialik, writers Shaul Tchernichovsky and Yaakov Klatzkin, and editor Moshe Kleinman, placed him in the center of Berlin's Zionist intellectual life. Those with the power to shape Zionist opinion also clearly considered his voice part of the larger conversation about the meaning of Jewish nationalism, even if he advocated a contrarian position. For instance, Ha'olam, the journal of the Zionist movement, regularly published Rawidowicz's proddings to place Jewish culture in Palestine and the rest of the world on equal footing.[21] The Israeli author Amos Oz related in his recent autobiography that he remembers Sabbath visits to the Jerusalem home of his uncle Joseph Klausner, the scholar of Hebrew literature and candidate for president of Israel, who was eagerly awaiting the next issue of Rawidowicz's journal Metzudah.[22] Rawidowicz viewed himself, and was viewed by others at the time, as very much a part of the fluid discourse of Jewish nationalism that belied a rigid diaspora–Zionist bifurcation.

Debates about Hebrew culture represent only one component of Rawidowicz's intellectual pursuits during this period, however. He pursued secular studies, spending seven years completing his university education. His doctoral dissertation, which focused on the intellectual influences and development of Ludwig Feuerbach's philosophy, was published in 1931.[23] But Hitler's rise to power in 1933 terminated Rawidowicz's fecund intellectual career in Berlin. At the same time, negating the increasingly dominant negation of the diaspora rhetoric alienated him from the trajectory of Hebrew culture.

After settling in London in 1933 following the early Nazi anti-Jewish ordinances, Rawidowicz wrote a remarkable and telling essay that encapsulated his position on the relationship between Zionism and the diaspora.[24] "Kiyum hatefutzah" (The endurance of the diaspora) decried those Zionists who viewed Hitler's rise to power as the final fulfillment of Zionism's repeated warnings about the ultimate destruction of diaspora Judaism.[25] Rawidowicz acknowledged the grave seriousness of the Nazi takeover. He also expressed his growing frustration at Zionism's ideological rejection of diaspora Jewish life and its claims of having found a solution to the Jewish problem. One of the fascinating questions about Rawidowicz's intellectual biography is why this personal experience of exile failed to change his view on the role of the diaspora in Jewish national life. In fact, as his career progressed, his belief in the role of diaspora communities actually burgeoned. What began as an observation that Jews will remain outside the homeland developed during his career toward an increasingly clear position that made that reality a positive attribute of Jewish national life.

Rawidowicz continued his scholarly research and his active support for the Hebrew language in the diaspora as a faculty member at Jews' College in Great Britain and later, from 1941 until 1948, as a member and later head of the Semitics department at the University of Leeds. In an attempt to keep Hebrew alive while its traditional centers in Europe were being destroyed, Rawidowicz founded a second Hebrew publishing company, Ararat. The company, which he symbolically viewed as a refuge for Hebrew amid the anti-Semitic deluge of Nazism, published a series of books on various Jewish topics. In 1948 he began teaching at the College of Jewish Studies in Chicago, before being recruited by the president of the new Brandeis University in 1950 to join its faculty as a professor of Hebrew literature and Jewish philosophy. He remained at Brandeis, serving as chair of the department of Near Eastern and Judaic Studies until his death in 1957.

Babylon and Jerusalem

While Rawidowicz's early essays indicated the direction of his future work, the final formulation of his ideas of diaspora Jewish nationalism did not appear until 1957. *Babylon and Jerusalem,* Rawidowicz's last project before his untimely death, reworked decades of polemical debates about Zionism, updating them to reflect his frustration with the State of Israel's early decisions and his disappointment with the American Jewish community. As one of the period's most insightful, critical, and Jewishly knowledgeable observers, Rawidowicz penetrated the ebullience of Israel's creation in order to highlight what he considered the ideological contradictions, moral challenges, and fundamental Jewish identity questions that accompanied statehood.

Outside of a small group of committed followers, however, the book received little attention. There are several possible technical reasons for the poor reception. The book was repetitious, lengthy (over nine hundred pages), and written in a prolix Hebrew style laced with rabbinic and medieval philosophical references. However, even a more accessible version would not have overcome the ideological reasons for the work's underwhelming reception and its inability to enter the popular or even scholarly canon of modern Jewish thought. By the time of its publication, there was no potential readership for this work. Zionist intellectuals and activists would most likely have found the content deeply problematic. Those Israelis capable of reading the difficult style would have chafed at Rawidowicz's affirmation of independent diaspora centers, his sobering critique of Israel's policies, and his declaration that Jewish nationalism was not Zionism. But outside of Israel, only a rapidly dwindling number of Jews could even read Rawidowicz's writing, let alone feel passionate about his repudiation of American Judaism.

It is therefore easy to dismiss Rawidowicz's final project, and his life's work for that matter, as one man's stubborn refusal to recognize the incompatibility of his notion of Zionism based on his understanding of Jewish nationalism and the path solidified by the founding of the state. *Babylon and Jerusalem*'s style and tone reflect a complete misunderstanding of the realities of Jewish life after the Holocaust and the euphoria of 1948. Like other émigré intellectuals who failed to translate Old World ideologies into the language of the New World, Rawidowicz underappreciated the tremendous discontinuities in twentieth-century Jewish life. Without dismissing the trends and dramatic changes that he refused to acknowledge, it is valuable to consider what his marginalization from Jewish thought reveals about foundational biases in conceptualizing the modern Jewish experience. Although Rawidowicz firmly rooted his conceptions in a context forever altered by World War II and the founding of the State of Israel, in fact his work looked forward to theories of national identity formation that have become increasingly relevant in a post–Cold War era.

A Decentered Geography

Rawidowicz saw Jews' political uniqueness—the fact that "no other people has an outside house [a diaspora population]"—as the key to their "chosen" status.[26] This position posed a theoretical challenge of how to articulate a definition of nationality that downplayed place as the primary characteristic and boundary marker of communities. Global Hebraism, Rawidowicz's response to this dilemma, was unique for creatively reading and rereading religious symbols, myths, and words to build a new vocabulary, and with it an alternative geography, for imagining national boundaries that diminished the importance of location within the calculus of identity formation.

Although global is not the exact word Rawidowicz adopted to describe Jewish nationalism, it is a far more accurate term for his theory than diaspora nationalism. In fact, although his passion for the endurance of the diaspora could lead to his being categorized as a diaspora nationalist, it would be wrong to force this theory of nationalism into the very terminological orbit he hoped to escape. The most effective approach to fully appreciating Rawidowicz's conception of Jewish nationalism is to introduce the new term global. This provides a fresh lens for exploring the ways in which he departed from conventional readings of nationalism, both past and present. The process of developing novel terminology as a way of questioning assumptions encoded in scholarly and popular vocabulary reflects Rawidowicz's recognition that language and terminology color our perception of reality. Moreover, such key terms as homeland, diaspora, and even Jerusalem are so deeply ingrained in our perception of national identity that the ideological connotations they convey are taken for granted.

A global nationality required fresh terms (such as Babylon and Jerusalem), symbols (such as the rabbinic concept of eruvin), and words (such as *beinartzit,* or interland) to construct ties that bind outside of geopolitical markers. The terms Babylon and Jerusalem provide the most visible example of how Rawidowicz sought new terminology to replace the binary either/or opposition of homeland versus diaspora with an *and,* connecting multiple centers around the globe.[27] This vocabulary, firmly rooted within the Jewish textual tradition, reconceptualizes the relative weight of diaspora and homeland within the national imagination. Employing this language affirms the dominance of a generally erased chapter in Zionist historiography: the central authority that the rabbinic academy in Babylon held in crafting rabbinic tradition. Zionist ideology focuses on biblical experiences in the land and the humility of exile to mold the people of Israel into the territorial paradigm of modern nationalism. But Babylon offered another narrative, one that complicated the mapping of the people of Israel on a specific homeland or political model.

One of the central spatial metaphors that the Babylon and Jerusalem framework defied was the theorist Ahad Ha'am's center-periphery language (discussed in chapter 2). This had elevated the homeland as the source of cultural vitality and national regeneration. Instead, Rawidowicz insisted that diaspora Jews must "auto-emancipate" themselves from the cultural hegemony of Jews living in the Land of Israel. His argument stems from the insightful contention that national culture, unlike commerce and people, cannot successfully be imported and exported. A monolithic and homogeneous Jewish culture could not, by definition, allow Jews living in such diverse contexts to thrive. This constitutes quite a radical statement for a thinker writing in a period that considered cultural, linguistic, and political uniformity as the sine qua non of nationalism. Rawidowicz felt that the linguistic, artistic, and intellectual developments in the new state would not answer the needs of Jews living within another cultural milieu. In fact, he continued, the existence of a perceived center actually undermines the promulgation of national culture in other locations. A national cultural center strips responsibility and agency from those outside the community.[28] The perimeter, Rawidowicz demanded, must also have a role in the creation of sui generis national culture.[29] Rawidowicz developed several novel metaphors and symbols to map a geographical paradigm with a preference for multiple centers, rather than a single homeland center. In one of his most popular images, Jews in the Land of Israel and in the diaspora represent the two foci of an ellipse. In an ellipse the distance from all points along the curve to the two foci remains constant. Each geographical location and each approach toward Jewish life exerts a gravitational pull on the other points. Various expressions of Jewish national identity lie on the curve of the ellipse—some more closely tied to life in the land and some more to diaspora communities. Following Rawidowicz's geometrical calculus, the relative weighting of center and periphery disappears in this metaphor. Communities in the diaspora and the land are thereby transformed into equal partners in cultural production.

Rawidowicz shared Ahad Ha'am's belief that Jews have a unique relationship with the Land of Israel. Yet his formulation of local, self-sufficient communities opposed Ahad Ha'am's center-periphery philosophy of cultural dissemination.[30] In contrast to Zionist readings focused on the preexilic, biblical history, Rawidowicz turned to rabbinic and medieval texts that focus on God, the Torah, and Israel as primary to the land.[31] The land is sacred, he believed, but Jews living in the land are not superior, nor do they have a greater ability to create culture, than those living outside it. In recognizing the homeland as *one* of the centers of Jewish life, Rawidowicz also distinguished himself from the autonomism of Dubnow. Dubnow's theories viewed the center of national life in the diaspora, by affirming the value of the homeland community as part of the dyad of Jewish history.

The imagery in Rawidowicz's later work further decenters the spatial coordinates of Jewish nationality and display a more nuanced appreciation for the cultural interpenetration that takes place between Jews and their surroundings. One such image for describing the relationship between space and national identity formation is found in Rawidowicz's appropriation of the rabbinic concept of eruvin, which extends the realm of permitted movement during the Sabbath by creating a legal fiction extending the private boundaries of a home or city.[32] Rawidowicz dedicated an entire chapter of *Babylon and Jerusalem* to this concept, an analysis of which sheds light on the multiple levels at which he wrote and thought.[33]

Eruvin represented Rawidowicz's attempt to appropriate a traditional religious concept as the foundation for a corrective to state-seeking

Zionism's assertions about the nature of Jewish nationalism. He engaged the battle for the authentic model of contemporary Jewish nationalism by searching for traditional symbols to build a counternarrative to Zionism's historiography. The centrality of eruvin in Rawidowicz's thought was reflected in his claim that eruvin "are the ways of the people, the ways of every man in Israel and Israel itself for all generations."[34]

Yet, for Rawidowicz, the importance of eruvin had little to do with the observance of the Sabbath. He interpreted the institution of eruvin as establishing a myriad of semiautonomous Jewish communities not directly linked by geographical proximity or human interaction. Rabbinic law outlined the process by which members of a courtyard community placed a shared loaf of bread in the center of their dwellings. This created a self-enclosed collective without relying on external borders to facilitate communal unity. No hierarchy privileged certain eruv populations depending on geography or communal size. By building the eruv boundary, each community created its own cultural and social center. Acknowledging, and even celebrating, the independent existence of many self-enclosed centers of national life reveals a fundamental tenet of Rawidowicz's nationalism. In order to survive across geographical, cultural, and political boundaries, Jewish nationalism must take into account diverse expressions of national consciousness. Each community, he argued, "creates for itself its life both materially and spiritually; it forms its Jewish image as much as the reality permits it or demands upon it."[35] Rawidowicz exploited the flexible nature of the *eruv tehumim* (boundary eruv), which extended the horizon of local communities to include Jews outside the courtyard or village in one shared national community.

In addition to rereading rabbinic concepts, Rawidowicz also employed his creative skills at Hebrew wordplay to map spatial coordinates of the Jewish nation. Taking advantage of the amorphous nature of the Hebrew language, still in the process of rapid modernization, Rawidowicz developed an argument from within the inchoate national tongue to further rethink nation and territorial homeland. For instance, he referred to the boundaries uniting Jewish communities as *beinartzit* (interland),[36] inventing this term instead of using the standard *bein le'umit* (international), a term referring to relationships between sovereign nation-states. By replacing the word for state with the politically neutral land, Rawidowicz implicitly rejected political boundaries set by international treatises. This example demonstrates his sensitivity to the need to undermine the conflation of nationality and statehood by depoliticizing the nature of transnational bonds.[37]

From raising the visibility of Babylon in the Jewish narrative to tweaking linguistic details, Rawidowicz developed a new language for outlining the contours of a nation that transcended specific territory and a political order that carved up the map into nation-states. The novel vocabulary came from a variety of sources in different layers of the Jewish tradition. These inventions share a sensitivity to the importance of physical space that was not broken down into geopolitical units. The language and metaphors Rawidowicz introduced view space as a crucial backdrop for collective interaction. Social proximity is necessary for national identity formation. However, local relationships and community imbue space with its importance, not vice versa. The linguistic building blocks of Rawidowicz's notion of the nation of Israel establish a very different logic that undermines calls for an ingathering of world Jewry into one place. Babylon and Jerusalem, eruv borders, and beinartzit communities introduce terms that expand national membership to dispersed individuals living in multiethnic environments.

The ambiguous qualities of joining homeland and diaspora as equal partners, however, create a daunting theoretical challenge. What boundaries replace territory as the glue that unites national groups? Without a center it is difficult to ascertain the clear parameters or constituent elements of a national tradition. A homeland provides a clear set of boundaries, an imagined rallying point to link members, and a physical location to ensure social integration that builds national bonds. What would Rawidowicz propose? He solved this dilemma by replacing territory with a heterodox understanding of the function of the Hebrew language in creating a literary culture accessible across space and time.

A Permeable Hermeneutic Community

One of Rawidowicz's most memorable phrases, which he borrows from Hebrew literature professor Joseph Klausner, is his critique of Jews living in the state of Israel as "*Goyim shemedabrim ivrit*" (Non-Jews that speak Hebrew).[38] The juxtaposition of non-Jews and Hebrew speakers is a perplexing concept for a man who dedicated his life to the promulgation of the Hebrew language. How could a proponent of linguistic nationalism mock Hebrew speakers as potentially leaving the parameters of the people of Israel? This phrase forces readers to contemplate widely held and rarely challenged assumptions. In this case, Rawidowicz questions a basic premise about the role of language in defining national culture.

As the scholar Benjamin Harshav has pointed out, the renaissance of modern Hebrew and Zionist ideology provided a means to create a modern, universal culture that maintained particular boundaries through form, not content.[39] Thus the growth and vitality of Hebrew as the national language required the transformation of a primarily written form of communication into a spoken language heard from the streets to the halls of government. The critique of limiting Hebrew to its revival in Palestine, and later the State of Israel, reflects a fundamentally different (and certainly unique among both Yiddish and Hebrew advocates of linguistic nationalism) concept of the relationship between language and national culture.[40] Rawidowicz struggled to defuse the spatial preference and spoken function of the revival of Hebrew that was encoded within Zionist ideology as well as in Hebrew literature.

With the growing success of Hebrew as a spoken language, combined with the center of Hebrew literature moving from Europe to Palestine, Rawidowicz expressed grave concerns about the direction of the Hebrew revival. The conversion of a written language dedicated to legal, intellectual, and religious topics into the language of daily use, he predicted, would engender a dramatic change in the role of language.[41] Shifting Hebrew to a spoken language, he felt, would actually deprive it of its multiple layers rooted in Jewish sources. Language provided critical access to particular sources of Judaism (from rabbinic literature to medieval commentators to premodern maskilim). The importance of these sources, Rawidowicz must have concluded, would be marginalized by efforts to modernize Hebrew by translating universal texts (such as Greek classics) into the ancient tongue. There were also pragmatic realities of transforming a written language into the language of quotidian interactions. Thus, from the beginning of his publishing career as the founder of the Ayanot Press, Rawidowicz dedicated his energy to popularizing and perpetuating a style of post-rabbinic Hebrew philosophical and literary texts that interested neither Zionists nor Orthodox Jews. These texts were considered either too religious (for the former) or too secular (for the latter).

Why was Rawidowicz, a non-Orthodox Jew and a scholar of Ludwig Feuerbach (the atheist rationalist who humanized theology), so concerned with preserving rabbinic, medieval, and early modern religious sources? His interest in maintaining a transhistorical canon of Hebrew literature had little to do with a desire to promulgate Jewish law or theological creeds. In fact, the very assumption that there are distinct religious and secular strands in Hebrew literature is a binary distinction mapped on sources by modern thinkers (an approach still far too common in most popular and scholarly approaches) and implicitly rejected by Rawidowicz. The need to arbitrarily separate progressive rational strands of Hebrew language and literature from more primitive religious dimensions in order to fashion a modern national language was a symptom of a more fundamental break in the function of Hebrew as the vehicle of national cultural production. The secularization and removal of historical layers transformed the textual tradition from an expansive, permeable interpretive community designed for readers across time and space to a spoken language conceptualized as a finite boundary delineating one national group from another.

Historical typologies introduced by Sheldon Pollock, a scholar of Sanskrit and Indian studies, provide a helpful theoretical frame for appreciating Rawidowicz's concept of Hebrew's role in shaping collective identity.[42] Cosmopolitan languages, such as Sanskrit and Latin, Pollock contends, have historically created canons of literature, often based in oral traditions, which circulate freely across space and time. In these traditions, people are unified by shared modes of literary analysis and familiarity with certain canons that allow readers from diverse environments to engage in one conversation. The need to encompass multiple local experiences ensured that cosmopolitan languages remained heterogeneous and provided room for multiple levels of interpretation. The rise of the nation-state transformed the parameters of cultural belonging through the development of the vernacular. Instead of engendering an ever-expanding audience of readers, language thus became an instrument for marking spatial boundaries.

Framed in Pollock's language, the revival of modern Hebrew (as Harshav's earlier observations indicate) was an effort to create a vernacular tongue that serves primarily to create fixed criteria to distinguish between Jews and non-Jews.[43] Like delineating territorial markers, Zionist ideology and ultimately the state would maintain (and enforce) finite borderlines of national culture that promote a homogeneous membership. The vernacularization of Hebrew inspired by nation-state nationalism retards the dynamism and organic nature of languages spread by population shifts and transnational networks. From Rawidowicz's perspective, linking the growth of Hebrew culture with a specific place and political infrastructure erodes the cosmopolitan nature of Hebrew as the language that was practiced for centuries. Language promotes national culture by supporting shared textual canons and modes of literary analysis, which unite readers through the process of interpretation. To accomplish this, cosmopolitan languages require us to think about the relationship between language, national boundaries, and geography in a very different framework.

In this view, language serves as a permeable membrane that creates Jewish space and provides a nexus between Jews and their surroundings.[44] Rawidowicz conceptualizes linguistic boundaries as fluid rather than fixed, symbolic rather than physical, and process-based rather than content-based. The earlier discussion of eruvin also provides Rawidowicz with a metaphor for the ways in which language paradoxically creates and dissolves boundaries. He offered eruvin as the rabbinic counternarrative to an alternative Hebrew term *tehum* (border), which was preferred by state-seeking Zionist theorists. The eruv, Rawidowicz wrote, "establishes the people's tehum, and creates the tehum for Israel."[45] Here he is playing on rabbinic use of a word that etymologically comes from the root of mixing to construct borders. Mixing between Jewish communities and between Jews and non-Jews counterintuitively engenders a more vital national culture than a homogeneous environment created by territorial boundaries.

This is another attribute of the rabbinic notion of the eruvin boundary—it (or at least Rawidowicz's reading of the concept) included non-Jews as well as their cultural influences within the walls of the Jewish community. Rawidowicz refrained from explicitly discussing the rabbis' conversation regarding the process for building an eruv when non-Jews or apostates were present within the courtyard. However, he was certainly aware that the rabbis enabled an eruv to include non-Jews living in the same neighborhood. By symbolically renting the property for the Sabbath, a Jewish space could still be formed that included non-Jewish property. Within the rabbinic context, the eruv constructed an ethnic and religious space that was not hermetically sealed from the outside community. The institution of eruvin assumed a high level of integration in what Rawidowicz called "mixed urban neighborhoods." Living among non-Jewish cultures thus provided the intellectual fuel that propelled the tradition forward.

But how does Rawidowicz explain the counterintuitive logic that integration preserves national culture more effectively than static boundaries?[46] This is precisely the paradoxical "secret of the eruv," the essential process of creating distinct space by mixing boundaries. The deceptive rigidity of state boundaries actually represented the greatest threat to the survival of the Jewish people. Key to understanding this process is Rawidowicz's concept of interpretation. He outlined his philosophy of language and hermeneutic methodology in an essay called "On Interpretation," published shortly before his death in 1957.[47] According to his reading, Jewish sources did not constitute static legal doctrines or religious tenets. The core values and meaning of the Jewish tradition remained closed to those who approached sources to find their original intent. Instead, Rawidowicz described the authentic hermeneutic processes as "an attempt at reshaping either the 'document' interpreted or the world it came from. Here an act of transference is always involved. An invasion of one system by another takes place . . . [interpretation] derives its strength both from a deep attachment to the 'text' and from an 'alienation' from it."[48]

Only by creating friction between external systems and the texts themselves could an authentic understanding of traditional sources emerge. Outside stimuli from alien, or perhaps more specifically non-Jewish, influences facilitated discovering the essence and particular character of Jewish life. The requisite balance between alienation and attachment required the existence of clear yet permeable boundaries that differentiated Jews from their surrounding intellectual milieu. Flexible demarcations allowed for questions that might spark individuals to invade Jewish sources with relevant challenges. Impermeable boundaries, however, eliminated the non-Jewish interlocutors—the crucial ingredient for gaining insight into the depths of the Jewish people. The nation-state context hinders cultural development in another way as well. The state's support of a particular language and culture erodes a crucial catalyst—the perceived need to protect and nourish a cultural tradition against external threats.[49]

The advantages Rawidowicz aligns with diaspora and multinational settings have radical implications for rethinking the geography of cultural production. Maintaining cultural centers outside the homeland guaranteed a crucial conduit by which non-Jewish ideas and developments could enter Jewish national consciousness. Although lethal in large doses, outside influences suppressed by ethnonational conformity fuel the interpretive process that Rawidowicz considered a key to national survival. Counterstate national groups thus have the advantage of *not* commanding the political authority and social infrastructure to police cultural boundaries. Rawidowicz's iconoclastic notion that national unity not only *tolerates* but actually *demands* diversity rejects the need for static social, intellectual, or cultural boundaries. National preservation thrives when groups shift their focus away from explicit boundary maintenance and toward immersion, without any specific intended outcomes, with the texts, symbols, and narrative history of their traditions.

Global Hebraism imagines bonds created through *interpretation* rather than the day-to-day use of a particular spoken language. Hebrew therefore facilitates the construction of a hermeneutic community dedicated to a shared canon and commitment to remaining within its boundaries, but not necessarily the same interpretive conclusions. Moreover, Hebrew is a mode of generating culture fueled by engagement with the external environment. This differs significantly from other ideologies of nationalism, whose sovereign aspirations make heterogeneity and geographic dispersion among members of other nations anathema.

Delving more deeply into Rawidowicz's global Hebraism reveals that although the scholar had one foot deeply immersed in an early-nineteenth-century ideology of linguistic nationalism and its essentialist connection to delineating fixed collective boundaries, his other foot was gingerly placed to prefigure formulations of identity that resemble those of recent cultural theorists. Although language is a central pillar for Rawidowicz, his concept of cultural production does not assume essentialist or monolithic definitions of nationality. Precisely the opposite is the case. He considers language to be a form that promotes a diverse cultural matrix capable of encompassing a wide spectrum of possibilities. Shifting the role of language from content to process neutralizes a potential critique of collective boundaries as imagined, by acknowledging (and endorsing) the constructed nature of boundary markers. Interpretation engenders fluid boundaries that cannot be easily enforced by central institutions, ideological agendas, or state power.

Rawidowicz believed that mixing still maintains clear boundaries. The tension, especially clear in his metaphor of eruvin, serves as an excellent counterpoint to notions of hybridity.[50] The concept of hybridity views the constant erasure of boundaries as a reprisal against efforts to police the boundaries of identity. This approach tends to eliminate conversations about the value of collective preservation. In this view, hybridity dissolves collective ties. Eruvin, however, at least as Rawidowicz presented the concept, takes cultural preservation seriously while acknowledging acculturation as a crucial ingredient in the evolution of national culture. The options available to think about culture—either discredited notions of purity or a fluid mélange—engender an artificial dichotomy between separation and assimilation. Rawidowicz grappled with the possibility that national cultures can simultaneously mix and retain their distinction.

Rawidowicz's efforts to formulate a concept of the Hebrew language as serving as the permeable and nonspatial boundaries of Israel suffer from a number of weak points, however. Although the theoretical possibilities of a Hebrew revival occurring outside the homeland may be invaluable, it is highly unlikely that diaspora communities could sustain the degree of language proficiency necessary to create the bonds Rawidowicz advocated. Conversely, the revival and spread of the Hebrew language can be largely attributed to the role of educational, social, and economic infrastructure available only in Palestine and later the State of Israel. Rawidowicz thus ignored a crucial paradox: the survival of Hebrew as a language available to more than a small minority of scholars has primarily happened within the state's territorial boundaries. Yet this revival has the potential to endanger the very tradition it purports to be saving. Cosmopolitan languages may thrive in multinational empires, but they have far less chance of flourishing in the age of the nation-state and in a time of dominance of the vernacular.

Rawidowicz's romantic effort to recapture a premodern function of language as an instrument for creating hermeneutic communities directly challenges efforts in the nineteenth and twentieth centuries to link land, language, and nation. One could speculate that nostalgia, more than denial, fueled his own personal reluctance to relinquish his critique of Hebrew within the nation-state context and to recognize the limitations of linguistic boundaries within a diaspora setting. The world of rabbinic exegesis—characterized by wordplay, symbolic interpretations, and expansive possibilities—that Rawidowicz entered as a young man was increasingly threatened as his lifetime progressed. His own relevance and legacy depended on people carrying on an approach to Judaism that appreciated and respected the centrality of interpretation and textual tradition. Maintaining the tradition was thus a valiant effort to maintain the world he saw disappearing.

The Judaism Rawidowicz had experienced as a yeshiva student in Lithuania, however, could not be created with his undergraduate students at Brandeis University. Although his decision led to his marginalization, his persistence enabled him to diagnose the price that the desacralization of Hebrew would play in transforming the function of the Hebrew language. Rawidowicz saw how this desacralization contributed to a rift between the homeland population dedicated to Hebrew as the language of everyday life and the diaspora community that viewed Hebrew at best as the language of liturgy. Perhaps the greatest loss he lamented connected to this desacralization was the concretization of the mythic dimension of Israel's national life, specifically the deferred messianic vision of returning to the homeland in the distant future, into the political project of Zionism's state-building enterprise.

Myth and Messianism

Rawidowicz's *Babylon and Jerusalem* opens with a stand-alone essay on Jewish history called "Al parashat batim," which is known in English as "Israel's Two Beginnings: The First and the Second 'Houses.'" Jewish history, as Rawidowicz portrays it in the essay, exhibited two basic stages.[51] The first period—symbolized by the First House, the temple in Jerusalem—categorized the Jews' experience as a politically sovereign nation living in the Land of Israel. This era ended, Rawidowicz argued, with the first dispersion to Babylon. At this point the second period commenced, centered around the rebuilt temple in Jerusalem, infused with a new textual tradition developed during the Babylonian exile that galvanized Jewish life during the following millennia.[52]

At more than a hundred pages, this extended analysis offers a synthetic philosophy of Jewish history that stands alone from the rest of the chapters in *Babylon and Jerusalem*. The later chapters focus more explicitly on a contemporary critique of Zionism and American Judaism. Yet this opening chapter introduces a crucial thematic link in Rawidowicz's work between the role of language and myth in shaping the historical development of the people of Israel. The key to understanding the centrality of this essay is in exploring the distinguishing factors between the first and second periods. The historiographical division sets up a dialectical relationship in Jewish history between two opposing attitudes toward theology, religious life, geography, time, and other criteria. The crucial evolution is the development of a mythic consciousness, exemplified in the rabbinic notion of a deferred messianism. Unpacking Israel's historical commitment to maintaining a mythic realm, which retains a clear separation between reality and ideal aspirations, serves for Rawidowicz as both a partial explanation of twentieth-century exclusivist nationalism and an admonishment to Zionism's quest for sovereignty. Reading this essay as a contemporary commentary on the meaning of national identity formation, rather than as a history lesson, illuminates the integration of history, literature, philosophy, and politics within the theory of global Hebraism.

The First House, which technically encompassed the First Temple period, reflected Rawidowicz's understanding of the political and philosophical proclivities of nation-state nationalism. A particular geographical location and political control define the First House. The people of this period yearn for a king so they can become a "nation like all other nations." These kings, and the prophets who challenged their legitimacy, advocated a universalist outlook and humanistic concepts of morality. From a philosophical point of view, the chief characteristic of the First House remained its ability to view the world through "pure vision." Lacking the mediation of theoretical or speculative categories, the First House encountered reality directly through the senses. The meaning of place, events, and history remained limited to what could be directly observed about the object. This epistemological handicap indicated that the First House could rely only on concrete markers to delineate its identity from other national groups. At this stage, boundaries were fixed to place because no more sophisticated options existed for formulating a shared identity. Without the ability to create abstract categories, the First House conflated temporal distinctions between past, present, and future.

The Second House revolutionized Jewish history by discovering the power of ideas and concepts to order reality. Rawidowicz celebrated the intellectual transformation sparked by the Israelites' first experience with life outside of their homeland. He wrote: "The unfulfilled end of the First House and the seventy years in Babylon taught Israel a new and great teaching, a secret of existence which they did not know before, a secret of secrets. They provided a new reason for existence. That which Israel learned in those seventy years had no equal in the hundreds of years before them and after them."[53] What was the secret? The Second House developed the capacity to understand the world through the lenses of both myth-making and interpretation. This transformation directly opposed the First House's proclivity for political normalcy, homogeneity, and epistemological monism. Rabbinic hermeneutics generated symbolic and historical analogies to explore the deeper significance of specific events and experiences.

Rawidowicz focused on the development of Jewish law as an example of this novel approach to reality. Ignoring the theological implications of the yoke of commandments, he read the rabbinic tradition as marking and interpreting hidden philosophical truths through ritual acts. The rabbis during this period discovered the power of *revah derekh tzimtzum* (the universal through the particular). The commandments infused the material world with glimpses of the universal through engaging particular issues and questions that transcended quotidian reality. Rawidowicz read the rabbinic concept of messianism, specifically the deferred longing for a return in the distant future, as one of the most salient examples of Judaism's appreciation for distinguishing between the real and the ideal.

The religious imperative to defer political return to a specific homeland, and to privilege yearning rather than realization, created the basis for the people of Israel's philosophical and political orientation. The diaspora experience galvanized the development of this greater level of philosophical consciousness—the creation of a chasm between material experiences and other levels of speculation.[54] Without the ability to rely on a specific place or political union, the tradition was forced to seek national meaning on a more abstract plane. Following this reconstruction of Rawidowicz's philosophical tenets, however, suggests that he regarded this move toward symbolic boundaries as the richest intellectual development in Jewish history. Far from being a historical tragedy, exile thus pushed the Jewish people to a higher level of self-consciousness and philosophical awareness of the role of myth in understanding reality.

This chapter in *Babylon and Jerusalem* reflects an immersion in Jewish historiography and theories of modernity, as well as an effort to challenge these narratives. On the one hand, the account of the two houses is deeply indebted to a tradition of *Wissenschaft des Judentums* (the science of Judaism), an approach to history committed to locating thematic threads that trace historical progress and development.[55] This was part of the modern project of looking back over history to determine key turning points and define characteristics of national groups. On the other hand, this essay should also be read as a critique of the Enlightenment project and its political ramifications. The chapter inveighs against the eradication of myths by focusing on rational analysis and the limits of knowledge. The critical debunking of myth by reason, science, and history diminished the validity and truth claims encoded within textual traditions based on myths and symbols.[56] Myth, Rawidowicz wrote, is "a world view in which the rational is not the decisive element."[57]

The Second House demands the demythologization of Western philosophy, a position that reflects a curious amalgam of Nietzsche's return to Greek myth and postexilic rabbinic literature. Interpretation within mythic and literary traditions provides a crucial dimension for understanding reality and moral standards, even if they are not empirically verifiable or rational according to scientific standards. Myths nourished through forms of art and literature, and therefore open to infinite interpretations and reinterpretations, can illuminate truths without being real.[58]

The aesthetic and philosophical critiques also have significant political consequences. Although modernity debunked myths, nationalist ideologies resurrected many of the myths in a new form, as historical legitimizations of their national movements. The political process that accompanied national ideology—the resurrection of myths as concrete maps for political objectives rather than as material for speculation—distorts the mythic dimension. By appropriating the aesthetic realm, political ideologies exploited national myths for the purpose of galvanizing the state. Rawidowicz addressed this development by contrasting Jewish messianism with the messianic dreams woven into state-seeking national movements. The urge for immediate messianic completion and religious redemption erased the barrier between ideal and real by imbuing the state with a level of absolute meaning that had always existed as a future goal but never as current reality in mythic conceptions. Temporal realities, biological characteristics, and national identities acquired a false level of importance as a direct result of the blurring of these categories. The immersion in unrealized myth eroded the healthy bulwark between inner meaning and material manifestations, between present reality and the ideal future. One of the most disturbing manifestations of this tendency, in Rawidowicz's mind, could be found in modern states' endeavors to wrap their own political existence within a mantle of religious and redemptive significance.

One can read Rawidowicz's narrative of the two houses (published in 1957) as part of an ongoing diagnosis of a debilitating disease affecting nation-state nationalism. He had begun his critique of German national-ism and work on counterstate formulations of Jewish nationalism decades earlier. The 1934 series of essays known as "The Endurance of the Diaspora," written in installments from Rawidowicz's new home in London, offers a detached, scholarly analysis of the historical and philosophical roots of the rise of fascism in Germany. Rawidowicz did not believe that twentieth-century German nationalism should be understood as a completely irra-tional movement devoid of explanation. Instead, the exiled scholar and Hebraist proposed a historical and philosophical elucidation that linked Hitler's rise to power directly with Germany's political attempts to realize its messianic urges.

The Germans, suffering from the economic and political humiliation of World War I, turned toward reviving their internal religious spirit as a direct response to their predicament. Nazi ideology engendered the mate-rialization of deep-seated religious and messianic impulses in German cul-ture and thought. According to Rawidowicz:

> In the hearts of the German people, suffering after the war from political and economic difficulties, lives a messianic dream, a dream connected to ancient Germany. A dream for revival of [*tekuma*] a great, dominating and free Germany, whose freedom will find its expression in total control of its own land and outside its land. . . . The racial laws flowed directly out of the dream of freedom and redemption [*geulah*] of Germany, that lived in masses, the politicians and the poets of the nation.[59]

The feeling of German powerlessness, Rawidowicz theorized, triggered an attempt to project a dream of a utopian Germany onto contemporary political circumstances. The political state served as an instrument for the revival of an idealized past that had innocuously survived in fictional accounts and poetic nostalgia.[60] As a result of this fusion of political state and religionational yearnings, Germany radically altered its definitions of citizenship and embarked on a policy of territorial expansion. Politics aligned with messianic fervor completely undermined the basic universal principles of equality and individual rights that had been championed by eighteenth- and nineteenth-century idealism.

Rawidowicz developed his concept of the Second House in particular and global Hebraism in general during the years following his own exile as an antidote to the loss of a truly mythical dimension. By focusing on the symbol of Babylon, and the rabbinic theories crafted outside the homeland, Rawidowicz aligned Israel with a concept of collective cohesion based on the deferred concept of redemption. According to his reading of Jewish sources, the realization of redemption actually heralded "the desecration of messianism."[61] Rawidowicz read rabbinic texts as models of political philosophy that rejected imbuing political events or entities with theological significance.[62]

The clearly delineated gap between ideal aspirations and concrete possibility prevented the conflation of literary imagination and political doctrine that led to exclusivist and immoral theories of nationalism. Thus, one of the primary agendas in *Babylon and Jerusalem* is to deflate the messianic impulse in Jewish thought to defuse what Rawidowicz viewed as a primary cause of the discrimination that arises when national myths inform state policies. At the same time that he admonishes messianic tendencies in European nationalism, also encoded within the concepts of the two houses (and more explicitly elsewhere in *Babylon and Jerusalem*), is the effort to defuse what he sees as potential parallels between European nationalism's use of history and mythic language to articulate political ideologies and the messianic language of Zionist discourse.

By ignoring these fundamental principles of Jewish thought, political Zionism and the policies of the newly created Jewish state risked emulating the inequities implemented by those nations that persecuted Jews throughout the nineteenth and twentieth century in the name of national unity. Noting these connections in Rawidowicz's thought between his critique of German messianism, his affirmation of Jewish nationalism's deferred messianism, and his confrontation with Zionist ideology about the redemptive language does not imply that Rawidowicz equated the State of Israel with fascism or Nazi ideology. Rather, he was consciously concerned with the slippage between the liturgical, poetic, and philosophical yearning for a return to the homeland and the centrality of homeland (and the corollary demotion of diaspora) in modern theories of nationalism as a rhetorical tool adopted across many streams of Zionism. His frustration with the direction of the Zionist movement, particularly after the declaration of statehood, was fueled by a concern that the mythic aspect of Jewish politics would be severely undermined by statehood.[63]

Subsequent chapters in *Babylon and Jerusalem* offer a far more explicit critique of Zionism from the perspective of its attitude toward messianism. Confronting these claims of messianic import was so paramount for Rawidowicz that he included a central chapter entitled "Without Messiah?" in the work. This piece posed a rhetorical question: How could Zionists confuse the declaration of the State of Israel with the religious notion of complete redemption? Rawidowicz decried Ben Gurion's declaration that "we are living in the days of the Messiah." He also protested any corollary claims linking this redemptive moment with the ingathering of all world Jewry in the Land of Israel.[64] For Rawidowicz, the state's use of messianic language to justify its existence was a manifestation of one of his fundamental apprehensions about the nature of the new state's nationalism. Without rejecting the centrality of homeland in Jewish sources, he recovered traditional sources that reveal the alignment between religious notions of exile/homecoming and state-seeking Zionism.[65] The founding of the State of Israel, along with its attempt to declare partial completion of the political-religious dream, thus violated traditional restraints against hastening the end.[66]

The polemic with Zionism, specifically Ben Gurion's idea that statism represented a revolution in Jewish history, implicitly permeates Rawidowicz's concept of the First House. This is a response to Zionist historiography that focused on biblical Israel as the highest level of Jewish life, and postexilic Judaism as turning to religion as a temporary and far inferior substitute to land, language, and sovereignty. He inverts the negative vector of Jewish history from homeland to exile but highlights Babylon as the source of the "secret of secrets" that characterizes Israel. Rawidowicz's narrative highlights biblical selections that underscore origins not in the land, but instead focus on moments in Jewish history when Jews learned to develop culturally *outside* the land. The First House, like Zionism, views the present as the ultimate fulfillment. By couching Zionism's return to the land as a completion of the messianic yearning to return to Jerusalem, Zionism thus moves Jewish nationalism to a more primitive level of development.

These connections between the literary, philosophical, and political strands of Rawidowicz's thought delineate myth as a source of truth, cultural vitality, and the primary antidote to the dangers of modern nation-state nationalism. This indicates the multiple levels upon which Rawidowicz conceptualized global Hebraism. These connections also raise a question: How can myth, and a politics of deferred homecoming, be preserved in the modern period? Although Rawidowicz passionately defends the aesthetic realm of myth and yearning, he does so with a modern consciousness that rejects national mythic narrative as historically accurate. Here he finds himself in a conundrum that plagued a number of his contemporaries, including the philosophers Franz Rosenzweig and Martin Buber. How does one construct modern philosophical justifications for returning to pre-modern narratives? In particular, Rawidowicz's challenge was to overcome the debilitating effects of historicism and Enlightenment critiques of religion that undermine the validity of religious traditions, without embracing theological dogma or literal textuality of the religious sources. To put this another way, Rawidowicz struggled to consciously promote national culture as developing organically to reflect the lived experiences of its members. An appreciation for myth as true, but not real, presents a very nuanced position that lacks the certainty of embracing myth as history or rejecting the traditional account of Jewish history as primitive myth.

Rawidowicz's effort to maintain the myth and an awareness of its historically constructed nature provides another angle for understanding his decision to present his political theory through symbols and metaphors plucked from traditional sources, rather than directly importing Western philosophical terms. One avenue for addressing this fundamental challenge of consciously theorizing a dynamic relationship with the tradition is to present oneself as writing from *within* the tradition. Only by following his own theory of interpretation by remaining within the particular historical dimensions of the textual tradition can he demonstrate the viability of his theory. Thus Rawidowicz committed himself to a Hebrew style and Jewish vocabulary that gave the impression of a historical weaving together of multiple strands of Jewish sources.

Writing in English or in a style less rooted in language, symbols, and myths would have undermined Rawidowicz's own efforts by creating a critical distance between his own work and the interpretive tradition. Thus his Hebrew style, his rehabilitation of rabbinic symbols, and his hesitancy to acknowledge modern influences are all part of his conscious effort to produce a work of interpretation that downplays historical consciousness. Most of Rawidowicz's writing suppresses any explicit recognition of historical change or external influences. However, Rawidowicz did not lack a keen awareness of interactions between Jewish texts and their contexts and his own efforts to overcome the post-Spinoza crisis of a critical and historical approach to reading Jewish sources. This creates a tension in Rawidowicz's work between, on the one hand, the theoretical importance of external influence and the explicit rejection of external influences and, on the other hand, a preference for understanding changes in Judaism as completely internal in nature.[67]

The tension between Rawidowicz's commitment to intellectual dialogue and his strident denunciation of external influences denotes a real struggle in his thought. Jewish life in the diaspora, Rawidowicz bemoaned throughout *Babylon and Jerusalem*, had misunderstood the delicate balance between bringing outside ideas into the tradition and overwhelming the tradition with foreign concepts. Facing this reality, Rawidowicz found himself fighting a two-front battle against what he viewed as the polarization of modern Jewish life. Toward the state-seeking Zionists he voiced an argument for the importance and enduring viability of diaspora and the importance of creating national communities within other cultures and societies. Toward the American Jewish community he emphasized the deleterious effects of allowing outside influences to completely overwhelm Judaism's own vocabulary and conceptual framework. Rawidowicz derided those movements and ideologies that stressed either complete integration or complete separation. Eruvin, according to his logic, exemplified the complex equilibrium that the rabbinic tradition espoused.

The success of global Hebraism (and more broadly, counterstate nationalism), as Rawidowicz imagined it, thus demands maintaining the veneer of organic development, while acknowledging the epistemological limitations of the very myths that are supposed to be at the center of national culture. Perhaps an even greater weakness inherent within Rawidowicz's global Hebraism is its incompatibility with the sovereign mold as it developed during the twentieth century. The final section of this chapter explores Rawidowicz's explicit efforts to apply his literary imagination to the political realities as they drastically shifted during his lifetime.

The Right to Be Different

Here I consider some of the practical implications of how global Hebraism might interact with the reality of an international order dominated by sovereign nation-states and the existence of a Jewish state. Though not nearly to the degree exhibited by Mordecai Kaplan and Hans Kohn (the subjects of chapters 4 and 5, respectively), Rawidowicz did respond to the postwar reality and the shift in his own political environment after the war and the events of 1948. The success of global Hebraism, and other transnational nationalisms, would require the recalibration of the reigning theories of international relations and nationalism. But with what models of national sovereignty in general and Jewish statehood in particular is global Hebraism compatible?

Global Hebraism's approach to the disconnect between national sovereignty and transnational solidarity is to promote minority rights and the value of difference within the state. The clearest expression of this position is in a piece Rawidowicz wrote in 1945 called "Libertas Differendi." In this essay he contends that the four freedoms outlined by President Franklin D. Roosevelt during World War II—freedom of speech, freedom of religion, freedom from want, and freedom from fear—were not sufficient for guaranteeing liberty. The Jewish intellectual historian insisted upon a fifth freedom: The right to be different.[68] Democratic governments, he wrote, have an obligation not only to preserve individual freedoms protecting belief and physical security, but also to recognize and promote the existence of minority groups within their own borders and around the world. Rawidowicz explained: "One of the shortcomings of proponents of a liberalism and democracy based on the ideas of the eighteenth century is that they were unable to recognize the right of groups to differ and grant this right to the minorities in the world."[69] Modern political thought, with its equation of shared universal assumptions and uniformity, therefore misrepresented the meaning of equality.

Rawidowicz presented Israel itself as exemplifying this value of difference (a critique of liberalism he shared with the counterstate theorists explored in chapter 2). Jews, in both their insistence on remaining separate from non-Jewish society and their internal disparate expressions of Judaism, illustrate the basic paradigm of the right to be different. The Jews' political role in the world was to disseminate this political message. Rawidowicz expounded: "The more a Jewish community in a non-Jewish environment preserves its *libertas differendi* at heart and in practice, the greater a blessing it will be, not only to itself but also to its non-Jewish environment."[70] Herein lies a formulation of the Jewish political mission as the bearers of libertas differendi to the world. Rawidowicz even took the rare step of adopting a "foreign" term to give an authentic voice to this principle of Jewish nationalism. The term libertas, in a similar fashion to such terms as civilization (used by Kaplan), served as a bridge between Rawidowicz's internal conversation about Judaism and his endeavor to promote a Jewish nationalism that might influence external political considerations. Even the scholar obdurately committed to writing in Hebrew and to working within the parameters of the Jewish sources divulged his understanding that global Hebraism could only work by convincing a non-Hebrew-speaking audience of its universal implications and advantages.

The demand for integrating libertas differendi as a Jewish principle integral to the foundation of liberal democracies raises a potential conflict for Jewish nationalism, however: How does the right to be different play out in the Jewish state? And what is the relationship between Jewish character and non-Jewish citizens? Demanding that Israel remain true to its defining characteristic of libertas differendi, whether as a diaspora community or as a sovereign power, raised a taboo that even Rawidowicz hesitated to challenge. The manuscript of *Babylon and Jerusalem* included a final chapter called "Bein ever ve'arav" (Between Jew and Arab) that challenged the new State of Israel's policies, especially the decisions to refuse repatriation of Arabs following the War of Independence. However, Rawidowicz decided to remove this section from the book's final edition. Examining this text provides a sense of how Rawidowicz might have applied the concepts of global Hebraism to policy in the new state.[71]

Zionism's efforts to link the state with a particular national–religious identity troubled Rawidowicz. Commenting about the Law of Return (the 1950 Israeli law that provides automatic citizenship in Israel for Jews interested in settling in the State of Israel), he wrote: "The idea of a monolithic [national population] that has ambushed the state [of Israel] . . . teaches that no state is worthy of its name unless it is composed of one skin (read as, one nation)."[72] This language of one skin contrasts sharply with the right to be different. In fact, Rawidowicz's use of the term skin evokes racial concepts of Jewish nationality that promote a purity absent from his notion of collective boundaries. The passage of laws designed to welcome Jewish immigrants (the 1950 Law of Return and the 1952 Nationality Law), and to prevent the repatriation of Arabs who fled after 1948, perturbed Rawidowicz.[73] These government decisions clearly aimed to create a greater correlation between Jews and citizenship by promoting Jewish immigration and preventing the return of non-Jewish former residents.

Rawidowicz's controversial critique of these laws has only become more of a polarizing topic in modern debates about the future of Israel, the Palestinian Authority, and Palestinian refugees. Considering this critique is not intended to present a counterfactual historical narrative that ignores the possible price the nascent state might have faced if it had implemented Rawidowicz's suggestions. Valid concerns, especially a sense of existential threat following the Holocaust, postponed conversations about these tensions. Moreover, absent from Rawidowicz's analysis is an appreciation of the Palestinian rejection of the two-state compromise and the potential threat to Israel of large numbers of refugees returning. Yet sixty years after the founding of the state, Rawidowicz's questions about the Law of Return and what the Palestinians now call, echoing Israel's language, the Palestinian Right of Return, is a flashpoint in debates about the future of Israel and Palestine.

Rawidowicz grappled with the inconsistencies that marked Jewish expectations as both the majority population in Palestine and the minority community in the United States and other countries. As he watched the nascent state displace those who had lived in Palestine for generations and then discriminate against those minorities who had remained, he wrote: "But don't those who make this claim realize that it actually undermines the existence of the Jewish Diaspora?"[74] Such policies threatened the political well-being and ethical justifications for Jews living outside the new state.[75] The Jewish people, he demanded, must advocate a single, consistent political policy toward minorities. Diaspora Jewish nationalism would lose its ability to advocate a more tolerant attitude toward minority cultural, ethnic, or religious orientations if its own political homeland denied the rights of its Arab minorities. Thus his calls for the "State of Israel to have a spirit of inter-humanity [*bein ha'adamiyut*]" demanded the same recognition of the right to be different that he expected from President Roosevelt in the United States.[76] Global Hebraism thus illuminates a knotty situation in conceptualizing the meaning of Jewish peoplehood. Preserving a Jewish ethnoreligious demographic majority and cultural dominance provides a sense of security and a level of collective preservation. However, these cultural advantages would disappear if the state eliminated any preferences for Jewish citizens. Rawidowicz highlighted the fragmentation that this would create by declaring a set of shared collective values for Jews in both the diaspora and the homeland community.

Global Hebraism anticipated, decades before the term globalization was coined, the complications of preserving religionational identity through political boundaries. The bonds of solidarity shared by global communities would provide a constant thorn in the logic of the sovereign mold. Although the refusal to allow Arab refugees of the war to return ensured a sense of security, it may have also underestimated the power of nation-state nationalism to motivate a return among the exiled population that could erode long-term stability. Rawidowicz predicted that creating a more robust federation, or a system of minority rights, in the years immediately following the state's creation might have defused the tension. Global Hebraism is far less threatened by these processes than nationalisms built on the foundations of the sovereign mold.

Contemporary scholars and communal leaders have begun to observe, and lament, the decline in the fabric of a shared sense of Jewish peoplehood. Increasing a connection to the State of Israel is assumed as the most effective treatment for this phenomenon. Rawidowicz's work, however, suggests that the forces eroding Jewish collective consciousness arise for precisely the opposite reason—the prevalence of a narrative of nationality that centers on the state. He mapped the fissures that arise when a diaspora sense of collective identity is constructed through building a connection to a state. Underneath this assumed shared narrative, he exposed several actual and potential friction zones—the tacit agreement that the state serves as the cultural and political center of world Jewry, the difference between Jewish national culture as specific criteria (such as land or language) or dynamic process, and the questions of minority rights and the ethical positions of sovereign and subject communities.

Beyond these specific troubling issues, Rawidowicz also diagnosed a more fundamental error in the roots of mainstream conceptions of Jewish peoplehood; that is, the residue of either/or ideological choices in narrating modern Jewish history and politics. Understanding Jewish identity is problematic when viewed as a series of choices: religious versus secular, diaspora versus homeland, nationality versus religion, sovereigns versus subjects, premodern versus modern. At a crucial point in Jewish history Rawidowicz questioned the need for such distinct paths. The residue of these distinctions remains active today, still delineating the mainstream discourse of Jewish identity and Israel–diaspora relations. But by replacing mutually exclusive possibilities with the conjunction *and,* Rawidowicz tried to neutralize what he perceived to be a threat to Jewish peoplehood: the adoption of nation-state nationalism's political assumptions as the building block of Jewish identity formation. Ironically, the ideological differences at the poles are actually much more closely related than theorists might admit. Each extreme is rooted in the same set of assumptions about identity formation in the modern world as citizens of nation-states have. Reading *Babylon and Jerusalem* raises the possibility that the ideological extremes conceptualized in the either/or logic are actually more closely linked than many intellectuals think. Global Hebraism was therefore an effort—certainly from a critical, modern perspective—to illustrate how the binary choices are colored by the paradigm of the sovereign mold and not necessarily the language of Jewish tradition.

The way forward, following Rawidowicz's lead, is to develop a comprehensive counternarrative built on a new logic: an attempt to shift the discourse of nationality away from the ideological clarity of the either/or paradigm toward the fluidity of the both/and model. One of the few American Jewish thinkers who read Rawidowicz's work and appreciated his efforts to fragment the emerging synthesis between Jewish nationality and the sovereign mold was Mordecai Kaplan, popularly known as the founder of Reconstructionist Judaism. Folded up and paper-clipped to the inside cover of Rawidowicz's personal copy of Kaplan's landmark work *Judaism as a Civilization* still rests a handwritten note in Hebrew from 1936. "I realized that in a number of ways our outlooks are similar," Kaplan wrote.[77] After reading Rawidowicz's article "The Endurance of the Diaspora," written in 1934, Kaplan thought Rawidowicz would appreciate *Judaism as a Civilization.*[78] The two men shared an ambivalent passion for Zionism and rejection of its trajectory toward linking Jewish nationalism and statism. Yet, as chapter 4 explores, Kaplan's immersion in American life and thought contributed to quite a different approach to counterstate Zionism.

Mordecai M. Kaplan on board the S.S. *Excambion* working on the first essay in *Judaism in Transition,* titled "What to Live for as a Jew," ca. 1935. *Courtesy of the Archives, Reconstructionist Rabbinical College.*

4

Making American Democracy Safe for Judaism

Mordecai Kaplan, National Civilization, and the Morality of Zionism

The book *Who Are We? The Challenges to American National Identity* (2004) by international relations theorist Samuel Huntington makes it clear that the debate about what it means to be an American is still very much alive today.[1] Huntington expresses concern that the "substance" and "salience" of the "Anglo-Protestant" cultural core of American national identity has been eroded by a wave of multiculturalism and massive immigration from Latin America. This recent salvo in the critique of multiculturalism regards national, ethnic, and even religious diversity as potentially undermining the fabric of American society. Huntington's claims—sanitized of explicitly racial or jingoist overtones—echo anxieties about citizenship popularized a century ago that resulted in the promotion of Anglo-Protestant conformity and denounced so-called hyphenated identities as antithetical to the progress of American civilization.

When we consider the tension over the past century between the concepts of America as a unified nation or as a nation of many nationalities, the ineluctable force of these debates cannot be ignored. Also extraordinary, however, are the ways that notions of American identity and collective identity among minority communities have changed over the years. Today, voices like Huntington's write from a more marginal position in society. Warnings of the fragmentation of the United States are increasingly on the defensive against a mainstream that recognizes, and even values, multiple attachments and loyalties. Elementary school and high school curriculums, college campuses, and businesses alike welcome and even encourage ethnic, religious, and cultural diversity. Entire fields of scholarship—ethnic, diaspora, multicultural, and transnational studies—have developed since the 1960s and 1970s to analyze the interplay between minority groups and the federal government. The rise of these identity politics is often viewed as the catalyst in this transformation. However, the shift from American nationalism to multiculturalism had roots far earlier in a discourse (nationalism) and intellectual cohort (those individuals affiliated with Jewish and Zionist concerns) that has rarely been recognized as part of the central narrative.

This chapter attempts to fill that gap by recovering one such forgotten contributor to the narrative: the influential American Jewish thinker Mordecai Kaplan. He published, taught, and built institutions over a long lifetime. Born in 1881 in Lithuania, he died in New York more than a century later. Kaplan's concept of Judaism as a civilization helped ensure his legacy as one of the twentieth century's most significant Jewish thinkers and remains today one of the most influential contributions to modern Jewish thought.[2] Instead of linking Kaplan's famous concept of civilization to religion, however, this chapter places the key term within debates about nationalism, Zionism, and internationalism. Approaching Kaplan's conception of Judaism as a national civilization (rather than the term he himself made famous, Judaism as a religious civilization) more accurately captures his lifelong interest in aligning Zionism, and civilization more broadly, with a counterstate conception of Jewish nationalism.

Kaplan is remembered for his commitment, both theoretical and communal, to Zionism. Jewish historian Arthur Hertzberg has called him "the Summary of American Zionism."[3] This association belies a far more complex relationship with Zionism, however, as it fails to acknowledge Kaplan's deep reluctance about, and even opposition to, statehood. Kaplan's legacy as a religious thinker and American Zionist overlooks the two central motivating objectives of his work: the effort to formulate Judaism as the example par excellence of ethical nationhood and the attempt to reconstruct U.S. democracy to reflect the principles of Zionism.

Kaplan defined civilization as the totality of social interactions, cultural attributes, and religious folkways that historically have created the ties that bind Jews to one another. As a religious thinker, Kaplan offered the explicit acknowledgment that the Jewish religion was a cultural system that had evolved over time in response to internal changes and external contexts. He famously jettisoned the concept of a supernatural God, challenged Jews' self-perception as God's chosen people, and underscored the need to consciously reinterpret the tradition to meet contemporary challenges. During his long life, Kaplan promulgated his message through dozens of books and articles. He also taught homiletics to generations of rabbinic students at the Conservative movement's seminary (the Jewish Theological Seminary) and served as the founding rabbi of both the Jewish Center and the Society for the Advancement of Judaism. Kaplan's program solidified its position within American Jewry with the founding of the Reconstructionist movement, known as the fourth denomination of American Judaism, in 1955.[4]

As the debates about the meaning of nationality and sovereignty dominated the early decades of the twentieth century, Kaplan's most influential work, *Judaism as a Civilization,* was published in 1934. The phrase it popularized emerged from his passion for translating Judaism into an American context, but also from his belief that U.S. democracy threatened the preservation of Judaism. To address this predicament, Kaplan formulated the idea of civilization with a distinct mission in mind: to promulgate a concept of American democracy and ethical nationhood based on his vision of the Jewish paradigm of collective identity. Civilization therefore theorized a specific typology of nationalism that would encourage sovereign powers to promote national diversity within their borders and define moral parameters for neutralizing any potential tension between nationality and citizenship. Reconstructing nationalism, both locally and globally, was thus a crucial first step in the reconstruction of Judaism.

Addressing the relationship between Judaism, nationality, and ethical progress remained a central theme in Kaplan's writings—from his first article, "Judaism and Nationality" (1909), to his final book, *The Religion of Ethical Nationhood* (1970).[5] Yet the popular and scholarly reception of his *Judaism as a Civilization* (1934) into mainstream American Jewish life has clouded this dimension of his thought. The focus has almost exclusively been on Kaplan as a religious philosopher and institution builder. His effort to blur the categories of religion and nationhood through the introduction of the concept of civilization thus largely failed to overcome the very dichotomy he set out to challenge. The more radical possibilities he hoped the use of civilization would engender were effectively neutralized by integrating the term into the paradigm of Judaism as a religion and America as a nation of multiple religious communities (rather than multiple nationalities).

In contrast to his legacy, Kaplan interpreted civilization not as a theory of religious philosophy (or more specifically as a program of Jewish renewal), but as a strategic intervention in conversations about what it means to be an American and a member of a nation. Using the term Jewish civilization provided Kaplan with a conceptual vocabulary to try to dictate, or at least to negotiate, the terms of discussions about the meaning of American identity at a moment when the sociopolitical pressures of Americanization were radically reshaping the realities of Jewish life.[6] Kaplan faced the challenge of trying to translate the multivalent aspects of Jewish collective consciousness into modern social and political thought. His use of civilization introduced new language to mediate between both the possibilities and the threats posed by complex intellectual and social forces, including racial science, exclusivist theories of nationalism, American nativism and anti-immigration, the promise of Zionism, and religion's role in middle-class American identity formation. Historicizing the development of Jewish civilization within the hotly contested conversations about Americanization indicates that Kaplan intended that the term be embraced as a paradigm for making American democracy safe for Jews.

I argue that Kaplan selected a deliberately vague term and refused to reconcile contradictions in his description of that term for strategic purposes. This ambiguity enabled him to grapple with fundamental tensions between Jewish national preservation and American citizenship, involving irresolvable questions such as the relationship between individual rights and collective recognition, patriotic duty and national loyalty, religious creed and cultural cohesion, and voluntary association and coercive bonds. Kaplan thus found a unified term that would address a series of irreconcilable dilemmas. These strategic silences allowed him to blur the boundaries between such key categories as nation, religion, race, Americanism, and Judaism. The expansive connotations of civilization furthered his ability to appeal to multiple audiences. The fact that a larger audience never read his work does not undermine the importance of reading civilization as a term designed to teach Americans both about their own national identity and their obligations to minority groups through the characteristics of Jewish civilization with American nationalism. This chapter recognizes the specific intellectual, social, and political pressures within Kaplan's historical milieu and his mixed success at creating a category to resist these various factors.

My approach to national civilization raises three questions, each of which is addressed in detail in this chapter. First, how did the term civilization help Kaplan achieve his objectives of reconstructing the relationship between Americanism and Judaism? Second, how did Kaplan's formulation of national civilization develop pioneering strategies for legitimating the morality of national cohesion? Third, how did Kaplan's conclusions about nationhood, formulated from the perspective of Jews as a minority group in the diaspora, shape his understanding of Zionism and Jewish settlement in Palestine? That Kaplan's interpreters rejected this dimension of his political thought underscores his own misjudgment of the limits of shifting the language and self-perception of the relationship between American Jews and their host country. Rehabilitating this political and externally oriented dimension of Kaplan's work complicates a teleological reading of the development of the American Jewish synthesis as eschewing the possibility of Jewish nationhood as compatible with Americanization. Kaplan's push for redefining the theoretical language of the Jewish community, both in America and around the world, has new relevance today as the popular discourse of American multiculturalism and ethnicity swings closer to Kaplan's ideals of civilization.

Kaplan: An Intellectual Biography

Before examining these complex issues, let us begin with a brief look at Kaplan himself. The spectrum of theoretical positions incorporated within his civilization concept reflects his own personal struggle between his accommodationist reading of the reality of American Jewish life and his maximalist yearnings for a return to the romantic notion of premodern Jewish diaspora autonomy. Because he grew up deeply steeped in Jewish life, Kaplan intuitively grasped the power that religious communities, practices, and texts have in shaping allegiances. He believed that his program for the reconstruction of American Jewry—imbued with the American ideals of democracy, pragmatism, and progress—had something in common with Simon Rawidowicz's Hebrew ruminations on the endurance of the diaspora (which Rawidowicz had written in response to European Zionism and German nationalism).[7] The two men shared affinities in how they thought about the role of Jewish nationalism in transforming modern political thought, possibilities for minority national rights at a moment of political transition, and a vision of counterstate Zionism. Both men were also open to viewing religion and nationhood as intimately related concepts, rather than as rapidly polarizing categories of group identity.

Kaplan's sense of kinship with Rawidowicz's ideas has roots in their parallel life experiences (although the two probably knew about these overlapping contexts, it is difficult to determine if they surely did). Fifteen years apart in age (Kaplan was born in 1881, Rawidowicz in 1896), both thinkers were born into families that had been influenced by the intersection of traditional Jewish learning and innovations linked to the integration of secular studies and Zionism. One of the representatives of this intellectual and political foment was Rabbi Isaac Jacob Reines. Reines stirred controversy in two ways. First, he founded the religious Zionist party known as Mizrachi and was one of the early Orthodox rabbis to promote the Zionist movement and settlement in Palestine. Second, the yeshiva Reines founded in Lida in 1905 combined rabbinic training, specifically Talmud study, with secular subjects. Israel Kaplan (Mordecai's father) and Chaim Isaac Rawidowicz (Simon's father) were both ardent, learned devotees of Reines's heterodox efforts to integrate Orthodoxy, nationalism, and secular studies. Reines was the local rabbi in Sventzian, where Mordecai Kaplan was born and lived until age seven. Kaplan's father had been a close friend of Reines and offered his house (with Mordecai playing in another room as a toddler) as a place for the yeshiva's first meetings.[8] Rawidowicz's father had served as a delegate of the Mizrachi Zionist party (although he opposed Reines's vote at the 1905 Zionist congress to support the British offer for a Jewish homeland in Uganda).

Rawidowicz and Kaplan each had brief, direct interactions with Reines and his ideology: Kaplan traveled to Lithuania in 1908 during his European honeymoon to receive rabbinic ordination from Reines, and Rawidowicz spent a year studying at the Lida Yeshiva in 1910. Indirectly, however, the approach of fusing Torah and science championed by Reines influenced both men through their particularly close relationships with their fathers. Both fathers personally took charge of their sons' Jewish education, studying rabbinic texts with them throughout their formative years (and in Kaplan's case, until the end of his father's life).[9] From an early age, both Kaplan and Rawidowicz emerged from an intellectual environment that viewed the integration of nationalism, religion, Jewish texts, and secular studies as enriching rather than threatening. The possibility of weaving these poles together remained foundational for both Rawidowicz's global Hebraism and Kaplan's national civilization.

Another similarity was that Kaplan and Rawidowicz both rejected the binding authority of Jewish law that characterized the Judaism of their fathers and Rabbi Reines. They shared the lifelong intellectual challenge of articulating the immersion in Jewish sources and the passion for settlement in Palestine, which had dominated their fathers' approaches, with a far more critical reading of Judaism informed by secular studies. Each thinker grappled with translating his father's inchoate sense of emotional attachment into theories of identity formation that had to explain his own intimate, and not always logically consistent, sense of belonging to an increasingly diminishing number of Jews with similar educational experiences.

The contingent winds of early-twentieth-century Jewish history moved these two figures in disparate directions at different moments in history. Kaplan's journey was shaped by his immigration in 1889 at age eight to the United States.[10] Rawidowicz remained in Eastern Europe until he entered the university in Berlin at age eighteen and immigrated to the United States in 1948 after spending over a decade in England. It is one of the telling ironies of American Jewish history that Kaplan, whose rejection of a supernatural God led to his condemnation as a heretic by the American Orthodox community, emigrated to America as a result of the U.S. Orthodox community's effort to bolster religious observance and learning in the new world. His father was brought to America as part of Rabbi Jacob Joseph's entourage.[11] Facing increased pressure to acculturate, a group of Orthodox New Yorkers had invited the rabbi to nourish the area's dwindling observant community. Kaplan's father was brought along to serve on the rabbinical court. Shortly after Rabbi Joseph's arrival, however, his tenure abruptly ended, and Israel Kaplan was left with plenty of time to oversee his son's Jewish education. Mordecai received as close to a traditional Jewish education as a young man could find in the United States at that time. He studied the Talmud daily with his learned father, enrolled at a yeshiva that had been established to provide an East European–style immersion in traditional subjects, and took courses in Jewish studies at the Jewish Theological Seminary from age twelve until twenty-one.[12]

Kaplan would spend his life theorizing about the ideal of "living in two civilizations"—an East European world of Talmudic learning and the pragmatism of the Progressive Era, which was reflected in his own upbringing. He attended City College, where he learned Greek and Latin, philosophy, and logic. He entered a master's program at Columbia University in 1900, where he took courses with the sociologist Franklin Giddings and other scholars who inspired him with their optimistic belief in the powers of science, evolution, and rational thought. Kaplan decided to dedicate his life to articulating a program of Judaism that would bridge Americanism and Judaism. Recreating this equilibrium required what he began calling the "reconstruction of Judaism," a program first articulated in a 1927 article in the *Menorah Journal*.[13] This process, he argued, required the reconceptualization of Judaism to expand its definition from a creed to the totality of social, cultural, and political components.

By 1934, Kaplan had clearly defined and outlined his program in a book named after that very concept: *Judaism as a Civilization: Toward a Reconstruction of American-Jewish Life*. For another four decades, he reiterated many of the arguments popularized in his magnum opus. The central theme running through all of these works was his effort to understand and conceptualize the status of Jews (a national group unified by their connection to a homeland, shared language, folkways, and sacred values) and the purpose of Judaism (to reveal the possibilities of personal and collective self-fulfillment and salvation). One of the most untapped resources in understanding Kaplan's intellectual development in general, and his concept of civilization in particular, are the thousands of pages of journal entries that he kept meticulously and regularly throughout his lifetime. The journals portray a man swinging between a haughty sense of self-importance and a searing self-criticism, a certainty of mission and an insecurity about his own abilities. They reveal Kaplan's yearning for a private place to explore intimate feelings and the need for additional platforms to construct his own image for a public audience. The existence of such a unique window into the private considerations of this intellectual's public positions is an invaluable tool for Kaplan's biographers, for intellectual historians, and for students of American Jewry in general.

The journals narrate developments in American Jewry from the position of a man intimately connected to leading figures, central institutions, and decisive intellectuals for almost three-quarters of a century. They offer an unparalleled glimpse into the intertwined relationship between Kaplan's personal concerns and the concepts promulgated in his published work. The positions he publicly championed obfuscate a mind obsessively focused on evaluating the complexities of integrating reason and ritual, humanistic values and particular preservation, and pragmatic calculations and objective truths. Kaplan entertained the opposing possibilities of socialism and Jewish nationalism, passion for Zionism and rejection of the movement as "godless," and a desire to lead a secular movement of religious reform and to spark a Jewish renaissance.

These internal contradictions are particularly apparent in Kaplan's debates about Jewish observance. Despite his "heretical" theology, his journal bespeaks the deep bond that he continued to feel toward Jewish ritual and observance. His intellectual critique of traditional Jewish ritual and theology was out of step with his own emotional commitment to the Jewish religion. On one Friday evening in 1919, after the start of the Sabbath, for example, he realized that he had forgotten to write his weekly note to his mother. Torn about what to do—violate the prohibition against writing on the Sabbath or fail in his commitment to his regular update—Kaplan locked himself in the bathroom and penned a letter.[14] On another occasion, he acknowledged in his diary that he would consider moving the Sabbath from Saturday to Sunday to increase participation. A short while later, however, he wrote a scathing report about a congregation outside New York City that considered sponsoring a carnival following Sabbath services.[15]

Examining Kaplan's personal diaries reminds scholars to avoid projecting a consistent or rational position across this thinker's oeuvre (or even within the same text). Kaplan confidently drew clear distinctions in places without readily apparent logical justifications, and these distinctions could shift within a matter of days. His writings grappled with systematizing and categorizing his own experiences of reconciling the ambiguities of living in two civilizations. The product was far from systematic, but Kaplan's diary entries trace the theoretical and practical difficulties of articulating the spectrum of emotional attachments that he held toward various aspects of his American and Jewish influences.

Kaplan's journal illuminates the development of his key terms and concepts, specifically the cross-fertilization of ideas that he wove together in his own writings. His reflections on books he read or comments on texts he picked up in the library while researching sermons outline an intellectual field wider and more diverse than one might expect from a thinker so deeply rooted in a particular American milieu. Kaplan's theory of civilization, which one can gain important insights into by including his personal diaries and his footnotes in an analysis, illustrates the transatlantic exchange and the ways in which American thought translated and reconfigured these notions. Diverse intellectual streams—from European Zionism to British imperialism to American pragmatism to the social gospel movement—are assembled and added into the medley of approaches that Kaplan's civilization directly and indirectly emulates, resists, and rearranges. Piecing together these diverse conversations that formed his intellectual matrix suggests contextualizing civilization in debates about American democracy and theories of nationality.

Reconstructing Judaism, Reconstructing America

Published when Kaplan was already fifty-three, *Judaism as a Civilization* met with great success. The book won a prestigious prize and quickly went into a second printing. After years of frustration that his program for Jewish reconstruction would fail to influence American Judaism, Kaplan felt validated by the positive reception of his text. Surprisingly, however, he denied a publisher's request to reprint the book a third time during the late 1930s. Twenty-five years later, when he finally permitted a third printing of the book that had become a classic text of American Judaism, he explained his hesitancy: "Nationhood," one of the key terms he had used in *Judaism as a Civilization*, "had come to be closely identified with statehood, and was, therefore, in need of being replaced."[16] This conflation led Kaplan in later years to replace the term nationhood with numerous alternatives in subsequent publications.[17]

Kaplan's need to find alternate language signifies far more than a terminological shift. The centrality of the term nationhood in his mind places the evolution of civilization within the early-twentieth-century discourse of nationalism. If nationhood is central, why did he choose civilization, as opposed to nation or nationhood, as the book's primary category? How did he perceive the relationship between two words—nation and civilization—that both provide vocabulary for categorizing collective groups? Civilization was intended to describe a specific typology of nationhood pioneered by Jews and critically needed by the United States and other sovereign states around the globe. Long before Kaplan settled on the term as the book's foundation, he had diagnosed the problem it would have to address: namely, "political movements like democracy and nationalism."[18]

In 1918, Kaplan recorded his inner struggle about whether to accept a rabbinic position with a new synagogue in New York City called the Jewish Center. His extensive diary entries during this period reflect long deliberations over whether he could overcome disagreements—over a range of issues from mixed seating, institutional affiliation, and Zionism to the order of the service and the role of biblical criticism—with his potential congregants.[19] When it came down to making the decision, Kaplan accepted the position and justified his move by explaining that the center would function "to make democracy safe for Judaism."[20] This is a puzzling statement coming from one of the great synthesizers of Americanism and Judaism, a man whose work adopted fundamental themes of American democracy to define Judaism. The explosion of nativism and the monocultural nationalism of early-twentieth-century American history help explain Kaplan's pressing concern (see chapter 2 for a detailed discussion of the social and political currents in early-twentieth-century America).

One of the touchstones of the shifting concepts of what it meant to be an American at this time was the notion of the melting pot. In the play *The Melting Pot* (produced in 1908), Israel Zangwell, an immigrant Jewish intellectual with close ties to Jewish nationalism, popularized this metaphor of the United States as a great cauldron that would smelt away the differences that fragmented European societies. Zangwell's melting pot imagined the country as a society open to the various talents of immigrant groups melding together in a radically new environment. Yet, as the historian Philip Gleason has pointed out, a transition in the meaning of the melting pot occurred during World War I. The cauldron idea shifted from a pot welcoming multiple groups to one whose objective was to strip away the impurities of immigrants and to enforce conformity to Anglo-Saxon norms and racial purity.[21]

A circle of Jewish and non-Jewish pluralists countered that America was a nation of nationalities. Three of the most vocal champions of this message for a more pluralistic and tolerant view of what it means to be an American were Horace Kallen (discussed in chapter 2), Randolph Bourne, and John Dewey. Through publications such as the *Nation*, written for a general audience, and the *Menorah Journal*, intended for a more specifically Jewish audience, Kallen and Bourne promulgated the message that the United States had the potential to fulfill Europe's inability to integrate multiple nationalities. They argued for a greater appreciation of difference and immigrant groups, without undermining a sense of shared American national cohesion.[22] Jewish and specifically Zionist concerns helped shape this first wave of American pluralism. Their rhetoric constructed a cosmopolitan pluralism that yearned for difference under the umbrella of the Americanization process.

The *Menorah Journal* served as a central node for the intellectual community to redefine American democracy. The publication promoted Zionism and Jewish nationalism as the model for democracy and Americanism. The theories of nationality developed by such thinkers as Kallen and Bourne—transnational America, cultural pluralism, and civilization nationality—would serve as the antidote to President Franklin Roosevelt's "new nationalism" and its demands to dissolve so-called hyphenated Americans. Kaplan's early writing and the evolution of his civilization concept were integrally connected in both content and rhetoric to these attempts to fill in the conceptual gaps in increasingly contentious public debates about the nature of American nationality. The backdrop of efforts to resist the process of Americanization provides an important setting for Kaplan's early publications, a series of articles published in the *Menorah Journal* between 1915 and 1916.

Kaplan clearly viewed his work as participation in the discourse of making U.S. democracy safe for minority groups in general and for Jews in particular. The primary catalysts for the evisceration of Jewish life, he argued, were the political and social trends that dominated American nationalism and democracy during the early twentieth century. He expressed his anxiety that U.S. national life was suffocating the Jewish community. Kaplan's articles provide a crucial key for understanding the underlying factors motivating his innovative philosophical, theological, and religious contributions to modern Jewish life. Furthermore, they illustrate that the concept of "Judaism as a civilization" found its earliest expression in external political debates as much as in internal theological discussions. A study of these articles indicates that Kaplan breathed new life into Judaism not only to defend it against the threatening spiritual challenges of science and progress, but also to invent a political shield to parry the thrusts of American national unity.

Kaplan's *Menorah Journal* essays identified two diametrically opposed trends in American nationalism that threatened Jewish preservation: (1) the legal recognition of individuals rather than groups, and (2) the pressure to conform to a Christian model of American national culture. In his article "How May Judaism Be Saved?" Kaplan highlighted the modern political structure as the greatest hindrance toward spiritual peace. Modern democracy, he decried with passion, "is the principal cause of the undoing of Judaism."[23] Instead of considering the United States as the political entity that guaranteed Jews freedoms that had been unavailable to them in Europe, Kaplan admonished his readers that American democracy actually threatened to accelerate the demise of Jewish life. Prefiguring Bourne's fears of European nationalism (published the following year), Kaplan's gravest concern focused on the possibility that U.S. nationalism might emulate European models.

From this perspective in 1915, Kaplan considered the United States liable to debilitate Judaism through the ultimate fulfillment of European liberalism. He even deemed Jews in America as potentially worse off than those in European nations. Unprotected by any attachment to a particular land and overwhelmed by the pressures of immigration, he believed, national minority groups in the United States would succumb to the power of democratic nationalism far more quickly than their brethren in Europe had. American nationalism, he pessimistically asserted, promised a deadly blow for American Jewish life. Such "nationalism based upon the democracy of individuals," he averred, "is bound to prevent Jewish communal life from ever evolving to that degree of social autonomy which is indispensable to Jewish consciousness."[24] Theories of liberalism portended the dissolution of Jewish life by ignoring communal affiliations.

The development of a strong national identity in the United States, based heavily on religious notions, severely compounded this challenge associated with the atomization of liberal societies. According to Kaplan, a growing national self-consciousness—deeply rooted in religious motifs, language, and ideas—permeated the population and acted as a unifying agent. The nation's slow transformation into the role of religious icon and provider would ultimately lead to the loss of power among particular churches. Separating church and state, Kaplan asserted, represented only a temporary step toward a far more insidious predicament. The state, formerly the protector of diverse religious communities, "has become ambitious to develop its own soul and its own religion."[25]

This new fusion of nation and religion would ultimately replace the old boundaries between church and state. Kaplan even referred to the new religious language inherent in U.S. life as "the new nationalism," echoing the language Roosevelt had used a few years earlier to describe his political platform. Given this pervasiveness, Kaplan contended, "America will probably lead the way among the Western nations in the substitution of a home religion for an imperial one."[26] The traditional room for religion in liberal societies, guaranteed under the language of separation of church and state, would soon disappear in the United States under intense demands to meld national–religious identity with citizenship. Without halting this excessive trend in American nationalism, Kaplan held, no religious reform or theological innovation would be able to rescue Judaism.

Collective group consciousness was thus under attack from two opposing poles—liberal individualism and a homogenizing religious nationalism. Negotiating a middle-ground theory of nationality would have to emulate these extremes by affirming individual rights and religious collectivity but would also provide space for recognizing multiple substatist groups, such as the Jewish community. Kaplan's early essays present Jewish nationalism as an alternate path of Americanization that neutralizes both the individualism and collectivism that simultaneously eroded space for "being Jewish" within American life. The tradition most clearly suited for guiding this transformation was already being developed by Kaplan. As early as the late 1910s, he had conceived of Jewish political thought, embedded within its religious tradition, as part of the process of reforming American nationalism.

Not all religious traditions engendered national communities with the same quality of political aspirations or moral inclinations, Kaplan argued in his *Menorah Journal* essays. Some religions, particularly Christianity, had a tendency (both historically and currently), he felt, to retard human progress by enforcing a cultural and political imperialism on other religious communities. But some other religions, notably Judaism, propelled the forces of moral progress by striving to reach a telos of multiple national civilizations thriving in relationship with one another. Following a historiographical approach motivated by contemporary political considerations, Kaplan reduced Christianity and Judaism to mutually opposing political predilections: one inclined toward imperialism and the other, nationalism. Christianity had demonstrated itself as "a collective consciousness with imperialism for its method."[27] By celebrating the universal equality of humanity, Kaplan continued, Christianity actually threatened the rights of groups to declare their individual freedom. In contrast, Judaism's fundamental contribution to world history, he contended, was the political and moral ability to withstand the pressures of Christianity to guarantee the possibility of otherness in European society. From its historical origins, Judaism had "showed itself as a collective consciousness with nationalism for its method."[28] Judaism's inveterate struggle against imperialism indicated the tradition's recognition of the "vain delusion" of elevating cosmopolitan visions above particular national divisions.[29]

The specific terminology and general program Kaplan used for constructing Jewish nationality as an alternative to Christian imperialism and American nationalism shared a strategy and vocabulary with other intellectuals who regularly published in the *Menorah Journal*—namely, Bourne and Kallen. They held similar views about Jewish nationalism being an antidote to American nationalism. Bourne, a non-Jew, even championed Jewish nationalism as the most highly developed form of transnational cohesion. He aligned Jews with the "ardent effort for that progressive democratic reconstruction in America which is the ideal of all true Americans, no matter what their heritage."[30] Kallen defined the Jews' global mission as the catalyst for ensuring that political states would recognize federations of minority national groups within their political and territorial boundaries. Enacting this political transformation pioneered by the Jews would thus enable the world to progress toward a higher level of civilization. This utopian vision of civilization elevated diversity, distinction, and transnational communities over the uniformity of states grounded on ethnoreligious criteria.

It is interesting to note that such a diverse group of figures—Jewish professionals, deracinated Jewish public intellectuals, and non-Jewish antiwar activists—shared the opinion that Zionism would contribute to a post-nation-state era. At a moment of possibility, the end of World War I, Jewish nationalism was amorphous and malleable enough to provide an appealing theoretical platform for Jewish and non-Jewish intellectuals interested in transforming the relationship between nation and state. But why write about this issue through the lens of Jewish nationality instead of just writing about American nationality? Writing about the universal through the particular demonstrates the need to actually justify the Jews' ability to integrate at a time when they were being pushed out of the boundaries of American identity. The pressure to justify the tolerance of Jews within the acceptable boundaries of American identity necessitated a distinct explanation of how the Jews' very difference actually fostered their ability to integrate into American society.

In chapter 2 we discussed the use of civilization in the Zionist internationalism of Kallen and Zimmern. Both used civilization to describe a federation of nationalities that would maintain their distinct identities as citizens under the political control of a shared political entity. Note the relationship here between the key term civilization, the commitment to reformulating the nation-state model, and the unique role that Jewish nationalism has in transforming America into a state of nationalities. Jewish intellectuals were not alone in selecting civilization to serve the polemical purpose of challenging the increasingly monolithic definitions of American self-identity in the postwar years. The historian Gail Bederman has analyzed the ways in which disenfranchised intellectuals in the early twentieth century turned to the rhetoric of civilization as a strategy of resistance against the hegemony of racial, religious, and ethnic purity.[31] Such intellectuals and civil rights activists as W. E. B. Dubois and Ida B. Wells used similar discourse to reformulate the terminology so central in denying their community's full acceptance into American society. By "inverting the discourse" of civilization, these intellectuals challenged the term's meaning and proposed alternative definitions.[32] Instead of equating civilization with Anglo-Saxon, Protestant uniformity, they offered a counterdefinition that not only tolerated but actually celebrated the value of multiple national identities. The prevalence and parallel function of the term civilization in the works of Kallen, Zimmern, and Kaplan suggest that these Jewish thinkers adopted a similar strategy.[33]

In 1928, the year before he embarked on writing *Judaism as a Civilization,* Kaplan enthusiastically recorded the breakthrough that led to his adoption of the term civilization as the centerpiece of his book. He explained that he had finally found an important "new thought tool" that would address the need for a solution capable of "the deliberate attempt to modify the environment or reckon with it, even more than upon a repentant mood on the part of the Jews."[34] He sensed the polemical power of the word to transform the grounds of national cohesion from state and territory to elements compatible with dispersed populations and supportive of multiple nationalities. His theory of national cohesion was built on two pillars: first, he articulated a moral argument that viewed particular attachments as the most effective path toward guaranteeing individual rights and creating harmony between different groups. He thus turned the meaning of progress on its head by juxtaposing civilization with national diversity, not ethnocultural uniformity. Second, Kaplan viewed religious folkways, a connection to the Jewish homeland, social and legal institutions, and cultural engagement as the collective boundaries for minority communities.

This link between nationhood and civilization crystallizes in the section of *Judaism as a Civilization* entitled "The Nationhood of Israel," where

Kaplan defines nationality (directly citing Zimmern's essays) as a "body of people united by a corporate sentiment of peculiar intensity, intimacy and dignity, related to a definite home-country."[35] Zimmern's influence suggests a parallel use of both terms, civilization and nationhood. Zimmern's theory of nationality contrasted two paradigms: a civilization and a Kultur typology (see chapter 2 for a more detailed discussion of Zimmern's model). The two approaches to nationality stood for opposing concepts of the bonds of nationhood and the relationship between nation and state. The approaches are distinguished by a set of opposing characteristics—cosmopolitan and particular, ethical and nonethical, and pluralistic and exclusivist. The Kultur model, associated by Zimmern's World War I writings with Prussian nationalism, defined an exclusivist nationalism that linked nationhood with statehood. Citizenship demanded conformity to specific ethnonational criteria enforced by the state.

A civilization, however, created national bonds that thrived across political boundaries and eschewed a hierarchy of various ethnoreligious groups. Instead, it provided a cosmopolitan vision of difference that views the tolerance of other groups and the affirmation of particular identities as a defining characteristic of progress toward recognizing the moral possibilities of humanity. A national civilization thus becomes a conduit toward achieving a greater degree of universal integration. Kaplan's notion of civilization, as this fruitful comparison with Zimmern suggests, should not be read as introducing a unique category of identity. Rather, the term embodies what Kaplan considers the most progressive and ethical typology of nationality.

Delineating the civilization model of nationalism is a defining theme of Kaplan's *Judaism as a Civilization*. Despite being seen primarily as a theological and sociological reformulation of Judaism, the work includes extensive discussions about nationalism in general and American democracy in particular. Although they are not as plainly articulated as Zimmern's comparison between civilization and Kultur, Kaplan also outlined the contours of two typologies of nationhood in his magnum opus. The more pernicious stream, however, is not represented by German Kultur but by American democracy. Kaplan presented an unenthusiastic evaluation of U.S. "democratic nationalism" throughout the text. Paralleling Zimmern's and Bourne's critiques of Kultur nationalism, Kaplan considered contemporary expressions of American nationalism problematic due to burgeoning efforts to fuse the notions of nation and state.

Kaplan wrote: "Current concepts of nationalism are deeply problematic because they are based upon the misleading assumption that nationhood is synonymous with statehood, which makes it impossible for a people to be considered a nation unless it is represented by a state."[36] This fusion caused "every modern nation [to] expect[s] all its citizens to identify themselves completely with it, to accept its cultural values and to further its social aims and ideals."[37] Kaplan daringly compared American "democratic nationalism" to European völkisch nationalism—this only one year after Hitler's rise to power in Germany. "With the organization of modern nations"—including American democracy—"there has been a return to the sub-human principle of the herd."[38] From Kaplan's perspective, then, the difference between German theories of völkisch nationalism and the American melting-pot concept was only a matter of degree (ironically, although Kaplan rejected elements of German notions of nationalism, he simultaneously decided to place the concept of Volk at the center of his civilization model). His repeated references to the growing similarities between American and European models of nationalism indicate that he regarded opposition to these theories as a core objective.

National civilization served as the antithesis of völkisch nationality by creating boundaries for a "new type of nation" that is "international" in scope.[39] This interpretation of Jewish political thought supported Kaplan's conclusion that "the notion that allegiance to a state precludes identification with more than one nation will therefore have to be scrapped."[40]

National civilization required grounds of cohesion that would distinguish it from the exclusivist, militant, and illiberal typologies of nationality that Kaplan sought to replace. Kaplan accomplished this objective through a number of innovations that distinguished his criteria for cohesion from those developed earlier by Zimmern and Kallen. Kaplan's critique of national sovereignty rejected notions of descent, culture, or spirit as the primary criteria of membership and turned to religion as the basis of national solidarity. Although Zimmern and Kallen had rejected sovereignty as the primary criterion for nationality, a position that put them against the current of theoretical and practical developments in theories of nationalism, they adopted other dominant aspects of defining nationality. This first generation of pluralists in the United States relied on the language of descent and culture to describe group boundaries (although, as explored in chapter 2, they undermined the essentialist implications of this language).

Kaplan continued the trajectory begun by figures such as Kallen and Zimmern to distinguish national markers from racial characteristics. Yet Kaplan went even further in maintaining a clear distinction between the biological grounds of cohesion and the ties that linked co-members of a national civilization. Developing his theories at the high-water mark of racial science in the 1920s and 1930s, Kaplan was more consciously seeking an alternative to race than his predecessors. Taxonomies of race pushed Jews to the boundaries of whiteness.[41] On the one hand, race served as a powerful force for maintaining identity markers within the United States. On the other hand, however, writing after the 1924 immigration restrictions, the rise of discrimination at a variety of institutions, and the efforts to categorize Jews as Hebrews rather than as Caucasians, Kaplan recognized that the cost of racial otherness would inevitably diminish the standing of that group. As a result, Kaplan calibrated national civilization to offer a nonracialized discourse of difference that would share the robust and even involuntary boundaries of difference suggested by racial categories *without* the negative stigma and coercive nature of racial nationalism. Civilization would thus help transform American nationalism from a nation of *races* to a nation of *civilizations*.

Reversing the approach to civilization by looking at its *function* rather than its *content* helps explain Kaplan's definition of the term as well as the ambiguities he leaves unresolved. The constituent elements of a civilization are enumerated as such: land; language and literature; mores and laws; and folkways, folk sanctions, and folk arts.[42] Perhaps most important are the elements that are absent from this list: statehood, spirit or culture, and descent. However, Kaplan's notion of civilization also fails to fully discard these concepts. The elements stand in limbo between rejecting certain criteria and trying to reassert modified versions of them.

Kaplan's real focus is on the more dynamic elements of the modes in which a civilization operates. Social interactions produce traditions and mores that unite members of historical civilizations. National civilization generates cohesion through shared commitment to certain sancta, or principles, that are reflected in historical sources, practices, and communities. Civilization is fluid, and the constituent elements are expansive enough to include Hebrew and non-Hebrew speakers, homeland, and diaspora. Moreover, most of the key elements are actually processes for affirming, and when necessary, changing, collective ideals and values. The term thus provides a shell that introduces a theory with positive connotations of the epitome of progress and humanity without delineating clear parameters of membership.

Kaplan's development of folkways provides an interesting example of this process of addressing the dilemma of advocating for *distinct* national attributes without claiming *fixed* attributes. Folkways, as he defines them, represent the range of "social practices" by which groups express their "collective being."[43] One significant aspect of Kaplan's selection of this term is his implicit rejection of culture to define this category.[44] As a general term, one prevalent among European thinkers and popularized within American Jewry by the essays of theorist Israel Friedlaender, culture would have served as a far more obvious choice either to replace civilization as the general description of Jewish nationhood or in the specific discussion of folkways.

Yet culture would have suggested that the content of Jewish national cohesion was an abstract set of characteristics imbued within Jewish historical progression. Culture also connoted exclusivity—that is, one was primarily a member of one culture over another. But folkways, a term Kaplan most likely learned from Yale sociologist William Graham Sumner, are social norms and mores shaped by society.[45] One term stands as an a priori, innate quality, while the other affirms fluidity and external construction. Kaplan's selection of folkways, however, did not completely relinquish the concept of essential characteristics of particular civilizations. Ironically, the term originates in German nationalism's concept of the innate spirit that unifies members of a particular group.

In addition to downplaying descent and culture, Kaplan affirms the centrality of religion as the primary cohesive basis of national solidarity. One might read his juxtaposition of religion with civilization not as innovative, but instead as an indication of his ultimate kowtowing to expectations of the American Jewish synthesis. As a realist and pragmatist, he certainly knew that the recognition of religious groups remained far more compatible with American political realities than the acceptance of national corporate minorities.[46] Acceptance into middle-class American society was increasingly defined by affiliation with religion. In some ways, the recognition that religion would serve as the most effective language for difference and acceptance in America anticipated the theorist Will Herberg's classic *Protestant, Catholic, Jew: An Essay in American Religious Sociology.*[47] The more radical claims of nationality were thus mollified by juxtaposing religion with civilization.

Despite Kaplan's efforts to advocate a separation of nation and state in America, he still operated out of the basic assumption that difference in the United States is expressed through religious paradigms. He pushed hard for Jewish identity to transcend religious boundaries in America. At least implicitly, though, he acknowledged the limitations of this approach. Kaplan recognized that paradigms of minority nationality explicitly based on a multinational state model would have little success in the United States.[48] Yet the role of religion and its relationship to civilization and nationality is more complex than reading its use as a way of neutralizing Kaplan's maximalist efforts to create a new typology of nationality.[49] The use of religion in Kaplan's concept of national civilization has multiple functions and serves as another example of how he formulated terminology vague enough to support conflicting objectives and to negotiate, rather than resolve, complicated dilemmas.

Why did Kaplan risk undermining his clear desire to make a mark on theories of nationality by linking civilization and religion? Juxtaposing these ideas reflected Kaplan's personal connection to Jewish religious practice and themes as well as his calculated efforts to appeal to certain audiences by using the concept of religion. It was an effort to appease his potential audience, but it also reflected his own personal engagement with Jewish observance, themes, and cultural components. Kaplan's intellectual critique of traditional Jewish ritual and theology was out of step with his own emotional commitment to the Jewish religion. To some degree, this gap explains his insistence on emphasizing religion as the building block of national identity. Bonds formed through religious ritual and narrative are deeply personal and command observance. Out of a combination of his own psychological attachments and guilt at breaking from the past, Kaplan therefore needed to anchor his Judaism in religious categories, even if he had stripped away many of religion's defining characteristics.

This reflected Kaplan's strategic realization of his Jewish and American audiences and the optimal path for rethinking the synthesis between Judaism and Americanism. Kaplan's sensitivity to the pragmatic reality of religion as the accepted category of otherness for American Jews led him to express his theory in a language that would resonate.[50] Kaplan knew his audience well enough to know that couching his program as a religion would gain him readership, but he underestimated their interest in exploring the political implications of his definition of religion on the American Jewish synthesis.

Once Kaplan made the case for the category of religion, however, he translated the core of Jewish religion to reflect his larger political agenda. Religion itself served the functional purpose of providing the philosophical, and even theological, justification for the existence of particular national communities that operated outside nation-state categories. When we study Kaplan's conclusions about God, the Torah, and Israel, we see that the classic categories of Jewish religion suggest that not only intellectual but also political concerns fueled some of his more radical assertions. For Kaplan, a crucial shaper was the political question of resetting the equilibrium of Jews and their non-Jewish neighbors. The motivations for his theory of religion are best understood as a response to his concerns about the status of Jews within American society as well as that of Jews in the homeland.

The centrality of these concerns is evident in Kaplan's formulation of such primary concepts as God and salvation. One of his most well-known (and controversial) contributions to twentieth-century Jewish theology is the declaration that God was "the process that makes for salvation." Philosophical or theological discussions of the strengths and weaknesses of Kaplan's soteriology ignore the political and historical meaning of the term salvation, however.[51] Kaplan envisioned God as the political and social structure that would elicit the most rewarding type of communal life. The "God idea," he explicitly acknowledged, "functions . . . as an organic acceptance of certain elements in the life and environment of the group, or of reality as a whole in relation to the group, as contributing to one's self-fulfillment or salvation."[52] The divine infused the world through creating a healthy intergroup and intragroup equilibrium. The task of religion thus "consists in rendering that milieu efficacious in eliciting from its adherents the best that is in them."[53] From Kaplan's perspective, there can be no greater priority for religious thinkers than constructing political visions for their religion's adherents. Healthy national life remains the fundamental purpose of religious traditions and the prerequisite for salvation. Religious salvation would then emerge at the moment when the proper equilibrium between Jews and their host society would be restored.

The content of religious life existed solely as a tool to galvanize a higher level of communal solidarity. To support this claim, Kaplan reinterpreted the Torah, the central symbol of the Jewish tradition, as a detailed map outlining the ideal political structure of nationalism. The Torah, he concluded in *Judaism as a Civilization*, "especially as developed in practice and interpretation, is the full equivalent of what we understand by national civilization."[54] Kaplan applied a functionalist approach to determining the meaning of each individual religious belief or action outlined in the Torah. He also relied on the same lens to understand religion itself. Religion operated primarily as the glue that created and sustained the bonds of civilization nationhood. To put it another way, the folk religion of nations constituted the instrument by which "civilization reaches the point of self-consciousness essential to its perpetuation."[55]

At the same time that Kaplan used religion to promote distinct national groups, he also used it as a way of drawing parallels between the Jewish and the American nation. The source of this fusion reflects his observations about the relationship between religion and state in America. Kaplan's use of religion allowed him simultaneously to bring Jews closer to and to distance them from Americans. This model emulates the prevalent discourse advocating for the Christianization of America. Although the years in which Kaplan wrote *Judaism as a Civilization* corresponded to the final years of the social gospel movement (which reached its apogee in the first two decades of the century), the fluid boundaries between political reform and religious fervor continued to inform his intellectual and social context. In addition to the strong strains of racial nationalism that gained political strength after World War I, liberal Protestantism (particularly the social gospel movement) embraced progressive politics as a vehicle for Christianizing America and thus ensuring the social salvation of the entire nation.[56] The influence of predominantly religious figures such as Washington Gladden, Richard Ely, and Walter Rauschenbusch transcended church meetings and Bible study groups and influenced the national political and cultural scene. These leaders contended that only a Christian America could bring about religious salvation.

Kaplan mirrored the political implications of salvation developed by the social gospel movement and applied these concepts to his notion of Jewish civilization. This move had the benefit of creating parallel religious traditions dedicated to the concept of salvation. Of course, Kaplan had to tweak the specific aspect of salvation—from a universal acceptance of Christian doctrine to the embrace of national diversity. Emulating the approach of his Christian contemporaries accomplished two important polemical tasks. First, it gave Judaism legitimacy by translating Jewish nationalism into a form compatible with the discourse of the United States as a Christian nation. Second, it transferred the true carrier of national authenticity from Protestant Christianity to Judaism. Judaism was thus transformed from a community hindering American progress toward unification to the nation best empowered to implement the ideals of the Progressive period. Religion remained central for Kaplan—not to promote any particular Jewish praxis or belief, but to put Judaism on par with Christian nationalism, and ultimately to replace the conflation of America and Christian salvation (aligned with homogeneity) with Jewish salvation (characterized by heterogeneity).

"Can Nationalism Be Other Than Bellicose?"

After reading a 1933 *New York Times* article about Nazi propaganda minister Joseph Goebbels, Kaplan posed a question in his journal that reaffirmed his commitment to identifying the moral dangers of advocating for national preservation. He also raised the question of how to justify his own efforts to advocate for Jewish nationality at a moment when nationalist rhetoric was being used to justify the revocation of Jewish citizenship in Germany (two years earlier, as we shall learn in chapter 5, a lecture by Hans Kohn sparked a similar set of questions in response to the Arab revolt in Palestine). Kaplan wrote:

> The fundamental question is: Can nationalism be other than bellicose? If nationalism is—as [Reinhold] Niebuhr maintains in his recent book "Moral man in an Immoral Society"—irredeemably militant and hostile what does the world gain by the Jews' creating another source of group hatred and militancy? By retaining their nationhood they are bound to act as a corrective of the brutal and bellicose aspect of nationalism and are certain to serve the course of cosmopolitanism and international peace as they never could if they were to become assimilated internally.[57]

Clearly this was a burning question for Kaplan. Could affirming national boundaries be moral? In his 1932 book *Moral Man and Immoral Society,* Protestant theologian Reinhold Niebuhr, who taught at Union Theological Seminary across the street from Kaplan's home institution, the Jewish Theological Seminary, argued that national preservation was "selfish" and antithetical to individual rights and concerns. Niebuhr's work distinguishes between the "moral and social behavior of individuals and of social groups."[58]

Kaplan's diary reflects the attraction that he had to the universalist ideals promised by socialism and communism. In considering his follow-up to *Judaism as a Civilization,* Kaplan privately considered two alternatives in 1934: "the completion of the book on 'The Creed of the Modern Jew' and the formulation of a system of religious Communism."[59] He ultimately decided to pursue the former project, which became his *Meaning of God in Modern Jewish Religion.* However, from his perspective, the God idea in Judaism—the process that makes for salvation—was fully compatible with the ideals of universal humanity espoused by socialists and Marxists (Kaplan dropped his interest in Marxist ideology after reading a pamphlet called "Lenin and the Jewish Question," which argued that Jewish national culture and international culture are incompatible).[60] The interest in finding ethical language to talk about national survival was a central concern for him. The concept of national civilization was an effort to negotiate between these potentially conflicting possibilities of nationalism and internationalism, parochialism and humanism, and moral and immoral actions.

The necessity of formulating a new nationalism only gained greater urgency for Kaplan after his 1934 publication of *Judaism as a Civilization*. His subsequent personal ruminations and publications clarify the distinction he endeavored to make between various typologies of nationality. One might assume that Kaplan's two-year sojourn in Jerusalem between 1937 and 1939 might have caused him to reconsider his emphasis on the value of national diversity and the centrality of sovereignty. Amid growing Arab–Jewish hostilities in Palestine, the early indications of mass killings of Jewish communities in Europe, and the fervor of Zionist ideology and clamoring for independence, however, Kaplan only reaffirmed the viability of Jewish national minorities in the diaspora and the need to redefine theories of nationalism to make space for such communities.

Spurned by a 1939 discussion at Hebrew University on the meaning of Jewish nationality, Kaplan spent several weeks commenting on the topic in his diary. He explained his intense interest in nationalism in general and its relationship to Judaism in particular:

> The main task which confronts Jewish leadership today, is to define anew the meaning of nationality and national consciousness in terms that will not only render tenable but will invest with purpose and dignity, the status of the Jews who must indefinitely remain scattered among the various nations of the world. They must point the way to a conception of Jewish nationhood that would make it compatible with unquestioned loyalty to whatever non-Jewish nation they cast their lot with.[61]

In this project of defining anew, Kaplan questioned the assumption that each people required sovereignty to fulfill their national aspirations. He contested this by distinguishing between a "nationalism which insists on one's nation being sovereign . . . and recognizes no higher law than its own will and needs, and internationalism which, admitting a high degree of autonomy to each nation, advocates the submission of each nation to a sovereignty higher than its own and representative of a group of nations but preferably of all nations."[62] Kaplan refers to the second type of nationality, the one compatible with multinational states, as ethical nationhood rather than civilization nationhood. Although he had already used the term ethical interchangeably with civilization in a few instances, the switch in terminology indicates a shift in his focus.[63] Whereas Jewish civilization allowed him to address notions of nationality through the medium of the meaning of Judaism, ethical nationhood more directly confronted the need to redefine nationality *without* the mediation of a program for Judaism.

Ethical nationhood rejects political control and territorial possession as criteria for group affiliation. Instead, it argues that the former will most likely lead to homogenizing demands and totalitarian means of enforcement. In his *Future of the American Jew*, Kaplan wrote about the moral dangers of connecting nation and state. "The doctrine of 'absolute national sovereignty,' with its assumption that the interests of one's own nation must always override those of other nations, is responsible for the international anarchy of the modern world, and is liable to bring about a catastrophe that will destroy the very foundation of human civilization."[64] (Note the enduring opposition in Kaplan's thought between human civilization and absolute national sovereignty.) Writing in the late 1930s, Kaplan certainly had German nationalism in mind when composing this trenchant critique. Nazi nationalism, however, was not a qualitative perversion of modern theories of Western nationalism; rather, the totalitarian regime represented the logical conclusion of theories of national sovereignty.

Ethical or civilization nationhood therefore offered the antidote to the impending disaster engendered by ascribing shared ethnic, cultural, or biological characteristics to a polity. Kaplan's correction envisioned a global order of multinational states or commonwealths consisting of a patchwork of national communities with members dispersed across political and territorial boundaries. The flourishing of such communities would fragment the sovereign political power's ability to enforce membership in one privileged national culture.

In order to juxtapose the ideals of ethical nationhood, Kaplan grappled with the question he posed in his diary: Can nationalism be other than bellicose? He responded to Niebuhr's claim indirectly throughout his subsequent essays by developing three arguments to demonstrate that man is most moral when attached to a particular national group. Kaplan asserted: (1) that corporate groups actually provide the most effective path toward ensuring individual ethical behavior; (2) that there are grounds for legal protections for specific groups within liberal democracies; and (3) that minority groups can practice a form of voluntary coercion to highly encourage membership without negating the free choice of their members. Such recent works as Robert McKim and Jeff McMahan's *The Morality of Nationalism*, Yael Tamir's *Liberal Nationalism*, and David Miller's *On Nationality* indicate that the basic challenge Kaplan faced—to justify the moral probity of national affiliation—had moved from the margins of political theory to the center of conversations about nationality in a global era. The assumption that liberalism and nationalism clash had evolved from a constellation of modern cosmopolitan political and intellectual currents. National identification confronts liberalism's deeply rooted concerns about promoting public expressions of difference.[65]

Maintaining partiality toward a particular group reflects clannish tendencies, often motivated by irrational and even erroneous fictional national narratives, and galvanizes feelings of superiority that inflame global ethnoreligious strife and war. Acknowledging particular loyalties threatens universal rights and individual autonomy. Expressions of cultural difference and national partiality rub against the commitment to uniformity around a shared set of political principles and shared values. Liberal advocates for national partiality face the theoretically daunting task of justifying collective cohesion as fully compatible with free choice and opposed to national hierarchies.

This is precisely the challenge in which Kaplan engaged in constructing the theory of Judaism as a national civilization as an ethical alternative to the dominant theories of nationality. He entered this gray area of modern political thought when few theorists blurred the clear divide between ethnic, or clannish, nationality and cosmopolitan visions that equated nationality with Enlightenment universality (in fact, his contemporary and the subject of chapter 5, Hans Kohn, who was struggling with the same tension between nationalism and humanism, would soon popularize the normative distinction between civic and ethnic paradigms with the publication of *The Idea of Nationalism* in 1944). Kaplan was keenly aware of having to negotiate between the poles of irrational, familial preferences and the impartial principle of human equality.

His strategy transforms the latter into an instrumental force calibrated to engender the former. In other words, collective affiliation ensures the highest degree of moral and pragmatic value. Only through the particular, Kaplan suggested, could universal ethical ideals be fully realized.[66] Accordingly, nationhood "qualifies the human being not only for the group but for human life, and, though the means are necessarily particularistic, the aim is universal."[67] In order for individuals to contribute to humanity, they must gain through religious education a deep self-awareness of their distinct identity as "other." Individuals are most effective as moral agents when they remain embedded within particular human networks that connect them through shared narratives. Promoting uniformity therefore actually diminishes the ability to react to the needs of an undifferentiated universal humanity.[68]

Just as individuals have a natural affinity toward family, Kaplan asserted, so too is it fully justified to prioritize obligations to a specific group over equal affection for all humankind. "An obligation to the members of one's nationality," Kaplan explained, has no less moral validity than "cosmopolitanism which recognizes no such priority."[69] The overlap of cosmopolitanism and civilization is interesting because it suggests a parallel to the literature on cosmopolitanism that has been recently used to negotiate between particular nationality and universal concerns.[70] The universal connotations of cosmopolitanism have enabled such theorists as David Hollinger and Kwame Anthony Appiah to make particular claims without undermining their compatibility with ethical or moral issues that transcend a specific group's preservation.[71] Even though the nationalist scholar David Miller does not use the specific term, he reframes Kaplan's inchoate argument far more clearly by culling from recent ethical theory that distinguishes between an ethics of particularity and an ethics of universality. By endorsing the potential moral value of expanding the familial metaphor to include a much larger collective, ethical particularism promises to ensure the greatest level of moral efficacy.

Kaplan turns the charge of clannish particularity on its head by insisting that cultural rootedness actually creates the "milieu in which the individual's right of life, liberty, and the pursuit of happiness may be realized."[72] Obligating oneself toward a particular community facilitates *individual* autonomy and freedom—principles highly valued by liberal thought.[73] Communal ties create the structure that individuals require to imagine their possible choices and the context for deciding on their actions and beliefs. Removing these cultural contexts strips away individuals' capacities for making meaningful choices. National civilization, as defined by Kaplan, adopts a similar strategy to neutralize liberalism's critique of minority group rights. The theories also share a notable side effect acknowledged by the political philosopher Will Kymlicka. Liberalism can support minority cultures provided group identity serves an instrumental role in strengthening an individual's autonomy and commitment to universal rights. Thus, in justifying the preservation of national tradition, Kaplan erodes the authority of divine revelation by elevating individual choice and freedom as the ultimate criteria for delineating the outer parameters of behavior and belief.

The need to answer the charge that nations are bellicose had an important corollary impact on Kaplan's thought—namely, the elimination of any hierarchies between various collective groups. Kaplan insisted that one nationality "cannot advocate superiority over other nations" and that no nationality has exclusive "possession of salvation."[74] In the language of Anthony Smith, a scholar of nationalism, Kaplan advocated for a "polycentric" as opposed to "ethnocentric" theory of nationality.[75] Polycentric theories view the world as divided into autonomous communities of equal status. Ethnocentric communities, by contrast, focus solely on preserving each nation's culture at all costs and consider other groups inferior. Kaplan's emphasis on ethical nationhood as polycentric and voluntary reflects the association of ethnocentric criteria with *illiberal* political expectations.

This explanation of Kaplan's need to eliminate any specific claims about the relative merits of one nation over another sheds new light on understanding his rejection of the concept of "the chosen people." Harmonizing national partiality with individual right pushed him into direct conflict with this key principle. His diary acknowledges the tension between his ideal of ethical nationhood and the tenet of divine election as well as the acceptance of the Torah as the commanded path toward salvation. Thus the elimination of the notion of *chosenness*—one of Kaplan's most influential and contested contributions to Jewish thought—emerged as the necessary by-product of equating Jewish nationality with ethical nationhood.

There is an interesting parallel between the theory of liberal nationalism (as, for example, in the work of Israeli political philosopher Yael Tamir) and Kaplan's implicit decision to eliminate chosenness to make the claim that Jewish nationhood was ethical. Tamir explicitly identifies the same boundary in her effort to reconcile Jewish and liberal nationalisms. She singles out the theme of divine election as an example of a claim "that cannot be justified" in a theory of nationalism.[76] Like Tamir, Kaplan jettisons this aspect of Judaism: "We find it necessary to reject as obsolete the kind of nationalism taught by our tradition."[77] He was not willing to completely reject the unique contribution that Jewish nationality offers, however. Instead, he adopted a back-door approach to continuing to argue for the unique relevance of Judaism—specifically, that Jewish political thought offered the most developed path toward the next wave of nationalities that would facilitate toleration and cosmopolitan values.

The juxtaposition of civilization and nationality captures this paradox perfectly. Instead of siding with religious or leftist advocates of dissolving national bonds or Nazi efforts to affirm bellicose models, Kaplan adjusted the definition of both "ethical" and "nationhood" to argue for their full compatibility. This move had a clear disadvantage as well, however. The content of Jewish civilization was shackled by the need to justify its universal moral efficacy. The solution represented a collectivist twist on the mission theory that had been popularized in Reform ideology. Kaplan believed that Jewish nationhood "should also contribute toward the elimination from nationhood of its dross of collective selfishness and sacred egoism and render it essentially a means of social creativity and individual betterment."[78] This left him with a tenuous, and somewhat tautological, justification for advocating for the continuity of the Jewish people. In this view, Jewish national identity deserved continued adherence because it was the most effective path toward the universal mission of reforming modern political thought. National culture is reduced to an instrumental position as a facilitator for undermining the distinct elements of those cultures that might clash with universal ethical norms. To put it simply: Jews could be different, as long as they shared universal ethical norms with the rest of humanity.

Kaplan recognized but refused to acknowledge fully the implications of this statement for promoting and requiring participation in Jewish national life. The tension between the demands of ethical behavior and particular preservation is most evident in his ongoing debate about whether membership in the Jewish nation is voluntary or coercive. Following from the logic of a cosmopolitan expression of national difference, Kaplan had to insist on voluntary membership in order not to violate the free choice of individual members and to fully demonstrate his belief that all particular groups are equally valid. At the same time, however, he hoped to erase volunteerism from Jewish civic involvement. Instead, he insisted that the Jewish community restore the power of coercion over its members. Fully embracing volunteerism would erode what he called the "true index of a living civilization," defined not by its "ability to advise but its authority to command." As he confided in his diary, "the very freedom which will be won for the Jews will help to put an end to Judaism."[79]

This yearning for a level of social and cultural autonomy that Jews had enjoyed before their emancipation attempted to overturn the problems associated with volunteerism. These problems had eroded the authority of Jewish communities since the Enlightenment thinker Moses Mendelssohn had insisted in the late eighteenth century that only the government (and not the church) has the power to coerce its members. Mendelssohn had relinquished communal autonomy and turned civic legal matters into the hands of the state. At the same time, he desperately attempted to retain some communal authority for enforcing the ceremonial law by claiming that the Sinaitic revelation continued to be compulsory for the Jewish people. Kaplan overturned this formula. He rejected the historical binding power of revelation but attempted to return the civil power of coercion to the Jewish community. Without the theological basis of revelation, Kaplan's only recourse for challenging the voluntary nature of membership was to promote some degree of civic or communal coercion.[80]

Burdened by the measuring stick of defining an ethical nationhood, however, Kaplan remained unwilling to violate the basic premise of individual free choice to opt in or out of a community. Members, he conceded, at all times retain "the moral right to surrender such membership [in a nation] and become a member of another nation."[81] Violating an individual's freedom to choose his or her affiliations represented the clear boundary beyond which an ethical theory of nationality could not operate. That Kaplan was aware of this bind was evident from his private efforts to explore possible exceptions to the voluntary criteria of ethical nationhood: "When the nation to which one belongs is attacked then it is regarded as an act of treason to try to escape one's responsibilities to it, by becoming a citizen of another nation."[82] The global situation of Jews puts them in this category. They are thus exempt from the voluntary nature of nationality on account of the existential threats facing their community. No harmonious synthesis to resolve the tension between these conflicting convictions evolved in Kaplan's work. Instead, he let them rub up against one another. The best theoretical solution he could ever hope for would be a paradoxical arrangement of voluntary coercion, whereby individuals agreed to commit themselves to following the dictates of a minority national community. He did, however, consider more practical solutions that could make space for minority national groups without undermining their ethical mission.

Ensuring "social autonomy as a permanent factor in American life," Kaplan opined in 1916, would be possible "on the assumption [that] the American nation will prove to be a federation of nationalities."[83] Given Kaplan's personal experiences with the New York Jewish community during the previous decade, this statement advocating for social autonomy seems to reflect a romantic nostalgia for an East European model of self-government rather than a realistic analysis of the possibilities for distinct space within American democracy. Kaplan would have known the difficulties in advocating for communal autonomy by 1916. For ten years he had joined Rabbi Judah Magnes's effort to recreate a European model of Jewish self-government, the Kehillah, in New York City.[84] The Kehillah "envisioned a democratically governed polity which would unite the city's multifarious Jewish population."[85] The Kehillah experiment failed for a number of reasons, however, including accusations that the organization, based on a voluntary model of membership, was a body with too much power and control.[86]

Despite the failure of this experiment (the organization was defunct by 1922), Kaplan continued to express a desire for Jewish space within American political and social life that would ensure some degree of distinction. The absence of any mention of the Kehillah in his *Judaism as a Civilization* suggests that Kaplan struggled to come to terms with the implications of this failure on his more maximalist aspirations. His book not only made no reference to the Kehillah's demise, but it also advocated for an even more centralized and authoritative communal structure than that of the initial Kehillah. Kaplan continued to entertain programmatic and theoretical plans for creating distinct social and political space within U.S. society. For instance, he looked to the administration of certain "civic types of organization," specifically Jewish courts that would have the power to enforce their rulings on members of the Jewish community, to reinstate such political boundaries.[87]

In a 1927 *Society for the Advancement of Judaism Bulletin* editorial, Kaplan indicated that such a distinct legal sphere should certainly include the right to adjudicate on matters of marriage and divorce.[88] He responded to the U.S. government's refusal to recognize the validity of a Jewish divorce by claiming that "this business of refusing to give civic recognition to marriage and divorce laws of a group that is united by historic and religious association" was unreasonable. This implies that he envisioned two parallel legal systems that fully recognized one another's decisions as binding. Creating a dual system of courts, Kaplan continued, would help eradicate the "continual friction between the two loyalties which most people nowadays profess, loyalty to a religion and loyalty to a country."[89]

By maintaining such a separate legal network, Kaplan hoped, the Jewish community would no longer constitute merely a voluntary organization but would regain the power to enforce legal decisions. He ignored many of the difficult questions of negotiating the boundaries between two such systems.[90] Nettlesome issues remained unanswered—for example, which court would have ultimate authority or jurisdiction in particular cases, or how the U.S. legal system could handle a series of alternative judicial systems in other areas of civil or criminal law. Kaplan's analysis of the possibility of a separate legal track lacked sophistication and legal expertise.[91] However, despite his limited legal acumen and his frustratingly amorphous ruminations on this topic, his proposal of a separate legal sphere represents a noteworthy attempt to resist the state's legal power—one more manifestation of the enforcement of Americanization.

In other writings, Kaplan admitted that unifying such a variegated group of Jews into one polity and demanding some degree of official recognition proved a completely unrealistic goal. The demands of American conformity and unparalleled possibilities for integration made him realistic about the possibilities of autonomy within U.S. citizenship. He acknowledged that citizenship required limits to the demands of minority group recognition and cultural difference.[92] The political and cultural autonomy advocated by European diaspora nationalists, Kaplan felt compelled to admit, had no place in an American context.[93] Moreover, he appreciated liberalism's dichotomy between the public political and private religious spheres that ensured Jewish acceptance into American society.

This appreciation required a delicate dance that Kaplan engaged without ever fully staking a clear position. No doubt, the ambiguity of his position exposes his limitations as a political theorist. Yet Kaplan's failure illustrates his tenacious desire to address an intractable dilemma. Once again, Kymlicka's recent work on multicultural citizenship clarifies the middle-ground balance over the limits of diversity within liberal democracies. Kaplan's concept of civilization anticipated the distinction Kymlicka makes between "self-governing" and "polyethnic" rights. "Self-governing rights," Kymlicka states, demand some form of political autonomy or territorial jurisdiction. "Polyethnic rights," however, are "group specific measures . . . intended to help ethnic groups and religious minorities express their cultural particularity and pride without it hampering their success in the . . . institutions of the dominant society."[94]

Kaplan exhibited a tempered yearning for the former but demanded only the latter. He suggested that the minority national community primarily seeks recognition as a collective community with specific behaviors and practices that the state should not hinder. His *Future of the American Jew* calls on the state to extend "the principles of equality from individuals to groups."[95] In Kymlicka's language, Kaplan expects polyethnic rights, specifically the legal support to protect cultural and religious diversity. Kaplan wrote: "The principle of group equality must be translated into legal enactments prohibiting the propagation of racial and religious hatred, and removing all unjust discrimination in the treatment of members of religious and racial minorities."[96]

Note that Kaplan's call for legal recognition shares a second aspect with Kymlicka's theory of minority rights—namely, "external protections" without "internal restrictions." The state can and should, Kymlicka argues, ensure that members of minority national groups demand external protection for their cultural practices. However, polyethnic rights and even self-governing rights do not extend to illiberal practices that would in any way restrict an individual's rights, specifically freedom of choice. Kaplan anticipated the importance of limiting his call for external protections with the affirmation that ethical nationhood, best exemplified by Jewish nationality, is fully consonant with liberal practices. "As convinced Jews and loyal Americans," he wrote, "we should seek to incorporate in American life the universal values of Judaism and to utilize the particular sancta of Jewish religion as an inspiration for preserving these universal values."[97] Under pressure to restrain his demands to the confines of liberal theory and citizenship, Kaplan posited that minority rights are fully contingent on the liberalization of those particular national cultures. Jewish nationality—the exemplar of ethical nationhood in Kaplan's thought—must therefore demonstrate its full adherence to the political objectives of liberal democracy. Kaplan's theory legitimates multiple national communities within the state; however, legal protections and recognition only apply to those sharing specific political and moral guidelines.

Kaplan left his own questions unanswered about the nature of the boundaries between communities and their level of political independence. Nonetheless, exploring the contradictions between entertaining the possibility of separate legal systems and accepting the primacy of U.S. culture suggests a more complex view of Kaplan's approach to Americanization.[98] While Kaplan as the pragmatic communal leader understood the popular resistance any form of segregated civic life might have incited in the Jewish community, Kaplan the critic of liberalism espoused a Jewish civilization that commanded the devotion of its members.

National Civilization and Kaplan's Hopes for Zionism

The intellectual origins of national civilization are integrally connected to Kaplan's interest in formulating a counterstate variation of Zionism. Kaplan understood progress as the replacement of territorial, racial, and statist nationalisms with collective cohesion tied to religious traditions, shared values, and connection to a homeland. He endeavored to create an alternate, ethical ideal of nationhood that would affirm national partiality without undermining universal principles of individual rights, human equality, and free choice. One of Kaplan's inherent challenges in presenting civilization as a counter model to sovereign models that emphasize the intimate connections among nation, state, and territory was integrating his Jewish national civilization with Zionism. How to reconcile the ideological development of Zionism and the founding of the State of Israel was one of Kaplan's greatest intellectual and personal difficulties. Although he is remembered for his support of the Zionism movement, he had a major investment in creating a theory of Jewish nationality that would directly challenge Zionism's articulation of Jewish nationalism. A journal entry from 1924 proclaims: "The dream of my life . . . [is] to work out a clear formula for Judaism as a civilization both in Palestine and in the Diaspora, before my mental powers will begin to wane, which I understand is normally the case at 55."[99]

Kaplan's mental powers lasted far longer than age fifty-five; he continued to work on this dream for more than half a century. His last work, *Religion of Ethical Nationhood*, published in 1970, was dedicated to precisely this problem. It is difficult to appreciate that there was such a deep tension between the conflicting pressures of imagining a typology of nationality that would apply to Jews in both the homeland and the diaspora, given Kaplan's popular legacy as the "summary of American Zionism." He was an ardent supporter of Zionism, and the centrality of building Jewish national life in the homeland was a central component of both his *Judaism as a Civilization* and the *Reconstructionist* weekly magazine he edited.[100] Yet, as Kaplan himself admitted: "I realize fully the vacillating and paradoxical character of my attitude toward Palestine."[101]

Kaplan's relationship with Zionism and the developments in Palestine were far more contested than his passionate support for Zionism might suggest.[102] This tension indicates Kaplan's conscious effort to reconcile opposing definitions of Jewish life into one shared category that would be compatible with both diaspora and homeland experiences. He must have been reminded of the difficulty of realizing his dream on a boat to Palestine in 1925, en route to the inaugural ceremony of the Hebrew University in Jerusalem. Kaplan discussed the importance of the Mediterranean Sea with Chaim Weizmann, then president of the World Zionist Organization and future president of the State of Israel. This conversation left Kaplan quite distraught about Zionism's future prospects. According to Kaplan, Weizmann declared the Mediterranean to be "a Jewish sea." Kaplan recorded his negative reaction to Weizmann's "imperialistic attitude" in his journal. He retorted that "imperialism in the mouth of a Zionist has a hint of the chauvinism which reigns among modern nations."[103] Kaplan read into Weizmann's reasonably innocuous statement the same language of imperialism that *Judaism as a Civilization* had aligned with American nationalism.[104]

Developments in Palestine, specifically the Arab riots of 1929, further inflamed Kaplan's frustration with the Zionist movement. "The Balfour Declaration," Kaplan wrote in his diary that year, "has been like a foreign body in the system of Jewish revival, causing irritation and liable to set up a dangerous poison."[105] His volatile opposition to the declaration of a "national homeland in Palestine" highlighted the raw emotional conflict that the Jewish settlement in Palestine had sparked in his thinking. The abundance of such critical comments in Kaplan's journals during the 1920s and 1930s toward the political developments of Zionism suggests that such observations should not be disregarded as merely capricious reactions to disturbing contemporary events.

These reflections represent Kaplan's growing awareness that his moral argument for Jewish nationalism as an important corrective to American nationalism directly contradicted the political claims and military actions of Zionist leaders. Unlike Justice Louis Brandeis, whose Zionism was based on the claim that "to be good Americans meant being good Jews which meant becoming Zionists," Kaplan believed (although he certainly would never have voiced this in public) that to be a good Zionist meant to be a good Jew which meant to challenge America's own concept of nationalism.[106] For Kaplan, Zionism was not a reflection of the ideals of America. On the contrary, he believed that America should transform itself to reflect the model of nationalism being developed within Zionism.[107] Yet, he realized, Jewish nationalism could only succeed in challenging the hegemony of American nationalism as long as the Jewish settlement in Palestine remained solely a religious or cultural homeland. In his mind, the coercion of religious and ethnic minorities by Jews morally tainted the act of settlement in Palestine; therefore, Jewish civilization ceased to represent the apotheosis of national community.

As Kaplan's reaction to Weizmann's remarks on the steamer made clear, his faith in the Zionism movement was shaken. Kaplan's concept of Judaism as a civilization could only remain compatible with a Zionism that eschewed the doctrine of absolute sovereignty. He asserted this view up until the 1948 publication of *The Future of the American Jew*, which he finished writing shortly before the establishment of the state: "But the foregoing objectives of Zionism do not and need not require the sort of irresponsible and obsolete national sovereignty that modern nations claim for themselves. This doctrine of 'absolute national sovereignty' . . . is responsible for the international anarchy of the modern world, and is liable to bring about a catastrophe that will destroy the very foundations of human civilization."[108] (Note the exact repetition of Horace Kallen's language of associating national sovereignty with international anarchy discussed in chapter 2.)

As the leaders of the Jewish community faced the realities of Arab nationalism in Palestine and the Zionist movement became increasingly focused on political statehood, Kaplan found himself straddling two concepts of nationalism that could not be bridged. Desperately trying to illuminate a path toward a new nationalism, one that would guarantee a homeland to serve as a unifying center for world Jewry and would model the moral powers of national civilization, he sought a number of practical resolutions to this conundrum. In one passage in *Judaism as a Civilization*, he even imagined a situation in which Palestine would be "included and subordinated to a world state."[109] Such an international body would allow the Jewish transnational nation to have a cultural homeland, without necessitating the inevitable moral sacrifices that arise when nations marry states and strive to create a monolithic cultural and social identity.[110]

Setting aside the fact that Kaplan's world state idea had failed to materialize, this hypothetical proposition sheds light on his vacillating feelings toward Zionism. The notion of a world state represents one attempt to offer a potential solution to his own fundamental conflict concerning Zionism. How could the same definition of Jewish nationalism encompass both diaspora Judaism's historical role as the obstinate defender against political and cultural coercion as well as the political realities of building a sovereign Jewish state in a land with an indigenous population claiming national recognition? Only by dramatically altering the political realities of the international political order could Kaplan envision his concept of transnational nations. Just as addressing the Jewish question in America required adjusting ideas of American nationalism, so too would setting Zionism on the correct track involve adjusting the "equilibrium" between nations and states on a global level. However, in lieu of a political alteration of the global order, Kaplan's amorphous civilization concept incorporated the potential paradox of supporting both Zionism and diaspora nationalism. The parameters of civilization encapsulated the same conflict between advocating for the cultural benefits of political sovereignty in Palestine and for the separation of nation from state in the American context. As a Jewish thinker constantly reflecting on the implications of his work in two political milieus, Kaplan yearned for the benefits of a Jewish homeland that might come without the price of undermining his own justifications for diaspora Jewish life.

Reading Kaplan's theories as American Zionism par excellence dissolves the role of civilization as a nexus between American Jewish and Zionist categories of group solidarity. His perceived legacy as a Zionist, despite his ambivalence toward the movement, reflects Jewish historiography's tendency to conflate Jewish nationalism, Zionism, and national sovereignty. National civilization grapples with the inconsistencies dividing concepts of diaspora religion and statist Zionism. Supporting the yishuv and underscoring Zionism's role in the reconstruction of American Jewry was not a summary of American Zionism, but a criticism of efforts by both American Jews and Zionists to agree to disagree on the status of modern Judaism and the merit of life in the diaspora. Like Simon Rawidowicz before him,

Kaplan dreamed of an overarching status that would define national civilization as a cohesive force that would operate for Jews as both sovereigns and subjects, demographic majority and minority.

Kaplan's Legacy and the History of American Pluralism

Viewing Kaplan's national civilization as an effort to reconstruct both Zionism and Americanism offers rich dividends for historians and political theorists alike. The theory developed by Kaplan fills an important gap in tracing the evolution of ethnonational diversity in the United States. Kaplan tried to salvage a comprehensive definition of Judaism as more than a religious creed at a moment when such a multifaceted and all-encompassing reality was rapidly disappearing. How could Kaplan accurately translate the many aspects of Jewish collective life into the restricted categories of modern political thought? He diagnosed the problem correctly as first and foremost a limitation of the category of nationality. The introduction of the new term civilization would expand the discourse of difference by Jews' refusing to have their status dictated to them.

Torn by conflicting pressures to downplay nationalism in order to fit in as an American religious minority, coupled with his desires to compete directly with American religious nationalism, Kaplan refused to choose between the two very different paths. On the one hand, the term was intended to claim the status of nationhood for Jews and to use Jewish nationhood to decry the homogenizing force of American nationalism. When used for this objective, the language of civilization allowed Kaplan to compare American and Jewish nationalism on the same plane. By taking advantage of the amorphous meaning of civilization, he laid the groundwork for applying his assumptions concerning Judaism's political values to American nationalism as well. On the other hand, use of "religious civilization" played an opposing function: to strongly temper the claim for national status for diaspora Jews by replacing the language of nationality, laden with connotations of separatism that Kaplan knew would alienate American Jewry, with religion and civilization. These terms were far more compatible with American Jews' interest in promoting their ability to integrate and to share the universal, civilizing mission of their host country. Kaplan allowed these contradictions to thrive within the protean parameters of national civilization.

Kaplan's national civilization presented a cosmopolitan multiculturalism that bridges early-twentieth-century cultural pluralism with more recent concepts of cosmopolitanism. His view of Jewish civilization imagined membership grounded in consent rather than descent, shared memories rather than shared territory, liberal values rather than exclusivist claims, and social interactions rather than religious creed. His use of civilization thus anticipates the need to define a liberal theory of minority rights that specifies the balance between minority group recognition and the guarantee of individual rights. Unlike contemporary political theorists, whom Kaplan both echoed and anticipated, he probed the undertheorized area between religion and collective consciousness. His experience of Judaism as a living religiocultural system, rather than as a private creed, recognized the practical fallacy of Enlightenment thought's attempt to relegate religion to the private sphere. His view appreciated the fluid relationship between theology and politics—considerations that twenty-first-century theorists and practitioners will certainly have to reevaluate given the increasingly central role that religion has played in eroding national boundaries.

Civilization ran aground in Kaplan's inability to escape the orbit of the external political possibilities and social forces that exerted tremendous theoretical and practical pressure on his program. Civilization navigated between religion and nationhood by appropriating both terms to describe Jewish collective consciousness. Integrating these terms into the parameters of civilization allowed Kaplan to reach multiple audiences and to draw parallels between the Jewish and American contexts. This same strategy, however, also undermined the efficacy of a new key term by defining it based on the foundations of existing notions, whose connotations remained dominant. Judaism as a national civilization thus records Kaplan's desire to erase any tension between particular preservation and universal integration. Kaplan himself was struck by the daunting task of constructing categories that affirmed both poles. The recognition that he could not systematically reconcile voluntary and involuntary, familial bonds with cosmopolitan compassion, and self-government with citizenship led him to adopt a term fluid enough to affirm his competing aspirations.

Hans Kohn was also dedicated to linking these opposing forces of nationalism and humanism. Unlike Kaplan, however, Kohn decided, after years of active involvement in the Zionist movement, that reconciling Jewish nationalism with universal humanism was a naïve hope. He ultimately turned his scholarly abilities toward what he saw as a more achievable goal: to integrate his vision of Zionism into scholarly definitions of Western European and American nationalism. Kohn's political writings on Jewish nationality became the foundation of the study of modern nationalism. Kaplan correctly sensed the importance of shaping the external discourse as the primary goal in addressing internal Jewish concerns. What he did not fully accept, however, was the fact that a book on Judaism was the wrong vehicle to engage the ideas of Americanization and the nationalisms he hoped Jewish civilization could ultimately influence. Jewish concerns would have to be packaged in less parochial language to reach a general audience. Kohn's success can be partially traced to this very factor. He wrote for a general audience and translated his early writings on Jewish political thought into a narrative that only gave the smallest hint of its beginnings in the philosophy of Martin Buber and a small circle of German Zionists.

Hans Kohn sitting with a book at his desk in Jerusalem, 1925.
Courtesy of the Leo Baeck Institute, New York.

5

From German Zionism
to American Nationalism

Hans Kohn, Cultural Humanism, and the
Realization of "the Political Idea of Judaism"

On December 21, 1931, Mordecai Kaplan met Hans Kohn at a small gathering of American Zionists who had invited the visiting scholar to speak about the history of Arab nationalism in the Middle East.[1] Although Kohn agreed to speak to the group on the condition that he would not directly discuss the impact of Arab nationalism on Zionism, he eventually was compelled to address this issue directly. Kaplan's journal entry from that evening illustrates the tremendous impact that Kohn's "passionate condemnation of the Zionist futilities" had on Kaplan's feelings about the development of Jewish settlement in Palestine. Kaplan lamented, "I became convinced by his main talk that we Jews are in an awful mess with prospects in Palestine. . . . As I was walking home the thought occurred to me that the Jews have gotten themselves into such a tangle . . . by persisting to stand out as a distinct group."[2]

Kohn's lecture brought Kaplan to one of the lowest points of despair he expressed in his journal. Surprisingly, Kohn, an expert on Arab nationalism from Jerusalem and the sharp critic of "official Zionism," had been, until a few months earlier, the director of propaganda for Keren Hayesod (the fund-raising arm of the World Zionist organization). He had been a vocal proponent of Zionism and had contributed to leading journals and newspapers throughout Europe and Palestine. Kaplan encountered Kohn precisely in the midst of the activist's fascinating intellectual and biographical metamorphosis.

Inspired by the vision of Zionism as a movement dedicated to the cultural and spiritual renewal of Judaism promulgated by such figures as Ahad Ha'am and Martin Buber, Kohn embraced Jewish nationalism in the second decade of the century. After World War I, he traveled around Europe as a representative of Zionism and moved to Palestine in 1925 with the hopes of fulfilling his vision of Palestine as a place of international cooperation and peace. His pacifist conception of Zionism as an alternative to chauvinistic expressions of nationalism clashed with rising tensions and violence between Jews and Arabs there. Following the Arab riots of 1929, Kohn resigned from his official position within the movement and, a few years later, left Palestine for the United States. Failing to realize his vision of Jewish nationalism as an instrument for spreading universal humanism within the laboratory of Palestine, the German Zionist transformed himself into a leading American scholar of nationalism.

Kohn's prolific writings on the history of nationalism, both the concept in general and its development in specific geographical locations, and his broad appeal to popular audiences had a lasting impact on American scholarship and public opinion. Kohn wrote more than forty books (translated into many languages, including Italian, Japanese, and Korean), published hundreds of articles, shaped opinions through dozens of encyclopedia articles, and contributed to textbooks required for students of nationalism.[3] His books, especially *The Idea of Nationalism* (1944), received immediate recognition as pathbreaking contributions to historical scholarship.[4] The *New York Times* declared the book as "without hyperbole, the most brilliant, all-inclusive and incisive analysis of the ideological origins of nationalism which has yet appeared in any language."[5] More than half a century after the publication of his magnum opus, leading scholars of nationalism, including Benedict Anderson and Anthony Smith, continue to regard Kohn as one of the "founding fathers" of academic scholarship on nationalism.[6]

Kohn's scholarship focused on defining nationalism as a historical force for spreading universal principles, liberal ideals, and human integration.[7] This appears to represent a dramatic shift from the German Romantic conceptions of organic ties binding blood communities that characterized Kohn's Zionism in the 1920s. As one Kohn scholar has pointed out, Kohn's views on many issues—including liberalism, pacifism, socialism, colonialism, and the United States—changed radically.[8] Kohn's texts written after his immigration to the United States strike readers as far less sensitive to groupness and national culture than those written while under the influence of concepts in the early twentieth century.

Kohn's scholarship accentuated this break by popularizing a theoretical dichotomy between the ethnocentric nationalism of non-Western varieties and the civic, liberal nationalism of the West. This still widely accepted binary rubric of nationalism (discussed in chapters 1 and 2) located his nationalism as the antithesis of the tribal, ethnic, and cultural bonds that had shaped his intellectual development within the multinational context of the Hapsburg Empire. Moreover, his endorsement of a civic nationalism that eschews groupness based on historical grounds has little explicit interest in, and even potentially undermines the validity of, preserving Jewish solidarity. Kohn's Jewishness and Zionism appear less relevant because of his zealous universalism and challenges to the official positions adopted by the Zionist movement (especially regarding the goal of establishing a sovereign Jewish state in Palestine).

Kohn's personal disillusionment with Zionism and his theoretical distancing from his intellectual roots in Romantic, völkisch nationalism suggest a radical break between his careers as a German Zionist and an American scholar. As a result, like many émigré intellectuals, his intellectual development is bifurcated into two distinct stages.[9] Yet a close look at his scholarship reveals striking parallels with, and in some cases even exact translations of his earlier work into his American scholarship. Underneath the new heroes and histories, the fundamental content of Kohn's historical narrative remained consistent.

This chapter draws on Kohn's personal correspondence and publications from his involvement with Zionism to narrate the fascinating development of his formulations of nationalism and the biographical journey of this peripatetic polymath. He became a significant intellectual in Europe, Palestine, and then the United States over a period that spanned half a century. Tracing the origins of these scholarly innovations to Kohn's youth in Prague highlights a surprising source for his theories of nationalism. Remarkably, the foremost critic of ethnic, Romantic nationalism, particularly the Central and East European variety, developed his concept of political nationalism directly out of the assumptions and methodology of German biological and cultural nationalism. My goal in establishing thematic continuities in Kohn's intellectual biography is to correct a common misreading of his pioneering contributions to the study of nationalism. Interpreting Kohn's later work as a theory of liberal, humanistic, or civic nationalism overlooks his continued sensitivity to many of the concepts he promoted as a Zionist activist. Kohn's experiences as a Jew and a Zionist made him just as weary of cosmopolitan universalism as of chauvinistic nationalism. Both extremes engendered totalitarian ideologies that threatened Jews' individual and collective rights. Kohn responded to this observation by focusing his theoretical efforts on reconciling, rather than drawing a sharp opposition between, the commitment to national ties that shaped his formative years and the focus on humanity that characterizes his legacy.

This chapter highlights this aspect of Kohn's scholarship by focusing on two arguments that appear, although to varying degrees, across Kohn's careers as Zionist activist and American scholar: 1) equating nationalism with the recognition of human solidarity and a historical trajectory toward social integration; 2) contending that this vision is fully compatible with the recognition, and even promotion of, counterstate national ties, rooted in culture and historical allegiances. Cultural humanism, the term I use to refer to Kohn's conception of Zionism and nationalism, more accurately captures this dialectical tension that distinguished his life and thought.

The fact that Kohn's criticism of Zionism had such a powerful impact on Kaplan at his 1931 lecture (and that Rawidowicz expressed similar concerns about state-seeking Zionism and its implications for Arabs in Palestine) suggests that Kohn's formulations of Jewish nationalism are more closely linked to other counterstate theories of Zionism than it initially appears.[10] The first part of this chapter attempts to contextualize Kohn's cultural humanism within the transnational context of interwar Zionism that included Kaplan's national civilization and Rawidowicz's global Hebraism. These expressions of Zionism constituted parallel responses to similar historical events, intellectual influences, and debates within Zionism.

The three Jewish nationalisms developed from two basic assumptions. First, Jewish nationhood constituted an advanced form of nationalism committed to finding alternatives to sovereignty as the basis for Jewish cohesion. Second, Jewish concepts of national cohesion paved the most ethical path toward affirming human commitments. Thus, instead of viewing Kohn's nationalism as categorically different from religious civilization and global Hebraism, it is more historically accurate and conceptually beneficial to view these theories as delineating a spectrum of Zionists theorizing different solutions to a shared set of fundamental dilemmas. Although global Hebraism, religious civilization, and cultural humanism posit decreasing levels of separation and increasing degrees of integration, they all identify Jewish political thought as a site for negotiating the relationship between nation and state and between particular and universal allegiances. The second section of the chapter probes ways in which Kohn's counterstate Zionism continued to shape his pioneering view of nationalism. Indeed, reintegrating the disparate components of his intellectual biography highlights the way in which important aspects of his theory, especially his bifurcation between civic and ethnic nationalism, have been misunderstood.

Kohn: An Intellectual Biography

Born in 1891 to assimilated Jewish parents, Hans Kohn grew up in Prague. He attended the Altstädter Deutsches Gymnasium, the same school that Franz Kafka had graduated from the year before Kohn entered in 1902. Kohn grew up in a highly acculturated family and had little interest in his personal connection to Jews and Judaism.[11] The growing affirmation of national pride and ethnolinguistic factionalism within the Hapsburg Empire sparked his interest in Zionism.[12] Kohn, like other young acculturated Jews, got involved with the Prague Jewish student organization, the Bar Kochba society, beginning in 1908. He soon fell under the spell of philosopher, historian of Hasidism, and Zionist Martin Buber, who delivered a series of lectures between 1909 and 1911 to the society. These speeches, later published as *Three Addresses on Judaism*, called for a "renewal of Judaism" that emphasized the tradition's striving for unity and exemplifying a national ethical spirit dedicated to "interhuman" relationships.[13]

These lectures ignited a Zionist flame among many members of the Bar Kochba association of Jewish university students, especially Kohn. Buber's vision of Judaism and Zionism appealed to a young generation obsessed with the neoromantic possibility of creating *Gemeinschaft* (organic community) and pulled between competing national movements. Buber's Zionism focused on the spiritual revival of the Jewish people and Judaism's humanistic vision inspired by prophetic writings. For Kohn, the lectures "constituted a turning point in all my views."[14] Indeed, he would remain a lifelong disciple of Buber and published an intellectual biography of his teacher in 1930 (a new edition was published in 1961).[15]

Galvanized by Buber's Zionism, Kohn, along with his lifelong friend, journalist Robert Weltsch (the future editor of the Zionist newspaper *Jüdische Rundschau*), soon became a leader of the Bar Kochba society and edited an important collection of essays on Judaism and the future of Jewish nationalism called *Vom Judentum: Ein Sammelbuch* (Judaism: a collection of essays) in 1914.[16] Kohn's introduction to this series of essays by prominent intellectuals—including Buber, the non-Marxist socialist Gustav Landauer, and the philosopher Hugo Bergmann—demonstrated a deep desire to redirect the "destiny" of the Jewish people and to place Jewish renewal within a larger context of worldwide change. However, before he had the opportunity to further clarify his ideas, World War I broke out. The Austro-Hungarian army drafted him only a few months after the publication of *Vom Judentum*. Shortly thereafter, the Russian army captured the young officer and sent him to the Carpathian foothills. From 1915 until

1920, he traveled throughout the Russian Empire as a prisoner of war. From Poland to Siberia, Kohn walked, rode, and sailed through the great expanse of the empire and personally witnessed the destruction of the land during the 1917 revolution.[17]

Following the revolution, Kohn was stranded in Siberia. His letters from this period indicate that he spent his time as a Zionist organizer among fellow former prisoners of war: "We have organized here in Siberia a very vivid Zionist spiritual life," he boasted in a 1919 letter.[18] Nevertheless, Kohn was anxious to return to Central Europe, but he had no money for the journey. Desperate to secure transportation, and possibly even a new job, he turned to his old Prague friends, some of whom had already gained important positions in the Zionist movement. In a letter from Irkutsk to Leo Hermann, an older member of the Bar Kochba Society and a leader of the World Zionist Organization, Kohn pleaded for Hermann to "take him as a 'Zionist worker' to Europe or Palestine," since it would be terrible to "sit here in Siberia."[19] In the hopes of proving his Zionist credentials, Kohn continued in his newly acquired English language skills, "I began to work here as Zionist leader I can say with great success. I have grown up to be a very good orator and I have worked in many towns of Siberia and I'm well known in this country among the Jews. . . . The war once finished it is hard to be here when the building up of the new commonwealth in Palestine begins."[20]

With the help of Hermann, Kohn moved to Paris in 1920, and soon after, to London in 1921 to work as an employee for Keren Hayesod. The job entailed traveling around Europe, galvanizing interest in settlement in the Land of Israel and soliciting donations. His letters back to the central London office of Keren Hayesod illustrate his methodical analysis of the local Jewish community and detailed plans for maximizing contributions to the Zionist movement. Internal letters from Keren Hayesod executives indicate that Kohn was their most valuable fund-raiser and communal organizer (his boss referred to him as a "heavyweight" fund-raiser and propagandist).[21] In addition to his work at Keren Hayesod, Kohn contributed regular articles about Zionism, Jewish life, and nationalism more generally to Buber's important Zionist publication, *Der Jude*.[22]

At the same time, Kohn aligned himself with international socialism and cosmopolitan pacifism (specifically the socialist French Clarté movement, which proposed internationalism as an alternative to militant nationalism and capitalism). Writing under the pseudonym Paul Colin, he contributed regular columns from 1919 to 1922 on developments in the socialist internationalist movement for the movement's paper, *Clarté*.[23] Kohn's articles reviewed trends in the internationalist socialist's struggles against imperialism in various European countries. In addition, Kohn participated in socialist conventions and advocated for pacifism.[24]

The decision to write under a pseudonym suggests that, at least in his public persona, Kohn sought to preserve a clear distinction between his Zionist and pacifist activities. Yet, internally, he clearly viewed these two commitments as fully compatible ideologies. The peaceful integration of national groups outside of the nation-state framework and Zionism's call for the renaissance of the Jewish people were mutually consistent ideologies. But why align universal and particular programs? Why didn't Kohn reject his Zionist associations and fully align his utopian dream of a new paradigm of human integration with movements and ideologies that eschewed national cohesion completely? One reason may have to do as much with financial and social realities as with ideological decisions: his network of Zionist associates had helped rescue Kohn from Siberia and find him a stable job with the movement.

However, there was a more personal and practical reason as well. A letter Kohn wrote to his friend, the writer Berthold Feiwal, helps explain his attraction to Zionism as an outlet for his hopes of achieving universal integration:

> I and a group of friends saw in Zionism a moral-spiritual movement, in which we could realize our universal human convictions, our pacifism, our liberation and humanism. We were often criticized that amidst the European people we could not solely stand up for pacifism or ethical politics, or else we would be labeled as foreign people, as traitors. Zion was to be the site of fulfillment of our universal strivings.[25]

Kohn thus turned to Zionism as the medium for his universal vision because he felt excluded as a Jew within European social and intellectual contexts. Even internationalism's universalism struck Kohn as failing to fully welcome Jews. His autobiographical experience of the exclusionary possibilities of both nationalism and humanism made an enduring mark on Kohn's theoretical engagement. It helps contextualize the ambiguous relationship between the particular and the universal that characterized his future career. The paradoxical formulation of national ties as the catalyst for human integration directly mirrored his own lifelong struggle to reconcile Paul Colin's exclusion from European cosmopolitanism and Hans Kohn's frustration with state-seeking Zionism. He sought to reconcile theories of nationalism and humanism because he never felt fully at home at either pole.

In 1925, Kohn moved to Palestine to work in the Keren Hayesod office in Jerusalem. After advocating for Zionism and settlement in Palestine for almost a decade, the transition to Palestine was still a difficult one for Kohn. He acknowledged in his letters that he had found a nice house and had many visitors, but that he was also underwhelmed by the general quality of life in Palestine.[26] Yet he had great hopes for Palestine and the role of Jewish nationalism in transforming the land into a model of universal cooperation. Kohn viewed Palestine as the laboratory for the development of a form of nationalism that would unify, rather than divide, humanity. He rejected the concept of Palestine as a territorial homeland that the Jews had historical rights to reclaim. Nor did he yearn to ensure a Jewish majority in Palestine. Instead, Kohn imagined a spiritual homeland that would facilitate Zionism's role as the vanguard force spreading the Jewish political ideal at the crucial meeting point of the nationalisms of the East and the West.

Kohn's involvement in Zionism and the affairs of the yishuv went beyond his official capacity at Keren Hayesod. With a tremendous amount of dedication and zeal, he published numerous articles on Zionism, Judaism, and world affairs in such newspapers as the Labor Zionist *Hapo'el hatza'ir* (The Zionist worker) and the Palestinian periodical *Filastina*.[27] He was particularly concerned about the Arab question in Palestine and throughout the Middle East.[28] Palestine's Arab population provided Kohn with the perfect opportunity to highlight the revolutionary possibilities of unadulterated Judaism. "The fact that there is already a large non-Jewish population," he wrote in 1924, "poses an added challenge for the creation of the collective. The solution of which could be meaningful for the population that suffers from a nationalism delusion. Herein lies an element of the hardship, which is both a blessing and a curse."[29]

While few Zionist thinkers were even willing to acknowledge the existence of Arab nationalism, Kohn dedicated his scholarly energies toward evaluating the potential pitfalls of Jewish settlement in an area with a non-Jewish majority.[30] His research furnished a historical justification for his belief that ultimately the existence of two national groups in the same territory would be a blessing. He dedicated his scholarly energies toward tracing the evolution of Arab nationalism.[31] Kohn also attempted to advocate for his vision of a binational state in Palestine by participating in the creation of Brit Shalom, a small yet influential circle of intellectuals created to advocate for a binational state that would provide cultural and religious autonomy for Jews and Arabs alike.

The Arab riots of 1929 jolted the Jewish community in Palestine. For the majority of Zionist leaders there, this rude awakening galvanized a renewed political and military effort to pressure the British to implement the Balfour Declaration and to consider new ways of defending the yishuv against the threats of the Arabs in Palestine. The riots hardened the positions of liberal Zionist leaders, such as Chaim Weizmann and Brit Shalom founder Arthur Ruppin. They replaced their hope in the ability of the two communities to coexist peacefully with a more pessimistic vision of the future of these two peoples. The riots forced members of Brit Shalom to address the tensions between their vision of Zionism and the realities of Jewish settlement in Palestine. Instead of dissolving differences and diminishing particularities, the yishuv in Palestine had planted the seeds of a deeply divided national conflict. Moreover, their demands for a binational state were attacked in the wake of the riots as tantamount to treason. Kohn's fellow members of Brit Shalom, including his collaborator Hugo Bergmann, remained silent in response to these criticisms. Kohn, however, refused to relinquish his push for continued dialogue with the Arab population. His stance brought a public outcry directly upon him that pressured him to resign from his position in the movement.

Kohn penned a letter of explanation to Buber concerning this decision to quit his post. In a moving remark, he wrote: "Zionism as it is today . . . is unacceptable. . . . I am not concerned about Ishmael, only about Isaac, that is, our aims, our life, our actions. I am afraid [that] what we support we cannot vouch for. And because of false solidarity we shall sink deeper into the quagmire. Either Zionism will be pacific or else it will be without me. Zionism is not Judaism."[32] Kohn expressed his deep disappointment and anguish in this letter and a number of others written during this period. Zionism's effort to solve the tragic failings of nationalism created a more militaristic manifestation of Jewish nationalism. Whereas Kohn had hoped that the movement would become the ultimate bearer of the Jewish political idea, he felt betrayed by the perversion of the tenets he considered central to Judaism. Buber, who considered Kohn one of his prize pupils and certainly empathized with elements of Kohn's frustrations, found Kohn's resignation disappointing. Buber considered Kohn's "basic moral position to suffer from a 'doctrinaire idealism.'"[33] Moral idealism, Buber averred, had to be balanced with real-world political considerations. For Buber, Zionism's inability to realize his idealistic vision of creating a peaceful coexistence between Orient and Occident did not undermine the entire project. Kohn, however, had intricately linked his Zionism to the fulfillment of a utopian dream that clashed with political realities and dwindling support for Arab–Jewish dialogue within the yishuv.

Still unaware of what his next step might be, Kohn spent the next four years living in Palestine and traveling throughout Europe, America, Russia (where he served as a correspondent for the *Frankfurter Zeitung*), and the Middle East. One of his speaking engagements brought him to the United States, where he delivered the talk Kaplan attended. Thanks to his old friend Judah Magnes, the American-born Zionist who served as one of the founders of the Hebrew University in Jerusalem, Kohn received an invitation in 1934 to teach history at Smith College in Massachusetts. His new position as a scholar of nationalism in the United States enabled him to explore the possibility of expanding the idea of Judaism, expressed by Jewish thinkers, to a much wider audience.

Kohn reinvented himself as a leading American scholar of nationalism who would go on to publish important works on the history of nationalism and the nature of American nationalism. With astounding flexibility, Kohn replaced Moses, the Baal Shem Tov, and Buber with the Sophists, Rousseau, and Jefferson as the prophets of modern nationalism. The German-educated scholar mastered an entirely new corpus of historical material in under a decade. Biblical sources and Zionist ideologies were swapped for an in-depth intellectual history of England, France, and the United States. Kohn downplayed his past activism in the Zionist movement in his publications on nationalism. Over the next forty years, Kohn taught history at a number of American universities, including Smith College (1934–1948), City College of New York (1948–1961), and Harvard Summer School, where he served periodically as a visiting faculty member for over two decades (1935–1958). Kohn was a popular teacher and an incredibly prolific writer.[34]

As the historian Hagit Lavsky has pointed out, Kohn himself character-ized his move to the United States as a "break" with Zionism that would give him the opportunity to find "completely new paths."[35] Recent schol-arly interest in Kohn's intellectual biography tends to accept this assertion of discontinuity between the German Zionist and the American scholar of nationalism.[36] Was it a complete break, as he himself claimed? If not, how did the concepts and research endure in his work? Before address-ing this question, it is necessary to explore Kohn's understanding of Zion-ism and its affinities with other interwar counterstate theories of Jewish nationalism.

"Nationalism as the Ultimate Ordering Principle Is Dead"

In a 1921 article, "Nationalism," Kohn predicted: "The time will come when 'national sovereign independence', the goal of the age of political national-ism, will vanish because mankind will have realized that . . . the noninter-vention of the 'foreigner' in 'our' affairs, is a dangerous phantom that, under the suggestiveness of the myth of the nineteenth century, has become an article of faith."[37] Kohn's essay, published in the influential Zionist journal *Der Jude,* presented a scathing critique of European "egoistic" nationalism and a profound antipathy toward the claims and actions of European nation-states. The equation of nation and state, he contended, created an exclusivist logic that engendered belligerent actions toward other states and threatened the individual rights of citizens. His critique of nationalism, however, did not lead him to reject the historical or normative importance of national identity. Although "nation and state are distinct," Kohn insisted that "the nation in its vital utterances, in its culture and development must be protected even without national independence, without the national state."[38] Kohn's task as an interpreter of Jewish political thought and a Zionist was to advocate for the depoliticization and deterritorialization of concepts of nationalism, past and present.

During the eighteenth and nineteenth centuries, Kohn argued, nationalism played an important role in the historical development of Enlightenment ideals. The nation-state spread humanistic values across large populations and thereby enabled world history to proceed to a higher level of ethical development. However, as political leaders appropriated nationalism for their own ends, the antipathy stirred by nationalism led to the vast destruction of World War I. This historical cataclysm actually represented the end of a more primitive stage of nationalism and signified the beginning of a new period in human history. The epoch would enable more authentic, humanistic strains of national identity to shine forth.

Kohn's historical schema suggested that such historical turning points required transition periods. During this intermediary epoch, Kohn contended that a particular nation would model the future typology of ethical nationalism. Such a nation would "announce the future road, the new, purified, primarily human value of the nation, its release from politics and from suggestiveness, and its elevation into clarity . . . it [the nation] knuckles under to moral laws, eternal valuations; it dares to look into its own eyes with ultimate clarity."[39] The advanced stage of national identity, purified of the dross of political greed and moral indifference, would eventually catalyze a transformation eliciting a worldwide "feeling of social unity."

According to this narrative, "state-nationalism" defined as "the attachment of a sovereign people to a specific territory that it owned and possessed" would disappear and a more authentic national solidarity based on "a context of a group of people held together through a common descent and common or similar historical destinies" would reshape the political order.[40] Kohn contrasted those authentic national groups that exemplified a cohesion based on culture and "natural ties" with those that made dubious political claims based on historical claims to land and collective identity.[41] Creating a new "pure" nationalism served in Kohn's periodization as the transitional mechanism for ensuring the transformation from the age of malevolent nation-states to his vision of a more cosmopolitan world order. The authentic nation unified by moral probity and organic social bonds would serve as the corrective to the völkisch extremism of European nation-states.

This antipathy toward privileging states' political ends over moral concerns echoed contemporary discussions among German-speaking intellectuals about the relationship between right and might in political thought. In 1924 Friedrich Meinecke, for example, the founder of German political intellectual history, published *The Idea of Reasons of State*.[42] This book traced the historical development of the relationship between ethics and realpolitik from Machiavelli through World War I. In his conclusion, Meinecke critiqued the notion of the "power state" and denounced the "false idealization of power politics."[43] Kohn adapted Meinecke's admonition against the use of force or moral coercion as the basis for political entities.

Kohn's distinction between cultural or moral and political expressions of nationalism reflects another example of how significantly early-twentieth-century German thought shaped Kohn's formulations. His dichotomy between organic and political ties reflects sociologist Ferdinand Tönnies's distinction between two types of groups—*Gemeinschaft* (community created by organic bonds between members) and *Gesellschaft* (societies united by instrumental relationships between individuals). These were categories highlighted by Buber in the so-called Prague lectures that Kohn helped organize before the Great War.[44]

Other romantic conceptions and imagery—such as *Blut* (blood), *Kultur* (culture), and *Volk* (people)—also reverberate through Kohn's descriptions of the ties that bind members of national groups. "National sentiment, detached from its territorial state-faith," Kohn averred, "will help determine the destiny of mankind through the power of the traditions of blood."[45] Yet this statement also illustrates his tension with the very intellectual milieu that shaped his vocabulary and concepts of nationalism. Kohn internalized the terminology of organic national bonds at the same time that he employed these concepts to undermine the historical importance of the nation-state as the optimal carrier. By separating nation from state, Kohn subverted the fusion of the two concepts that even liberal interwar intellectuals such as Meinecke viewed as destined to come together.

Indeed, Kohn's historical narrative applied the tools of German idealist historiography to challenge the integration of nation and state as the final stage in the development of political theory (a narrative shaped by such seminal German intellectuals as the philosopher Hegel). Kohn's periodization and analysis of the rise and (he hoped) fall of national sovereignty was a polemical call for the normalization of stateless national groups, such as the Jews. This emphasis was far different from that of such influential German thinkers as Ernst Troeltsch, who defined the spirit of German culture (Kultur) as a concept advocating for the national freedom of the state, rather than the liberal freedom from the state.[46] Jewish national culture signified the future type of nationalism that retained the higher moral status associated by German thinkers with the völkisch emphasis on the collective over the individual. However, it rejected the centrality of the state, or the fatherland, in guiding the national spirit through history.

Kohn undermined the assumptions of an organic hierarchy of national spirits in another way: he neutralized the exclusivist connotations increasingly linked with völkisch expressions of nationalism. National identity was not a reflection of historical objectivity or ascriptive characteristics. Kohn called such "myths" of collectivity based on past traditions and characteristics "subjective" illusions that create a false sense of unity.[47] His definition of Jewish nationalism reflects this important critique: "Zionism is not a science, not a logical conceptual system; it has no racial theories of definitions of people."[48] Judaism focused on dynamic unity in the present, thus avoiding the danger of reifying particular criteria of inclusion and diminishing the tension between national autonomy and international integration. Kohn adopted the antiliberal language of German political thought. In particular, Kohn internalized the terminology associated by his German-speaking contemporaries with the rejection of Western European concepts of freedom from collective authority. As a result, his theoretical basis differs from the counterstate Zionists associated with the Allied powers during World War I.

Horace Kallen, Alfred Zimmern, and Mordecai Kaplan all aligned themselves with British civilization, with its emphasis on individual rights and equality, over the authoritarian demands of Prussian or Kultur nationalism. Kohn identified Jewish nationalism primarily with German Kultur and opposed (at least until the mid-1920s when he aligned his idea of nationalism with Western civilization against German nationalisms) the liberal individualism and freedom associated with British civilization.[49]

Yet the alignment of Zionism with opposite intellectual traditions is not quite as sharp as the bifurcation suggests. Counterstate Zionists on both sides of the civilization–Kultur debate appropriated their political milieu's highest conception of nationalism, separated this theory of nationalism from sovereignty, and associated its true fulfillment with Zionism. Moreover, Zionists on both sides sought to find compromise positions that reconfigured the stark dichotomy between individual and collective freedoms. Kohn's early writings focus on equality, universal concepts of justice, permeable national boundaries, and minority rights far more unequivocally than his German nationalist contemporaries. Conversely, Zimmern, Kallen, and Kaplan all integrated the language of spirit and culture into their formulations to demonstrate the compatibility of liberalism and communal recognition.

Kohn's personal correspondence contextualizes the existence of this parallel. Counterstate Zionists engaged Jewish and general concepts of nationalism as a response to their personal experiences as Jews of the limits of nation-state nationalisms, in both their liberal and ethnic variations. Revealing his own awareness as a Jew of the source of his interest in nationalism, Kohn wrote: "Our [Jewish] tensions are stronger, our sensitivity stronger, our homelessness deeper than among others. . . . Scattered throughout the world, we carry the suffering of all mankind."[50] His anxiety about the position of Jews as the primary victim of the totalizing logic of nation-state nationalism motivated his early engagement with Zionism and remained a driving force throughout his career. Solving the Jewish question within the parameters of nationalism demanded a middle-ground approach that sought areas of compromise between liberal individualism and völkisch collectivism. At the same time, their very anxiety about ethnic exclusion motivated Jewish thinkers to align themselves with precisely the discourse that had the potential to alienate them in order to fit in. As a result, figures from various intellectual milieus expressed Jewish political thought through competing perspectives on nationalism but ended up with far more in common than their identification with one pole or the other might suggest. One such area of overlap was the creation of a synthesis of Zionism and humanism.

Jews: A Nation One with Humanity

Kohn's lifelong interest in demonstrating nationalism's role as the primary carrier of the principle of a shared human solidarity through history originated in his understanding of Zionism. Hungry for a transformation of Judaism and the extant social and political order, he believed that Zionism constituted an integral part of a larger change in the basis for social integration within European society. Kohn wrote in 1913: "Today, there is a general yearning of the individual to go beyond the individual, to prepare oneself for the superindividual connection. All the indications are that in our day a change is coming, not only for Judaism but for all of mankind."[51] These "superindividual connections" would transcend biological, national, religious, and linguistic categories. Jewish national culture signified the first step toward spreading the human spirit. Kohn developed his concept of the Jewish idea of nationalism through constructing a sacred history of the Jewish people, from biblical prophets to the prophets of Zionism. He developed these in a number of works, including a 1924 German pamphlet called *Die Politische Idee des Judentum* (The political idea of Judaism) and the two-volume Hebrew book, *Perakim letoldot hara'ayon hatzioni* (A history of Zionist thought), which was published in 1929.[52]

Die Politische Idee des Judentum interpreted Jewish sources as prescribing the fundamental principles of the future stage of humanistic, counterstate nationalism described in his 1921 "Nationalism" essay. To demonstrate the core principles of Jewish ethical, humanistic, and integrative nationalism, he highlighted three pillars of the Jewish political idea in this work: covenant, humanity, and messiah. The covenant signified the acceptance by both individual Jews and the larger community of an absolute sense of justice rooted outside of the selfish concerns of other individuals or the state. Kohn claimed that the Israelites distinguished themselves in the annals of history as the first nation to spread their own divinely inspired social legislation toward all of humanity.

The most important pillar for Kohn, the messianic principle, tracked Jewish and early Christian calls to build the messianic kingdom within the extant political order. Kohn cited the prophets, and particularly his favorite Jewish prophet, Jesus, as evidence of the centrality of the call for this-worldly redemption (Kohn does clearly reject Jesus as the Messiah; instead, he interprets the founder of Christianity as a Jewish activist in line with other Hebrew Bible prophets). In this reading of salvation, freedom and equality would dissolve national boundaries, bringing about the crowning achievement of the Jewish idea. From Moses to Isaiah, Kohn documented the gradual proliferation of the divine in the world as an evolving political recognition of universal brotherhood. According to Kohn, the doctrine of Israel taught that "in the last reason, all are the same, all are related."[53] By tracing the biblical stories of the Garden of Eden and the Flood, Kohn contended that the Bible recognizes that ultimately all people come from the same stock. This ability of divine justice and universal love to permeate quotidian reality through an enlightened political structure constituted the core of Kohn's idea of Jewish messianism. He traced the political idea of Judaism to the Bible's calls for higher levels of integration and a greater consciousness of the underlying unity that binds humankind.

This understanding of the political idea of Judaism and its relationship to theories of nationalism outlined in his "Nationalism" article illustrates

Kohn's tremendous intellectual debt to his teacher Martin Buber. The "Nationalism" article borrowed almost directly from Buber's famous 1921 speech, with the same title, which was delivered at the Twelfth Zionist Congress. Buber's lecture made a similar distinction between false nationalism, which "exceeded the function it was destined to" and has "become too sick and thus [is] beginning its decline," and Jewish nationalism, whose task is to point the nations toward a "super-national sphere." "We live in the hour," Buber concluded, "when nationalism is about to annul itself spiritually."[54] Buber introduced the concept of a supernational Jewish nationalism as the conduit between false nationalism and a future without nationalism, which reappeared as the central theme in Kohn's subsequent essay.

Buber linked these political claims to his reading of Judaism and religious thought. Underlying the apparent duality of the world, Buber averred, lies a deeper spiritual unity that integrates humanity. It is the Jewish obligation, he wrote, to "strive for unity within individual man; for unity between divisions of the nation and between nations," and to turn "the Jewish question into a human question."[55] Buber expressed Judaism's cosmopolitan appreciation through his interpretation of the core concepts of unity, the messianic future, and deed. These same three principles of Judaism appeared in slightly altered form in Kohn's *Die Politische Idee des Judentum* as covenant (which paralleled Buber's deed category by promoting the commitment to act in the political realm), humanity (a call for equal justice based on the unity of all mankind), and messiah.

Yet Buber balanced his vision of a supernational nation and human integration with an emphasis on the cultural and religious revival of Judaism and vibrant Jewish communities.[56] Kohn, in contrast, transposed this religious vision into a political plan that primarily utilized the cosmopolitan implications of Buber's philosophy. One direct example of this move manifested itself in Buber's and Kohn's varying interpretations of messianism. Messianic fulfillment, Buber argued, paradoxically served as a goal to orient action in the world and yet remained forever unreachable. The messianic moment remained "eternally remote and eternally immanent."[57] Buber maintained an appreciation for the power of messianic deferral at the same time that he highlighted its central role in Judaism. Kohn completely overlooked this dialectical vision central to Buber's messianism. For Buber, religious unity existed as a religious and theoretical ideal, not as an immediate political program.

Disregarding these important hesitations, Kohn read the messianic future as a utopian social and political blueprint that demanded immediate realization. The prophets, he claimed in a clear departure from Buber, "see the coming of the messianic reign as a historical act, carried out in a living generation."[58] Not particularly interested in the philosophical or religious dimensions of Buber's thought, Kohn appropriated one pole of his teacher's work to serve as the foundation for a universal humanism based on Jewish nationalism. Kohn's Jewish nationalism served a primarily instrumental purpose: to spread the political idea of Judaism to the other nations. When it finished its mission to the world, the Jewish idea would eliminate the need for a Jewish nation (a political analogue to Reform Judaism's concept of ethical monotheism).

Kohn fused his political idea of Judaism with the evolution of modern Zionist ideology in *Perakim letoldot hara'ayon hatzioni*. This analysis of the history of Zionist thought presented an intellectual counternarrative to the Zionist idea as it was playing out in Palestine.[59] Foregrounding Zionist theoreticians usually relegated to the boundaries of the Zionist narrative, Kohn claimed that all of these thinkers, beginning with Moses Hess, recovered the ancient message of Judaism that had been lost in the wake of the Emancipation. In Kohn's interpretation of modern Jewish intellectual history, the Emancipation distanced Jews from the Jewish political idea. Ironically, Jews had lost their particular identity in the modern period by ignoring Judaism's universalistic core. Kohn lionized Hess as the first Jewish intellectual to reconnect Judaism with its commitment to humanity. Jewish nationalism emerged from Hess's work as the return to Judaism's authentic role as the unifier of humankind. Subsequent chapters of Kohn's treatise linked the growing unity between Jewish nationalism and humanism through the work of Joseph Salvador, Nathan Birnbaum, Martin Buber, and A. D. Gordon.

The book's final chapter transformed the mystical and land-connected Zionism of A. D. Gordon into the pinnacle of Kohn's political idea of Judaism.[60] Gordon had gained cult status among young Zionists for his mystical appreciation of labor and land. Kohn, however, focused his analysis on Gordon's concept of nationalism and particularly on the notion of *am adam* (people-mankind). This Hebrew wordplay equated the two concepts that Kohn had desperately been trying to fuse since the conclusion of World War I: humanity and nation. Kohn found Gordon's "synthesis of the national foundation and the human foundation" inspiring, and defined the profound significance of the term in the following manner: "*am adam*: the name is new, the idea is old. It is the message that the nation of Israel brings to the world. From our prophets until our own period we have not lost the faith that man, as he is man, fulfills the cosmic task, the task that was imposed upon all those who were created in the image of God, and because of this creation the unity of all humanity comes before differences of nations, race and religion."[61]

Zionism, the highest stage of national development, took the grouping principle that had united nations and elevated the sense of cohesion to all humanity. Kohn praised Gordon in the conclusion of his history of Zionist thought for his understanding that "the nation is the natural pipe, the life that creates human life."[62] This pipe infused each individual with a cosmic connection that sparked love for the other and eliminated the desire to wage war. Kohn considered am adam to be Zionist thought's ultimate realization of the Jewish political message—the centrality of the national group in promoting human solidarity.

In order to mold Gordon's Zionism to fit his comprehension of human history, Kohn overlooked one of the most important elements in Gordon's work—the centrality of the Jewish land. The connection to humanity in Gordon's thought emerged through labor on Jewish soil. Am adam thrives when the nation exists on its own land. Kohn exploited Gordon through his political idea of Judaism. As with his appropriation of Buber's work, Kohn focused on Gordon's mystical concept of humanity and ignored his prerequisite of connection to a particular people or place. The idea remained the distorting lens through which Kohn read nuanced theories of Jewish nationalism as clear declarations of a humanistic vision that mitigated cultural or religious differences.

Kohn's polemical efforts to synthesize Judaism and humanism can also be understood as a motivating factor in his groundbreaking research into Arab nationalism. From his arrival in Palestine, Kohn distinguished himself even from his Brit Shalom colleagues in his idealistic and unwavering commitment to addressing the Arabs living in Palestine.[63] The Zionist movement would have to make two crucial concessions in preparation for realizing Kohn's lofty aspirations: renouncing their calls for a Jewish majority and agreeing to a binational state. Kohn's letters fulminated against attempts to increase immigration so that a Jewish majority in Palestine might be obtained. He believed that the Arabs had no inherent antipathy toward the Jewish settlers; instead, they feared that the Jews would take over Palestine completely. If only the Zionists would limit immigration and recognize Arab national claims, the Arabs would embrace their arrival. Jews and Arabs would then build a binational federation with complete cultural autonomy under British protection.

In 1926, Kohn published a book called *Toldot hatenu'ah hale'umit ha'aravit* (A history of the Arab national movement). This book, one of the first on Arab nationalism in any language, let alone in Hebrew, documented the recent development of national self-consciousness of the Arab population in Palestine, Syria, Trans-Jordan, and Iraq. Kohn maintained that the Arabs constituted a primitive "Oriental" society whose tribal organizational structure, economic development, and legal statutes required Europeanization. In spite of the problematic expressions that plagued European nationalism, Kohn firmly believed that the Arab population had to pass through the stage of nationalism to gain the moral, economic, and legal lessons espoused by the European Enlightenment. Jewish settlers in Palestine, Kohn suggested, would shepherd the Arabs through this process toward a higher level of national consciousness. This symbiotic relationship, at least in Kohn's eyes, would not only spread harmony between two disparate nations, but would also bridge the economic, industrial, and political chasm separating the Orient from the Occident. Analyzing Arab nationalism served as a platform for Kohn to present Zionism as an integrating force of tremendous importance.[64]

Kohn's analysis was both prescient (Zionism did in fact catalyze Arab nationalism) and naïve (Jewish settlement in Palestine led to increased tensions between Jews and Arabs—although, to be clear, Kohn did believe that Jews would have to curtail immigration and remain a minority community for the envisioned cooperation to take place). From a historical perspective, the relevance of Kohn's engagement with Arab nationalism at this point in his career is twofold. First, his Orient-modernizing narrative, a topic that would remain a central theme in his subsequent scholarship on nationalism, developed out of his efforts to support a vision of Zionism as a humanistic enterprise. He had a vested interest in highlighting the rapid development of nationalism in the Middle East to validate Zionism. Zionism's mission was contingent on a parallel process of national renaissance in the region (later in this chapter, we will return to the ways in which this idea played out in his subsequent dichotomy between civic and ethnic nationalism). Second, Kohn's explanation of Jewish nationalism's role as a modernizing force in the Middle East integrated tropes of European Orientalism and colonialism. He borrowed aspects of the European civilizing mission to explain Zionism's role relative to Arabs in Palestine and the Middle East. In 1925, for example, he commented, "it will take many years of education work in many fields until the Arab nation can find its place among the cultured nations of our time."[65]

One also needs to mark important differences between Kohn's affinity with European views and the category of Orientalism as defined by postcolonial theorists.[66] First, Kohn himself decried European colonialism, especially its deleterious and deadly effects in Africa. Second, his view of the

East was not completely negative. Kohn, following Buber's lead, had credited the ancient Oriental civilization with imbuing Judaism with a number of its fundamental characteristics. He viewed aspects of Eastern culture, specifically the organic communities, as models for correcting the individualism of Western societies. Third, Kohn also lacked the political will-to-power that postcolonial scholars such as Edward Said argued motivated the construction of European Orientalism. Kohn claimed no metropol, or imperial state, that he hoped to see profit from his venture in the Middle East. With his insistence on allowing only a small number of Jews to settle in Palestine, he clearly had no claims to any sort of colonialization program. Furthermore, his goal was not to enslave or persecute the Arab population in any way.

Kohn's published and personal writings indicate that he remained deeply motivated by a utopian impulse to act in this world to end the moral inequality and political egoism generated by nation-states. Moreover, the civilizing mission (shared with other Zionists such as Kallen and Zimmern) was complicated by Jewish intellectuals' own perception of alienation and outsider status. Aligning Jewish nationalism with European civilizing force normalized the Jewish people by demonstrating their own ability to integrate into the status of an elite racial, ethnic, or national group within a ranking system that increasingly marginalized Jews. One effective path up the ladder of colonial hierarchies was to adopt the very logic of classification against the standard of European civilization used to disenfranchise Jews as not ready for citizenship within the European context. Counterstate Zionists exhibited a complex relationship to colonialism and imperialism that demanded more analysis than other expressions of European Orientalism.

Palestine as the Model of the State of Many Nations

Kohn did not leave his idealist hopes for Zionism, and its role in facilitating the interaction of East and West in Palestine, to theoretical scholarship. He also explored the potential political structure of a binational state in a series of articles that appeared in the socialist Zionist paper *Hapo'el hatza'ir* in 1926.[67] Kohn envisioned the future "political shape of the Land of Israel" as a society that would recognize cultural, religious, and linguistic differences and encourage cooperation and tolerance between different groups. The government of Palestine would take the form of a multitiered, binational federation, roughly organized around a canton system. Since the majority of villages, cities, and regions in Palestine already had divided populations, the local inhabitants would democratically elect representatives. Above the local political structure, Kohn proposed two "general autonomous institutions" (*mosdot ha'otonomi'im*) that would concentrate on developing national social and cultural life. These institutions would operate independently and would have the power to control personal, religious, and civil law, to oversee education, and to tax citizens. A democratic national council would serve as the liaison between these institutions and the British authorities. The British would retain the power to supervise foreign policy and security.[68] Kohn hoped to adjust the political realities of Palestine to match his high expectations for the realization of the idea in Palestine by using this complex formulation for ensuring productive coexistence between the two groups.

For Kohn, this model of a binational state in Palestine was not an exceptional political compromise, forced by the demographic reality of a large Arab population. Instead, it was to serve as the vanguard of a federative model of internationalism that would usher in a transition from a world divided into national states to one organized by states of many nations. Moreover, these national groups, exemplified by the Jews, would retain cultural autonomy across geographic and political territories. Thus Kohn demanded an "interterritorial solution to the Jewish question" that strongly affirmed the national status of Jews as minority citizens.[69] Unlike Ahad Ha'am, Kohn did not see the preservation of the diaspora as a fact, but as part of his global vision of national solidarity. "When Ha'am partially said yes to the exile," Kohn wrote, "he did it out of weakness of the unbelieving, out of lack of consequence. . . . When we say a partial yes today, we do it with belief in the creative power of the entire people."[70] Kohn's decentered vision of Jewish national culture resembles the vision Rawidowicz was developing at this moment. However, Kohn did not see the existence of national centers around the globe as a way of preserving Hebrew culture. He did view Zionism as a model of multinational existence that demonstrated how integration was not tantamount to assimilation.

There are a number of possible sources for Kohn's interest in multinational federations as a political model. One approach, explored by the historian Yfaat Weiss, is to link Kohn's interest in binationalism to his exposure to the multinational Hapsburg Empire of his youth.[71] Kohn had witnessed the possibility of creating a federation of nationalities in the context of the multinational Austrian Empire, where various successful attempts at national autonomy had taken place (certainly an explanation that would apply to Rawidowicz, who had been born into the multilinguistic backdrop of late imperial Russia as well).

While Kohn's formative experiences should be taken into account, it is also worthwhile to note that he began to identify his understanding of a federation of nationalities with the British model of a commonwealth and internationalism. During the mid- to late 1920s, a strong anglophile tendency emerged in Kohn's essays. For instance, the "Commonwealth of India Bill" serves as the blueprint for Jewish and Arab autonomy in Palestine, England exemplifies the "minority country that supplies humanity to the world," and Great Britain should remain in charge of foreign policy and border policing.[72]

Even though Kohn saw the limitations of imperialism, he also believed that the nation-state was not an option. This left him with little choice: only a supranational power could ensure political order and secure collective rights outside of national sovereignty. Some variation of imperialism remained the only alternative to the inconceivable options of demolishing national solidarity or seeking a Jewish nation-state. Such a system would recognize the practical and moral necessity of separating political power from the development of national culture. Caught between the exclusivism of nation-state nationalism and the risk of imperialism's excesses, Kohn sided with the later, imagined as a benevolent and ethical imperialism.[73]

The synthesis of Zionism and forms of internationalism based on a supranational political power (especially the British Empire) was not atypical, or limited to Zionists who had grown up in the Central European context. The promise of an international federation based on the British commonwealth paradigm appealed to counterstate Zionists discussed earlier in the book, specifically Zimmern, Kallen, and Kaplan. From Kohn's correspondence, we can conclude that it is highly likely that Kohn was aware of Anglo-American Jewish intellectual circles, especially conversations in the *Menorah Journal* discussed in chapter 2.[74] There is evidence that Kohn read *Zionism and World Politics* (Kallen's 1921 book critiquing national sovereignty and highlighting the promise of internationalism) and knew about Zimmern's essays on nationalism and the British internationalist's 1920 translation of Buber's lectures (the same ones that had such a profound effect on Kohn in the second decade of the century) into English. These connections between intellectuals indicate affinities and even shared conversations about the implications of Jewish political thought for interwar political organization.

Within a few months of each other, Kohn, Kallen, and Zimmern each attempted to introduce the lessons they attributed to cultural Zionism to wider audiences: their works included Kohn's *Nationalism: Concerning the Meaning of Nationalism in Judaism and in the Present* (1922), Kallen's *Zionism and World Politics: A Study in History and Social Psychology* (1921), and Zimmern's 1923 article in *Foreign Affairs*, "Nationalism and

Internationalism." All three thinkers understood (and shaped) the revival of Jewish nationalism and the ideas they attributed to their mentors, Ahad Ha'am and Buber, as "a general discovery of the being of Nationalism."[75] Zionism promised to normalize the Jewish people by ushering in an age of international federations and multinational states, rather than promulgating the identity logic of national sovereignty. This overlapping vision shared by Kohn (the head of propaganda for the Jewish National Fund in Palestine), Kallen (a leading American Zionist and an adviser to Judge Louis Brandeis, the head of the Federation of American Zionists), and Zimmern (the world's first professor of international relations and an adviser to the British government) reflect the capacious boundaries of interwar Zionism. In particular, Jewish communities in Palestine and the diaspora did not signify groups with opposing schools of thought, but necessary partners for underlining the possibilities of nation beyond state in a world of international federations. Ironically, as Kohn moved westward, his affinities with his earlier British and American Zionist contemporaries grew far less obvious. Yet the positions Kohn developed during this Zionist period in his intellectual development remained an anchor for his later scholarship.

The Idea of Nationalism

In 1931, at the start of his trip to America, Kohn lamented to his friend, the philosopher Hugo Bergman, from a Chicago hotel room: "But I don't like the USA and I don't really like the type of people here. I don't want to live here. Jerusalem is preferable for me."[76] Kohn's disparaging comments do not convey a particularly positive first impression for a man who would soon hail America as a "new type of nation, apparently without past or precedent, but endowed with a great future."[77] As these quotations suggest, Kohn did not immigrate to America out of ideological commitment or even a desire to live there. He could no longer support himself and his family after he left his job in the Zionist movement, and German publishers refused to print his articles and books when Hitler came to power. Kohn sailed for America with his wife and son primarily out of economic necessity.[78]

Kohn's attitude toward America changed drastically when he returned to the United States two years later as a new immigrant. A few months after arriving in New England, he admitted to Buber, "strange that I should call America homeland . . . that a new life begins in many aspects. In midlife: Vita nuova [new life]. . . ."[79] On both a social and emotional level, Kohn embraced his new life in the United States. America provided him with the academic position, financial wherewithal, and audience that he lacked in Palestine, where his scholarship and political activism had alienated him from mainstream Zionist circles. Kohn was particularly frustrated by his rejection for an academic chair in peace studies at the Hebrew University. In a letter encouraging Weltsch to follow him to America, Kohn admitted that he was tired of being a martyr for Jewish nationalism in Palestine.[80]

At Smith College, Kohn was extremely well liked by his students; he found publishers for his articles and books, and enjoyed a community that was similar to "the circle of friends he had found in Palestine."[81] He gained a sense of security and acceptance in America that he had never received in his forty years of wandering throughout Europe, Asia, and the Middle East. Kohn's burgeoning personal appreciation for the United States translated directly into his scholarship. He transferred the political transformation he fought for in Palestine into his new career as an American academic. This substitution of America for Palestine was evident in a letter to Weltsch. "In spite of all the problems," Kohn wrote, "there is no other land in which people endeavor towards liberal grounds. . . . Here it is possible and permissible, to educate a new generation in a new spirit. . . . Here there is hope that a new ideology can be successfully created. . . . In Palestine there is no hope."[82]

For Kohn, Palestine had failed to produce the new nationalism. America, however, exhibited the proper political potential and remained open to a new spirit. Kohn even invited Weltsch to join him in defining and spreading this new spirit in America; however, Weltsch declined and continued his work as editor of the German Zionist paper, the *Jüdische Rundschau*, and moved to Palestine in 1938. If Zionism would not support Kohn's idealization of Judaism, America would have to serve as Judaism's proxy. In less than a decade, Kohn would resurrect a generalized version of his understanding of Zionism's political mission as the idea of nationalism, with American nationalism embodying the former role of Zionism.

Backdrop, details, and context would all change dramatically. However, three areas remain that anchor Kohn's subsequent contributions to the study of nationalism: first, a counterstate definition that equates nationalism with an integrating force rather than a political or territorial boundary; second, an analysis based on the role of a particular national group that carries this concept of nationalism through each epoch in history; and third, a subtle but important contention that preserving national cultural distinctiveness outside of statehood strengthens human solidarity.

A close comparison of Kohn's most influential contribution to American scholarship, *The Idea of Nationalism* (1944), with Kohn's Zionist writings indicates that the new spirit exemplified by American nationalism was not new at all. Instead, the idea of nationalism echoed many aspects of his understanding of the political idea of Judaism and mirrored the concept Kohn had developed under the mentorship of cultural Zionists Ahad Ha'am and Martin Buber in Europe and later in Palestine. As the name of the book suggests, *The Idea of Nationalism* focused on the progressive evolution of an "idea-force" that manifested itself in models of political integration that transcended tribal, geographic, and religious boundaries. Through the ebb and flow of this idea in time, Kohn discerned the clear development of national groups that exemplified the integration of individuals around "a political idea, looking towards the common future that would spring from their common efforts."[83] The narrative suggested that the Enlightenment and early stirrings of seventeenth-century national movements signified the realization of these ancient yearnings toward unity. Despite the situation in Europe in 1944, Kohn retained his belief in a historical trajectory from tribalism to universalism.

The object of Kohn's historical analysis had clearly widened its scope from Judaism and Zionism to world history. Nevertheless, the approach paralleled his earlier texts, especially *Die Politische Idee des Judentum* and *Perakim letoldot hara'ayon hatzioni*, in its vocabulary, methodology, and content. The repetition of the language of the idea remained the most obvious link to Kohn's earlier efforts. Heavily influenced by the German intellectual tradition, Kohn viewed his role as interpreting, not chronicling, the significance of historical events. "The historian," Kohn later commented, "should represent on the one hand the consciousness, the self-awareness of an epoch or of a people, and on the other hand its conscience."[84] This approach demanded that Kohn imbue his vision of the past with his own historical schema for narrating the past and projecting it toward the future. His methodological emphasis on the historian's role in elucidating the particular nature of a period or people provided the key for understanding how Kohn discovered such similar ideas permeating different epochs. As long as his fundamental ideal of nationalism as the humanizing historical force remained his historiographical compass, he had to discover examples of its manifestation in the past.

Kohn also retained the paradoxical claim that true nationalism expresses itself through promoting solidarity with those beyond its particular boundaries. He had previously singled out Jewish nationalism as the primary example of this conception of nationalism. By 1944, Kohn equated the general category of national consciousness with what had previously been the foundation of the political idea of Judaism—"the love of humanity or of the whole earth."[85] National identity did not erect boundaries between people, but instead bridged the superficial and primitive claims of biological, cultural, and religious adherence. Nationalism, as the carrier of the idea of unity, galvanized populations to appreciate their human connections. In language that echoed his discussion of Gordon's am adam, Kohn summed up his "idea of nationalism" as follows: "Nationality, which is nothing but a fragment of humanity, tends to set itself up as the whole. Generally this ultimate conclusion is not drawn, because ideas predating the age of nationalism continue to exercise their influence. These ideas form the essence of Western civilization—of Christianity as well as of enlightened rationalism; the faith in the oneness of humanity and the ultimate value of the individual."[86]

Notice the new addition of Christianity and Western civilization to the basic concept of nationality and humanity familiar from his Zionist period. This important addendum reflected Kohn's effort to universalize the source of the idea and to make it palatable for an American audience. At the same time, he demonstrated a continued attachment to his own intellectual roots in the Jewish tradition, a tradition that continued to represent a critical stage in the development of the idea of nationalism. In "Israel and Hellas: From Tribalism to Universalism," the second chapter of the book, Kohn contends that Jews and Greeks were the only people of antiquity that had developed "an attitude of universalism and humanism which left behind it all difference of race and national civilizations."[87] This chapter commences with an analysis of the ancient Hebrews' understanding of covenant, humanity, and Messiah. These categories and the rest of his description of the Jewish understanding of the idea of nationalism closely resemble the description of Judaism in *Die Politische Idee des Judentum*.[88]

This similarity resulted from the fact that Kohn incorporated large sections of his previous work on Jewish nationalism into this classic study of nationalism. The most substantial differences between the pieces, written twenty years apart and for radically different audiences, lie in Kohn's attitude toward Hellenism. In the earlier work, Kohn used the Greeks as a foil to illustrate the merits of the Jewish idea. For example, he directly contrasted the Jewish conception of justice with that of the Greeks, whose conception he considered "far more limited," and he criticized the Greeks for making a distinction between themselves and the "barbarian" others.[89] By 1944, Kohn decided to include the Greeks as partners in the early evolution of humanistic nationalism. By updating the earlier text through eliminating sentences that explicitly presented Greek philosophy in opposition to biblical wisdom and adding a few paragraphs praising the later Greek tradition, Kohn included Athens in his narrative.[90] Clearly, he felt the need to universalize the origins of his Jewish political idea and to diminish the centrality of Judaism. However, these cosmetic changes only superficially altered his early thoughts and writings on Zionism.

Kohn made few other explicit references to the role of Judaism in *The Idea of Nationalism*. However, the historical teleology followed the progression outlined in his 1920s work. For Kohn, "the age of nationalism represents the first period of universal history."[91] By spreading concepts of universal justice, individual rights, and shared philosophical assumptions, the nation ushered its citizens toward higher levels of transnational integration. National sovereignty was only a temporary stage in the development of nationalism. The final stage of national identity eschewed cohesion based on political or territorial ties.

Kohn himself admitted this debt to his earlier formulations. "[The 1921 essay] 'Nationalism'," he acknowledged in the preface of *The Idea of Nationalism*, "contained already in outline form some of the main conclusions of *The Idea of Nationalism*."[92] Probably aware that few readers of his 1944 book would have the wherewithal or the interest to locate and read his German article, Kohn overlooked a fundamental difference. The 1921 essay concluded with the suggestion that Jewish nationalism, on the basis of its political tradition, would model transformative nationalism. In his later formulation, Kohn implied that Western nationalism, with Britain and the United States at the forefront, would stimulate a new world order. The Jewish mission persisted, but the centrality of Zionism faded away.

One of the most significant and lasting historiographical contributions of Kohn's *The Idea of Nationalism* constituted his distinction between two typologies of nationalism: the illiberal, ethnic nationalism of non-Western traditions and the liberal, Western, civic model. Kohn recognized that national groups shared certain linguistic, biological, cultural, social, or religious similarities as a result of living in proximity. However, he flatly rejected these criteria for national identity by claiming that these ethnographic groups may define tribes or clans but did not delineate national groups.[93] Politicians, historians, and intellectuals who gave absolute value to any of these criteria misled themselves and their followers by confusing irrational myths and primitive conceptions of reality with absolute political principles. These "ethnographic" groups masquerading as nations were in actuality merely ephemeral communities whose precise identities fluctuated throughout time.[94] Kohn demoted culture, language, and biology from unifying criteria to stumbling blocks to authentic nationalism.

One of the great contributions of Kohn's scholarship on the history of nationalism, which distinguished his work from that of his contemporary, historian Carleton Hayes, was a critique of such ties based on an analysis of the historically constructed nature of essentialist distinctions between various national groups.[95] Politicians and scholars who valued any of these criteria misled themselves and their followers by confusing irrational folklore and archaic conceptions of reality with absolute political principles. Kohn's theory of nationalism thus transposed the ideal type of nationalism from categories of descent to voluntary membership, from cultural identification to political will, and from organic unity to universal social contract.

When Kohn's more nuanced, Zionist-inspired critique of völkisch nationalism is taken into account, his apparent transformation is not as stark. As discussed earlier, Kohn's antipathy toward essentialized definitions of nationalism had deep roots in his Zionist writings. In 1919, Kohn (demonstrating his own conflicted relationship with Ahad Ha'am, whom he celebrated for introducing the idea of an ethical Judaism) critiqued Ahad Ha'am's notion of a Jewish spirit because it did not go far enough in affirming the dynamic nature of Jewish life. The unique aspect of the Jewish political idea for Kohn could be found in its universal orientation and ability to overcome particular cultural, historical, or religious identities. This same understanding of Jewish nationalism served as Kohn's paradigm for defining the Western nationalism of England, France, the Netherlands, and the United States.

Another parallel with his earlier work is the very concept of a dichotomy between good and bad expressions of nationalism. The opposing typology of nationalism—referred to as "Eastern European and Asian"—can be linked to Kohn's view of Arab and Oriental nationalism. Clearly, the distinction between Occident and Orient, as represented by Jews and Arabs in his history of Arab nationalism (*Toldot hatenu'ah hale'umit ha'aravit*), did not map directly onto the non-Western typology of nationalism that had made Kohn famous a few years later. Arab nationalism merely required European support to reach the next level of national existence. German nationalism, on the other hand, epitomized an irredeemable theory of nationalism, the antithesis of Western nationalism.

Yet once Kohn left Palestine and Hitler took over Germany, the problematic nation par excellence shifted westward from Arabia to Germany. The non-Western variety described in *The Idea of Nationalism* mirrored his critique of the tribal bonds in Arab society that had prevented the Arab population from embracing European Enlightenment values. The basic dichotomy of East and West, Occident and Orient, which was so central for Zionist intellectuals in the orbit of figures such as Buber, permeated Kohn's more mature work. For Kohn, Palestine served as the bridge between advanced political conceptions and primitive social organization. Jewish nationalism, based in this critical location, would catalyze rapid growth in Eastern nationalism toward the Western model. The specific geographical location diminished in importance for Kohn; however, the fundamental mission of Jewish nationalism remained to transform nationalism from tribalism to universalism.

America, Kohn's New Canaan

Before immigrating to the United States, Kohn exhibited a Eurocentric disdain for what were perceived as America's inferior cultural and political characteristics. A series of published and unpublished critiques in the 1920s of America as emphasizing economic success, parochial interests, and assimilationist tendencies reflected this unflattering perception.[96] By the time he published *The Idea of Nationalism*, however, Kohn presented the country in a very different light. America, or "the new world," emerged as the carrier of the historical idea of nationalism Kohn had developed two decades earlier in Palestine. He posited, "One thread runs through the history of the New World from its beginning to the present day: to be a new Canaan for those who wished to throw off the yoke of Egyptian oppression, to seek the haven of liberty in escaping authoritarianism."[97]

References to America as the promised or holy land have clearly resonated throughout American intellectual history. Kohn could have been appropriating his language from these traditions; however, the direct link with Kohn's intellectual biography made these references to Canaan and Jewish history particularly significant. Still attached to the geographic and mythical vocabulary of Jewish nationalism, Kohn used this imagery to convert the United States into his new Canaan. American nationalism permitted him to continue dreaming about the possibility of creating the form of national integration and freedom he had failed to achieve in Palestine.

As the reference to America as a new Canaan suggested, American nationalism increasingly took on the role previously assigned to Zionism in Kohn's narrative as the "idea-type" of collective solidarity. The clearest expression of the transformation of German Zionism to American nationalism is seen in Kohn's 1957 book, *American Nationalism: An Interpretive Essay*. Direct links to Judaism, Zionism, or the Hebrew political tradition cited in *The Idea of Nationalism* have been almost completely excised from this text (I discuss the one exception below). Instead, the source of American nationalism is said to have emerged directly out of English political philosophy, not the Bible. The American Revolution, Kohn argued, enabled the United States to realize the humanistic ideals of English nationalism. By rebelling against England, the colonists were actually fighting to implement the "tradition of rational liberties" that the English nation had created but failed to actualize fully.[98]

The new United States was able to overcome the rigid social hierarchy of European social life and create a country with levels of social equality impossible even within England. "In that sense," Kohn claimed, "the United States has been from its beginning, and is today, the frontier land of both the English tradition of liberty and modern Western civilization."[99] The American Revolution transferred the beacon of international light across the Atlantic.[100] By rising up in defense of universal liberty, the American colonists created the binding philosophy, the political idea, of a revolutionary nation. America constituted "a universal nation . . . in the sense that the idea which it pursued was believed to be universal and valid for the whole of mankind."[101]

Kohn wove an intellectual narrative documenting the development of American political thought that has different historical turning points and philosophical sources than his writings about Jewish nationalism. Nevertheless, the content of American nationalism and its role in history remains identical to the way he described the attributes of Jewish nationalism. For instance, the argument that the United States constitutes a "universal nation" directly reflects an almost direct translation of Gordon's am adam that Kohn highlighted as the culmination of Zionist thought in his earlier intellectual history of the movement into the key principle of American identity.[102]

Kohn's attempt to read his ideal of nationalism through U.S. history manifested the same weakness that characterized his earlier work. This dedication to tracing the idea through historical events and intellectual trends forced Kohn to avoid or reinterpret realities that deviated from his master vision for world progress. In a discussion of the rise of American nativism at the end of the nineteenth century, Kohn hesitantly admitted that "America did not escape this general [European] current although the radicalization of the intellectual climate did not go so far as in continental Europe."[103] The United States did diverge from the trajectory of its idea. However, he insisted, the minor deviation from its political idea paled in comparison to the ongoing distortion of the idea prevalent in Europe. Kohn refused to reconcile *The Idea of Nationalism* in America with the scars left by slavery and segregation. In *American Nationalism,* he addressed the "Negro-problem" by pointing to recent civil rights legislation and court rulings that further indicated the ethical progression of the idea.

This evaluation of the state of U.S. civil equality was particularly stark in comparison to Kohn's contemporary theoretician of American nationalism, Gunnar Myrdal. Unlike Myrdal, who coined the notion of "American

Creed" in 1944 as a corrective to the sorry state of race relations in America, Kohn traced U.S. history as the very model of his idea of nationalism.[104] By explaining fundamental moral flaws in the fabric of American life as "occasional aberrations" in U.S. history, Kohn kept his universal-oriented trajectory in place. He hailed America as the inheritor of the European Enlightenment project without acknowledging America's own penchant for racial, gender, and religious prejudice, suppression of minorities, and inequality. This historical account of nationalism appeared blind to the possible weaknesses of American political life that abounded in the past and continued to surround Kohn even up to the years of the book's publication. His "doctrinaire idealism," critiqued by Buber in 1929, continued to define Kohn's scholarship throughout his life.

At first glance, one major change between American nationalism and German Zionism in Kohn's work is his tendency to focus on cultural assimilation within the state, rather than on the preservation of minority groups or counterstate nations. Kohn's Zionism emphasized humanism and fulminated against the nation-state paradigm of nationalism; yet, following his mentors Ahad Ha'am and Buber, it also recognized the particular ties that bind national groups outside political or territorial boundaries. Kohn had no desire to turn Palestine into a melting pot, at least not in the immediate future. Palestine would serve as a model for human integration through building international relationships, rather than dissolving ethnonational solidarity. As discussed, Kohn dedicated considerable energies to constructing a system of government in Palestine that would recognize national autonomy.

In contrast to Kohn's writings in Europe and Palestine, his theory of American nationalism adopts the melting-pot idea to describe the country's success at integrating immigrants from diverse backgrounds. The melting-pot metaphor provided Kohn with a concrete example of America's commitment to humanistic nationalism. A discussion of the French-American farmer Hector St. John de Crèvecoeur, originator of the term, figured prominently on the first page of the book and remained a theme throughout. Kohn even dedicated a few paragraphs in his work toward supporting the immigration restrictions of the early twentieth century. These severe restrictions served as necessary measures to ensure that the melting pot had the "required time to operate."[105] Kohn also applauded legislation aimed at denying citizenship to those immigrants who might disturb the assimilation process of the American political idea.

Kohn's narrative emphasized America's success in integrating different religious, ethnic, and cultural groups around the idea of nationalism in a way that Zionism had never been able to achieve. A biting comment at the end of *American Nationalism* (the only explicit allusion to Jews or Judaism in the book) hinted that Kohn's strong rejection of particular cultural identification in American nationalism remained connected to correcting what he saw as the failure in Palestine. Kohn jabbed at his old Zionist comrades with the comment that "in spite of the call from Israel, few American Jews left their country to settle in a land where their ancestors probably lived two thousand years ago."[106] Instead, they came to America and developed a strong sense of belonging to the United States and the American political idea. The American idea of liberty has "proved a stronger national cement and a more secure basis for ordered liberty and economic prosperity than bonds of a common blood or religion or the uniformity of a closed society."[107] Kohn insisted that American nationalism would fulfill the role of transforming nationalism from primitive tribal bonds to enlightened political ideals. Ultimately, the United States succeeded in welcoming Jews and fulfilling the Jewish idea in a way that Zionism never could.

Kohn also made an explicit point of differentiating his concept of the American idea of nationalism from the most well-known opponent of the melting pot, Horace Kallen, whose concept of cultural pluralism advocated for the retention of ethnonational identity within the state. Kohn took Kallen to task for "practically demanding the introduction of the rights of national minorities as they existed in central and eastern Europe, on the basis of an ethno-linguistic nationalism unknown to the Anglo-American tradition."[108] This reading of Kallen's famous essay "Democracy versus the Melting-Pot" indicated that Kohn considered Kallen's claims threatening to the vitality of American nationalism. The fruition of the national idea, Kohn suggested, was at odds with the division of social or cultural life into particular national groups. Such a fragmentation threatened to undermine the primacy of individual rights by fueling ethnonational tensions.

Kohn's adoption of the melting pot as a term for describing American nationalism, and his discrediting of the notion of cultural pluralism, directly contradict his own earlier statements published in the Hebrew press. A 1924 *Hapoel hatza'ir* article denounced American Jewish immigrants invested in the "melting pot of the cultureless general Americanness."[109] Instead, Kohn insisted that the retention of national identity in general and Jewish solidarity in particular was important in the diaspora, as well as in Palestine. Kohn's specific language on the melting pot, and his awareness of a growing interest in Jewish topics by a group of intellectuals associated with the *Menorah Journal,* suggest that he read Kallen's "Democracy versus the Melting-Pot" and supported his vision of America as a nation of nationalities. Kohn's professed rejection of autonomous cultural or national spheres within the political idea represented a shift from his activism in Palestine, where he advocated the construction of autonomous national cultural communities in the Land of Israel.

Did Kohn make a clear break from his earlier views, especially around the question of the role of group solidarity in promoting ethical progress and humanism? If so, it would be quite easy to understand his hesitation to define America as a nation of nationalities. The stubborn refusal of ethnic, religious, and national bonds to dissolve their sense of solidarity undermined his vision for Zionism and peaceful integration in Palestine. Despite his idealistic blinders and tremendous faith in the power of the idea—the force that strips away differences by upholding the cohesive power of unity—Kohn had witnessed its limitations. The realization of the idea of nationalism, he concluded after witnessing a failed experiment in Palestine, demanded the eradication of particular solidarity, not national cultural autonomy.

Promoting counterstate nationalism threatened the universalizing trajectory of the idea of nationalism. Unlike Kaplan and Rawidowicz, Kohn no longer championed the paradoxical conclusion that national cohesion outside of statehood paved the way for human integration. America would avoid the error of Zionism by discouraging the retention of multiple ethnic, historical, and religious groups that might challenge the principles of liberal democracy as primary grounds of national cohesion. Jettisoning the theoretical contortions necessary to reconcile Jewish nationalism with universal integrationism—a logical inconsistency that remained unresolved in Kohn's Zionism—would have most likely brought welcome relief. Kohn would have been able to fully embrace the conclusion of the classic political thinker John Stuart Mill that ethnonational uniformity within the polity is a necessary condition for establishing and safeguarding liberal principles. In America, the cultural nationalist became a cosmopolitan humanist. Such a reading also fits well into Kohn's reputation as the founder of a civic nationalism that stands in direct opposition to ethnic, or cultural, varieties. Kohn, this narrative suggests, redefined American nationalism in direct opposition to the cultural basis he had championed during his Zionist stage.

"A Nation of Many Nations": Kohn's Enduring Commitment to Cultural Particularism

Kohn's apparent journey from being an advocate of ethnonational diversity within the polity to promoting the melting pot was not a complete reversal of his earlier position on the importance of national solidarity at a substate level. *American Nationalism* (and other writings from the last two decades of Kohn's life) includes a subtle counternarrative that nuances an association of Kohn with a level of complete assimilation suggested by the melting-pot concept. Indeed, comments throughout *American Nationalism* suggest a vision of diversity in the United States that was quite close to Kallen's nation of nationalities that Kohn described as "going far beyond anything envisaged by the American national idea."[110] Kohn retained a proclivity toward ethnocultural diversity within the framework of the state. The tension-filled link between particular cultural solidarity and universal political rights did not disappear in his work. It is Kohn's very ambiguity about the relationship between the particular and the universal that demonstrates the continuity with his similarly conflicted relationship with Zionism.

Only a few pages before rejecting Kallen's vision of America as a nation of nationalities, Kohn defined the character of America as "a land with open gateways, a nation of many nations," characteristics that "became as important for American nationalism as its identification with the idea of individual liberty and its federal character."[111] Indeed, the book's penultimate chapter, "A Nation of Many Nations," highlights the centrality of multiplicity in his concept of American nationalism. To support his claims about the importance of national diversity, Kohn cites one of Kallen's closest conversation partners, fellow Zionist Sir Alfred Zimmern. "The people of the United States," Kohn quotes Zimmern as writing, "awoke to the strange reality that, in spite of all the visible and invisible agencies of 'assimilation,' their country was not one nation but a congeries of nations such as the world has never seen before within the limits of a self-governing state."[112] A "congeries" implies a far less organized mix of national groups than the "federation of nationalities" language that Kallen included in his "Democracy versus the Melting-Pot."[113] Yet anyone familiar with Zimmern's writings on nationalism would have linked the comments about the congeries to his broader vision of creating commonwealths or federations of nationalities that would recognize collective groups and secure individual rights as the basis for international cooperation.

Kohn's enduring appreciation for the position that denounced assimilation and instead viewed national diversity as a necessary condition for the spread of liberalism is evident in his emphasis on British liberalism as the tradition he associated with the idea of nationalism.[114] Kohn's allusion to Zimmern as a "British student of nationalism" accompanied other direct references to British political thought as the bedrock of American nationalism. Kohn reminds his readers that, in opposition to the progressive public intellectual Randolph Bourne's concept of American nationality, "the foundation of American national life was not a new cosmopolitanism but the universalization of the English tradition of liberty." The anglophilic tendency in Kohn's discussion of liberalism represents a critique of homogenization and uniformity and an enduring yearning for a federated approach to international integration.

The British model (along with Swiss nationalism), he explained a few years later in his autobiography, "has set an example of an affirmative nationalism that emphasizes cohesive collective power, and yet is compatible with the preservation of individual liberty and a non-militaristic society."[115] Two models that occur throughout Kohn's post-Palestine career are the British commonwealth period and Swiss federalism—both examples of governments that recognized the enduring relevance of nationality outside of the state-seeking paradigm. They are precisely the two models that a number of interwar counterstate cultural Zionists, including Kallen and Zimmern, highlighted as the most progressive and ethical typologies of nationalism.[116] Kohn remained enamored with the models that served, in addition to his earlier interest in Zionist binationalism, as exemplars of nonstatist national autonomy within a multinational setting. References to Zimmern, Kallen, and Bourne—all active participants in debates about Zionism and internationalism in the early 1920s—suggest that Kohn's thinking about the United States remained shaped by the reference points and intellectual positions that advocated for the preservation of national identity in the United States, Europe, and Palestine.

Why does Kohn explicitly reject cultural pluralism as a pillar of democracy and liberalism, while integrating aspects of its message and even references to thinkers he must have known shared many of Kallen's views? One possibility is that Kohn viewed the United States as exceptional—a country that did not need to pass through the temporary stage of a federation of nationalities necessary for other political entities to reach a higher level of integration. I suggest an alternate possibility: Kohn intentionally downplayed his support for the preservation of minority groups. This move makes sense within the historical context within which he published *American Nationalism*. Written in 1957, the book was formulated immediately after the McCarthy era. Kohn's having experienced these official probes of "un-American" activities made him realize that this was a delicate moment to advocate for ethnonational diversity as a challenge to a unifying principle of U.S. nationality (especially for a Jewish thinker who had identified with socialist circles in the 1920s).

Kohn's critique of Kallen and his integration of the popular notion of the melting pot provided cover to make a muted argument against ethnonational conformity and to endorse a vision of pluralism within the United

States. Kohn strategically aligned the melting-pot concept with sharing common political ideals instead of cultural or ethnic ties. As a result, the outcome of social integration was not ethnic, religious, ideological, or cultural uniformity. The melting-pot concept in the political sphere left open, and even encouraged, preserving the collective consciousness of minority groups.[117] Kohn transvalued the melting-pot idea to more closely match his own idea of nationalism as unity through multiplicity, rather than uniformity. The distinction between political and cultural expressions as the basis for American democracy and nationalism was far closer to the distinction articulated in Kallen's classic "Democracy versus the Melting-Pot" than Kohn acknowledges.

Kohn's expression in his later work of nationalism as political, rather than cultural, seems to represent a complete reversal of his earlier position. Yet the value of cultural diversity, while certainly muted, remains visible in his formulations. It is evident in Kohn's ambiguous position regarding the role of counterstate national groups. Whether strategically thought out or unconsciously included as a reflection of his own internal ambivalence, this tension underscores an important dimension in Kohn's political thought. He is not opposed to cultural diversity; he is against nationalism that leads to a "distortion of perspective and to the over-valuation of the distinctiveness of national history and of national character."[118] This is a subtle distinction, clarified by viewing Kohn in the larger context of his lifelong sense of allegiance to the Zionism of Buber and Ahad Ha'am.

Kohn's association of nationalism with liberalism, universalism, and civic principles does not entail cultural uniformity. Nor does the replacement of tribal ethnonationalism by political civic nationalism imply the elimination of groupness and cultural diversity. Universal political ties uniting citizens of the state and the preservation of particular cultural ties are not either/or positions.[119] Collective attachments, as the cultural Zionists had taught, promoted moral ends. Making this differentiation in his later work is crucial because it prevents the error of linking rejection of Zionism with a rejection of the importance of preserving groupness outside of statehood. This was Kohn's understanding of the lasting relevance of such thinkers as Ahad Ha'am, who taught that one could live "fully and freely only as a member of a nation."[120] Even though Kohn describes Ahad Ha'am as "equal to Mill," he makes a clear distinction in the implications of Ahad Ha'am's liberalism as distinct from Mill's variety.

Cultural diversity across political and territorial boundaries was a key ingredient in preserving individual freedom. Gone from Kohn's references to Zionism are the references to "blood," but, at the same time, he shows far stronger appreciation for Jewish peoplehood, historical links, and religious community. Kohn's position on Ahad Ha'am in 1962 was even more sensitive to the need of preserving a particular historical and religious culture.[121] Ahad Ha'am's message—promoting a liberalism that recognizes, and even endorses, counterstate nationalism—remained relevant until the end of Kohn's career.

Kohn never fully resolved the tension between universal political principles and national cultural attachments. But his unwillingness to consistently distinguish between the competing outlooks represents a fundamental continuity with his earlier work and reflects the enduring mark of his efforts to square Jewish nationalism with humanism. The theoretical challenge of creating an inclusive, tolerant, and progressive paradigm of nationalism prevented the construction of a systematic reconciliation of particular and universal allegiances. Instead, the Zionist Hans Kohn and his internationalist alter ego Paul Colin tugged the cosmopolitan wanderer in opposing directions throughout his career.

A New Perspective on Kohn's Legacy

By the end of his career, in defining his ideals of Zionism and American nationalism Hans Kohn appeared to have taken intellectual paths diametrically opposed to those of Mordecai Kaplan or Simon Rawidowicz. Kohn's emphasis on replacing religious, ethnic, or racial concepts of Americanness with an affirmation of individual equality (as opposed to European ethnic nationalisms) contributed to a narrative of what it means to be an American. In contrast to Europe, the United States would promise its citizens an unprecedented degree of tolerance by promoting integration and dissolving "groupness."

The distinction between civic nationalism and ethnic nationalism generated a dichotomy that questioned the moral efficacy of national attachments other than those of citizenship and civic rights. Kohn's formulation of universal humanism as the basis for American nationalism in 1957 helped set the foundation for Jewish communal life in the United States as a religious minority group with full individual rights.[122] Kaplan and Rawidowicz sought narratives of liberalism and nationalism that would empower American Jews to imagine their own collective status outside the limited personal sphere of religious creed. Ironically, Kohn's integration of a stream of German Zionism committed to breaking the sovereign mold contributed to shaping a discourse that would suppress the possibility of Jewish collectivity by aligning patriotism and particularism.

Clearly there were other major differences between these thinkers. Kohn lacked the same attention to the experiential, day-to-day attributes of group life and national culture. His theory suffered from a relative insensitivity to the power that religious and cultural bonds hold over individuals. As a result, he considered it possible to externalize his own cosmopolitan ability to effortlessly travel between various linguistic and cultural worlds as a citizen of the world. His interest in national cohesion was primarily theoretical (the idea of collective ties) and instrumental (providing security against totalizing claims of nationalism). This difference certainly reflects the biographical contrast between Kohn, Kaplan, and Rawidowicz. From their formative years of studying Judaism with their fathers, both Rawidowicz and Kaplan developed strong personal and familial ties to Jewish life. This attachment nourished their enduring commitment to national boundaries even in the face of strong humanistic impulses that challenged the moral validity of particular preservation.

These emotional and psychological attachments to Judaism motivated an intellectual project to develop a concept of nationalism that also celebrated particular tribal differences as an integral component of fulfilling the Jewish political mission. As the child of highly acculturated Czech Jews, Kohn lacked the connection to Jewish traditions and Jewish community that anchored Kaplan's (and also Rawidowicz's) universal visions of Jewish communal life. Kohn lacked the historical pull, emotional attachment, or religious convictions that characterized the particular connections instilled in Rawidowicz and Kaplan.

But Kohn also expressed sentiments in the last fifteen years of his life that suggest an additional dimension of his understanding of Jewish peoplehood than the one implied by his legacy. Far from getting further detached from the question of Jewish nationalism as time passed from his earlier involvement in Zionism, Kohn reengaged with the Jewish nationalism that had shaped his formative thoughts. He tempered his own earlier declarations of rejecting Zionism (expressed in letters and comments written immediately after the painful process of leaving Palestine) with the insight that his subsequent scholarship owed a debt to his Zionist mentors. Kohn contributed articles to the *Menorah Journal* and *Commentary* on Zionism, Jewish nationalism, and Israel. He edited and introduced a volume of essays on Ahad Ha'am, and reprinted (with a new foreword) his biography of Martin Buber—the two Zionists who shaped his earliest writing.[123]

Writing for Jewish audiences, and through the mediation of discussing the intellectual history of Zionism, Kohn acknowledged the central role that Zionism had on his political thought. In a new 1961 edition of his

Buber book that notes that even though Kohn (he refers to himself as the "author") parted ways with Buber, he nonetheless acknowledges the impact of "this unique Jewish German teacher upon him and all the generation."[124] Two years earlier he had written an article in *Commentary* about the relevance of Ahad Ha'am that concluded:

> But there cannot be any doubt that this little-known Hebrew writer belongs in the age of nationalism to the small company of men of all tongues who in their unsparing search for truth and in the sobriety of their moral realism are the hope of the future. Perhaps none has expressed their attitude better than he did as far back as 1907 when few other men recognized these danger signals as clearly as he.[125]

The relevance of the prophetic, ethical Zionism promulgated by Buber and Ahad Ha'am did not dissipate in importance.

These later ruminations on Jewish nationalism shared noteworthy parallels to the ongoing efforts by Kaplan and Rawidowicz to reorient post-1948 Zionism. Kohn used the introduction to his essays on Ahad Ha'am to demonstrate the validity, and enduring relevance, of his 1919 call for an "interterritorial solution to the Jewish question."[126] Kohn commented: "Might not perhaps the 'abnormal' existence of the Jews represent a higher form of historical development than territorial nationalism? The Diaspora has been an essential part of Jewish existence."[127] Kohn went on to exhort:

> In both Israel and the Diaspora, the need to re-define this puzzling relationship, to insure that it neither becomes narrowly political nor degenerates into a vague sentimental attachment, has become increasingly pressing. Ahad Ha'am's type of compromise may someday be reached between the Diaspora's desire to be a free and equal partner in the making of modern Judaism, and a Zionist Israel's claim to historical and religious uniqueness.[128]

Kohn still believed in the value of affirming a Jewish peoplehood that transcended homeland and diaspora settings. His vision of Zionism in this 1962 piece envisions a type of Zionism not so radically different from the concept articulated in Kaplan's *New Zionism* (1955) and Rawidowicz's *Babylon and Jerusalem* (1957). All three thinkers focused on the disconnect between the theory of statist Zionism and the reality of Jewish peoplehood around the globe. Nation-state nationalism did not solve the Jewish question. Kohn, echoing Rawidowicz's concerns about the process of desacralizing the Jewish tradition, lamented that the Israeli-born youth "no longer feel any particular affinity with the Jewish past."[129] Even though Kohn framed his comments in the context of explaining Ahad Ha'am's position, his emphasis on a "free and equal partnership" implicitly rejected the center-periphery model advocated by the cultural Zionist (reflecting the same frustration Kohn had had with Ahad Ha'am since the 1910s).

The passionate connection that Kohn retained with the Zionists that inspired his intellectual journey suggests that, from his perspective, Zionism moved away from him far more radically than he moved from it. Despite Kohn's marginalization from the organized Zionist movement, he remained passionate about spreading his understanding of Judaism and its political message. As Kohn himself wrote about his teaching plans shortly after officially breaking with the Zionist movement, "I wish to give the basis for a deeper understanding of the eternal forces, of the spiritual and ethical values of Judaism."[130] Although Kohn felt that Zionism could not be the rightful bearer of the political idea of Judaism, he still believed that his interpretation of the Jewish political idea, shaped by the cultural Zionism of Ahad Ha'am and Buber, had an important role to play. Note Kohn's willingness to distinguish between his frustration with the direction of the Zionist movement and his enduring commitment to the thinkers and ideas he had associated with Zionism. While breaking from the former, Kohn would continue to align himself with many of the teachings espoused by the latter.

This bifurcated relationship to Jewish political thought reveals itself in Kohn's nuanced understanding of his relationship to Zionism, which is far more subtle than the assumption that his departure in 1929 signified a radical break. At various points in his post-Palestine writings, Kohn uses Jewish nationalism itself to represent both sides of the dichotomy between good and bad nationalism. He did not reject Zionism; rather, he rejected "the pseudo-messianism and modern nationalism [that] had gained the upper hand over the realism and the ethos of Ahad Ha'am's Zion."[131] Kohn continued to make a distinction that became less and less relevant as counterstate Zionism moved beyond the parameters of Zionism. There is a lot at stake for historians in considering to what degree Kohn's two careers (as a German Zionist and as an American nationalist) represent intellectual continuity or discontinuity. Figures like Kohn are the most difficult to integrate into Zionist history. Borderline cases, who might not have been so borderline in their own lifetime, raise questions about the ideological clarity of Zionism in the prestate period. Understanding Kohn as abandoning Zionism and going in a radically new direction reinforces a historical picture of Zionism neatly defined as a state-seeking ideology in all its pre-1948 expressions.

Kohn's case has an interesting parallel in understanding another émigré German Jewish intellectual, the influential political theorist and Zionist Hannah Arendt. As the Jewish historian Steven Aschheim has explained, until rather recently Arendt's intimate relationship with Zionism had been largely erased from the Zionist narrative as well as from the history of her political thought.[132] When Kohn arrived in America, he found in Arendt a thinker who shared both his passionate connection to Zionism and a frustration with developments in the yishuv. In the early 1940s the two worked together to prepare a volume of essays dedicated to Judah Magnes, one of the founders of Brit Shalom. They were both involved in the Judah Magnes Foundation, which promoted the ideas of Ihud, the organization that succeeded Brit Shalom in advocating for a binational state solution for Palestine.

Although Kohn was about fifteen years Arendt's senior, the two shared a similar path from German Zionism to American scholarship. Arendt never moved to Palestine; however, she became interested in Zionism in the early 1930s (precisely the moment that Kohn officially left the movement), as the Nazis rose to power in Germany. Her work on totalitarianism shared Kohn's critique of "tribal nationalism" and hailed the "decline of the nation-state."[133] Her liberal nationalism and critique of national sovereignty was, as the historian Amnon Raz Kotzkin has explained, integrally connected to her views on Zionism. "She developed her binational views as she thought about and wrote *The Origins of Totalitarianism*," wrote Kotzkin, "and should thus be considered as part of the same project, an attempt to implement the conclusions of her historical analysis in a concrete realm."[134]

Kotzkin's conclusion about the intimate relationship between Arendt's Zionism and her contributions to modern intellectual history (part of a larger trend in Arendt historiography to underscore the role of her Jewish experiences in her work) recovers the importance of considering ethnic concerns in the production of mainstream scholarship. Intellectual biography is crucial for revealing the personal experiences and intellectual relationships that shaped Zionist thinkers, even those who ultimately differed with the direction of the movement. A more expansive view of historical Zionism provides the opportunity to trace the far wider circles that Zionist thought touched, precisely among those figures whose concepts of Zionism needed to find alternate areas after Zionism marginalized their own position. Failed visions of Zionism developed into highly successful theories of nationalism, modernism, and political history.

Reintegrating Kohn's career has important normative implications outside of Jewish history in the field of political theory. The continuities in

Kohn's concept of nationalism correct a misconception associated with his legacy. Kohn is remembered for a sharp refutation of cultural nationalism. As a result, a number of recent works have been written partially as correctives to the dichotomy associated with Kohn's legacy. For example, John Hutchinson's study of cultural nationalism specifically attacks Kohn for engendering a deep scholarly antipathy toward cultural nationalism. Kohn undermined the importance and moral attributes of cultural nationalism, Hutchinson argues, by insisting that tribal or cultural bonds remained far less sophisticated grounds for national identity than the cosmopolitan premise of political nationalism. In opposition to Kohn, Hutchinson cites cultural nationalism's roles as "moral innovators" in the modern struggle for ethical progress.[135] Another sharp critique of Kohn considers his idea of universal progress as misleading and ultimately detrimental for achieving his own vision of equality.[136]

The legacy of the Kohn dichotomy between civic and ethnocultural concepts overemphasizes the categorical distinction between universal bonds nourished through citizenship and particular bonds that transcend state and territorial boundaries. Indeed, Kohn grappled with precisely the core issue of contemporary theories of nationalism—the yearning to understand the place of groupness within the liberal polity. His legacy got caught in precisely the choice he avoided (often by retaining contradictory claims) between cultural autonomy and integration, national chauvinism and universal humanism, diaspora and homeland, and liberalism and nationalism. It is a great historical irony that Kohn popularized the conceptual terminology that erased the ambiguities he upheld until the end of his life.

Associating Kohn's legacy with cultural humanism more accurately reflects Kohn's interest in reconciling what have become oppositional poles. Kohn did erode the historical legitimacy of certain assertions made by national groups—particularly those linked to territorial or biological claims. He did not, however, believe that retaining national culture and solidarity was antithetical to liberal principles or greater levels of human integration. Establishing an opposition between civic and ethnic typologies erases this crucial distinction in Kohn's thought.

If Kohn's legacy is connected to a dichotomy, it should be one that differentiates between counterstate and statist conceptions. For Kohn, counterstate nationalism was an important protection against the totalizing threat of national sovereignty, whether grounded in an ideology of universalism or particularism. Zionist thought, and the personal experience of alienation Kohn encountered as a Jew in early-twentieth-century Europe, left him with an appreciation for the limits of both liberalism and Romantic nationalism. Preserving a categorical distinction between nation and state, rather than blurring the lines between the political and cultural concepts, would ensure an appropriate balance between diversity and equality. Kohn, like Rawidowicz and Kaplan, understood Zionism as a framework for contesting the sovereign mold and affirming the morality of counterstate nationalism. The lessons learned from these three approaches to addressing the dilemmas of nationality are the subjects of the final chapter of this exploration of Zionism and the roads not taken.

6

Zionism, Jewish Peoplehood, and the Dilemmas of Nationality in a Global Era

In 1955, only a few years after the establishment of the State of Israel, Mordecai Kaplan lamented the absence of a "concept of a uniting bond which so far has not received official recognition, nor achieved general understanding."[1] In order to address this pressing problem, Kaplan urged those reading his book *A New Zionism* to heed his call for a future world conference that would agree on a particular category "as the appropriate one for the Jewish corporate entity to assume."[2] Unwilling or unable to settle on one specific recommendation, Kaplan proposed a number of possibilities, including "people," "corporate entity," "international group or fellowship," "transnational group," "spiritual organism," "ethical nation," and "national civilization."[3]

Why was Kaplan so desperate to introduce, and legitimate through a world conference, a new language of Jewish collectivity a few years after the creation of a Jewish state? Why not speak of Jewish nationalism or Zionism as the key terms for describing Jewish unity in the new age of statehood?

The establishment of the state left Kaplan deeply conflicted. Until the United Nations passed a resolution in 1947 calling for the establishment of a Jewish state (and even throughout the War of Independence), statehood was not certain and the ideological parameters of Zionism remained malleable. The signing of the Israeli Declaration of Independence presented a major obstacle to the hope that Zionism would introduce a radically different model of nationalism, a new political program, into the world. Kaplan, and other theoreticians of Zionism who had pioneered alternate collective boundaries (such as shared language, religious folkways, and civic principles) now had to contend with a plot of land and national sovereignty. The conceptual vocabulary of Zionism as it was now understood would no longer provide enough ambiguity to highlight the unique political mission of Judaism as a national civilization.

As a result, Kaplan needed to alter his strategy for disarticulating nation and state as the universal message of Zionist ideology. Only by distinguishing state-seeking Zionism from his counterstate variety could Kaplan realize his vision of reconfiguring the relationship between Americanism and Judaism and between Jews living inside and outside the borders of the State of Israel. Thus, despite the title of his book (*A New Zionism*), Kaplan's conception of Zionism was not new at all. What was new was his perceived need to differentiate his own understanding of Jewish nationalism from the now victorious state-seeking paradigm. The struggle to theorize appropriate terminology to preserve national status for Jews (as well as the centrality of the Jewish homeland) as Zionism's association with sovereignty solidified occupied him for the rest of his career.

Broader historical trends further compounded Kaplan's search for a new language of Jewish collective identity. World War II eroded the remnants of multinational empires that had continued to maintain political control of diverse populations through the so-called mandate system. Moreover, the economic and political influence of the Cold War superpowers reinforced the doctrine of national sovereignty as the dominant organizing principle of international relations. States, supported by one of two superpowers, exerted political control over their own populations and muffled the nationalist claims of ethnic minorities. These forces further eroded the analytical distinction between nation and state. Without conversation partners in American and European political thought, Kaplan not only had to alter how Jews thought about national identity, but also had to confront the greatly constricted meaning of nationalism in political thought more broadly.

As fellow proponents of the ideal of counter-state nationalism, Kohn and Rawidowicz also experienced similar moments of recognition that the roads they envisioned Zionism taking—namely, working toward the distinction between nation and state—had been blocked. Their interwar visions of a third road in Jewish life, one that navigated between national assimilation in the diaspora and national autonomy in the homeland by formulating boundaries of Jewish national membership as a form of cohesion distinct from political bonds and territorial boundaries, could not bridge the historical and ideological ruptures of the mid-twentieth century. But few others shared their concerns. No meeting to find a vocabulary for the "Jewish corporate entity" ever took place. Few practitioners cared as deeply as they did about theorizing nation beyond state in the 1950s.

Would it make sense to convene such a conversation today as the correlation between nation and state has once again become increasingly blurry? Yes, this conclusion argues. Global Hebraism, national civilization, and cultural humanism decades ago addressed what remains a key question: What does national identity, or more broadly, a primary sense of solidarity and allegiance to a particular group, mean when disconnected from the purely political objective of self-government? In addition to anticipating many of the issues and strategies now being explored by scholars and politicians, these formulations of Jewish nationalism also reveal important weaknesses and limitations of the contemporary discourse of difference. Moreover, one specific strategy utilized by Rawidowicz, Kaplan, and Kohn for negotiating dominant categories of identity is still in use. All three contested categories of Western political thought by constructing theories of Judaism and Zionism. This program reveals a subterranean strategy in modern Jewish political thought that endures in the writings of a number of leading American Jewish and Israeli public intellectuals today. Finally, rehabilitating global Hebraism, national civilization, and cultural humanism offers a diagnostic tool and sample road map for considering a new language of Zionism and Jewish peoplehood that meets present realities. Before addressing these issues, let us return briefly to Rawidowicz, Kaplan, and Kohn to explore the insights gleaned by analyzing the fate of their legacies in Jewish and non-Jewish thought during the second half of the last century.

What Happened to the Roads Not Taken?

Rawidowicz would have sympathized with Kaplan's call to introduce new language for defining the "Jewish corporate entity." As discussed in chapter 3, Rawidowicz expressed his terminological concerns directly to David Ben Gurion by denouncing the prime minister's decision to name the new state Israel—a choice heavily influenced by Ben Gurion's need to link nationhood and statehood (whether or not Rawidowicz would have been interested in attending Kaplan's conference is another question. I imagine he would have still considered Kaplan far too much of an adapter of the American concept of religion and not sufficiently committed to the diaspora as a complete equal to Jewish life in Palestine to have joined Kaplan's plan for a conference).

Prime Minister Ben Gurion, even with the duties of running the young country, took time out to write a handful of responses to Rawidowicz indicating his firm belief that Israel was in fact the appropriate name for the state (see chapter 3). Other than the retort directly from the prime minister,

Rawidowicz's opposition to the name of the state fell on deaf ears. Few today would even realize that the name of the state was ever up for discussion, let alone an ideologically charged decision with repercussions for what it means to be a member of the nation of Israel.

Rawidowicz's decision to leave the final chapter of *Babylon and Jerusalem* unpublished indicates that by the 1950s he already recognized that his questions about the state's legal efforts to limit the Arab population were touching an emerging communal taboo. Rawidowicz conceded that his own ideal of holding Jewish theories of nationalism to the same standards regarding minority populations was already far outside the parameters of either an Israeli or American audience.

But Rawidowicz was less willing to acknowledge that it was not only his particular criticism of the new state that marginalized his views. Indeed, *Babylon and Jerusalem*'s vision of a Hebrew-speaking, textually rich Jewish culture with centers in the homeland and diaspora was itself completely out of synch with the ideological direction of American Jewish and Zionist politics. For opposite reasons, both communities had deeply vested interests in aligning Jewish nationhood with statehood. The statist paradigm strengthened both communities' developing self-narratives as Israeli sovereigns and American Jewish subjects. Recognizing that the vast majority of the Jewish nation had no intention of moving to the new state, Prime Minister Ben Gurion responded by creating an ideology that overcompensated for the exceptional characteristics of Jewish nationalism,[4] and sought a term that more closely linked the state to the existential condition of the Jewish people.[5] The concept of statism affirmed that the state was not only instrumental for promoting national culture and integrating members of the nation, but was actually the most significant criterion for Jewish nationhood.

Why did the American Jewish community welcome Zionism's post-1948 ideological opposition to the concept of nation beyond state? Ben Gurion's pronouncements about the risks of diaspora life and the centrality of *aliyah* (immigration to Israel) certainly did not appeal to American Jewish immigrants, the majority of whom had no desire to leave the opportunities the United States afforded them. Nation-state logic did appeal to American Jews' interest in denationalizing Jewish identity. The more closely Zionism was aligned with the new state, and not with a national community in the diaspora, the easier it would be to assuage anxieties about dual loyalties and to promote a program of Americanization.

Focusing on the state normalized the construction of American Jewish identity in a second way. A recognized national homeland supported claims that American Jews had parallel experiences to those of other immigrant groups, such as Irish, Polish, and Italian people. Echoing the rhetoric of

Israel as homeland—despite the obvious fact that the vast majority of Jews had emigrated from European countries rather than from Palestine—bolstered the American–Jewish synthesis by facilitating the construction of an ethnic identity linked to a homeland.[6] Internally, support for the State of Israel as the center of Jewish national life provided another benefit as well: it became a symbol of the shared agenda of the community that galvanized philanthropy and collective ties among a diverse population of American Jews. Embracing a Zionism that rejected the notion of nation beyond state matched the ideological agenda of both models of Jewish life. Both American Jewish and Israeli leaders had a vested interest in defining Zionism through the logic of nation-state nationalism.

The legacies of Kaplan, Rawidowicz, and Kohn demonstrate the profound effect that these narratives had on shaping popular and scholarly memory in such a way that it erased, or domesticated, formulations of counter-state nationalism in modern Jewish thought. Of the three, Rawidowicz was least interested in compromising his position, especially on Hebrew language, in order to have an impact on a wider audience. As a result, his global Hebraism was firmly outside the parameters of either diaspora Judaism or state-seeking Zionism. Rawidowicz's considerable distance from either ideological pole left his reputation completely absent from both camps.

A more complex process of interpretation characterized the reception of both Kohn and Kaplan—two figures whose work was far too central to American Judaism and Americanism to ignore fully. However, their legacies have been cleaned up and reshaped to fit precisely the rigid categories of Zionism and Americanism they struggled to complicate. Kaplan's preeminence as the American Jewish religious thinker par excellence and his vocal support for Zionism erase his painful struggle with the definition of Jewish nationalism espoused by state-seeking Zionists and his keen interest in reforming American nationalism.

Kohn's reception was fashioned in the opposite direction. The ambiguity in his work between universal integration and particular solidarity chronicled in chapter 5 had little impact on the lessons learned from his scholarship. Instead, Kohn's success at replacing religious, ethnic, or racial concepts of Americanism with an affirmation of individual equality (as opposed to European ethnic nationalisms) contributed to a narrative of assimilation as the hallmark of liberal nationalism. Instead of confounding the dominant narratives of the American–Jewish synthesis or of American liberalism and civic nationalism, Kaplan and Kohn stand as paradigmatic examples of these ideological trends.

Interwar Zionism and Identity Politics Today

Assessing the shared quandaries that Rawidowicz, Kaplan, and Kohn faced and contrasting the responses they formulated reveal the dilemmas of defining, legitimating, and negotiating categories of difference that arise when what has become a fundamental assumption of nationalism—the one-to-one correspondence between nation and state—disappears. The theoretical benefit of the nation-state paradigm is its ability to provide concrete boundaries—such as citizenship, border controls, educational systems, cultural policies, and language requirements—that mark expectations of national membership. The nation-state model tends to diminish the relevance of maintaining more than one primary national allegiance. An individual can simply be categorized as a member or not. Identifying grounds for national cohesion beyond the material characteristics typically underscored by the doctrine of national sovereignty compels theorists to identify grounds of solidarity outside geopolitical criteria. But what cohesive grounds delineate the boundaries of national membership beyond these concrete features?

One of most interesting aspects of Zionists seeking to define nation beyond state is their pioneering effort to grapple with this question. Their theoretical challenge was compounded by the need to differentiate between Jewish nationality and other potential categories of group difference, such as religion and race. The process of translating the imprecise grounds of what it meant to be a historical member of the people of Israel failed to clearly match the established categories of Western political thought. Nationality, at least in the minds of Rawidowicz, Kaplan, and Kohn, had semantic elasticity that mirrored geographical diversity, complex connections to the Jewish tradition, and commitments to the particular and universal. Thus, all three theories sought hybrid categories sensitive to diverse components of collective identity formation. For instance, they grappled with finding theoretical vocabulary to explain psychological allegiances, sociological attachments, and dimensions that could not be neatly divided into religious, cultural, or ascriptive categories.

In articulating substitute conceptions, Rawidowicz, Kaplan, and Kohn faced a language and logic problem: how to reconcile the positions they regarded experientially as compatible with categories that regarded their conflicting yearnings as incompatible. They responded by attempting to alter the logic of national cohesion. This logic, especially as seen in dichotomies such as religion versus nation, diaspora versus homeland, and human versus particular allegiances, remains deeply embedded in the discourse of nationalism and liberalism to this day.

Indeed, these categories continue to make it difficult for Jewish thinkers to define collective boundaries that negotiate the poles of autonomy or assimilation. The fact that Jews remain exceptions from categories of collective exceptionalism indicates the enduring dominance of racial and territorial criteria for articulating the grounds of difference. This is not merely an issue for Jewish thinkers and leaders seeking a language for describing Jewish collective solidarity. It also highlights a much more general bias that fails to fully address the ties that bind communities not based around these limited criteria.

With the ascendancy of multiculturalism, ethnic identity, and criticism of cultural homogeneity, interest in rethinking the boundaries of groupness has grown dramatically. Ethnic studies have expanded the narrative of American history in important ways. However, Jews' perceived position of privilege and racial integration places the Jewish case on the boundaries of ethnic studies and the history of American pluralism. Trained during the 1960s and 1970s, the founders of ethnic studies justified the new field by mapping hierarchies of power within the United States and giving voice to disenfranchised communities. By the 1970s, American Jews had reached a mainstream position. Because of this success, identifying the Jewish case as exceptional helped distinguish the new field of ethnic studies from mainstream American historiography.

Defining group identity through oppression, race, and class has been a way to correct for historical mistreatment among minority groups. But the tendency to focus on categories of identity as formulations constructed to control or categorize certain populations severely limits the ability of scholars and practitioners to justify grounds for solidarity other than victimization or resistance.[7]

Scholars such as David Hollinger, Werner Sollors, and Kwame Anthony Appiah have attempted to conceptualize group boundaries beyond the racial paradigm so dominant in scholarship and public discourse today. But Jewish collectivity once again finds itself in an awkward position vis-à-vis models that advocate for "post-ethnic" groups formed by voluntary engagement rather than descent-based criteria. In Judaism, there has always been a tradition defined by both descent (through maternal line) and consent (conversion). The Jewish case falls through the cracks of ethnic and multicultural studies: Jews are too well integrated into the mainstream for consideration as a minority group, but too attached to descent models for inclusion within the post-ethnic conceptions of difference.

There is a parallel problem raised by the specific criteria for collective preservation and national identity proposed by one of the leading scholars of multiculturalism, Will Kymlicka. Kymlicka, a strong supporter of minority rights, draws a clear distinction between immigrant groups and groups whose territory has been disposed by an occupying power. Although the latter may demand self-government, the former groups are expected to integrate into their new homelands. Substantial differences may be socially and legally tolerated; however, the ties that bind immigrants or religious groups to one another remain secondary to patriotic uniformity. This is a definition that does not apply well to the Jewish case, characterized by a population divided by geography and language.[8]

Neither, surprisingly, do Jews have a clear place in the new field of Diaspora Studies. Whereas immigrant Jews are too landless for Kymlicka's model, American Jews' associations with the State of Israel leave them on the margins of Diaspora Studies. Diaspora Studies has grown rapidly in the last decade as a result of the tremendous interest in understanding the identity construction of increasingly robust stateless communities. Diaspora constructions of identity tend to be defined in contrast to those engendered by state models. Diaspora has come to represent identity grounded in ethical bonds rather than state power, and geographically dispersed networks rather than territorial homelands.

By defining itself in opposition to nation-state nationalism, diaspora is actually the flip side of assumptions about nationalism.[9] The binary construction of diaspora theory as the antithesis to national sovereignty thus paradoxically limits the construction of diaspora to the very discourse it attempts to overcome. Even scholarly usage of the term diaspora is actually a reflection of the same logic that creates a distinction between homeland and periphery. This rubric leaves Jews perceived as linked to Zionism's nation-state identity, rather than identities of stateless and disenfranchised populations.

Making the case for Jewish boundaries between national autonomy and assimilation is quite difficult even at this moment of great interest in diversity. On the one hand, Jews face the same challenges as other groups in justifying particular preservation outside territorial and political boundaries. The critique of essentialism and tribal allegiances undermines the historical and moral basis for retaining particular solidarity. Yet Jews face an added challenge. Categories of otherness that have moved into mainstream scholarship and popular discourse to address the particular concerns of certain groups, largely those linked by racial or geographic bonds, do not apply to the Jewish case.

Global Hebraism, national civilization, and cultural humanism suggest four ways to think differently about difference that would more accurately reflect Jews and the increasing number of other groups whose collective identities will endure despite challenges to their historical narratives. New conceptual possibilities will continue to become more important as historical forces lead more groups to confound the rigid categories of difference still based on racial and territorial distinctions.

First, the unmasking of essentialist claims that associated particular characteristics with each national group does not necessarily erode collective consciousness. The historical turn in scholarship has contributed to a severe critique of static collective boundaries or essentialist claims. This trend undermines the validity of delineating collective borders and advocating preservation of particular communities. Decades before the historical turn, and the consequent analysis of nationality as historically constructed, imagined, and invented, Kaplan, Kohn, and Rawidowicz challenged notions that groups' identities are constant, pure, and distinct.[10] Their awareness of this issue can most likely be traced to two factors: direct experience of the exclusionary tendency of essentialist definitions of nationality, and a long-standing intellectual commitment to historicism. Jewish political thought, each contended, exemplified the possibility of balancing between fixed and dynamic characteristics. Kohn established nationalism as the corrective to descent-based definitions. The centrality of evolution in Kaplan's description of Jewish national civilization and Rawidowicz's interest in hermeneutic communities linked by dynamic interpretation rather than established boundaries demonstrate both men's attention to this dilemma. All three arrived at a parallel strategy: the particular spirit that defines Jewish collectivity is the process of dynamic change.[11]

As a systematic justification for national preservation, this paradoxical definition of dynamism as the essence of Judaism has serious limitations. But it demonstrates a desire to create a theoretical framework capable of establishing the importance of national cohesion above other attachments (such as citizenship or geographic proximity) and disabuses primordial claims of changeless characteristics or fixed criteria of membership. The lived experience of primary collective attachment has little to do with the collective's historical truth claims or the degree of acculturation, blurring clear distinctions between groups that claim unique genealogies. Global Hebraism, national civilization, and cultural humanism suggest the moving of nationalism studies beyond deconstructing the historical validity of nationalists' claims. Studying the Jewish experience demonstrates the importance of evaluating the political role that constructions of nationalism actually play in negotiating the relationship between majority and minority populations, the psychological reality of particular allegiances even for cosmopolitan intellectuals, and the enduring social power that collective allegiances hold on individuals.

Second, religion has the potential to sustain primary allegiances across nation-state boundaries. One of the clearest aspects missing from conversations about nationalism, ethnicity, and multiculturalism is religion. Many political theorists today minimize the role that religion plays as a fundamental element in imagining national identity.[12] Despite the increasingly political, social, and cultural role that religious communities play in today's world, the enduring and robust ties that religious communities create are largely underappreciated within debates about the politics of difference.[13] The marginalization of religion is even more apparent within the discourse of nationality, which rarely considers religion as one of the primary criteria defining national consciousness. The hesitancy to fully take into account the potential cohesive power of religious traditions illuminates a limitation in Western political thought's dichotomy between religion and nation. Religious traditions, such as Judaism, have the potential to construct cultural, social, and legal norms that promote bonds of solidarity that transcend personal creed, voluntary associations, and territory.

The theory of national civilization reflects Kaplan's interest in blurring the categorical boundaries erected to distinguish between religion and nationality. He championed religion not only as the unifying criterion of the Jewish nation but also as the determinative element in any national definition. For him, religion served as the basis for national identity because he felt that religion fuels a far greater sense of shared identity than models that rely on territorial cohesion or descent. The rigid dichotomy between religion and secular nationality reflected Western political thought's compromise with the theological–political dilemma. The characteristics distinguishing these two categories, as imagined by political theorists of the time—private and public, this-worldly and next-worldly, coercion and voluntary, secondary and primary—failed to match Kaplan's experience of Jewish collective identity. In reducing religious communities to voluntary groups unified by private creed and moral education, religious bonds lose the power of coercion and the possibility of demanding primary allegiance from their constituents.

Rather than opposing categories, Kaplan posits religious traditions as the cohesive core of national groups. This use of religion reflects his desire to reconfigure the theological–political underpinnings of modern Jewish thought and political thought more generally. Instead of accepting a separation of church and state, Kaplan saw the coexistence of parallel religious civilizations. By bridging religion and nationhood in this way, he demonstrated that the separation of religion and nationality into distinct categories, with the latter creating more powerful cultural and political ties, was a rather arbitrary division that failed to match religion's claims in many social, political, and cultural aspects. At the same time, he internalized the limited role of religion that he struggled to overcome. Judaism as a religious civilization could at best expect its members to submit to voluntary coercion.

The overlapping rather than mutually exclusive relationship between religion and nation in Kaplan's thought anticipated the lasting force of religious communities as consequential challenges to the nation-state's authority. The specific path that the fusion of religion and collective ties would take, however, has not developed as Kaplan predicted. His civilization model augured an increasing link between religion and nationhood that would affirm the cosmopolitan, pluralistic, and constructed nature of both categories of group identity. However, in overcoming the dichotomy created following the Enlightenment, an illiberal model of religious ties has erupted to challenge the dominance of nationality as a primary allegiance. Kaplan deeply underestimated the role that a commanding, antimodern, and particularistic God would play in fracturing the theological and political compromise that had been worked out in the eighteenth and nineteenth centuries. Considering religion as an integral component in galvanizing collective solidarity complicates efforts to synthesize liberalism and nationalism. Yet, to ignore religion's cohesive power, which transcends race, citizenship, and space, undermines nationalism's ability to address an increasingly critical basis of individual allegiances to minority communities and transnational groups.

Third, territorial models must be replaced by global conceptions of national networks. Diaspora Studies itself remains too integrally linked to the sovereign mold to consider the possibility of erasing the concept of center-periphery based on geography. Neither position fully escapes the assumptions of the sovereign mold: one must either accept its assumptions or define itself in direct opposition to those assumptions. Although the conceptual vocabulary for considering nationality is quite large, the possibility of a nationality that views diaspora and homeland as *equal* participants in the national drama remains a neglected area of study.

Counterstate Zionists, particularly those adhering to the theory of global Hebraism, offer another approach that more accurately reflects the interconnectedness rather than the unidirectional movement of social, intellectual, and political networks. Rawidowicz rejects a categorical distinction between homeland and diaspora as a false dichotomy. Space and territory contribute to national membership. But he also affirms the possibility of creating such spaces in multiple locations that eschew hierarchies based on center and periphery criteria. This model of heterogeneous, fluid, and local communities, rather than a fixed territorial center, offers a conception that has few analogues in contemporary political theory. The spatial dimension of national cohesion does not necessarily reflect an all-or-nothing choice between total national life in the homeland and attenuated national cohesion in the diaspora. Collective cohesion can be experienced, as it was by Rawidowicz, through more local and permeable boundaries. Acknowledging the links between homeland and diaspora communities is necessary for formulating an organizational principle of collective identity.

Finally, one must reconsider the link between liberalism and nationalism. The tension between these was not avoidable for counterstate Zionists writing during the interwar period. Nationalism held out the promise of collective recognition for Jewish minority populations, but also the threat of promoting exclusive loyalties among the host population that could undermine Jews' individual rights. Conscious of both audiences, all three thinkers constructed Jewish political thought on a precarious theoretical foundation that affirmed national solidarity as a primary allegiance for Jews, without relying on grounds of national inclusion, such as coercive criteria or ascriptive characteristics that might jeopardize liberal principles.

Rawidowicz, Kaplan, and Kohn developed a basic strategy for rationalizing this somewhat precarious theoretical position: Jewish nationalism has always distinguished itself by espousing a particularism dedicated to promoting equality and tolerance. The national mission of the Jewish people was paradoxically rooted in the shared commitment to individual rights, universal equality, and free choice of associations. Jewish particularism stood on the vanguard of progress toward higher degrees of individual autonomy and freedom from discrimination. Following this logic, Western theories of liberalism and nationalism would have to adapt to more closely reflect the Jewish model of ethical nationalism.

Rawidowicz and Kohn shared Kaplan's conviction that national partiality was fully compatible with an allegiance to humanity. For all three men, their sense of Jewish national cohesion was intimately linked to their passion for addressing human concerns. The centrality of bridging the universal and particular through theories of national solidarity is evident in the key terms they introduced. Rawidowicz's right to be different, Kaplan's ethical nationhood, and Kohn's idea of nationalism all focused on the juxtaposition of universal ideals (rights, idea of ethics, and civic duties) as fully compatible with particular allegiances. This synthesis is one that liberal political theorists remain hesitant to adapt. Zionism's exploration of nation beyond state anticipated one school of communitarian thinkers who have tried to justify collectivity not through concrete boundaries of territory, descent, or language, but through the moral efficacy of collective solidarity.

Global Hebraism supported the compatibility of liberalism and nationalism by critiquing the association of universal rights with universalism. Rawidowicz viewed the preservation of the particular web of relationships nourished by national bonds as a necessary component of individual decision making and freedom. Highlighting language and interpretation as the basis of national membership made his conception of boundaries permeable and dynamic enough to avoid the exclusivist claims of illiberal nationalism. Language and textual immersion provided a robust apparatus for uniting individuals, without building impermeable or coercive boundaries. Rawidowicz's strategy failed to take into account the erosion of the linguistic fabric of collective life in the United States, however.

National civilization operated in the middle of the spectrum, in what scholars now tend to call liberal nationalism or liberal multiculturalism. Yet Kaplan struggled with a central conclusion articulated by subsequent theoreticians: the severe restrictions on the internal authority of minority groups to erect cultural or social signs of distinction. As discussed above, the contemporary political theorist Will Kymlicka, for instance, has rejected national rights for immigrants, and the nationalism scholar David Miller has eschewed any efforts of "radical multiculturalism." Miller cites Jonathan Sacks, the chief rabbi of Great Britain whose book *The Dignity of Difference* advocates for tolerance of religious differences, as his example of minority communities making "unrealistic demands upon members of the majority group."[14] Similar to immigrant groups, as opposed to colonialized populations or oppressed racial groups, Jews fall into a category that even theories of multicultural citizenship and liberal nationalism have a difficult time granting anything more than a public sphere free of discrimination. Kaplan's move to national civilization may also have been influenced by the knowledge that within the logic of immigrant acculturation, religious traditions have a much clearer claim on maintaining a distinct status than other markers, such as homeland, language, or specific cultural practices.

Kaplan fell into a bind symbolized by the blurred boundaries between patriotism and cultural or social autonomy. There is no reason that a definition of ethical nationhood should be defensive about acknowledging the embrace of a particular language, culture, or even legal system. Yet the forces of cultural uniformity as the measure of political unity continue to dominate liberal theories of minority rights. Kaplan may have had a better appreciation for the psychological power of cultural and linguistic retention among immigrants than those writing about ethical nationhood today. As global demographic shifts continue to accelerate, communications and travel improvements allow groups to retain a strong sense of interconnectedness. Kaplan's pushing the acceptable limits of cultural difference within the rubric of individual rights suggests the development of more robust theories of multiculturalism that encourage particular ties and recognize separate rights for minority groups.

Is this a sustainable balance? At the end of a century that has seen nationalist rhetoric fuel expansionist territorial claims, aggressive programs of homogenization, and even ethnic cleansing, the morality of nationalism, and especially religious expressions, remains a subject of much debate today.[15] Is it possible to argue that collective cohesion engendered principles of toleration and equality? Can one be a member of a particular group and remain committed to the liberal principles of individual rights and equal opportunities?

The Kohn dichotomy between ethnic and civic nationalism has been interpreted as providing the theoretical basis for answering these questions with a resounding no. Yet although Kohn did as much as any other modern scholar to solidify the dichotomy between particular and universal, he himself was deeply ambivalent about their absolute opposition. Kohn's conclusion can be read as a cautionary tale about reifying the very delineation between civic and ethnic typologies of nationality that he introduced. On a personal level, the civic and ethnic were integrally linked and shaped his scholarship. His own experience as an intellectual able to simultaneously publish theories of Jewish nationalism in Hebrew and international socialism in French demonstrates that formulations of collective cohesion and universal integration coexisted quite amicably for interwar intellectuals. Kohn's biography may ultimately have far more to teach about the compatibility of an enduring connection to a particular group and a commitment to humanity than his theoretical musings on a clear dichotomy between ethic nationalism and civic nationalism.

"Make Room for Us":
Jewish Concerns and the Shaping of Nationalism

One of the most noteworthy lessons gained from analyzing global Hebraism, national civilization, and cultural humanism is the opportunity to better understand the relationship between Zionism and mainstream conceptions of American identity and theories of nationalism. Particular formulations of Zionism were calibrated to shape the meaning of key terms to make space for Jews within the discourse of citizenship and nationalism. National civilization, global Hebraism, and cultural humanism should not be read as formulations attempting to overcome their proponents' multiple allegiances, geographic dislocation, or conflicting attitudes toward the state; rather, these theories negotiated, legitimated, and normalized them.[16]

Thus, Jewish intellectuals did not passively translate Judaism into the existing social and political spaces delineated by the state, concepts of liberal democracy, or expectations of American nationalism. Zionist thought has to be understood not only as the emulation and internalization of dominant paradigms of identity formation but also, counterintuitively, as a calculated strategy for resisting and reshaping external categories. Marginal voices motivated by ethnic concerns thus played an integral role in constructing the mainstream discourse of Americanism and narratives of nationality more generally.[17]

The fluid interchange between Jewish concerns and specifically Jewish and specifically non-Jewish theories of collective identity allows a more complex appreciation for the ways in which Jewish thought is shaped by external categories permitted to Jews as minority groups in the United States or citizens of a Jewish state. We can also see more critically how mainstream counterproposals have reflected the perceived needs of the Jewish community.

But why respond to these perceived limitations in notions of American political thought and launch complex negotiations about the meaning of minority collective recognition within the state by theorizing about Zionism or Jewish political thought? Turning to the sources of Judaism is not the most obvious path toward advocating for greater space within the sociopolitical framework of the host country. Rawidowicz, Kaplan, and Kohn each had the training, interest, and opportunity to contribute to general political theory without writing directly about the Jewish case. Despite their ability, and at times their interest, in writing directly for a non-Jewish audience, these thinkers (including Kohn, at least until he moved to the United States) opted for a strategy of subverting mainstream political thought through the specific lens of Judaism.

As noted within the preceding chapters, as much as global Hebraism, national civilization, and cultural humanism claimed to emerge directly from Jewish sources, in reality each theory imputed various ideological positions and existing political vocabularies to Judaism. Challenging the parameters of American nationality or augmenting the boundaries of Jewish solidarity was far from a declaration of separatism or a rejection of the existing paradigms. Indeed, the gravitational force of the desire for integration kept each theory tethered to the language and assumptions it ultimately hoped to subvert. At the same time, Jewish nationality is portrayed as the exemplar of the next stage in the development of nationality. This creates an effective straw-man position that can resist dominant theories of nationality by universalizing the Jewish experience.

Would anyone outside the Jewish community have paid attention to a book on Jewish civilization as a serious work of scholarship on nationalism? Rawidowicz's and Kaplan's inability to gain even the attention of the Jewish community as political theorists indicates the difficulty of finding an effective balance between highlighting and erasing Jews as an alternate model of national cohesion. Kohn's successful penetration, and the absence of Kaplan or Rawidowicz from considerations of the evolution of American national identity or pluralism, also reflects this reality. Ultimately, Kohn was the most successful at translating his vision of Jewish nationality into public and scholarly debates. Yet his intellectual commitment to the Jewish political tradition is only visible to readers aware of his earlier work or cognizant of his placement of Jewish and Greek nationality as the progenitors of what he considered the idea of nationality. To gain mainstream acceptance, Kohn understood, Jewish intellectuals must downplay specifically Jewish concerns and present their work as addressing general issues. This leads to a counterintuitive strategy for those intent on promoting Jewish political thought as a vehicle for outlining additional space for Jewish concerns within the liberal state: the optimal path to make room for us, it seemed to Jewish intellectuals like Kohn, is to write *for* and *about* them.

This subterranean strategy—explored decades ago by Kaplan, Kohn, and Rawidowicz to varying degrees of success—has created an enduring stream of modern Jewish political thought. This stream of thought can be observed among the disproportionate number of American Jewish and Israeli political theorists whose Jewish concerns are evidenced by their strong desire to bring Jewish political thought to a larger audience. The explosion of interest in Jewish political thought among scholars indicates a parallel quest for a new conceptual vocabulary of Jewish nationalism in the theoretical literature.

Political theorist and public intellectual Michael Walzer provided a glimpse into this rarely acknowledged phenomenon when he was asked in 2006, "How does your interest in Jewish political studies relate to your other research?" Walzer joked that he found Jewish studies an excellent "escape" from the "endless business of studying John Locke." He then continued: "All my writing about group attachment, cultural pluralism, and the different 'regimes of toleration,' is, whatever else it is, an effort to develop and defend a picture of the political world that makes room for us—specifically, for a stateless people."[18]

Walzer's response suggests that the interwar intellectuals committed to remapping the relationship between nationality and statehood left a paradoxical legacy. The specific typologies of Zionism developed by Rawidowicz, Kohn, and Kaplan have been forgotten; however, the strategies they pioneered for addressing the dilemma of reconciling national and human allegiances have reemerged in new forms at the center of today's debates about identity formation. One of the primary vehicles for reshaping the landscape of sovereignty, nationalism, and citizenship is theorizing about the Jewish experience and its relevance to twenty-first-century scholarship and politics. Making the case for how and why liberal societies can be more sensitive to preserving minority groups is often argued by referring directly to Jewish political thought as an alternate paradigm of national cohesion. Walzer is part of a small, but highly influential, group of Israeli and American Jewish scholars seeking to disarticulate nation and state both inside and outside of Jewish studies. Walzer has played a seminal role in promoting this view through his editing, along with Israeli scholar Menachem Lorberbaum, a four-volume compendium of sources and commentaries that explore various aspects of Jewish political thought.[19] Walzer's stature in the field helped him assemble a group of well-known political theorists (including Harvard University professors Michael Sandel and Hilary Putnam, as well as political scientist and University of Pennsylvania president Amy Gutmann) whose participation in the project gives it unique validity. The compendium also gives validity to Jewish political theory as a tradition worthy of general scholarship.

The ambitious four-volume series, *The Jewish Political Tradition*, has gathered an unprecedented anthology of writings on this topic. The diverse selections, contextualized with commentaries by leading Jewish thinkers and political theorists, provide a counternarrative to the ineluctable link between centuries of Jewish political life and thought and statehood. The volumes highlight the rich historical examples of Jewish polity in diaspora communities, such as the existence of the Council of Four Lands that organized East European life for centuries. These sources demonstrate that Jews in the diaspora were in fact political actors who developed sophisticated strategies for preserving boundaries and communal polities outside of concrete spatial and political borders.

Walzer's explicit attempt to introduce the Jewish political tradition as a relevant paradigm is not a phenomenon limited to such explicit efforts. Indeed, parallel, yet slightly more subtle, examples of underscoring the unique aspects of Jewish history and collective solidarity can be found in the works of the disproportionate number of Jewish and Israeli intellectuals theorizing about nationalism, liberalism, and communitarianism. This cadre includes figures such as the author of *Liberal Nationalism*, Yael Tamir (known in Israel as Member of Knesset Yuli Tamir), leading communitarian advocates Amitai Etzioni and Shlomo Avineri, and nationalism scholars Chaim Gans, Leah Greenfield, and Aviel Roshwald.[20] These individuals, many with clear links to Jewish or Israeli concerns, play a leading role in developing vocabulary for categorizing shared identities, critiquing liberalism's focus on the individual at the expense of the collective, promoting theories of nationalism that recognize enduring ties of solidarity, and advocating for the pragmatic and moral necessity of nourishing distinct collectives within democracies. Linking these public intellectuals with mid-twentieth-century Jewish intellectuals and their theories of nationality raises fascinating questions about how Jewish concerns shape mainstream scholarship in ways that make space for stateless communities within liberal democracies.

What unifies this field of intellectual inquiry is a common interest in probing ambiguous areas that push the conceptual vocabulary of both nationalism and liberal political theory. In particular, these theorists erode core assumptions of national sovereignty by questioning many of the same dichotomies closely scrutinized by Rawidowicz, Kaplan, and Kohn, such as sovereign versus subject, homeland versus diaspora, and patriotism versus particularism. Jewish intellectuals formulate more expansive definitions of religion that blur the boundaries between national and religious solidarities and reconcile the invented and historically constructed nature of national solidarity with the preservation of group identity.[21] Another common thread is the implicit claim that the Jewish political experience is universally relevant as a model for collective cohesion as the forces of globalization accelerate the erosion of national communities within political boundaries.[22] The adoption of Jewish political thought echoes the efforts of Kaplan, Kohn, and Rawidowicz to normalize Jewish tradition by transforming its exceptional qualities into universally applicable models.

But why is there a resurgence of Jewish intellectuals interested in breaking the sovereign mold at a moment when the Jewish question has been resolved? Walzer's perceived need in 2007 to make room for us is a surprising echo of Kaplan's call almost a century earlier to make American democracy safe for Judaism. Surely U.S. democracy has proven itself quite safe for Jews since Kaplan penned his warning. Moreover, there are far more theoretical avenues for fragmenting the claims of national homogeneity than the interwar period during which Kaplan, Kohn, and Rawidowicz wrote. A rich discourse of multiculturalism, minority rights, and pluralism now exists to categorize groups and to challenge monocultural claims. Walzer's reference to Jews as a stateless people is also perplexing, now more than sixty years after the establishment of the State of Israel. Thus neither the explosion of interest in the politics of difference nor the establishment of a Jewish state has successfully addressed the question of Jewish collective membership in an age of two thriving, and fundamentally different, Jewish polities.

Although Jews are not the only stakeholders in this conversation, several characteristics of the Jewish population—such as the split between homeland and diaspora, the centrality of a religious tradition, the high degree of social and economic integration, and the categorization as white—marginalize Jews from the scholarly discourse of difference. The case of Jewish collective identity within the liberal state is doubly marginalized. First, American Jews do not fit the model of a diaspora community who emigrated directly from the homeland. Second, the Jewish experience does not fit clearly into rubrics of multicultural citizenship and ethnic identities.[23] Making space for Jews requires forging concepts of "otherness" that reflect these attributes. Jewish intellectuals bring specific concerns to debates about boundaries and identity formation. There is thus a theoretical bridge between Jewish thinkers' efforts to break the sovereign mold in the interwar period and American multiculturalism today. The formulation and promulgation of a Jewish politics of difference recognize Jews as a collective group in U.S. society, without the stigma and biases connected to marking specific groups as "other." Jewish political thought endeavors to formulate a politics of difference that is both more cosmopolitan and more particularistic than formulations proposed by other stakeholders.

The effort to bridge the human and the national represents a cosmopolitan multiculturalism with two seemingly conflicting agendas: on the one hand, Jewish intellectuals embrace liberal principles and democracy. Difference, they argue, is not a rejection of universalism, but instead is the most effective path for realizing Western political ideals. Finding universal justifications for the particular serves to engender the construction of fluid boundaries, such as religion, culture, and psychological attachment, rather than the potentially separatist categories of race or ethnicity.[24] At the same time, however, we can also notice the opposite trajectory—imagining more vigorous categories of difference that advocate for particular preservation. Communities with deep historical roots, including religious associations, have a legitimate interest in preserving more robust social and cultural networks. The boundaries of Jewish collective identity may be permeable, but they remain authentic, distinct, and reflective of how acculturated individuals continue to experience strong ties.

Historicizing the relationship between Zionism, Jewish nationalism, and Western political thought thus also sheds light on the subtle, yet consequential, relationship between ethnic concerns and mainstream identity categories. The historical strategy traced through this book of expressing Jewish concerns through general theories of nationality has defined the subsequent discourse of difference. Twentieth-century Jewish ideologies forged a largely undetected intellectual tradition that has shaped (and continues to shape) central narratives of national identity and citizenship. Students of American Judaism and American history alike might be surprised to find significant vestiges of Jewish political ideologies—often stripped and sanitized of their more separatist, idealistic, or explicitly nationalist claims—embedded in the writings of American Jewish thinkers and leading public intellectuals never explicitly connected with Jewish nationalism. Late-twentieth-century Jewish intellectuals, inspired by particular ethnic concerns, have had a decisive impact on the transformation from nation-state nationalism to multicultural citizenship. That Jews have largely been erased from a discourse they themselves pioneered and continue to shape is more than a historical irony. In reality, Jews' tremendous success at translating Jewish identity into the sovereign mold after World War II by creating American Judaism and Israeli nationalism has left them out of mainstream conversations about difference in the twenty-first century. This reflects the limited language of difference that characterizes scholarly and public conversations about identity today.

"What Will Become of the Jewish People?"

Since the late 1990s, the fragmentation of Jewish peoplehood has been perceived as a pressing issue in Jewish communal discourse. "What will become of the Jewish people?" was the topic of conversation at the United Jewish Communities General Assembly in 2007, which included the comments by A. B. Yehoshua that sparked the controversy discussed in chapter 1. A year earlier, sociologist Steven Cohen and historian Jack Wertheimer asked, "Whatever happened to the Jewish people?" in a provocative article lamenting an attenuated sense of collective solidarity among today's

American Jews.[25] Jewish and Israeli communal leaders drew up a covenant declaring the "enduring ties that bind" the two centers of world Jewry.[26] Most recently, the chancellor of the Jewish Theological Seminary, Arnold Eisen, highlighted the promotion of a sense of peoplehood as one of the primary goals of his tenure. There is a palpable anxiety about a diminishing sense of ties that bind Jews to one another, and a concerted effort to address what is perceived as a pressing issue in Jewish identity formation. But what does peoplehood mean and how is it measured?

Kaplan never succeeded in organizing a conference to define the language of Jewish collective organization. Yet he did succeed in contributing the term peoplehood that has gained rather widespread currency as the term for referring to Jewish solidarity and collectivity. However, his term has been adopted today without a historical consciousness of Kaplan's hesitancy about statehood and his desire to promote a theory of nationality compatible across the diaspora–homeland divide. As discussed at the start of the chapter, Kaplan proposed peoplehood to stand in for nationhood after his initial term became too closely associated with statehood. There is a telling historical irony in the fact that one of the primary barometers of peoplehood today is measured by interrogating diaspora Jews about their sense of connection to the Jewish state. This shift in the connotations of peoplehood—from an alternative to nation-state nationalism to a partial measure of American Jewry's support of the state—reflects a historical process that demonstrates the influence of the sovereign mold on both American Jewish and Israeli notions of Jewish solidarity. It is also another example of how Kaplan's legacy has been sanitized to reflect synthesis rather than fragmentation in the American–Jewish and Judaism–Zionism historical narrative.

Kaplan's interest in replacing, rather than emulating, the nation-state logic of post-1948 Zionism provides a fresh perspective for considering "what happened" to and "what will become" of the Jewish people. In rejecting the validity of nation beyond state as an organizing principle for Am Yisrael, Zionism actually contributed to the attenuation of Jewish peoplehood. Contemporary conversations about Jewish collective identity remain rooted in theories of peoplehood shaped by state-seeking Zionism, rather than conceptions made possible by clearly demarcating political citizenship from national consciousness. As a result, there are limited theoretical and practical resources to define the meaning of Jewish solidarity outside the terms established by Ben Gurion's statism and American Jews' acceptance of many of its fundamental tenets. To thrive, collective notions of Jewish identity must confront the primacy of the State of Israel (without fully negating its existence), affirm the value of diaspora consciousness in the construction of national culture, and posit alternatives to land and language as the sine qua non of Jewish nationalism.

The creation of the State of Israel and the state-seeking Zionism that crystallized in its wake engendered the creation of two distinct organizational structures for Jewish political life: hereafter, Jews would either constitute an ethnoreligious minority group in liberal states (America) or a sovereign nation within the Jewish state (Israel). This split reinforced a clear distinction in the cohesive parameters of Jewish identity. Citizens of Israel would possess passports with Israeli written under their nationality.[27] Their Jewish identity would be intimately linked to a civic religion, to the Hebrew language, and to patriotic defense of their homeland. American Jews, however, could voluntarily decide to affiliate with a Jewish community as a religious minority group. American Jewish and Israeli narratives of themselves and each other have actually contributed to increasing the rift between the two centers of Jewish life, thus retarding efforts to galvanize strong ties between diverse Jewish communities.

Zionism generated opposing identity constructions for immigrants to Israel and the United States, who came from similar places and shared exposure to the same range of modern Jewish religious and political movements. The process of acculturating into two distinct organizational principles offered by the sovereign mold—the dominant national population or a religioethnic minority in a liberal state—constructed hierarchies of values, identity categories, and communal narratives that had distinct and at times even mutually exclusive agendas. The very meanings of Judaism and Jews were refracted through these disparate lenses as well. American Jews, committed to understanding Judaism as a religion rather than as the basis for a national group, marginalized political elements of textual and historical tradition to emphasize the compatibility of Judaism with minority citizenship and ethical behavior. American Jews envisioned Jewish associations as voluntary communities built around religious institutions, thus championing an ethical creed committed to equal justice.

Zionist ideology formulated a definition of Judaism that emphasized national culture, language, a pioneering labor ethos, self-defense, and self-determination. Historians and politicians turned to biblical narratives to underscore precedents for statehood within the biblical tradition, eliminating two thousand years of political thought from relevance. Criteria for the new Hebrew national culture actively rejected characteristics perceived to be associated with Jewish life in the diaspora—religious practice, passive victimhood, and lack of control. These distinct typologies reflect a set of dichotomies already noted as by-products of the sovereign mold, such as nation and religion, diaspora and homeland, universal and particular.

There was a tremendous hesitancy to address the theoretical and practical wedge created by aligning each community with both sides of the sovereign mold. In fact, in 1950 two Israeli and American Jewish leaders, Ben Gurion and Jacob Blaustein, even made an agreement to disagree on the meaning of Judaism and Zionism. Ben Gurion promised to mitigate his rhetoric of aliyah and negation of the exile in exchange for the support of the American Jewish community. Given the historical circumstances, the decision to suppress prickly differences made sense at the time. After decades of tremendous dislocation, demographic transformation of the global Jewish community, and unprecedented persecution, both Jewish communities had a vested interest in focusing on bolstering their own situations rather than debating their ideological and practical differences. The immediate exigencies of building a state and securing the American Jewish position after the Holocaust justified suppressing unresolved issues. Moreover, the existence of close family ties and the euphoria of the establishment of a Jewish state that transcended ideological differences diminished the need to address such challenging questions.

Historical forces in the decades after 1948 reinforced the tacit contract to agree on the centrality of the sovereign mold but to disagree on the implications of equating Jewish nationhood with statehood. The Cold War—specifically its effect on the concepts of nationalism, religion, and America's policy toward Israel—contributed to the solidification of the unifying rhetoric and divergent underlying paths. The Jewish state gained legitimacy as the increasing control of two superpowers enforced the intimate link between nation and state around the globe, suppressed minority national voices, and reinforced the perception of an intimate link between citizenry, nationality, and state. For American Jews, the fight against "godless communism" united the Jewish community around viewing itself as a religious group and led to the disappearance of the diverse streams of secular, national, and socialist Jewish organizations that had thrived during the first half of the century.[28]

The pride American Jews felt about Israel as their homeland was boosted through the popular and political transformation of Israel's image in the United States. The 1960 film *Exodus* (starring Paul Newman) popularized the notion that Israel's founding reflected core American values of freedom and liberation as well as the drive to overcome oppression. A lightning military victory in the Six Day War, as the United States was facing its own morass in Vietnam, elevated Israel's military and moral status among

American Jews. As Israel became a central ally of the United States, the perception of the State of Israel as the national homeland of the Jewish people grew stronger. These developments legitimated American Zionism's claim (popularized by the Supreme Court justice and American Zionist leader Louis Brandeis throughout the second decade of the twentieth century) that Israel reflected America's highest values. Attachment to the State of Israel supported a narrative that emphasized unity, synthesis, and close ties rather than addressing the divergent paths, conflicting definitions of Judaism, and unresolved differences between the communities.

This shared acceptance of the slogan "We Are One" as the premise of Jewish peoplehood as reuniting the Jewish nation with political sovereignty masked systemic differences between these two organizational structures of Jewish life that would flower in future decades. Despite scholarly claims and social-scientific data sets demonstrating that the two centers of world Jewry—Israel and the United States—have developed "divergent Jewish cultures," leaders from both communities continue to articulate a strong rhetoric of unity.[29] Strategically ignoring these unresolved issues may no longer serve as an effective strategy for articulating the ties that bind the global Jewish community.

As the sovereign mold diminishes in import around the world, its effectiveness as the cohesive glue that binds Jews to one another will also likely decrease. The economic and social forces of globalization have eroded Israel's ability to control all aspects of Jewish national life, an integral part of Zionism's vision of mamlakhtiyut. Although present-day forces accentuate the divergent paths, they are merely symptomatic of the more systemic issue of diagnosing what happened to Jewish collective consciousness. Part of the answer to Cohen and Wertheimer's question is that the ideological assumptions of the sovereign mold, espoused by both American Jews and Israelis, hindered the development of a robust and global language for articulating Jewish solidarity. Although creative explorations of Jewish political thought have developed as a way for Jewish intellectuals to introduce ethnic concerns into the discourse of difference and national identity, they have not made nearly as strong inroads into Jewish communal life.

One area where cracks appear in this popular overlay of unity, revealing inner contradictions and tensions, is in the assumption of the centrality of the state in defining national consciousness. The center–periphery hierarchy between homeland and diaspora is one aspect of the sovereign mold that continues to shape American Jewish life. When teaching adult Jewish education courses about the Israel–diaspora relationship, I ask students to participate in an exercise. I hand out several short quotations about the nature of the relationship as written by historical figures—Ben Gurion, Ahad Ha'am, and Rawidowicz, as well as by such contemporary scholars as Jacob Neusner and David Hartman. I ask them to read, discuss, and then decide which perspective most closely reflects their own position. Some gravitate toward Ben Gurion's claim that the goal of Zionism is to make an end of exile, others appreciate Rawidowicz's model of the ellipse with two foci, and a few sheepish participants select Neusner's statement that the United States is the promised land for Jews.

But a significant number of my (American) students always look toward Ahad Ha'am's statement that "Zion is a cultural center radiating life-giving impulse to an ongoing Diaspora . . . a symbolic circle with a center in Israel and a circumference in the Diaspora." They see this view as the one that most closely mirrors their own. I tend to press them by asking a few questions: Have they visited Israel? Do they have any exposure to Israeli culture? Can they understand any Hebrew? Inevitably, a few have visited Israel; far fewer have extensively engaged Israeli music, literature, or film; and hardly any speak Hebrew with enough fluency to engage with Israeli culture outside of translations. In reality, Israeli culture is completely foreign to most American Jews. Nevertheless, they believe that Israel remains, at least in their conscious perception, the cultural center of their Judaism. Although this is only a tiny anecdotal sample, the results of this classroom exercise suggest the enduring internalization of Yehoshua's assertion that national identity can only thrive within the state. Despite American Judaism's tremendous accomplishments in various aspects of Jewish religious, cultural, and intellectual life, American Jews hesitate to acknowledge the United States as a Jewish cultural center.

The residue of Zionism's negation of the diaspora ideology is deeply ingrained in the self-definition of American Jews and reflected in the most visible projects in the American Jewish community.[30] Since its inception in 2000, for example, the organization known as Birthright Israel has sent more than 150,000 young Jewish adults (between the ages of eighteen and twenty-seven) on an all-expenses-paid, ten-day trip to Israel. This program is one of the most revolutionary and innovative developments in American Jewish life. It has reached a tremendous number of Jewish young adults at a crucial time in their development, provided them with the opportunity to visit Israel, and sparked conversations about Jewish identity. Yet the logic behind the program arises from a vision of Jewish solidarity that views the homeland as the catalyst for the survival of Jewish life in the diaspora. The rhetoric employed by such programs as Birthright Israel propagates the idea that Jewish experiences and Jewish continuity for diaspora communities require a shot in the arm of a pilgrimage trip to the state. Engagement with Israel arises from the perceived need to use it as an educational backdrop for diaspora Jewry's failure to sustain Jewish continuity.

A brief thought experiment will drive home the hierarchical connotations of associating a Jewish birthright with a trip to Israel. Can one imagine the response to funding a birthright trip for Israelis to visit American Jewish communities after their army service? Such a plan would appear absurd to Israeli and American Jews alike because it contests the unidirectional model of influence from homeland to diaspora. Having solved the question of Jewish identity, Israelis believe they have little to learn from American Jews (although they typically have a lot of interest in other aspects of U.S. society). Jewish life in the diaspora is perceived as irrelevant to the self-identity of most Israeli Jews. The mismatch, promoted by the educational systems of both communities, maintains at best a symbolic connection between diaspora and homeland communities that reflects the perceived needs of each community rather than a desire to develop mutual partnerships.

Despite its internalization, analyzing Jewish life through the prism of the homeland–diaspora dichotomy has limited precedent in the Jewish tradition and was not a foreordained development. Returning to the interwar period, and specifically to theories such as global Hebraism and national civilization, allows us to historicize the dichotomy between homeland center and diaspora periphery. Of the two theories, Kaplan's national civilization remained far more invested in the centrality of the homeland. Heavily influenced by Ahad Ha'am, Kaplan envisioned Zionism as a global movement whose success in Palestine would invigorate members of the Jewish civilization in the United States. He acknowledged that the realities of the American Jewish setting would limit its ability to compete with Jews in Palestine for national creativity. However, he attempted to distinguish between the possibilities for the culture center and negating Jewish life in the United States. Kaplan had great hope (and also felt many frustrations) for American Jewry and viewed possibilities for national culture in Palestine and beyond.[31]

Global Hebraism (perhaps the theory discussed in this book that remained most firmly rooted in an early-twentieth-century European milieu of linguistic nationalism) articulated an understanding of culture most relevant to a post-ideological age of hybrid identity formation. Rawidowicz exploited his textual and historical training to insist on the replacement of the homeland–diaspora model, rather than advocating Kaplan's modifications. There are two primary limitations of basing national identity on geography. First, the emphasis on spatial coordinates and political structure emerged as a way of weighting the validity of national life rather recently with the rise of Zionist ideology. Rawidowicz's work reminds readers that the closest categorization of place within Jewish sources, Babylon and Jerusalem, lacked the elevation of one territory over another. In fact, over time the Babylonia tradition entered the rabbinic canon, while the rabbinic literature developed in the Land of Israel largely disappeared. Moreover, other dichotomies not based on geography or political organization had far greater currency historically. Taxonomies for categorizing Jewish communities included language (speakers of Yiddish, Judeo-Arabic, Ladino, and so on), geographic origins (Ashkenazi and Sephardic), and religious traditions (Hasidic, Mitnagdic, and Musar).

More important than the recognition of the historicity of a center–periphery model are the potential limitations Rawidowicz highlighted of such a model to promote national life and reflect the reality of cultural development. The very concept of one center influencing peripheries, Rawidowicz argued, failed to capture the local, fluid, and temporal nature of cultural production. National culture, he insisted, could not be generated in one location and exported to other places. His perceptive analysis of the risks of Ahad Ha'am's hierarchy between diaspora and homeland suggests the possible corrosive effect of such an assumption. Cultural life, Rawidowicz insisted, cannot be imported or exported but instead must be developed locally. The nature of collective culture in America will therefore differ from developments in Israel or other geographies. The flow nourishing diaspora Jewish life through the cultural production of the homeland community will not answer local needs. Israeli culture cannot sustain Jewish life built on a foundation of voluntary membership and without the language resources to participate in Hebrew. His prognostication was correct: the Hebrew culture created in Israel has had almost no impact on American Jewish life. The vastly different demographic, political, and social reality of Jews living within an autonomous territory necessitates the existence of multiple national cultures. But Rawidowicz underestimated the enduring power of the idea of a center without actual social, cultural, or intellectual ties. Israeli Hebrew culture would thus not translate into American Jewish life; however, the very existence of such a culture could sustain collective solidarity among American Jews.

What relevance does Rawidowicz's analysis have today? Global Hebraism points to several strategies for minimizing the role that spatial and territorial considerations play in the construction of national cohesion. A basic principle is the promotion of local Jewish centers, rather than the outsourcing of American Jewish vitality to a distant homeland. The notion that Jewish culture thrives only in the homeland clashes with the reality that centers of Jewish culture exist outside Israel. The self-negation of Jewish vitality outside the state has the potential to obfuscate the existence of innovative cultural production. As a sense of solidarity erodes among American Jews, the logical response is to renew emphasis on a unifying center. Although such a strategy may have short-term advantages, over the long term it will only accelerate the attenuation of collective solidarity. The dissolution of a sense of peoplehood outside the homeland thus becomes a self-fulfilling prophecy as a distant center is conceived as the preserver of diaspora life and resources are directed to nourishing a culture that will have minimal relevance in the diaspora. Relying on a symbolic homeland disempowers local initiatives to galvanize sustainable models of communal affiliation. Moreover, it drains creative energy and financial resources that could invigorate local, self-sustaining cultural centers.

Recognizing multiple centers does not mean that Israel would no longer be an anchor point in the global Jewish community. As the home to the largest Jewish community, and in the not-so-distant future the majority of the world's Jews, Israel will surely constitute a core of Jewish life. However, there are no gated communities in a global world that produce, create, and sustain cultures. In a global era, spatial location has far less control on identity formation. Decentering national identity formation would facilitate the creation of subgroups within the national community that have parallel interests, rather than seeking a unified national culture that emanates from the homeland to the rest of the globe. Jewish nationalism in a global era can be imagined like a computer network—multiple nodes with a variety of paths connecting those nodes. Such a model not only disregards a geographic center, but also ignores a corollary assumption that the notion of center suggests—namely, the existence of a unified national culture.[32] The overlay of one particular master narrative or cultural center ultimately detracts from possibilities of unity. Rawidowicz's oft-repeated statement "the two that are one" reinforces this paradox about collective identity: collective cohesion is maintained only if local groups sustain a sense of larger community in particular fashions.

The primary advantage of moderating the state's centrality in constructing national culture is the possibility of facilitating mutual exchanges that bridge diverse expressions of Judaism. One of the most crucial subjects Jews in America and Israel can learn from each other is how to expand their rather limited conceptions of Judaism. When it comes to Judaism, the majority of American Jews and Israelis have little to say to one another beyond recognizing a shared history of persecution. This is a tragic by-product of the shaping of Judaism to meet the demands of the sovereign mold. A false dichotomy has developed between Judaism as a religious faith and Judaism as the basis of a secular national identity. The distinction, as discussed earlier, emerged from theoretical and practical forces that motivated both communities to create their definitions of Judaism based on historical and political expectations. Thus, American Jews after World War II embraced the mantle of a religious community, even if many of its members most likely viewed membership as transcending theological assumptions. And the creation of Israel's new Jew negated the perceived religious nature of diaspora Jewish life.

Jewish communities and institutions emerged that reflected these distinctions. American Jews built houses of worship, defined affiliation by membership in synagogue communities, and highlighted holiday observances and coming-of-age rituals as markers of Jewish identity. Religion in Israel, however, took two distinct paths regarding the relationship between religion and the state. For the majority of Israelis, Judaism became the basis of a civil religion that shaped the calendar and public rituals of the new state.[33] At the same time, Ben Gurion's status quo agreement in 1952 established Orthodox authority in all matters of personal status law in Israel. In all three instances Judaism was shaped, either directly or indirectly, by the state's expectations. In one case a secularized Judaism served as the basis of the cohesive national glue of the state, and in the other cases a depoliticized Judaism described a community fully compatible with the liberal state under the doctrine mandating the separation of church and state.

National civilization and global Hebraism viewed the religious–secular nationalists' vocabulary as a problematic distinction with limited precedents within Jewish sources. The distinction confounded their own experience of Judaism and formalized a categorical distinction between Jewish communities. Instead, both Kaplan and Rawidowicz invented terminology and conceptual possibilities that rejected these divergent interpretations of Judaism. As a sociologist, Kaplan recognized that social networks and communal ties would each play central roles in constructing group boundaries. The sovereign mold, as well as Western Enlightenment thought, polarized secular national and religious expressions of Judaism. From the Hebrew Am Yisrael—an ambiguous term that refers to a community with theological, cultural, tribal, and historical bonds—emerged a rather simplistic mode for interpreting Judaism into two mutually exclusive categories. Individuals grouped as religious Jews, a category that includes a spectrum of Jewish ideologies from ultra-Orthodox to Reform, often have less in common with one another than they might have with those considered representative of the opposite category of secular nationalism.

Despite Kaplan's and Rawidowicz's warnings about the danger of defining Judaism as either a religion or a nation, historical and ideological currents have reinforced very different definitions of Judaism. Building a sense of shared experience and collective attachment across the religious–secular nationalists' divide is a challenge that needs to be addressed. I believe putting aside the need to equate Judaism with either religion or secular nationality will encourage innovation in both communities. A program for global Jewish nationalism following the logic of Kaplan's and Rawidowicz's Zionism will catalyze these trends by promoting mutual learning opportunities. American Jewry can learn a tremendous amount about the possibilities for Jewish culture, including Hebrew language, through learning from the Israeli model. Sparked by trends in spirituality, Israeli Judaism would benefit from a concerted effort to share the innovations of liberal Judaism with a population that has very little exposure to this great innovation in modern Jewish life. Jewish national cohesion will benefit greatly from a shared interest in mining the sources of Judaism—from ancient to modern—as a set of shared materials to debate, create, and engage.

There are already signs that such changes are taking place. New Israeli institutions provide venues for Israelis to engage with the Jewish textual tradition. In the United States, vibrant Jewish cultural expressions are flourishing.[34] These changes will be slow, because they go against the grain of basic assumptions that have become second nature for both Israeli and American Jewish communities. However, blurring the religious–secular divide has the potential to reinvigorate both communities and build new bridges across the binary categorization that previous generations developed.

Perhaps the most enduring, yet difficult to address, rift preventing efforts to theorize Jewish collective solidarity is a fundamental divide between American Judaism and Israeli nationalism when it comes to the relationship between Jewish and universal concerns. American Jews, particularly the majority affiliated with liberal denominations, emphasize the universal liberal values of social justice, equality, and tolerance as the fundamental message of Judaism. Hence the concept of *tikkun olam* (repairing the world) is one of the most widely articulated definitions of Jewish values. From its origins in European cosmopolitan ideologies, Zionism (and later the State of Israel) saw itself as promoting universal and democratic values.[35] The realities of creating a Jewish state, however, created existential threats that made the practice of realizing the ideal of preserving both Judaism and democracy a complicated endeavor.

Although Kaplan, Kohn, and Rawidowicz sensed a potential conflict between the self-definition of American Judaism and Israel's deteriorating relationship with Arab minorities and neighbors before 1948, their concerns were largely ignored. The American Jewish community was able to fully embrace Zionism precisely because of the argument that the Jewish state espoused the same set of liberal values that American Jews had championed. Several factors have raised the tension between the two ideals—national and the human—in popular and academic circles. Israel's position as an underdog in a belligerent part of the world between 1948 and the 1970s has been challenged. A younger generation of American Jews, raised on pictures of Israeli troops in tanks patrolling Gaza and the West Bank rather than the Six Day War, experienced a clash between two narratives. The war in Lebanon and the First Intifada complicated the perception of moral clarity. Occupation and systematic restrictions on the collective rights of Arab-Palestinian Israelis have the potential to create a conflict between a commitment to Judaism's mission as spreading universal ideals and Israel's responses to policies.

Israel's increasing position as a flashpoint in popular and scholarly debates about the morality of nationalism further engenders rifts in theorizing shared grounds of Jewish national cohesion inside and outside the state. Liberal scholars and activists disproportionately select Israel to illustrate the limits of national sovereignty and the excessive power of Jewish lobbying groups. These claims have generally failed to evaluate Israel in a comparative perspective or to appreciate the ways in which other states disenfranchise certain populations by their national, religious, or cultural expectations. Nevertheless, it has become a politically charged moment to think about the limits of the sovereign mold as the basis for envisioning Jewish collective identity.

Theorizing a shared basis for Jewish collective identity cannot avoid this issue, but we must also recognize the explosive nature of raising difficult questions about the potential conflicts between repairing the world and maintaining a Jewish state. Kohn presented an excellent example of why engaging the relationship between the particular and the human is a risky topic to address. His focus largely shifted to creating nationalism centered solely on human values and the erosion of other particular bonds. His decision, based on the incompatibility of Zionism and his perception of Judaism as a force of integration and harmony, adumbrates one potential repercussion of opening this conversation. To this day, many cosmopolitan Jews in prominent intellectual positions have followed Kohn's decision.

It would be wrong, however, to let Israel's critics silence internal Jewish conversations about divergent, and even potentially conflicting, attitudes about minority rights and Jewish obligations toward non-Jews. Such an approach will ultimately create greater fragmentation in the Israeli–American Jewry relationship. A central component of Israeli life is debating the tensions between protecting the Jewish state and recognizing claims of its minority citizens and populations under the control of the Israeli government. These tensions shape the political and social fabric of Israeli society. Silencing debates about these strains distances American Jews from their Israeli counterparts, who live in a society that openly debates these questions.

Kaplan and Rawidowicz provide a middle-ground option for constructing theories of Zionism that look seriously at the potential conflicts between Jews as a minority community sensitive to individual rights and a majority community sensitive to security and preservation. Both men made controversial stands about whether certain policies of the yishuv or the state toward Arab minorities were justified.[36] Nevertheless, engaging different objectives did not lead them to reject Zionism or (once it was a fact) statehood. Kaplan and Rawidowicz grappled with how to reconcile principles and claims across very different political milieus. This is certainly a road that risks further alienating Jews from Zionism and the State of Israel. The price of ignoring a gap between commitments to social justice as a minority community and preserving the ethnonational identity of a state as the sovereign power may increase superficial levels of allegiance, but it will also hinder a fully open and meaningful relationship.

The paths explored in this book provide fertile theoretical ground for rethinking Zionism's historical and normative possibilities. Rawidowicz, Kaplan, and Kohn mined the Jewish traditions to defend very different claims about Jewish nationalism than those that eventually determined its accepted meaning. While we may or may not agree with their conclusions, their visions remind us of the relatively recent and historically conditioned nature of what have become fundamental, and rarely questioned, tenets of Jewish identity.

Expanding our vision of the past to include the wide range of state-seeking and counterstatist varieties discussed in this book inspires a more pluralistic approach to reconsidering what it means to be a Zionist today. Indeed, the future of Zionism, and a sustainable model of Jewish peoplehood, depends on reengaging the basic principle of Zionism's roads not taken—the distinction between the Jewish nation and the Jewish state—as well as the accompanying questions of what boundaries can substitute for the state in defining membership in Jewish national life.

NOTES

1. Breaking the Sovereign Mold

1. From A. B. Yehoshua's speech given on May 1, 2006, at the American Jewish Committee's centennial annual meeting in Washington, D.C. A full transcript of Yehoshua's comments, as well as articles written by more than a dozen leading American and Israeli scholars and other leaders who have been moved to respond to Yehoshua's claims, are in "The A. B. Yehoshua Controversy: An Israel-Diaspora Dialogue on Jewishness, Israeliness, and Identity," available online at www.ajc.org.

2. For more information on Ben Gurion's ideology, see Kedar, "Ben Gurion's Mamlachtiyut"; and Eliezer Don-Yehiya, "Political Religion in Israel: Ben Gurion's Mamlachtiyut," in *Israel: The First Decade of Independence*, ed. Ilan Troen and Noah Lucas (Albany: State University of New York, 1995), 171. Pnina Lahav, "A 'Jewish State . . . to Be Known as the State of Israel': Notes on Israel Legal Historiography," *Law and History Review* 19 (2001): 387–88.

3. "The A. B. Yehoshua Controversy: An Israel-Diaspora Dialogue on Jewishness, Israeliness, and Identity."

4. See David N. Myers, "'Beyond Statism': A Call to Rethink Jewish Collectivity," lecture delivered at the University of Washington, October 10, 2006.

5. One important scholarly exception is a recent collection of essays edited by Deborah Dash Moore and Ilan Troen, *Divergent Jewish Cultures*.

6. My own interest in expanding the historical record of early-twentieth-century Jewish nationalism and Zionism builds on several recent studies. Steven E. Aschheim, in his *Beyond the Border*, has highlighted Zionists, such as Hannah Arendt and Hans Kohn, who challenged statehood as the primary goal of Zionism. For a more general discussion of the diversity of early-twentieth-century views on Zionism and Jewish nationalism, see Myers, "Can There Be a Principled Anti-Zionism?" Michael Stanislawski, in his *Zionism and the Fin de Siècle*, has focused on the surprising relationship between cosmopolitanism and nationalism in the works of several leading Zionists.

7. For example, see cultural theorist Stuart Hall's equation of Jews with Zionism

and his conclusion that therefore Jews have no place in the discourse of diaspora. Stuart Hall, "Cultural Identity and Diaspora," in *Identity: Community, Culture, Difference*, ed. J. Rutherford (London: Lawrence & Wishart, 1990), 235.

8. There is a growing polarization between diaspora theorists who challenge the moral validity of the nation-state and supporters of national sovereignty who advocate for the state's right to promote particular ethnic or religious communities. This polarization politicizes efforts to foreground the fluid continuum of nationalities that existed between statist and nonstatist or diasporist positions during the first half of the twentieth century. Jewish leaders and scholars, facing a perceived attack from anti-Israel advocates, may be hesitant to promote the importance of a political tradition that complicates the conflation of Zionism and Jewish nationalism. See Judt, "Israel: The Alternative"; and Wieseltier, "Israel, Palestine, and the Return of the Bi-National Fantasy."

9. The historian Steven Aschheim has argued that it was only in the 1940s that "political statehood became the official goal of the Zionist movement." See Aschheim, *Beyond the Border*, 9.

10. See Myers, *Between Jew and Arab*, 23 and 249n5.

11. For example, Gideon Shimoni defines a pillar of Zionist ideology as the "territorial ingathering of Jews" seeking homeland sovereignty. See his *The Zionist Ideology*, 85.

12. This does not constitute an exhaustive list of thinkers within the broad orbit of Zionist intellectuals in the early half of the twentieth century who were dedicated to conceptualizing nationality outside of statehood. Other thinkers include the pioneering Jewish educator Samson Benderly, the rabbi Abba Hillel Silver, the philanthropist Jacob Schiff, the communal leader Louis B. Marshall, and the World Jewish Congress executive Nachum Goldman.

13. On February 2, 1929, Robert Weltsch wrote to Kohn and asked him to review an article by Rawidowicz for the *Jüdische Rundschau*. Weltsch reports that Rawidowicz was particularly pleased that Kohn would be reviewing his article. See AR 6908 1/1, Hans Kohn–Robert Weltsch Correspondence, Weltsch Collection, Leo Baeck Archive, New York City. Kaplan reports meeting Kohn at a lecture in his December 21, 1931, diary entry; see Kaplan, *Communings of the Spirit*, 464. Folded up and paper-clipped to the inside cover of Rawidowicz's personal copy of Kaplan's landmark work, *Judaism as a Civilization*, still rests a handwritten note in Hebrew from 1936: "I realized that in a number of ways our outlooks are similar," Kaplan wrote. See chapter 3 for more information. In *Babylon and Jerusalem*, Rawidowicz praised aspects of Kaplan's book, *New Zionism* (see p. 672).

14. For a discussion of recent scholarship on Rawidowicz, see chapter 3, note 7.

15. See, for example, Charles Liebman, "Reconstructionism in American Jewish Life," in *American Jewish Yearbook*, ed. Morris Fine and Milton Himmelfarb (Philadelphia: Jewish Publication Society of America, 1970).

16. For more on Kohn's legacy, see chapter 4.

17. Here I follow historian Michael Stanislawski's caution against a "teleological retrojection that effaces the complexity of human thought and development" (see Stanislawski, *Zionism and the Fin de Siècle*, xx).

18. Seton-Watson, *Nations and States*, 1.

19. Gellner, *Nations and Nationalism*, 1. Within the field of nationalism studies, there are a few exceptions to the tendency to conflate nationhood with statehood.

One of the first scholars to underscore the limitation of the doctrine of national sovereignty as a description of nationality was the historian Walker Connor. Connor claimed that this phenomenon distorts the realities of national attachments, which in his thinking have little to do with political independence or geographic borders. Instead, Connor suggested a category of ethnonationalism that acknowledges the nonpolitical ties that bind national groups outside of political and territorial borders. One problem with the terminology Connor uses, however, is that his conception of ethnic ties pays insufficient attention to the relationship between nation and state. See Connor, *Ethnonationalism*. On the importance of separating the cultural and political aspects of nationality, see also Hutchinson, *Dynamics of Cultural Nationalism*.

20. Hobsbawm and Ranger, *Invention of Tradition*. The scholars Elie Kedourie, Anthony Giddens, and John Breuilly have also contributed to make the modernist paradigm the dominant approach to nationalism since the 1970s. See Kedourie, *Nationalism;* Giddens, *The Nation-State and Violence;* Jon Breuilly, *Nationalism and the State* (Chicago: University of Chicago Press, 1982). See also Anderson, *Imagined Communities,* and Anthony D. Smith, *Theories of Nationalism*. Political theorist David Miller's *On Nationality* expands the constitutive core of nationality to include several additional elements, such as common beliefs and historical experiences. Yet even his conclusion favors "national self-determination" as the most effective structure for preserving national identity (see p. 98).

21. Smith, *Nationalism and Modernism,* 24.

22. Scholars of nationalism, such as Anthony Smith, who views the nation as "perennial," are more sensitive to theorizing the nation as a cultural community with ethnic, or historical, roots in the premodern period. See, for example, Smith, *Nationalism and Modernism*.

23. Hans Kohn, the subject of chapter 5, popularized the scholarly distinction between Western civic and Eastern ethnic strains of nationalism. See Kohn, *Idea of Nationalism*. Kohn envisioned the ethnic path as a strain that diverged from the Western trajectory oriented toward increasing levels of integration and shared universal principles. The enduring influence of these two categories, as well as the biases linked to each typology, can still be found in the work of such scholars as Anthony Smith. The influential theorist adopts, with a few important caveats, Kohn's distinction between rational and organic versions of nationalist ideology. See Anthony D. Smith, *National Identity: Ethnonationalism in Comparative Perspective* (Reno: University of Nevada Press, 1991), 81. Popular accounts of nationality also reflect the notion that these two paths lead to good and bad nationalisms. See Ignatieff, *Blood and Belonging*.

24. John Stuart Mill, "Of Nationality, as Connected with Representative Government," in his *Considerations on Representative Government* (1861), chapter 16, quoted in Vincent P. Pecora, ed., *Nations and Identities* (Oxford: Blackwell, 2001), 145.

25. Taylor has questioned whether Gellner was right to make the "state focus definitional for modern nationalism." He concludes "we gain nothing by excluding this phenomenon from our purview by definitional fiat" (see Taylor, "Nationalism and Modernity," 35). Kymlicka is another example of a theorist sensitive to national identity at the substatist level, but only for communities rooted in territorial attachment who were displaced by settlers. Yet both Taylor and Kymlicka (who are Canadian scholars) focus on language and land (characteristics of the Québécois) as alternate criteria for national cohesion. See chapter 6 for a further discussion of why this is a

definition that does not apply well to the Jewish case, characterized by a population divided by both geography and language. Two scholars with ties to Israel, Gans and Roshwald, advocate attributes that transcend land and language by focusing on non-statist nationality grounded in culture, history, and the psychology of collectivity. See Gans, *Limits of Nationalism,* and Roshwald, *Endurance of Nationalism.*

26. Brubaker, *Ethnicity without Groups,* 145.

27. Jewish historian Ezra Mendelsohn's concise overview of modern Jewish politics, *On Modern Jewish Politics,* provides an excellent example of this rubric. The historiographical distinction between nationalist and integrationist paths can be found in historian Jonathan Frankel's classic study of Eastern European nationalism as a postliberal phenomenon (see Frankel, *Prophecy and Politics*). In attempting to blur the distinction between national particularism and liberal integration, my investigation resembles historian Ben Nathans's study of Russian liberal jurists who advocated for Jewish minority rights during the early decades of the twentieth century. See Benjamin Nathans, "The Other Modern Jewish Politics: Integration and Modernity in Fin de Siècle Russia," in Gitelman, *The Emergence of Modern Jewish Politics.* Social historians, particularly those focused on the immigrant experience, have also demonstrated the limitations of the integrationist versus nationalist binary by exploring Jewish subcultures and social networks that enabled Jews to mitigate the pace of acculturation. Jewish intellectuals were not uprooted from their social and intellectual contexts, but instead they relocated and created a dialogue between European theories and their American environment. See Hyman, *Gender and Assimilation in Modern Jewish History,* and David Sorkin, *The Transformation of German Jewry, 1780–1840* (Oxford: Oxford University Press, 1987).

28. See Mendelsohn, *On Modern Jewish Politics,* 6–36. Mendelsohn does acknowledge that some "Diaspora Zionist leaders" did not clearly fit into the mainstream rubrics. He briefly mentions such figures and calls them "centrists" and "moderates." My book attempts to expand on the characteristically brief mention of such thinkers whose positions do not clearly match the ideological poles. See ibid., 35.

29. For a concise overview of major themes in Zionist historiography, see Penslar, "Narratives of Nation Building." Diaspora nationalism has a variety of expressions in addition to Simon Dubnow's autonomism, such as territorialists, who advocate for a Jewish political autonomy, but not necessarily in Palestine; diaspora nationalists; and Bundists, socialists who considered national Jewish organization as the first step toward international proletariat revolution.

30. The historian David Myers has described Rawidowicz as "continually traversing the border between Zionism and diasporism." This description applies to a far greater group of interwar Jewish nationalists that includes Kohn and Kaplan. See Myers, *Between Jew and Arab,* 55.

31. I provide an in-depth example of this phenomenon in chapter 2, by exploring the affinities between the diaspora nationalist Simon Dubnow and several early-twentieth-century Zionist thinkers.

32. On Ahad Ha'am, see Zipperstein, *Elusive Prophet;* for more information on Ahad Ha'am's influence in American Jewish thought, see Zipperstein, "On Reading Ahad Ha'am"; Friesel, "Influence of American Zionism on the American Jewish Community."

33. Indeed, this is precisely how the American Jewish historian Arthur Goren has defined Kaplan, whom he considers a "cultural Zionist." Goren is correct to designate

Kaplan as a Jewish thinker deeply involved in cultural Zionism. However, this stance diverts attention from an analysis of Kaplan's political challenges to American nationalism by underscoring Kaplan's Zionism as focused on cultural or religious innovations. See Goren, *Politics and Public Culture of American Jews,* 148. Zionist historian Evyatar Friesel's distinction between "inward" and "outward" Zionism creates an even deeper, and more misleading, gap between political and cultural Zionists. According to this dichotomy, American Zionists could be divided into two camps: those who focused their efforts on preparing Zionism for its presentation to a non-Jewish audience and those who dedicated their energies toward injecting elements of cultural Zionism into the American Jewish community. Such figures as Brandeis and Kallen fit into the first category, while Jewish communal activists like Kaplan and Friedlaender constitute the "inward" group. This false bifurcation suggests that those Zionists interested in transforming Judaism operated within the narrow confines of the Jewish community and made no effort to influence the American community. I challenge this claim, particularly in the case of Kaplan, in chapter 4. See Friesel, "Influence of American Zionism on the American Jewish Community," 143.

34. Here I disagree with Hagit Lavsky, who views Kohn's reading of Ahad Ha'am as sui generis. See Lavsky, "Hans Kohn: Nationalism between Theory and Practice." As the subsequent chapters in this book argue, especially the discussion of Zimmern and Kallen in chapter 2, a number of leading Zionists viewed Ahad Ha'am as an influential figure in their efforts to disengage nation from state. The quotation is from Kohn, *Living in a World Revolution,* 55.

35. The historian Samuel Moyn has captured this approach to interpreting theories of Jewish nationalism. He writes: "Collective identity is partly invented from within, partly imposed from without, and is best considered as a field of conflicting forces" (see Samuel Moyn, "German Jewry and the Question of Identity Historiography and Theory," *Leo Baeck Yearbook* [1996]: 291–308).

36. Jewish historian Amos Funkenstein's concept of the "dialectics of assimilation" guides this reading of theories of nationality as a dialectical process between assimilation and self-assertion. In particular, Funkenstein has pointed out that even language explicitly oriented toward asserting the difference between Jewish and non-Jewish traditions is generally deeply rooted in the language of the particular intellectual context. See Funkenstein, "Dialectics of Assimilation." More recently, David Myers has written about the importance of organizing historical research around the "criteria of interaction and exchange" within a specific milieu. See David Myers, *Resisting History: Historicism and Its Discontents in German-Jewish Thought* (Princeton, N.J.: Princeton University Press, 2003), 166. My goal is to extend this historiographical approach to modern Jewish political thought in general and to theories of nationality in particular.

37. Such postcolonial theorists as Partha Chatterjee have pioneered a shift in the study of nationality away from focusing on political movements. Instead, Chatterjee has argued that expressions of nationality served as a rhetorical instrument for disenfranchised intellectuals attempting to mitigate coercive political or cultural demands. See Chatterjee, *Nation and Its Fragments.* The development of Jewish nationalism is not fully analogous to anticolonial varieties; European and even Russian Jews were not subject to the levels of enslavement, violence, and land confiscations that European imperial powers inflicted on the indigenous populations of Africa, Asia, and the

Middle East. However, it is still fruitful to explore the applicability of postcolonial theory on the Jewish experience. One of the most interesting explorations of the Zionist–colonial comparison can be found in chapter 5 of Penslar's book *Israel in History*.

38. Theories of both liberalism and nationalism implicitly undermined efforts to preserve corporate identity and at their logical extremes defined difference as antithetical to their fundamental projects. That the universalist claims of liberalism cover up a compassionate theory of elimination for particular groups is a theme touched on by scholars from a variety of fields. See, among other works, Smith, *Spinoza, Liberalism, and the Question of Jewish Identity* (New Haven, Conn.: Yale University Press, 1997); Gilroy, *Black Atlantic* (Cambridge, Mass.: Harvard University Press, 1993); and Jeff Spinner-Halev, *The Boundaries of Citizenship: Race, Ethnicity, and Nationality in the Liberal State* (Baltimore: Johns Hopkins University Press, 1994). The threats posed by völkisch or ethnic strains of nationalism are more readily apparent. Explicitly prioritizing the state's primary role as preserving a particular national tradition diminished the validity of individual freedom for all citizens. See chapter 2 for a more detailed discussion of the challenges posed by liberalism and nationalism.

39. See Brubaker, *Ethnicity without Groups*, 10.

40. The historian Malachi Hacohen has argued that historical narratives tracing the evolution of modern political theory are too often constrained by "nationalist claims to an authentic closed tradition." See his "The Limits of the National Paradigm in the Study of Political Thought: The Case of Karl Popper and Central European Cosmopolitanism," in *The History of Political Thought in National Context*, ed. Dario Castiglione and Iain Hampsher-Monk (Cambridge: Cambridge University Press, 2001), 247.

41. Cohen, *American Jews and the Zionist Idea*, 26.

42. Immigrant Jews, social historians have shown, navigated paths of integration that allowed them to balance between Americanizing and preserving a distinct identity. Historians of Jewish political thought, however, have been far less interested in applying the same principle to document the ways in which Jewish thought took a stand against the state and its expectations of citizenship.

43. As a number of scholars have pointed out, at the turn of the twentieth century the Atlantic was very permeable indeed. Examples include Gilroy, *Black Atlantic,* and Daniel T. Rodgers, *Atlantic Crossings: Social Politics in a Progressive Age* (Cambridge, Mass.: Harvard University Press, 1998).

44. Matthew Frye Jacobson has described this general phenomenon quite well. He writes: "Part of the gravitational pull into this essentially nationalist orbit, as I have said, is accounted for by the citizenly concerns of many of the scholars involved, and the extent to which scholarship on immigration—like that in African American Studies or Ethnic Studies—invariably represents an engagement in a civic politics and a discourse of diversity, inclusion, exclusion, social equity, and the like, which itself is inflected or even fully bound by the logic of the nation-form" (see Jacobson, "More 'Trans-,' Less 'National,'" 79).

45. Mendelsohn has urged historians of modern Jewish politics to "make the connection between politics and geography" (see Mendelsohn, *On Modern Jewish Politics,* 37). Key distinctions that emerge between locations are the rather striking disjunctures when it comes to the influence of nationality. Scholars of American Jewish history, East European Jewish history, and Zionism agree that theories of Jewish nationality gained little traction in the United States. See Cohen, *American Jews and the Zionist Idea*, xvi; and Shimoni, *Zionist Ideology,* 395. Gideon Shimoni does not include any American

thinkers in his book, however, and mentions only two theorists who did not move to Palestine: Moses Hess and Yaakov Klatzkin. Hans Kohn appears in Shimoni's book, but only for his later work as a theoretician of nationalism. The fact that Kohn was also an active member of the Zionist intellectual circles is overlooked. In contrast, Arnold Eisen's study *Galut* deals extensively with Kaplan and briefly considers Rawidowicz. See also Gitelman, *Emergence of Modern Jewish Politics,* 183. Another example of evaluating American Zionism on the criteria of *aliyah* (immigration) and the negation of the exile is Evyatar Friesel's claim that American Zionism's inability to galvanize aliyah to Israel represents a failure of the Zionist movement (see Friesel, "Influence of American Zionism on the American Jewish Community," 130–48).

46. This shift toward emphasizing transatlantic continuities has emerged in a number of recent works by American Jewish historians and American historians. See Michels, *A Fire in Their Hearts;* King, *The Liberty of Strangers;* and Kobrin, "When a Jew Was a 'Landsman.'"

47. Several scholars across multiple disciplines have discussed this phenomenon. For example, see Appadurai, *Modernity at Large.*

48. One of the most vocal prognosticators for a postnational political order is the anthropologist Arjun Appadurai, who has argued that media and migration have shifted the centers of cultural production from the homeland to various diaspora centers (see ibid.).

49. In addressing the relationship between the sovereign state and minority populations, such political theorists as Yael Tamir, Chaim Gans, David Miller, Will Kymlicka, and Charles Taylor have introduced definitions of sovereignty that differentiate between nation and state. Theories on multicultural citizenship, liberal nationalism, and peoplehood have pushed for varying degrees of recognition for minority groups, from a set of legal protections for minority groups to more substantial systems of autonomy, including self-government. These theorists debate the limits of ethnonational diversity, the role of the state in preserving a shared national culture, and the criteria that delineate minority national groups from other allegiances. See Kymlicka, *Multicultural Citizenship;* Nina Glick Schiller and Georges Eugene Fouron, *Georges Woke Up Laughing: Long-Distance Nationalism and the Search for Home* (Durham, N.C.: Duke University Press, 2001); Hollinger, *Postethnic America;* Appiah, *Ethics of Identity;* Tamir, *Liberal Nationalism;* McKim and McMahan, *Morality of Nationalism;* and Gans, *Limits of Nationalism.* Such scholars as Paul Gilroy have strongly advocated for considering diaspora communities, with their dynamic interaction with disparate cultural contexts, as a paradigm for understanding modernity (see Gilroy, *Black Atlantic,* 29).

2. "Sovereignty Is International Anarchy"

1. Kallen, *Structure of Lasting Peace,* 34. According to the book review in *The Nation* magazine, although Kallen "traverses the familiar ground of Wilsonian liberalism," his account differs in a crucial way: "It discusses a pluralistic and non-sovereign state, the divorce of the Idea of freedom of nationalities from that of individual political statehood, international guarantee of the rights of minorities, and the release of education from governmental control" (see *The Nation,* November 23, 1918, 629).

2. See chapter 1 for a discussion of counterstate nationalism.

3. See Frankel, "An Introductory Essay—the Paradoxical Politics of Marginality."

4. Ibid., 4.

5. According to Carole Fink: "The most ardent nonstate proponents of international minority protection during this period were the Jews of Western Europe and the United States" (see Carole Fink, *Defending the Rights of Others*, xvii). Ultimately, the victorious powers refused to include a formal policy within the League of Nations' charter because they feared challenges to their own sovereign authority. Instead of obligating member states to guarantee minority rights, the League underscored the importance of universal human rights.

6. I am indebted to the historian Steven Beller for highlighting the "either/or" logic of nationalism in his discussion of the relationship between anti-Semitism and European nationalism. Beller, "Is Anti-Semitism an Eternal Hatred?" lecture delivered at the University of Washington, January 27, 2009.

7. Taylor, "Nationalism and Modernity," 40.

8. Smith, *National Identity: Ethnonationalism in Comparative Perspective*, 8. The notion that ethnic nationalism represents a dangerous and divergent path can also be found in journalistic accounts of nationality. See Ignatieff, *Blood and Belonging*.

9. Yack, "The Myth of Civic Nationalism."

10. See Rogers Brubaker's critique of the ethnic–civic dichotomy in his *Ethnicity without Groups*, 132–147.

11. The American Jewish historian Jonathan Sarna has discussed the unique aspects of the American Jewish experience in the introduction to his *American Judaism*, xii–xx.

12. See Gerstle, *American Crucible*, 104.

13. Ibid.

14. As Matthew Jacobson, an American Studies scholar, has illustrated in his book *Whiteness of a Different Color*, the increasing forces of nativism during this period manifested themselves in the invention of new categories of whiteness. Jews were certainly included in these changing taxonomies of race, which pushed them to the fringes of whiteness. See Jacobson, *Whiteness of a Different Color*. For a more recent discussion of Jews negotiating racial categories in America, see Goldstein, *The Price of Whiteness*.

15. Hector St. John de Crevecoeur, *Letters from an American Farmer* (London: T. Davies, 1782), Letter III.

16. Sollors, *Beyond Ethnicity*, 83.

17. See R. Jeffrey Lustig, *Corporate Liberalism: The Origins of Modern American Political Theory, 1890–1920* (Berkeley: University of California Press, 1982); Martin J. Sklar, *The Corporate Reconstruction of American Capitalism, 1890–1916* (Cambridge: Cambridge University Press, 1988); James Weinstein, *The Corporate Ideal in the Liberal State: 1900–1918* (Boston: Beacon Press, 1968); and Eldon J. Eisenach, *The Lost Promise of Progressivism: American Political Thought* (Lawrence: University Press of Kansas, 1994).

18. Smith, "Beyond Tocqueville, Myrdal, and Hartz," 549.

19. Eisenach, *Lost Promise of Progressivism*, 7.

20. Croly's work is discussed in David M. Kennedy, *Progressivism: The Critical Issues* (Boston: Little Brown, 1971), 39.

21. Higham, *Strangers in the Land*, 198.

22. The "100 percenters" are discussed in David M. Kennedy, *Over Here: The First World War and American Society* (New York: Oxford University Press, 1980), 69.

23. See Handy, *Social Gospel in America*, 12; Robert T. Handy, *A Christian America:*

Protestant Hopes and Historical Realities, vol. 2 (New York: Oxford University Press, 1984); and Robert T. Handy, "Protestant Theological Tensions and Political Styles in the Progressive Period," in *Religion and American Politics from the Colonial Period to the 1980's,* ed. Mark A. Noll (New York: Oxford University Press, 1990).

24. Handy, *Social Gospel in America,* 135.

25. Hollinger, *Postethnic America,* 91.

26. Friedlaender, *Past and Present,* 389.

27. See Article 11 of the Kadet Party program, quoted in Weeks, *Nations and State in Late Imperial Russia,* 24.

28. Dubnow himself used these two terms, among others, to refer to Jewish nationality in a series of letters he published between 1897 and 1907. Known as the "Letters on Old and New Jewry," these writings outlined Dubnow's philosophy of nationalism. A translated compilation of the letters appears in Dubnow, *Nationalism and History,* 143.

29. For more on the Folkspartei and its journal, see David Fishman's discussion in David Fishman, *The Rise of Modern Yiddish Culture* (Pittsburgh: University of Pittsburgh Press, 2005), 79. For more on Dubnow's political thought, see Weinberg, *Between Tradition and Modernity.*

30. Dubnow, *Nationalism and History,* 86.

31. Writing in Russian, Dubnow directly addressed an East European audience. However, his essays engaged the literature on nationalism written by the leading Central and West European nationalists, including the French scholar Ernst Renan, the Austrian Marxist Karl Renner, and the German nationalist Johann Gottlieb Fichte (see ibid., 79, 87).

32. Hacohen, "The Limits of the National Paradigm in the Study of Political Thought," 247–79, 251.

33. For a more detailed discussion of Renner's model, as well as the contemporary implications of early-twentieth-century theories of substate nationalism, see Nimni, *National Cultural Autonomy and Its Contemporary Critics.*

34. Ibid., 27.

35. Ibid., 28.

36. Ibid., 25.

37. See Friedrich Meinecke, *Die Idee der Staatsrason* (The idea of reasons of state) (Berlin: R. Oldenbourg, 1925).

38. Ibid., 500.

39. See Weiss, "Central European Ethnonationalism."

40. See Mendes-Flohr, *Land of Two Peoples.*

41. Examples of this phenomenon include Herbert Samuel, member of Parliament and first High Commissioner of Palestine; Sir Montague Burton, successful businessman and internationalist (he funded the chair in international studies at Oxford, later held by Zimmern); Sir Matthew Nathan, an elite member of the Colonial Service; Sir Hersch Lauterpact, one of the leading legal theorists of the past century; and Sir Louis Namier, the historian and British government official.

42. For more on Zimmern's biography and theories of internationalism, see Rich, "Alfred Zimmern's Cautious Idealism: The League of Nations, International Education, and the Commonwealth"; Carr, *The Twenty Year Crisis, 1919–1939;* Markwell, "Sir Alfred Zimmern Revisited: Fifty Years On"; and Morefield, *Covenants without Swords: Idealist Liberalism and the Spirit of Empire.*

43. Zimmern, *Nationality and Government*, 65.

44. Zimmern, "Jews and Nationality," 1915, MS Zimmern 177, folio 13, Sir Alfred Zimmern Papers, Bodleian Library, Oxford University, Oxford.

45. Overall, Jewish historians have overlooked Zimmern. One of the few exceptions is Philippa Stroum's brief mention of Zimmern in the context of the relationship Zimmern forged when accompanying Judge Louis Brandeis on his first trip to Palestine. See Philippa Stroum, *Louis D. Brandeis: Justice for the People* (Cambridge, Mass.: Harvard University Press, 1984), 240–43.

46. Evidence suggests that Kallen served as an intermediary between Zimmern and the *Menorah Journal*. Zimmern wrote: "I had a cable from Hurwitz [the editor of the *Menorah Journal*]. . . . Would you mind sending the enclosed on to him. My Menorahs, with the address are out of reach before the mail goes" (manuscript collection #1, Box 32, File 20, Horace Kallen Collection, American Jewish Archives, Cincinnati, Ohio).

47. Zimmern corresponded regularly with Kallen for more than a decade following his return, on issues ranging from international relations to Zionism and personal concerns. The Kallen–Zimmern correspondence is in ibid. I would like to thank Fred Krome of the American Jewish Archives and Colin Harris of the Bodleian Library for their help in locating Zimmern's archival material.

48. Kallen, "Zionism and the Struggle towards Democracy," 379.

49. Kallen, "Democracy versus the Melting-Pot."

50. The phrase has appeared as the title of several studies tracing the development of Zionism in America and reflects a theme that permeates the narrative of American Jewish history. One prominent publication that popularized this phrase is Halpern's "The Americanization of Zionism, 1880–1930." For a more recent example, see Cohen, *Americanization of Zionism*.

51. See chapter 1, note 41.

52. Recently, American Jewish historians complicated the notion of the American Jewish synthesis by highlighting the cracks and fissures that existed underneath the rhetoric of a harmonious process of integration. My interest in probing the relationship between American Zionists and American Jewish exceptionalism was sparked by a conference paper given by the historian Tony Michels at the University of Washington on February 28, 2008.

53. American Jewish historians have begun to bridge the historiographical gap between Kallen's contributions as both a Jewish and an American thinker. Daniel Greene has considered the relationship between Kallen's cultural pluralism and notions of chosenness. He concludes that Kallen rejected Jewish exceptionalism as a necessary compromise for including Jews within conceptions of American pluralism. See Greene, "A Chosen People in a Pluralist Nation: Horace Kallen and the Jewish-American Experience." William Toll has helped situate Kallen's notion of descent within the American Zionist's personal Jewish journey. See Toll, "Horace M. Kallen: Pluralism and American Jewish Identity."

54. This was not only a phenomenon involving Jewish intellectuals. A number of non-Jewish intellectuals also adopted the position that Zionism represented the paragon of national identity. See, for example, Bourne, "The Jew and Trans-National America."

55. Edward Alsworth Ross, *The Old World in the New: The Significance of Past and Present Immigration to the American People* (New York: The Century Company, 1914), 165.

56. Kaplan enumerated the constituent elements of Jewish civilization nationalism in his *Judaism as a Civilization* (see chapter 4 in this book for a more in-depth discussion).

57. Dubnow, *Nationalism and History,* 94. See also p. 87.

58. Zimmern, "Nationality in the Modern World," 210.

59. Ibid., 211. Kallen's debt to Ahad Ha'am for his central concept of Hebraism is evident in the clear overlap between the concept of Hebraism quoted in the text and the explanation of Ahad Ha'am's theory offered by Kallen in 1921: "Each nationality, Ginsberg holds, is characterized by a spirit, an essence, a central spontaneity, which expresses itself in all the inverse forms of the national life: economic, social, political, religious, literary, and so on . . . no Jew of modern times has had so profound an influence upon the Jewish people [as] Achad Ha'am" (Kallen, *Zionism and World Politics,* 76). Despite these claims, however, such historians as Naomi Cohen have concluded that Kallen "dismissed the theories of Achad Ha'am" (see Cohen, *American Jews and the Zionist Idea,* 18 and 220). The ingrained assumption that Kallen, like other American Jewish intellectuals, dismissed Ahad Ha'am reflects a larger bias that the cultural Zionist had little influence in American Jewish circles as a political thinker.

60. Ahad Ha'am introduced the idea of imitation in an 1894 essay, "Imitation and Assimilation." The article distinguished between a positive and negative expression of imitation. "Self-effacing" imitation seeks to copy the "spirit" and "personality" of the dominant nation. In the former model, "competitive" imitation, "the whole desire of the imitator is to reveal his own spirit or personality. He therefore endeavors to change the original impress, according as his personality or his position differs from that of his model." Zimmern integrated the competitive model into his discussion of Ahad Ha'am and the importance of promoting national communities. See Ahad Ha'am, "Imitation and Assimilation," in *Selected Essays of Ahad Ha'am,* ed. Leon Simon (Philadelphia: Jewish Publication Society, 1894), 111–12.

61. Ahad Ha'am, *Selected Essays by Ahad Ha'Am,* 112.

62. Zimmern, "Theodore Harzl and the Jewish Renaissance," 23.

63. Kallen, "Nationality and the Jewish Stake in the Great War," *Menorah Journal* 1, no. 2 (1915): 113.

64. Kallen, "Democracy versus the Melting Pot," 218.

65. Ibid., 220.

66. Both Hollinger and Sollors have developed parallel critiques of Kallen as a progenitor of trends in ethnic studies that view membership as heavily based on biological grounds, rather than on dynamic individual decisions. Kallen, Hollinger concludes, wants "to reduce the United States to an administrative canopy under which a variety of old-world clans could perpetuate themselves" (Hollinger, *Postethnic America,* 162). Note the derogatory connotations of clans and old world. These words suggest a blind adherence to a set of antiquated allegiances incompatible with the fluidity of identity in a society based on the liberal values of free choice and cultural amalgamation. Sollors defines Kallen's position as "most given to considering descent-based identifications eternal and static" (see Sollors, *Beyond Ethnicity,* 183). Sollors also argues that Kallen's notion of cultural pluralism engenders "a biological insiderism" that rejects a "shared history" and minimizes "human empathy" (ibid., 151). Sollors criticizes what he perceives as a biological rhetoric of difference, which he fears promotes a false sense of collective authenticity and obscures shared interests across group boundaries.

67. Kallen, *Structure of Lasting Peace,* 34.

68. Dubnow, *Nationalism and History,* 126.

69. Ibid., 127.

70. Ibid., 122.

71. Dubnow's footnotes in his *Nationalism and History* indicate that he was aware of an even more explicit rejection of Jewish national minority status. He referred directly to an 1883 essay by Renan called "Judaism as a Race and a Religion." Renan, an architect of civic nationalism and clearly one of Dubnow's influences throughout his essays, penned this essay about the Jews who rejected their national character and concluded they will "of necessity assimilate with other nations" (see ibid.).

72. John Stuart Mill, *The Collected Works of John Stuart Mill,* ed. F. E. K. Priestley, vol. 19 (Toronto: University of Toronto Press, 1977), 547.

73. Zimmern's vehement disagreement with Mill is clear from this critique: "I believe from the bottom of my heart that Mill's idea is fundamentally wrong—wrong in fact, and wrong as an ideal, and that all forward-looking men who desire better international relations and a better political organization of the world must rest their hope, not in the Nation-State, which is only a stage, and in the West an outworn stage, in the political evolution of mankind, but in states which, like the great governing religious systems of the past, like mediaeval Christendom and Islam, find room for all sorts and conditions of communities and nations" (see Zimmern, *Nationality and Government,* 64).

74. Smith, *Spinoza, Liberalism, and the Question of Jewish Identity,* 26.

75. Ibid.

76. Jewish nationalism's analysis of liberalism's failure to recognize an individual's ties to a particular group context, as articulated by Dubnow and other counterstate theorists, anticipated the communitarian critique developed over the past decade. See Etzioni, *New Communitarian Thinking;* Avineri and De-Shalit, *Communitarianism and Individualism;* and Walzer, "Communitarian Critique of Liberalism."

77. Zimmern, *Nationality and Government,* 67.

78. Ibid., 77.

79. Ibid., 15. See also his "Nationality in the Modern World."

80. Kallen, "Zionism: Democracy or Prussianism."

81. Kallen himself made the precise link between his melting-pot critique of the United States and the typology of German Kultur developed in Zimmern's writings in 1924. The introduction to a book of Kallen's essays, including a reprint of "Democracy versus the Melting-Pot," explicitly contrasted his vision of America with German Kultur (see Kallen, *Culture and Democracy in the United States*).

82. Morefield, *Covenants without Swords,* 219.

83. One recent collection of essays explores the tension between liberalism and nationalism. See McKim and McMahan, *Morality of Nationalism.*

84. Morefield, "A Liberal in a Muddle: Alfred Zimmern on Nationality, Internationality, and Commonwealth," 105.

85. "All aristocrats have one motto—it is *noblesse oblige.* This must be the motto of the Jew." Horace M. Kallen, "Address to the Third Menorah Convention," *The Menorah Journal* 1, no. 2 [1915]: 130.

86. Kallen, *Zionism and World Politics,* 294.

87. Kallen as cited in Rafael Medoff, *Zionism and the Arabs: An American Jewish Dilemma, 1898–1948* (Westport, Conn.: Praeger, 1997), 29.

88. Kallen, *Zionism and World Politics,* 294.

89. Neither did Kallen implement his vision of equality and diversity in the American context. African Americans, for example, had no clear place in his orchestra of humankind. See Gleason, "American Identity and Americanization," 107.

90. Kallen, *Zionism and World Politics,* 294. It is important to note that a degree of bicultural appreciation accompanied Kallen's sense of *noblesse oblige.* For instance, Kallen advocated for the creation of a "Department of Arabic Life and Letters" in the future Jewish university to promote Jewish–Arab understanding. Given his attitude about the Arab inhabitants of Palestine, however, the bicultural learning program was most likely a tool for catalyzing the process of integration, rather than maintaining two distinct national cultures within the Jewish homeland.

91. By the time Kallen published this program for Palestine in 1921, the Arab national movement had already made vocal claims contesting Jewish immigration and advocating for Arab national autonomy. Yet these developments did not, at least publicly, deter Kallen's optimism that the indigenous population would voluntarily and enthusiastically embrace Jewish culture.

92. Kallen, *Zionism and World Politics,* 294.

93. Zimmern's article critiquing the 1905 British Alien Act makes clear his own awareness of the marginal status of Jews as a national group worthy of inclusion within British civilization. See Alfred Eckhard Zimmern, "The Aliens Act: A Challenge," *Economic Review* 21, no. 2 (1911): 195.

94. One prominent example of a counterstate theorist who explicitly rejected the national status of Jews was Austrian cultural autonomist Otto Bauer. See Jack Jacobs, "Austrian Social Democracy and the Jewish Question in the First Republic," in *Austrian Socialist Experiment: Social Democracy and Austromarxism, 1918–1934,* ed. Anson Rabinback (Boulder, Colo.: Westview Press, 1985).

95. The Zionist philosopher and publisher Yaakov Klatzkin articulated one of the classic expressions of the negation of the diaspora ideology in *Tehumim,* his collection of essays published in 1928.

96. Zimmern, "Nationality in the Modern World," 210. For a slightly different variation of Zimmern's definition of nationality, see Zimmern, *Nationality and Government,* 52: "a body of people united by a corporate sentiment of peculiar intensity, intimacy and dignity, related to a definite home-country."

97. Horace Meyer Kallen, *Judaism at Bay,* 40.

98. Zimmern, *Nationality and Government,* 84.

99. Kallen only selectively affirmed his appropriation of Ahad Ha'am's long-distance link to another territory. Sensitive to the possibility of bolstering attacks on the patriotism of American Jews, Kallen downplayed the importance of the national homeland in the conception of nationality published for non-Jewish audiences. His article "Democracy versus the Melting-Pot," for instance, completely ignored the concept of the homeland, which played a critical role in the concept of nationality outlined in articles published in the Jewish press. Kallen's self-censorship reflects the delicate balance between the need for a broad appeal to legitimate differentiation as an American value, and making claims that would further fuel nativist attacks on the dual allegiances of American Jews. Transforming U.S. public opinion to recognize the value of pluralism in general and Jews in particular demanded the strategic silencing of certain elements of his understanding of Jewish political thought.

100. Kaplan, *Judaism as a Civilization,* 245.

3. Text, Not Territory

1. Rawidowicz, *State of Israel, Diaspora, and Jewish Continuity*, 198.

2. Ibid., 188. The longer Hebrew version of this article sent to Ben Gurion appeared under the title "Yisrael," in *Metzudah* 7 (1954): 11–61. Although he published under the Hebrew name "Shimon Rawidowicz," for the sake of consistency, I use the English name "Simon Rawidowicz" throughout this book.

3. Ibid., 194. Ben Gurion and Rawidowicz exchanged several letters between October 1954 and May 1955. An abridged English translation of these letters, compiled by Benjamin Ravid, appears in Rawidowicz, *State of Israel, Diaspora, and Jewish Continuity*, 194. The complete Hebrew correspondence was published by Rawidowicz in *Babylon and Jerusalem*, 872–909.

4. Ibid. For information on the debate over the name of the state and its relationship to Ben Gurion's theory of statism, see Kedar, "Ben Gurion's Mamlachtiyut"; Eliezer Don-Yehiya, "Political Religion in Israel: Ben Gurion's Mamlachtiyut," in *Israel: The First Decade of Independence*, ed. Ilan Troen and Noah Lucas (Albany: State University of New York Press, 1995), 171; and Pnina Lahav, "A 'Jewish State . . . to Be Known as the State of Israel': Notes on Israel Legal Historiography," *Law and History Review* 19 (2001): 387–88.

5. Jewish historian David Myers has called Rawidowicz "one of the twentieth century's great and neglected Jewish thinkers" (see Myers, "A Third Guide for the Perplexed?" 75). Scholarship on Rawidowicz primarily relates to his research on the medieval philosopher Moses Maimonides, historian Nachman Krochmal, diaspora nationalist Simon Dubnow, and poet Haim Nahman Bialik—and occasional references to his well-known essay "Israel: The Ever-Dying People." See, for example, the discussion of Rawidowicz's work on Krochmal in Harris, *Nachman Krochmal*. See also Sarna, *American Judaism*, 17. A number of essays were written after the publication of "Israel: The Ever-Dying People" in 1988. See Gordon Tucker, "Israel, Canaan, and the Diaspora," *Judaism* 37 (1988): 364–75. Myers's publication, *Between Jew and Arab*, is the most recent contribution to recovering Rawidowicz's thought, specifically an unpublished chapter from *Babylon and Jerusalem* that analyzes the Israeli government's treatment of the Arab question. See note 7 below for a list of other recent studies of Rawidowicz's life and thought. I am particularly indebted to Professor Benjamin Ravid, Rawidowicz's son, for taking the time to speak with me about his father, to review earlier drafts of this chapter for factual accuracy, and to provide me with access to his private collection of archival material.

6. Rawidowicz, *Babylon and Jerusalem*, postscript. Translated in Rawidowicz, *State of Israel, Diaspora, and Jewish Continuity*, 204.

7. For an account of Rawidowicz's life, see *Israel: The Ever-Dying People and Other Essays*, 13–50, and reissued in paperback under the title of *State of Israel, Diaspora and Jewish Continuity*. For a more detailed Hebrew version and a bibliography of Rawidowicz's major writings, see *Iyunim bemahshevet yisrael*, 1: 17–82 and 83–92 (Hebrew pagination), respectively. Myers's *Between Jew and Arab* includes a comprehensive biographical sketch that places Rawidowicz's life and thought in the context of wider intellectual and historical developments. Unfortunately, *Between Jew and Arab* appeared too late for me to fully integrate Myers's analysis and translation of Rawidowicz's unpublished essay into this chapter. I have, however, tried to provide some references in the notes to relevant sections in Myers's book. More general

information about Rawidowicz can be found in Ravid, "The Human Dimension of Wissenschaft des Judentums: Letters from the Rawidowicz Archive," in *Studies in Arabic and Hebrew Letters in Honor of Raymond P. Scheindlin*, ed. J. Decter and M. Rand (Piscataway, N.J.: Gorgias Press, 2007), 99–144; and the entry "Simon Rawidowicz," in *Metzler Lexikon Juedischer Philosophen*, ed. A. Kilcher and O. Fraisse (Stuttgart: Metzler, 2003), 389–91.

8. Rawidowicz edited and published two scholarly editions that were particularly well received: an edition of *Sefer hamada*, the first book of Maimonides' *Mishneh torah*, and the publication of Nachman Krochmal's *Moreh nevukhei hazman* (Guide to the perplexed of the time). The release of the Krochmal volume constituted the first annotated edition of this nineteenth-century historian's work. The work, together with Rawidowicz's introductory chapter on Krochmal's intellectual biography, contributed to the revival of this important historian, who had died before his major work was completed. Harris (see his *Nachman Krochmal*) has acknowledged the importance of Rawidowicz's work in Krochmal scholarship.

9. Rawidowicz, *Babylon and Jerusalem*, 784.

10. Simon Rawidowicz, "Book Review: A Theory of Jewish Nationalism," *New Judea*, September 1938, 194.

11. Simon Rawidowicz, "Simon Dubnow in memoriam."

12. Rawidowicz met his future wife, Esther Eugenie Klee, the daughter of the German Zionist leader Dr. Alfred Klee, in one of his Hebrew courses. For more information on his circle in Berlin during the early 1920s, see Brenner, *Renaissance of Jewish Culture in Weimar Germany*, 209–210. Rawidowicz's personal account of this period can be found in A. Ravid, "From the Letters of Simon Rawidowicz" and Rawidowicz, *Sihotai im Bialik*.

13. According to Rawidowiz's explanation in his *Sihotai im Bialik*, he declined the offer, however, because Bialik, concerned about competition from Rawidowicz's other editorial and publishing work, demanded that Rawidowicz relinquish his position at his own press, Ayanot.

14. The reasons for this shift in the center of Hebrew literature were both ideological and economic. Hebrew publishing actually benefited greatly from the rapid inflation in Germany that allowed foreign funds to make such publishing economically viable. The end of this rapid inflation diminished the economic advantages of publishing in Germany. Rawidowicz's relationship with Bialik during the 1920s and early 1930s provides a good barometer of how attitudes shifted during this period. Bialik told his protégé in 1932 that Jews "do not need a homeland" and claimed that Hebrew culture was possible wherever a minyan was present. (From *Merriam-Webster's 11th Collegiate Dictionary*, a "minyan" refers to the quorum required for Jewish communal worship, consisting of ten male adults in Orthodox Judaism and ten adults, male or female, in Conservative and Reform Judaism.) See Rawidowicz, *Sihotai im Bialik* (Conversations with Bialik), 47. Bialik clearly changed his position after his arrival in Tel Aviv: "There is no Hebrew literature outside of the Land of Israel," he wrote to Rawidowicz in 1929 (ibid., 92).

15. Rawidowicz to his brother, February 5, 1930, *Iyunim bemahshevet yisrael*, vol. 1, 32–33.

16. Myers suggests that despite Rawidowicz's very strong credentials, he was only considered as an alternate candidate for the Hebrew University position. See Myers, *Between Jew and Arab*, 51.

17. Benjamin Ravid reports that his father decided not to stay in Palestine in 1925 for two reasons. First, he wanted to complete his doctoral degree (and book on the philosopher Feuerbach) in Berlin. Second, as mentioned above, Rawidowicz had failed to obtain a faculty position at the Hebrew University in 1933. Despite these setbacks, Rawidowicz remained committed to eventually moving to Palestine. In fact, Rawidowicz purchased land in Palestine as an investment property. He thought that the income from several rental units on the property would be sufficient to support him and his scholarly endeavors in Palestine. Unfortunately, the plan failed to generate sufficient income. Conversation with Benjamin Ravid, May 8, 2009.

18. Rawidowicz's colleagues and friends in his circle of Zionist writers and speakers did not appreciate his enduring affirmation for Hebrew language in the diaspora. Rawidowicz's position led to his marginalization from the very organization and movements he had founded. For example, Rawidowicz's name disappeared from the masthead of the Hebrew World Union, the Hebrew-speaking organization he created. There is even some evidence that the poet Haim Nahman Bialik had a role in erasing Rawidowicz's founding position. Rawidowicz's dismay that his name was pushed off the masthead is expressed in *Sihotai im Bialik* (Conversations with Bialik), 14. Another reference to these events is found in a student's recollection of a conversation with him (see Greenbaum, *History of the Ararat Publishing Society,* 68).

19. See, for example, Rawidowicz's series published in *Ha'olam* in December 1931. See Rawidowicz, "Law and Practice: Remarks on the Hebrew Conference in Berlin," *Ha-Olam* 19 (1931): 936–37, 958–59, 978–79, and 998–99. These articles argue that Hebrew in the diaspora is necessary for Jewish survival. They also introduce the idea of two centers, specifically Babylon and Jerusalem, which remained a central theme (and symbols) for Rawidowicz through the publication of *Babylon and Jerusalem* in 1957.

20. As quoted in Myers, *Between Jew and Arab,* 59. The original can be found in "Le'irgun hagolah ha'ivrit," *Moznayim* 3, no. 10 (1931): 3.

21. Myers, *Between Jew and Arab,* 67.

22. See Amos Oz, *A Tale of Love and Darkness* (Orlando, Fla.: Harcourt Books, 2005).

23. See Rawidowicz, *Ludwig Feuerbachs Philosophie* (Ludwig Feuerbach's philosophy). The book was reprinted in 1964, indicating its scholarly significance. In the future Rawidowicz would turn away from his earlier interest in German philosophy. According to his son Benjamin Ravid, Rawidowicz later regretted the fact that he had published a book in German.

24. The essay was published as fourteen chapters between 1933 and 1934. See Simon Rawidowicz, "Kiyum hatefutzah" (Endurance of the diaspora), *Moznayim* 3, no. 2 (1934): 125–39, 265–76, 581–609.

25. The word choice of Rawidowicz's essay title suggests a polemical response to Yaakov Klatzkin's 1914 essay "Ha'galut bat kayam" (There is no future for the exile), in Klatzkin, *Tehumim,* which had by then become an influential tenet of political Zionist ideology. See note 45 for a longer discussion of the relationship between Rawidowicz and Klatzkin.

26. Rawidowicz, *Babylon and Jerusalem,* 218.

27. Benjamin Harshav, a scholar of Hebrew literature, has contended that attitudes about place, time, and identity tended to polarize toward extreme, often mutually

exclusive, formulations. Perhaps the most well-known dichotomy grew out of the clear distinction between here (diaspora) and there (the Land of Israel). See Harshav, *Language in the Time of Revolution*. The historian Ezra Mendelsohn has made a similar claim in his work *On Modern Jewish Politics*.

28. Rawidowicz wrote a series of articles in the Hebrew Journal *Ha'olam* that directly criticizes Ahad Ha'am's conception that life in Palestine can contribute to national culture in the diaspora. See, for example, Rawidowicz, "Leshem hidush sifruteinu" (Toward the renewal of our literature).

29. Only by fully separating from the hopeless reliance on the state's ability to produce relevant formulations of Judaism will "Torah [emerge] from the State of Columbus" (Rawidowicz, *Babylon and Jerusalem,* 259).

30. Rawidowicz had been making this argument against Ahad Ha'am for many years. One of the earliest examples of this debate is found in a 1931 speech inaugurating the Brit Ivrit Olamit. The motto for the organization directly challenged the ideological schisms. Adapting one of Rabbi Hillel's famous dictums, Rawidowicz declared this motto: "If not here—where? If there is nothing 'here' there is nothing 'there.' Here and there, there and here—this is the law of partnership between the land and the dispersion." The speech was published as Rawidowicz, *Im lo kan hekhan* (If not here, where?).

31. Rawidowicz claimed that his reading follows the interpretation of Maimonides. See Rawidowicz, *Babylon and Jerusalem,* 783.

32. The third chapter of *Babylon and Jerusalem,* "Eruvin," refers to *Masechet eruvin,* a volume of the Talmud dealing with two rabbinic institutions permitting certain behaviors normally forbidden on the Sabbath. First, the eruv hatzerot ("the courtyard eruv") is a legal argument that permits items to be carried between private domains and public realms. Eruv tehumim ("the boundary eruv") constitutes the second category. This legal loophole extends the distance an individual can walk outside the boundaries of a residential neighborhood on the Sabbath by placing a small amount of food on the outskirts of his town to symbolically extend his dwelling place. Rawidowicz quoted Maimonides' *Mishneh torah* to define the process by which families sharing a courtyard could enlarge their permitted sphere for carrying on the Sabbath by bringing a set amount of food to one communal place. Thus, Maimonides continued, "all those who contribute food are all joined in one property" (see Maimonides, *Hilkhot Eruvin* 1:6). For basic information on the eruv, see "Eruvin," in *Encyclopedia Judaica* (Jerusalem: Keter Publishing, 1973).

33. Rawidowicz based his explanation of eruvin on these two rabbinic typologies; however, he adapted the general concept for his ideological purposes and disregarded its legal details, especially its relevance for the Sabbath and holidays.

34. Rawidowicz, *Babylon and Jerusalem,* 197.

35. Ibid., 265.

36. Ibid., 198.

37. Rawidowicz's effort to establish the term interland instead of interstate would parallel an effort in the English language to change the term transnational to trans-statist. This shift would overcome the confusion that a transnational group describes a community whose national bonds transcend state boundaries.

38. Although Rawidowicz adopts this term from Klausner, he contends that Klausner misunderstands the source of this phenomenon. For Rawidowicz, the goyish

element stems from the "rejection of all of the galut-continuity." See *Israel, the Ever-Dying People*, 178.

39. Harshav, in his *Language in the Time of Revolution*, understands language as a "way of assimilating content by altering form," 41.

40. Although the language wars of the early twentieth century pitted Yiddishists and Hebraists, both implicitly agreed with the assumption that social autonomy and linguistic modernization were necessary for national culture.

41. See, for example, the article "Leshem hidush sifruteinu," which laments the negative impact that spoken Hebrew had on the written language.

42. Pollock, *The Language of the Gods*.

43. This point is one of the major differences between Rawidowicz's conception of national culture and Mordecai Kaplan's conception of Jewish peoplehood (discussed in detail in chapter 4).

44. Rawidowicz claimed that "the eruv is so powerful that it actually overcomes space" (Rawidowicz, *Babylon and Jerusalem*, 198).

45. Although Rawidowicz did not make this explicit link, there are a number of clues demonstrating eruvin's purpose as a challenge to Zionist rhetoric. The play between the terms eruvin and tehumim (boundaries) in this chapter certainly hints at a polemic against leading European Zionist ideologue Yaakov Klatzkin's emphasis on defining Israel's tehumim. Klatzkin published a collection of his essays called *Tehumim* in 1928. He insisted that the Jewish nation's only hope for survival was a return to its "natural tehumim: land and language" (see Klatzkin, *Tehumim*, 54).Perhaps Klatzkin, the son of a Talmud scholar, adopted the term to indicate the centrality of fixed spatial demarcations in traditional Jewish law. Applying this principle to political discourse, Klatzkin translated the notion of tehumim into the basic boundary for a modern nation-state—territorial sovereignty. In direct opposition to Klatzkin, who viewed territorial boundaries as the key to Jewish survival, Rawidowicz used the concept of eruv to challenge the assumption made by Zionist theorists that nation-state tehumim remain the sine qua non of Jewish nationalism.

46. A recent article analyzing the origins of the rabbinic concept of the eruv by the Talmud scholar Charlotte Fonrobert in fact highlights the eruv's role "as a project of constructing, maintaining and re-enacting a collective identity in relation to the residential space of the mixed urban courtyard" (Fonrobert, "From Separatism to Urbanism," 32).

47. Rawidowicz, "On Interpretation." A revised version of the essay appears in Rawidowicz, *Studies in Jewish Thought*, 45–80. Myers offers an in-depth analysis of this essay in his "Third Guide for the Perplexed?"

48. Rawidowicz, "Interpretation," in his *Studies in Jewish Thought*, 47.

49. See Rawidowicz, "Toward the Renewal of Our Literature," 994.

50. The scholar Mitchell Cohen has picked up on a similar metaphor in his discussion of *shaatnez* (a Torah prohibition against wearing garments made of wool and linen) as a model for Jewish politics in multicultural America. See Cohen's essay "In Defense of Shaatnez" in Biale, Galchinsky, and Heschel, *Insider/Outsider*, 34–55.

51. Myers has suggested that Rawidowicz's choice of the term house instead of temple might indicate his desire to move these categories away from their roots in religious institutions (see Myers, "Third Guide for the Perplexed?"). Indeed, Rawidowicz uses the term house to refer to a period longer than that of the First and Second Temple.

52. Rawidowicz's periodization—which categorized the return to Jerusalem and

the rebuilding of the temple and Jewish autonomy in the Land of Israel as part of the Second House period—closely mirrored Krochmal's breakdown of Jewish history (see Harris, *Nachman Krochmal*).

53. Rawidowicz, *Babylon and Jerusalem*, 72.

54. The focus on the importance of myth had a philosophical analogue for Rawidowicz in the erosion of philosophical idealism at the start of the twentieth century. He lamented specifically "a new generation in Germany arose that knew not Kant, Goethe, Luther, humanism and idealism." He concluded that the need to revitalize utopian visions of the past had eroded the central distinction in German thought, separating the theoretical values of humanism and liberalism from such concrete categories as blood, land, leader, and state. This strict Kantian separation between the real and the ideal had guaranteed two crucial safeguards that heavily influenced the status of Jews in modern European society. Positing the existence of universal, a priori moral criteria—even if they did not always manifest themselves in the concrete realities of quotidian interactions and political affairs—served as an orienting ethical force in human affairs. Idealism, the notion that real and ideal are separated, serves the parallel purpose to myth in religious traditions. See Rawidowicz, "Kiyum hatefutzah," 131.

55. Despite the Hebrew terminology and specific historical context, Rawidowicz's categorization of the philosophical developments of the First and Second Houses corresponded quite closely to Hegelian accounts of historical idealism. The Second House, to translate Rawidowicz's thought back into secular philosophical discourse, developed an epistemological approach that integrated the divine spirit into history. The rabbinic tradition strove to discern the absolute within historical developments. Their idealism manifested a level of philosophical self-consciousness of the dialectical relationship between current reality and ultimate historical meaning.

56. Rawidowicz wrote that myth has become "materialized" by the "stamp of pragmatism and positivism" (see Rawidowicz, *Studies in Jewish Thought*, 419).

57. Ibid., 418.

58. This effort to remystify the tradition echoes what the intellectual historian Allan Megill has termed the aesthetic dimension in Nietzsche. See Allan Megill, *Prophets of Extremity* (Berkeley: University of California Press, 1987).

59. Rawidowicz, "Kiyum hatefutzah," 128.

60. The cultural historian Carl Schorske has made a similar argument about political developments in Europe at the turn of the twentieth century. See Carl E. Schorske, *Fin-de-Siècle Vienna: Politics and Culture* (New York: Vintage, 1980).

61. Rawidowicz, *Babylon and Jerusalem*, 172.

62. The Hebrew literature scholar Sidra Ezrahi has articulated a parallel argument regarding the dangers inherent in Zionism's move to equate the political return to the Land of Israel with literary expressions of homecoming. Ezrahi explores the intersection of fiction and reality in twentieth-century Jewish literature. See Sidra Ezrahi, *Booking Passage: Exile and Homecoming in the Modern Jewish Imagination* (Berkeley: University of California Press, 2000).

63. This illuminates Rawidowicz's grievance that the new state "consists of a new foundation that is a complete reality: the State of Israel—from Judaism was taken . . . the foundation of foundations: the foundation of the messiah in its hidden form" (see Rawidowicz, *Babylon and Jerusalem*, 182).

64. For a discussion of Ben Gurion's messianic claims, see Eliezer Don-Yehiya and Charles Liebman, *Civil Religion in Israel: Traditional Judaism and Political Culture in the Jewish State* (Berkeley: University of California Press, 1983), 86. Rawidowicz's generalizations about the centrality of the messiah in Zionist ideology appear reductive and disingenuous, particularly from a sophisticated secular thinker. Rawidowicz reduced the complexities of Zionist thought to create a straw-man position for his argument that Jewish messianism eschewed political realization. In doing so, however, he ignored the complexity and range of views within the Zionist movement itself toward the historical and religious import of the founding of the state. Ideas of messianism certainly reverberated through both secular and religious theories of Zionism, but not all of these visions embraced 1948 as ushering in the messianic moment in Jewish history. Such highly visible thinkers as Gershom Scholem joined Rawidowicz in the efforts to "neutralize the apocalyptic sting" of messianism. See Gershom Scholem, *The Messianic Idea in Judaism and Other Essays on Jewish Spirituality* (New York: Schocken Books, 1971).

65. For more on the distinction between political and religious exile in Jewish thought, and its multiple interpretations in the modern period, see Eisen, *Galut*.

66. According to Rawidowicz's interpretation of rabbinic and philosophical traditions, a political return to the Land of Israel had to be integrally linked with metaphysical, or messianic, redemption. In an attempt to prove the fallacy of messianic claims, Rawidowicz listed the political compromises forced on the nascent state—the lack of massive aliyah (immigration) from the Western diaspora and the internecine tensions stirred up by the return of large numbers of Jews to the Land of Israel. The founding of the state thus failed to fulfill the primary criteria for redemption as described in the Jewish sources. For an extended discussion of the tension between Jewish sources and Zionism, see Aviezer Ravitzky, *Messianism, Zionism, and Jewish Religious Radicalism* (Chicago: University of Chicago Press, 1996).

67. Rawidowicz experienced the need to warn against external influences because he worried about the complete dissolution of traditional sources and knowledge. Judaism, he stressed throughout his work, operated with little influence from non-Jewish sources. He first introduced this methodological approach in his pathbreaking essay on Krochmal, which argued that the great Jewish historian was not influenced by Hegel's philosophy of history. His defense of Krochmal's intellectual purity was part of his battle against integrating words and concepts he considered foreign into Jewish life. Rawidowicz wrote that the role of Zionism is to engage in a "battle against *lo'az*" (that is, foreign language). He explained the resonances between Jewish thought and other intellectual currents as proof that Jewish sources already contained the seeds of later philosophical and religious innovations. See Rawidowicz, *Babylon and Jerusalem*, 261. Unlike his younger contemporary, Gerson Cohen, who insisted on the productive effects of adopting new forms and ideas in his 1966 address "The Blessings of Assimilation," Rawidowicz had little patience for the extent to which Western philosophy had undermined a familiarity and respect for traditional Jewish sources. Cohen's speech was first delivered at the Hebrew Teacher's College commencement in 1966. For a reprint of the lecture, see Gerson D. Cohen, "The Blessing of Assimilation in Jewish History," in *Great Jewish Speeches throughout History*, ed. Israel Forman (Northvale, N.J.: Jason Aronson, 1994), 183–91. Rawidowicz's own perception of the relationship between contemporary ideas and events and the Jewish tradition

remained far more nuanced. Other aspects of his work clearly indicate the importance of dialogue between text and context in his thought.

68. See Simon Rawidowicz, "Kiyum lelo tenai," *Metzuda*. The English translation remained unpublished, but Rawidowicz used it as a text for lectures. A revised English translation based on Rawidowicz's original is in Rawidowicz, *State of Israel, Diaspora, and Jewish Continuity*, 118–29.

69. Rawidowicz, *State of Israel, Diaspora, and Jewish Continuity*, 124.

70. Ibid., 128.

71. See ibid., 43. Special thanks to Benjamin Ravid for making the unpublished Hebrew manuscript of this chapter available for my use. The full translated text of this essay has recently been published for the first time by Myers in *Between Jew and Arab*. Myers translates the title of the essay "Between Jew and Arab" (rather than a more literal Between Hebrew and Arab) to reflect Rawidowicz's expansive use of the word Hebrew to refer to the Jewish people. Myers speculates on Rawidowicz's motivations for censoring the chapter, but concludes that the actual reason remains a mystery. See *Between Jew and Arab*, 24–31.

72. Rawidowicz, *Babylon and Jerusalem*, 459.

73. Myers includes full translations of these laws in his appendix in *Between Jew and Arab*, 194–202.

74. Rawidowicz, "Between Hebrew and Arab," 15a. Rawidowicz, "Bein ever ve'arav" unpublished manuscript, 15a. Translation quoted from Myers, *Between Jew and Arab*, 154.

75. Rawidowicz also offered a number of practical problems arising as a result of preventing the return of the 1948 Arab refugees. He noted that the refugee problem would be a blessing for Arab states that hoped to destroy Israel. Rawidowicz argued that six hundred thousand Arabs *outside* Israel were far more dangerous than six hundred thousand *inside* the new state (see ibid.). Striving for a particular ethnonational makeup, at the price of exiling those who had occupied the land, struck him as ethically out of line with his understanding of Jewish nationalism. He wrote: "where are the commandments of the 'ethical nation' in whose name Zionism waved its flag? Isn't the first command of all chosen people: Thou shalt not uproot man from his land, whether a member of your people or not?" (see ibid., 21).

76. Rawidowicz, *Babylon and Jerusalem*, 459.

77. The handwritten note is addressed to Rawidowicz and signed by the author, Mordecai Kaplan. This copy of *Judaism as a Civilization* can be found in the Simon Rawidowicz Archive, Newton, Mass.

78. Rawidowicz, "Kiyum hatefutzah."

4. Making American Democracy Safe for Judaism

1. Samuel Huntington, *Who Are We? The Challenges to American National Identity* (New York: Simon & Schuster, 2004).

2. See Sarna, *American Judaism*, 247.

3. See Arthur Hertzberg, *The Zionist Idea* (Philadelphia: Jewish Publication Society, 1997), 536. Hertzberg acknowledges Kaplan's fundamental differences with political Zionism, such as his affirmation of diaspora life as a creative value and his insistence on a more "tradition-minded" community in the Land of Israel. These important

distinctions, however, fail to acknowledge Kaplan's deep reluctance about, and even opposition to, statehood.

4. The Reconstructionist movement joined the Reform, Conservative, and Orthodox movements as the fourth major denomination of American Judaism.

5. Kaplan, "Judaism and Nationality," 61–63; and Kaplan, *Religion of Ethical Nationhood*.

6. This reading of civilization is meant to complement recent scholarly interest in identifying the influences shaping Kaplan's thought. An article by Deborah Dash Moore and Andrew Bush has drawn parallels between his adoption of the prominent position of the term and the language of civilization present in two influential works by American intellectuals published in the years preceding the publication of *Judaism as a Civilization* in 1934: John Dewey's *Philosophy and Civilization* (1931) and Charles and Mary Beard's *The Rise of American Civilization* (1927). By adopting the popular use of civilization, these interpretations suggest, Kaplan succeeded in translating Judaism into the language of American thought and in elevating Jewish history to the same status as American history. See Moore and Bush, "Kaplan's Key." Such readings support the claim that Kaplan turned to the use of civilization as part of his efforts to rewrite Judaism in an American key. This scholarship warrants serious consideration. As even a cursory glance through Kaplan's journal or footnotes indicates, Kaplan read widely and had most likely encountered the well-known definitions of civilization that had been offered by Dewey and the Beards.

7. This was not the first time that Kaplan had encountered Rawidowicz's work. His diary entry from June 9, 1927, refers to reading the edition of Krochmal's *Guide for the Perplexed of the Time*, which was edited and introduced by Rawidowicz. See "Mordecai Menahem Kaplan, 1881," box 1, vol. 3, File ARC 65, Kaplan Diaries and Papers, Jewish Theological Seminary, New York.

8. See Scult, *Judaism Faces the Twentieth Century*, 25.

9. Benjamin Ravid's biography of his father, Simon Rawidowicz, claims that the name Rawidowicz was "derived from the position of an ancestor, who had served in the capacity of *Rosh Av Bet din* (head of rabbinical court)" (see Rawidowicz, *State of Israel, Diaspora, and Jewish Continuity*, 13). Ravid relates that Rawidowicz's father was deeply committed to the education of Simon, whom he wanted to become a rabbi. Father and son would awaken before dawn every day to study together (see ibid., 15). Kaplan's father was considered a "brilliant and erudite" young scholar and received rabbinic ordination from Rabbi Naphtali Zvi Judah Berlin, known as the Netziv, and the rabbi of the Volozhin Yeshiva, one of Lithuania's most prestigious institutions of religious learning in the nineteenth century.

10. Scult, *Judaism Faces the Twentieth Century*, 30. Kaplan spent one year in France with his mother en route to New York City.

11. Ibid.

12. Ibid., 39. Kaplan, *Communings of the Spirit*, 108.

13. Kaplan, "Toward a Reconstruction of Judaism."

14. Kaplan, *Communings of the Spirit*, 170.

15. Diary entry, August, 24, 1914, "Mordecai Menahem Kaplan, 1881," box 1, vol. 1, File ARC 65, Kaplan Diaries and Papers.

16. The preface to the 1957 edition appears on page xxvii of the 1994 edition of Kaplan's *Judaism as a Civilization*. See Kaplan, *Judaism as a Civilization*, xxvii.

17. One of those replacement terms—peoplehood—became intimately linked with Kaplan's legacy. Thus a term closely associated with civilization did not actually appear in his initial formulation of the concept and obfuscates his intentional use of the language of nation in his magnum opus.

18. Kaplan, "How May Judaism Be Saved?" 41.

19. See Mel Scult, ed., *The American Judaism of Mordecai Kaplan* (New York: New York University Press, 1990), 156.

20. Diary entry, July 22, 1918, "Mordecai Menahem Kaplan, 1881," box 2, vol. 1, File ARC 65, Kaplan Diaries and Papers. This is not the first time Kaplan mentioned problems with democracy in his diary. An entry from March 30, 1913, argued: "democracy threatens the very integrity of the Jewish social group" (ibid.).

21. See Gleason, *Speaking of Diversity.*

22. See Kallen, "Democracy versus the Melting-Pot"; and Bourne, "The Jew and Trans-National America."

23. Kaplan, "How May Judaism Be Saved?" 38.

24. Kaplan, *Judaism as a Civilization,* 37.

25. Kaplan, "Future of Judaism," 160.

26. Kaplan, "Judaism and Christianity," 112.

27. Ibid.

28. Ibid., 115.

29. Ibid.

30. Bourne, "The Jew and Trans-National America," 284.

31. See Bederman, *Manliness and Civilization.*

32. Ibid., 57.

33. For a broader discussion of Kaplan's use of civilization in the context of expressing the Jewish contribution to civilization, see Biale, "Louis Finkelstein, Mordecai Kaplan, and American 'Jewish Contributions to Civilization'"; and Myers, "Discourses of Civilization."

34. Scult, *Judaism Faces the Twentieth Century,* 261.

35. Kaplan, *Judaism as a Civilization,* 264.

36. Ibid., 233.

37. Ibid., 20.

38. Ibid., 413.

39. Ibid., 234.

40. Ibid.

41. See Jacobson, *Whiteness of a Different Color.*

42. This list of criteria for the elements of a civilization was not thoroughly consistent across Kaplan's various publications, but he never strayed too far from the list that he introduced in the third section of his *Judaism as a Civilization.*

43. Kaplan, *Judaism as a Civilization,* 432.

44. Kaplan does not completely avoid the term culture in his discussion of folkways, however. He distinguishes between two levels of folkways—cultural and religious. See ibid., 433.

45. Kaplan links his definition of civilization as a paraphrase of William Graham Sumner's definition of ethos, from his book *Folkways: A Study of the Sociological Importance of Usages, Manners, Customs, Mores, and Morals* (Boston: Ginn, 1907). See Kaplan, *Judaism as a Civilization,* 535.

46. The political theorist Michael Walzer has made a similar move in his analysis of religious community as the basis for his model of thick difference that exemplifies multicultural citizenship. See, for example, Walzer, *What Does It Mean to Be an American?* and his "Multiculturalism and the Politics of Difference."

47. Will Herberg, *Protestant, Catholic, Jew: An Essay in American Religious Sociology* (Garden City, N.Y.: Doubleday, 1955).

48. Kaplan mentions the incompatibility of the diaspora nationalist Simon Dubnow and the project of East European diaspora nationalism for American Jewish life. See Kaplan, *The Future of the American Jew.* Interestingly, as mentioned earlier, Kaplan ultimately aligned himself far more closely with Ahad Ha'am's cultural Zionism than with Dubnow's diaspora nationalism.

49. This is precisely the argument correctly made by such scholars as Charles Liebman: that Kaplan, despite his claims to the contrary, articulated a theory of Judaism that was not so dissimilar from concepts of Judaism as a religion (such as the Reform ideology) that he inveighed against. See Liebman's "Reconstructionism in American Jewish Life." Similarly, Kaplan scholar Arnold Eisen has noted that Kaplan "demanded a 'maximalist Judaism' of his readers but then, under pressure from the 'reality principle,' quickly retreated to the recognition that every maximum would be a function of what the surroundings would allow and the individual would undertake" (see Arnold M. Eisen, "The Problem Is Still with Us," *Conservative Judaism* 56, no. 2 [2004]: 21).

50. Ultimately, the concept of religious civilization resonated too clearly with Kaplan's followers, however. The religious component of his work, rather than the theory of nationality, is remembered.

51. Harold Schulweis, "A Critical Assessment of Kaplan's Idea of Salvation," in Scult, *American Judaism of Mordecai Kaplan.*

52. Kaplan, *Judaism as a Civilization,* 199.

53. Ibid., 322.

54. Ibid., 259.

55. Ibid., 342.

56. See Richard Wightman Fox's critique of Protestant historiography that "misconstrues the depth and character of the linkage between secular and religious forces throughout this period," in his article "The Culture of Liberal Protestant Progressivism, 1875–1925," *Journal of Interdisciplinary History* 3 (Winter 1993): 645.

57. Diary entry, May 10, 1933, "Mordecai Menahem Kaplan, 1881," box 2, vol. 7, File ARC 65, Kaplan Diaries and Papers.

58. Reinhold Niebuhr, *Moral Man and Immoral Society* (New York: Charles Scribner's Sons, 1932), xi.

59. Diary entry, May 8, 1934, "Mordecai Menahem Kaplan, 1881," box 2, vol. 7, File ARC 65, Kaplan Diaries and Papers.

60. Diary entry, May 6, 1934, "Mordecai Menahem Kaplan, 1881," box 2, vol. 7, File ARC 65, Kaplan Diaries and Papers. However, he was still enamored with the communist movement a year later, when he wrote in his journal: "Because of my keen desire to see it survive I cannot conscientiously advise against joining the Communist movement on the ground of anything that Judaism teaches." (Diary entry, March 9, 1935, "Mordecai Menahem Kaplan, 1881," box 2, vol. 7, File ARC 65, Kaplan Diaries and Papers.) See also V. I. Lenin, *Lenin on the Jewish Question* (New York: International Publishers, 1934).

61. Diary entry, February 18, 1939, "Mordecai Menahem Kaplan, 1881," box 3, vol. 8, File ARC 65, Kaplan Diaries and Papers.

62. Ibid.

63. Kaplan continued to use the terms interchangeably in his writings until the publication of his last book, *Religion of Ethical Nationhood*.

64. Kaplan, *Future of the American Jew*, 125.

65. Will Kymlicka has explained the challenge clearly when he states his goal of demonstrating "how minority rights coexist with human rights" (see Kymlicka, *Multicultural Citizenship*, 6).

66. One of Kaplan's 1939 diary entries says that Jewish nationhood "should also contribute toward the elimination from nationhood its dross of collective selfishness and sacred egoism and render it essentially a means of social creativity and individual betterment." (Diary entry, February 7, 1939, "Mordecai Menahem Kaplan, 1881," box 3, vol. 8, File ARC 65, Kaplan Diaries and Papers.)

67. Kaplan, *Judaism as a Civilization*, 244.

68. This strategy is strikingly similar to the defense of national cohesion outlined by the political theorist David Miller. Miller, drawing from recent ethical theory, distinguishes between an ethics of particularity and an ethics of universality (see Miller, *On Nationality*).

69. Diary entry, February 19, 1939, "Mordecai Menahem Kaplan, 1881," box 3, vol. 8, File ARC 65, Kaplan Diaries and Papers.

70. See Hollinger, *Cosmopolitanism and Solidarity: Studies in Ethnoracial, Religious, and Professional Affiliation in the U.S.;* Appiah, *Ethics of Identity;* Mitchell Cohen, "Rooted Cosmopolitanism"; and Carol A. Breckenridge et al., eds., *Cosmopolitanism* (Durham, N.C.: Duke University Press, 2002).

71. Appiah, *The Ethics of Identity*.

72. Kaplan, *Future of the American Jew*, 143.

73. Kymlicka has adopted the approach of linking liberal values with national identification. The commitment to freedom of choice and personal autonomy, he argues, "is not only consistent with, but even requires, a concern with cultural membership . . . [I]ndividual choice is dependent on the presence of a societal culture, defined by language and history, and . . . most people have a very strong bond to their own culture" (see Kymlicka, *Multicultural Citizenship*, 8).

74. Diary entry, February 18, 1939, "Mordecai Menahem Kaplan, 1881," box 3, vol. 8, File ARC 65, Kaplan Diaries and Papers. Kaplan, *Future of the American Jew*, 154.

75. Anthony D. Smith, *Theories of Nationalism*.

76. Tamir, *Liberal Nationalism*, 80.

77. Diary entry, February 19, 1939, "Mordecai Menahem Kaplan, 1881," box 3, vol. 8, File ARC 65, Kaplan Diaries and Papers.

78. Diary entry, February 7, 1939, "Mordecai Menahem Kaplan, 1881," box 3, vol. 8, File ARC 65, Kaplan Diaries and Papers.

79. Diary entry as cited in Kaplan, *Communings of the Spirit*, 102.

80. Kaplan himself acknowledged this predicament: "Since they can no longer claim the right to cultivate a corporate Jewish life on the traditional basis of being the sole possessors of supernatural revelation, they must be able to base that right on their interpretation of nationhood" (see Kaplan, *Judaism as a Civilization*, 251).

81. Diary entry, February 18, 1939, "Mordecai Menahem Kaplan, 1881," box 3, vol. 8, File ARC 65, Kaplan Diaries and Papers.

82. Ibid.

83. Kaplan, "Future of Judaism," 170.

84. Kaplan supported the Kehillah and served as a member of the education committee. The Kehillah had a number of small successes, including Kaplan's work in the bureau of Jewish education. However, by 1922 the organization was defunct; see Scult, *Judaism Faces the Twentieth Century*, 116–19. For an in-depth account of the failure of the Kehillah experiment, see Goren, *New York Jews and the Quest for Community*.

85. Goren, *New York Jews and the Quest for Community*, 3.

86. Scult, *Judaism Faces the Twentieth Century*, 116.

87. Kaplan, *Judaism as a Civilization*, 293. In addition, Kaplan insisted, "if Jewish life is to exercise an educative influence upon the character of the Jew, it must possess the instrumentality of Jewish self-government and opportunity of law-making" (ibid., 468).

88. Mordecai M. Kaplan, editorial, *Society for the Advancement of Judaism Bulletin* 7, no. 12 (1927): 3.

89. Kaplan, *Judaism as a Civilization*, 234.

90. Kaplan accepted the limitations of Jewish legal courts within the U.S. system by suggesting that even though Judaism wished to "exercise authority in the matter of separation and divorce it cannot afford to ignore the superior power of the state." Nevertheless, he still insisted that "Judaism can so adapt its laws that its authority will be felt" (ibid., 424).

91. The anthropologist and lawyer Jonathan Boyarin's ruminations on the possibility of promoting the recognition of "genealogical and diasporic loyalty" in U.S. constitutional law provide a more nuanced contemporary example of an argument for separate legal spheres within the courts. While Kaplan envisioned a parallel legal system, Boyarin analyzes the far more plausible possibility of altering the extant legal approach to adjudicate based on the specific needs of particular diasporic communities rather than applying standard rulings to all citizens as equal individuals. See Boyarin and Boyarin, *Powers of Diaspora*, and Goren, *New York Jews and the Quest for Community*.

92. For instance, Kaplan acknowledged the fact that a U.S. citizen "derive[s] his political values, his language, literature and the arts from the civilization embodied in the state" (see Kaplan, *Judaism as a Civilization*, 234).

93. Kaplan directly talked about the difficulty of creating the right to self-government in his discussion of Dubnow (see Kaplan, *Judaism as a Civilization*, 25). He also acknowledged that the Jewish community can no longer demand "full legal jurisdiction" (see ibid., 109).

94. Kymlicka, *Multicultural Citizenship*, 27.

95. Kaplan, *Future of the American Jew*, 143.

96. Ibid., 158.

97. Ibid., 129.

98. Goren's conclusion that Kaplan "acknowledged the prior lien of America and its civilization on the individual's loyalty and interest" underestimated Kaplan's tormented relationship with the process of acculturation (see Goren, *Politics and Public Culture of American Jews*, 16). Goren has also commented that "living in two civilizations the American Jew, in Kaplan's celebrated analysis, subordinated the Jewish to the American" (ibid., 160).

99. Diary entry, December 14, 1924, "Mordecai Menahem Kaplan, 1881," box 1, vol. 2, File ARC 65, Kaplan Diaries and Papers.

100. There is no doubt about the centrality of homeland in Kaplan's concept of nationalism. He asserted that land remained a "constituent element of Judaism as a civilization" and insisted that the Bible has "in it a perfectly recorded deed to the possession of *Eretz Yisrael*" (see Kaplan, *Judaism as a Civilization*, 186 and 264). The masthead of his own *Reconstructionist* magazine read: "dedicated to the advancement of Judaism as a religious civilization, to the upbuilding of Eretz Yisrael, and to the furtherance of universal freedom, justice and peace."

101. His concerns about Zionism ranged from the pragmatic (Jews historically were able to develop a "far stronger bond of unity" than nations "living unmolested on [their] own native soil") to ethical ("I became convinced that we Jews are in an awful mess with prospects in Palestine. . . . Jews have gotten themselves into such a tangle . . . by persisting to stand out as a distinct group"). See Kaplan, *Communings of the Spirit*, 465; and *Judaism as a Civilization*, 190.

102. Goren's article "Spiritual Zionists and Jewish Sovereignty" (in Goren, *Politics and Public Culture of American Jews*) acknowledges and analyzes Kaplan's wariness toward statehood. My argument builds off Goren's important research by delving more deeply into the specific characteristics of Kaplan's formulation of ethical nationhood.

103. Kaplan, *Communings of the Spirit*, 201.

104. Kaplan's ire at Weizmann's statement is particularly interesting given Weizmann's history as a founding member of the Democratic Faction and a man quite sympathetic to the Arab plight in Palestine. See Lavsky, "German Zionists and the Emergence of *Brit Shalom*." Kaplan's emotional bond to the Zionist project and its potential was reflected in the journal entry that immediately preceded his diatribe against Weizmann. He described the tears that welled up in his eyes while singing "Hatikvah" in Italy and conveyed his joy and excitement at "the effort of our people to come back to life" (Kaplan, *Communings of the Spirit*, 201).

105. Kaplan, ibid., 377.

106. Goren, *Politics and Public Culture of American Jews*, 16.

107. This reading of Kaplan's Zionism as a corrective to the Americanization process directly challenges historian Ben Halpern's claim that Kaplan's Zionism "produced the most thoroughly American variant of Zionism" (see Ben Halpern, "The Americanization of Zionism, 318–36).

108. Kaplan, *Future of the American Jew,* 125.

109. Kaplan, *Judaism as a Civilization*, 243.

110. Kaplan's vision of a world state that would ensure the peaceful coexistence of distinct national groups fits squarely into the idealistic hopes of the left wing of the internationalist movement during the interwar years. Nevertheless, it must have been seen as woefully utopian only a few years after the publication of his magnum opus.

5. From German Zionism to American Nationalism

1. For Kaplan's full description of the meeting, see Kaplan, *Communings of the Spirit,* 464.

2. Ibid., 465.

3. For example, Kohn scholar Ken Wolf has pointed out that the 1970 edition of the *Britannica* contained the following articles by Kohn: "Atlantic Charter," "Communism," "Fascism," "Theodor Herzl," "National Socialism," "Nationalism," "Minorities,"

"Pan-Germanism," "Pan-Slavism," "Pan-Turanism," and "Zionism." Kohn also contributed to the *Britannica Book of the Year* and the *Encyclopedia of the Social Sciences.* See Wolf, "Idea of Nationalism," 353. A full list of Kohn's publications is listed in ibid., 321–53. Another bibliography of Kohn's publications appears in Kohn, *Reflections on Modern History: The Historian and Human Responsibility,* 357–59.

4. Koppel S. Pinson hailed the book as "an epoch-making work in American historiography," and the *New England Quarterly* considered the book "the most significant contribution that has yet to be made to the study of the subject." See Koppel S. Pinson, "Book Review: The Idea of Nationalism," *Journal of Modern History* 16, no. 3 (1944): 224; and Solomon Willis Rudy, "Book Review: The Idea of Nationalism," *New England Quarterly* 17, no. 3 (1944): 468.

5. Frederick L. Schuman, "Review of Hans Kohn, *The Idea of Nationalism,*" *New York Times Book Review,* April 30, 1944, quoted in Liebich, "Searching for the Perfect Nation."

6. See Anderson, *Imagined Communities,* 4. Anthony Smith regularly refers to Kohn's theory as "the best-known example" of the "influential distinction between 'Western' and 'Eastern' nationalisms." (See Smith, *Nationalism and Modernism,* 16.) Kohn's historical narrative, and especially his distinction between two varieties of nationalism, made him, in the words of the political scientist Craig Calhoun, "the most influential source of both the opposition of civic and ethnic nationalism and of its association with a parallel opposition between western and eastern varieties of modernity" (Craig Calhoun, "Foreword," in Kohn, *Idea of Nationalism,* ix). See also Kohn, *Idea of Nationalism,* and Ignatieff, *Blood and Belonging.*

7. The first, and for many years only, sustained scholarship on Kohn's theory of nationalism was produced by Ken Wolf. See Wolf's "Idea of Nationalism" and "Hans Kohn's Nationalism." Scholars of nationalism, such as Craig Calhoun and Andre Liebich, have recently demonstrated renewed interest in Kohn's work (see Liebich, "Searching for the Perfect Nation," and Calhoun, "Foreword" in Kohn, *Idea of Nationalism*). Jewish historians Hagit Lavsky, Steven Aschheim, Shalom Ratzabi, George Mosse, and Yfaat Weiss have contextualized Kohn's theory of Zionism within a larger context of German Jewish Zionism, European nationalism, and the Brit Shalom circle in Palestine. See Weiss, "Central European Ethnonationalism and Zionist Binationalism"; Lavsky, "Hans Kohn: Nationalism between Theory and Practice"; Aschheim, *Beyond the Border;* Mendes-Flohr, *Land of Two Peoples;* and George Mosse, "Central European Intellectuals in Palestine," *Judaism* 45, no. 2 (1996): 134–43. Also of relevance is Adi Gordon's dissertation; see "New Politics in an Old Key: Arnold Zweig, Hans Kohn and the Central European Jewish Generation of 1914."

8. Adi Gordon, "The Serial Convert and the 'Mythology of Coherence': The Contradictory Hans Kohn and His Multiple Metamorphoses," lecture delivered at the Legacy of Hans Kohn conference, March 11–12, 2009, Jerusalem.

9. Narratives written by scholars of Zionism tend to abruptly end with Kohn's decision to leave Palestine in 1933. Analysts of Kohn's later work, such as Wolf and Calhoun, include details about Kohn's involvement with Zionism; however, they focus on the discontinuities in Kohn's intellectual development between the two stages of his career.

10. One can even read *Judaism as a Religious Civilization,* which Kaplan was writing at the same time that he attended Kohn's lecture in 1931, as a response to Kohn's challenge. As Kaplan's subsequent works (specifically *Religion of Ethical Nationhood*)

suggest, however, *Judaism as a Civilization* did not fully satisfy his own continued need to grapple with the critique of Jewish nationalism as universal humanism.

11. Kaplan recalled hearing Kohn describe his childhood relationship to Judaism during his lecture as follows: "[u]ntil the age of eighteen Judaism meant nothing to him [Kohn] because he had come from an assimilationist background. At every Christmas there was a Yule tree in his home and they sang Christmas songs." Although many acculturated Hapsburg Jews had Christmas trees, Kohn's decision to share the information in the context of explaining the level of his family's acculturation demonstrates his lack of connection to Judaism before his introduction to the Bar Kochba Society in 1908. Kaplan, *Communings of the Spirit*, 466.

12. Weiss, "Central European Ethnonationalism and Zionist Binationalism," 100.

13. The three essays were published under the title *Drei Reden über Judentum* (Three addresses on Judaism). For an English translation of the lectures, see Martin Buber, *On Judaism*. For recent scholarship exploring Kohn's involvement with Prague Zionism, see Shumsky, "On Ethno-Centrism and Its Limits: Czecho-German Jewry in Fin-de-Siècle Prague and the Origins of Zionist Bi-Nationalism," and Zohar Maor, "Mysticism, Regeneration, and Jewish Rebirth: The 'Prague Circle' in the Beginning of the Twentieth Century."

14. See Nahum Glatzer and Paul Mendes-Flohr, eds., *The Letters of Martin Buber: A Life of Dialogue* (New York: Pantheon Books, 1991), 130.

15. Hans Kohn, *Martin Buber: Sein Werk und seine Zeit, Ein Versuch über Religion und Politik*.

16. Kohn et al., *Vom Judentum*.

17. Kohn provides a rough account of this journey in his autobiography; see Kohn, *Living in a World Revolution*.

18. Hans Kohn to Leo Hermann, October 3, 1919, Collection KH1, Folder 674, Central Zionist Archives, Jerusalem.

19. Ibid.

20. Ibid.

21. Letter from the New York office of Keren Hayesod to Leo Hermann, February 18, 1922, Collection KH1, Folder 245, Central Zionist Archives, Jerusalem.

22. See, for instance, Kohn, "Das kulturelle Problem des modernen Westjuden"; Kohn, "Zur Araberfrage"; and Kohn, "Nationalismus."

23. Copies of Kohn's regular contributions to *Clarté*, written under the pseudonym "Paul Colin" in 1920 and 1921, can be found Box 28, Folder 2 on Reel 26, AR 259, in the Hans Kohn Collection, Leo Baeck Archive, New York.

24. For example, he gave a speech entitled "Aktiver Pazifism" at the "Zweiten Konferenz der Internationale der Kriegsdienstgegner auf dem Sonntagsberg" (Second conference of the international pacifists) in July 1928. A copy of the speech is in Box 2, Folder 9 on Reel 2, AR6908, Hans Kohn–Robert Weltsch Correspondence, Weltsch Collection, Leo Baeck Archive.

25. Hans Kohn to Berthold Feiwel, November 21, 1929, ARC 376, Folder 224, Jewish National and University Library, Jerusalem.

26. See Kohn–Leo Herman correspondence from October 2, 1925, and June 26, 1926, File KH1, Folder 674, Central Zionist Archives.

27. Copies of Kohn's articles in *Filastina* are in File A 187 Folder 36, the Central Zionist Archive.

28. For an in-depth look at Kohn's writings on the Arab question, see Anya Sieg-mund, "German and Prague Zionists and Their Idea of *Verständigung* with the Arabs in Palestine, 1918–1948," Ph.D. diss., University of Munich, 2005.

29. Kohn, *Politische Idee des Judentum* (The political idea of Judaism), 45.

30. Historian Anita Shapira has written, "[t]he Arabs remained outside the perim-eter of awareness and engagement of the Jews both as individuals and collectively . . . the Jews in Palestine were . . . creating a separate entity—to which the Arabs remained external" (see Anita Shapira, *Land and Power: The Zionist Resort to Force, 1881–1948*, trans. William Templer [Stanford, Calif.: Stanford University Press, 1999], 142).

31. Kohn, *Toldot hatenu'ah hale'umit ha'aravit* (A history of the Arab national movement).

32. Glatzer and Mendes-Flohr, *Letters of Martin Buber*, 96.

33. See Buber, *Land of Two Peoples*.

34. Kohn's personal files are filled with admiring notes from students who viewed their teacher as an intellectual inspiration and even a father figure. "Students Flock to Listen to Lectures" declared the headlines of a September 26, 1958, article about Kohn in the City College newspaper. See Box 2, Folder 9 on Reel 5, File AR259, Hans Kohn Collection, Leo Baeck Archive.

35. Lavsky, "Hans Kohn: Nationalism between Theory and Practice," 206. Lavsky quotes at length from a November 21, 1929, correspondence.

36. See Weiss, "Central European Ethnonationalism and Zionist Binationalism"; Lavsky, "Hans Kohn: Nationalism between Theory and Practice"; Aschheim, *Beyond the Border;* Mendes-Flohr, *Land of Two Peoples;* and George Mosse, "Central Euro-pean Intellectuals in Palestine."

37. Kohn, "Nationalism," 27. Kohn's "Nationalismus" essay was originally published in *Der Jude* 6 (1921): 746–64. The essay was later republished in a collection of Kohn's essays (see Kohn, *Nationalismus*). The essay has been translated into English and can be found in Arthur C. Cohen, *The Jew: Essays from Martin Buber's Journal,* Der Jude.

38. Kohn, "Nationalism," 29.

39. Ibid., 27.

40. Ibid., 21, 22.

41. Kohn lays out the distinction in ibid., 24.

42. See Friedrich Meinecke, *Die Idee der Staatsraison* (Berlin: Oldenburg, 1925).

43. Ibid., 500.

44. See Ferdinand Tönnies, *Gemeinschaft und Gesellschaft* (1897; reprint, Leipzig: Fues's Verlag, 1912).

45. Kohn, "Nationalism", 29. Kohn's immersion in Buber's concepts of Kultur and blood is evident throughout his articles in the 1910s and early 1920s. Kohn associated nationalism with Kultur in 1921, when he wrote: "Nationalism must be human nation-alism, human cosmopolitanism, which emphasizes the traditional *Kultur* unity" (see Kohn, "Aufgaben der Stunde" [1921], in Kohn, *Nationalismus*, 93). In another example from a personal correspondence, Kohn commented to Hugo Bergmann in 1922: "The nationalism of the diaspora is not a territorial or a power nationalism but a cultural and blood nationalism" (see Kohn to Hugo Bergmann, August 29, 1922, ARC 40, Folder 1502/1561, Jewish National and University Library, Jerusalem).

46. See, for example, Ernst Troeltsch, "Der Geist der deutschen Kultur in Deutschland und der Weltkrieg" (The spirit of the German culture in Germany and in the World War), ed. Otto Hintze et al. (Leipzig: G. G. Teubner, 1916).

47. "Nationalism," 22.

48. "Geleitwort" (Preface), in Kohn et al., *Vom Judentum* 8, and "Der Geist des Orients" (The Spirit of the Orient), in ibid., 13.

49. Kohn's association of Zionism with Kultur, rather than civilization, paralleled the dichotomy popularized among German-speaking intellectuals by Thomas Mann in 1914, and reversed the moral connotations of civilization and Kultur. See "Gedanken im Krieg" in Thomas Mann, *Friedrich und die grosse Koalition* (Berlin, 1915). Mann viewed the war as one of opposing principles between "morally oriented Germans and politically oriented nations" (see Hannelore Mundt, *Understanding Thomas Mann* [Columbia: University of South Carolina, 2004], 100). Kohn's later work reversed the opposing principles and aligned good nationalism with "civilization." For example, in *The Idea of Nationalism*, Kohn characterized the dominant political struggle of his day as "the deep gulf and unending struggle between Western universal civilization and German culture" (Kohn's *Idea of Nationalism*, 355). In championing Western civilization, rather than German Kultur, as the most ethical stage in the development, Kohn flipped the reference points but preserved the underlying structure of a hierarchy of good and bad nationalisms.

50. Kohn, "Nationalism," 30.

51. Kohn, *Nationalismus*, 11.

52. Kohn, *Perakim letoldot hara'ayon hatzioni*.

53. Kohn, *Political Idea of Judaism*, 54.

54. Buber, *Land of Two Peoples*, 51–54.

55. Buber, "Judaism and Mankind," in Buber, *On Judaism*, 27 and 25.

56. Buber's involvement in Judaism and Zionism was multifaceted and ripe with tensions. As a young man, he was raised by his grandfather, Solomon Buber. The elder Buber was the scion of a rabbinic family and a well-known scholar of rabbinic literature in his own right. Throughout the younger Buber's involvement in contemporary philosophical and political movements, he remained connected with the sources and experiences that defined his childhood. For example, the same Buber that advocated for new forms of nationalism was simultaneously engaged in a radical new Bible translation; the existential writer of *I and Thou*, a book that makes no references to particular religious traditions, was at the same time the editor of *Der Jude*, a journal committed to the renaissance of modern Jewish life. Buber's life work swung between particular commitments and universal yearnings. Kohn, whose childhood education consisted of more Greek than Hebrew and more philosophy than Midrash, lacked the visceral connection with a living community that exemplified the dialectical tension between particular and universal in Buber's work.

57. Martin Buber, "Renewal of Judaism," in Buber, *On Judaism*, 50.

58. Kohn, *Political Idea of Judaism*, 61.

59. See Kohn, *Perakim letoldot hara'ayon hatzioni*, 2.

60. For an in-depth discussion of Gordon's work, see Einat Ramon, "God, the Mother: A Critique of Domination in the Religious Zionist Thought of A. D. Gordon," Ph.D. diss., Stanford University, 2000.

61. Kohn, *Perakim letoldot hara'ayon hatzioni*, 57.

62. Ibid.

63. Lavsky has pointed out that Kohn was interested in a binational state not as a pragmatic reality, but instead as an ideological belief that it represented the fulfillment of Zionist aims (see Lavsky, "Hans Kohn: Nationalism between Theory and Practice," 196).

64. Once again, Buber's work played a key role in supplying the groundwork for this Orient–Occident distinction. Buber's article, "The Spirit of the Orient in Judaism," provided a methodological approach for Kohn's political analysis of nationalism. Buber also argued that Jews in Palestine faced the crucial task of bridging the fault lines between East and West. See Martin Buber, "The Spirit of the Orient and Judaism," in Buber, *On Judaism*, 78.

65. Kohn, *Toldot hatenu'ah hale'umit ha'aravit*, 47.

66. See Edward Said, *Orientalism* (New York: Vintage Books, 1994). Zionist historian Derek Penslar has written extensively on the Zionist–colonial comparison (see Penslar, *Israel in History*).

67. Hans Kohn, "The Political Shape of the Land of Israel," *Hapo'el hatza'ir* 19, no. 33 (1926): 11–12.

68. Ibid., 12.

69. Kohn, *Nationalismus*, 19.

70. Ibid., 20.

71. Weiss has argued that "the views Kohn developed of the future autonomy of the two peoples . . . in a unified Palestine were the direct result of his European insights," specifically the model of the "former Austrian state" (see Weiss, "Central European Ethnonationalism and Zionist Binationalism," 102).

72. Kohn, "Political Shape of the Land of Israel."

73. Kohn argued that the "Land of Israel does not need to be a Jewish state, rather, a community, in which two equal people will live together completely in their rights, without one ruling nation that can dominate the will of the other" (see Kohn, *Toldot hatenu'ah hale'umit ha'aravit*, 34).

74. Kohn was a reader of the *Menorah Journal* and was familiar with the work of Randolph Bourne, Horace Kallen, and Alfred Zimmern. Kohn's correspondence with Buber indicates that Kohn worked in the early 1920s to convince the editor of the *Menorah Journal* to print Buber's writings in translation. Kohn also certainly knew about Randolph Bourne's work. In fact, one of Kohn's articles in *Clarté* shared a page with a review of Bourne's writings. Kohn did read Kallen's *Zionism and World Politics* by 1928 (he mentions Kallen's book in the bibliography of his 1928 book, *Geschichte der Nationalen Bewegung im Orient* [A History of Nationalism in the East]); however, it is unclear if he read it before or after writing his own chapters on the history of Zionism. See Hans Kohn, *Geschichte der Nationalen Bewegung im Orient* (Berlin: Kurt Vowinckel Verlag, 1928). Kohn expressed his interest in meeting Kallen in a November 17, 1931, letter to Robert Weltsch, Arc 350, Folder 1561A, Martin Buber Archives, Jewish National and University Library, Jerusalem. Zimmern's writings also appealed to Kohn. In an October 26, 1924, letter, Kohn called Zimmern "a prominent public man in the League of Nations movement . . . prompted [to translate Martin Buber's essays] by sheer enthusiasm and love of the beauty of Judaism and of Dr. Buber's theories." ARC 350, Martin Buber Archives, Jewish National and University Library, Jerusalem. Special thanks to Romy Langeheine for bringing this letter to my attention.

75. Kohn, *Martin Buber: Sein Werk und Seine Zeit*, 94.

76. Hans Kohn to Hugo Bergmann, November 20, 1931, ARC 40, Folder 1502/1561, Hugo Bergmann Archives, Jewish National and University Library, Jerusalem.

77. Kohn, *American Nationalism*, 51.

78. Hans Kohn to Martin Buber, April 29, 1933, ARC 350, Martin Buber Archives, Jewish National and University Library, Jerusalem.

79. Hans Kohn to Martin Buber, February 13, 1934, ARC 350, Martin Buber Archives, Jewish National and University Library, Jerusalem.

80. Hans Kohn to Robert Weltsch, July 2, 1936, Weltsch Collection, AR 6908, Box 2, Folder 1, Leo Baeck Archive, New York.

81. Hans Kohn to Hugo Bergmann, February 14, 1935, ARC 40, Folder 1502/1561, Hugo Berman Archives, Jewish National and University Library, Jerusalem.

82. Hans Kohn to Robert Weltsch, July 2, 1936, Weltsch Collection, AR 6908, Box 2, Folder 1, Leo Baeck Archive, New York.

83. Kohn, *Idea of Nationalism,* 351.

84. The quotation is from the introduction of an unpublished 1962 work called "Historian and Human Responsibility." The text is in AR6908 Box 2, Folder 1, Leo Baeck Archives, New York.

85. Kohn, *Idea of Nationalism,* 9.

86. Ibid., 20.

87. Ibid., 35.

88. Kohn's *Nationalism: Its Meaning in History* also singled out the Hebrew tradition as the pioneering contributor to the development of nationalism. "The idea of the nation-state was unknown to them [the Hebrews] but they had the strong consciousness of a cultural mission" (see Kohn, *Nationalism: Its Meaning and History,* 11).

89. Kohn, *Idea of Nationalism,* 50.

90. A close comparison of the *Idea of Nationalism* and the *Political Idea of Judaism (Die Politische Idee des Judentum)* reveals a number of examples in which Kohn slightly altered the text to include the Greek tradition as equal to the Jewish tradition. For example, both texts share the statement, "the main current of Greek political thought, both with the leading philosophers and with the general public, remained aloof from humanitarian ideals down to the end of the fourth century BC" (see ibid., 56; and Kohn, *Political Idea of Judaism,* 50). However, Kohn left out the following line from *The Idea of Nationalism,* which directly contrasted the two traditions: "the Jewish legislation recognized the rights of the poor, the free, the slaves, animals and all of Nature. In contrast, Greek justice was not oriented towards the Absolute, the eternal God, it is therefore temporal and limited" (Kohn, ibid., 50). In another example, Kohn copied a section from *Die Politische Idee des Judentum* that contended that the Jewish God, unlike Zeus, was a god of history who imbued time with meaning and order. However, in the English version, the sentence in the middle of the paragraph that distinguished Zeus from the "Jewish God" did not appear. In another location, Kohn took paragraphs that initially dealt solely with Jews and added an introductory sentence that read, "The Jews and the Greeks were the peoples of Ancient Times with a sense for history" (see Kohn, *Idea of Nationalism,* 34–35; and Kohn, *Politische Idee des Judentum* 16–17). Analyzing Kohn's original essay clearly indicates that the Greeks were added much later to include them as progenitors of the *Idea of Nationalism,* but without changing any of the original content.

91. Kohn, *Idea of Nationalism,* vii.

92. Ibid., vi.

93. See ibid., 13.

94. Ibid.

95. This concept radically extended the definition of nationalism in a cosmopolitan direction. Unlike his fellow American scholars, such as Carleton Hayes, Kohn did not attempt to delineate the particular characteristics that constituted national identity (see Carleton J. H. Hayes, *Essays on Nationalism* [New York: Macmillan, 1926]).

96. For example, Kohn expressed his feeling that the people he met in the United States lacked intellectual depth and sophistication in a letter to Robert Weltsch during a visit to America. See Hans Kohn to Robert Weltsch, November 17, 1931, Weltsch Collection, AR 6908, Box 2, Folder 1, Leo Baeck Archive, New York.

97. Kohn, *Idea of Nationalism*, 310.

98. Kohn, *American Nationalism*, 32.

99. Ibid.

100. In another statement of American triumphalism, Kohn wrote, "[i]n the U.S. all nations, all churches and sects, all the good and evil powers of the old world, meet without blows or bloodshed; and while Europe began with paganism and barbarism, American begins with the results of Europe's two thousand years' course of civilization" (see ibid., 153).

101. Ibid., 144.

102. Ibid.

103. Ibid., 93.

104. See Gunnar Myrdal, *An American Dilemma: The Negro Problem and Modern Democracy* (New York: Harper & Row, 1944).

105. Kohn, *American Nationalism*, 172.

106. Ibid., 175.

107. Ibid., 154.

108. Ibid., 170.

109. Hans Kohn, "Yehudim americanim," *Hapo'el hatza'ir* 1–2 (October 12, 1924): 26.

110. Kohn, *American Nationalism*, 170.

111. Ibid., 135.

112. Ibid., 167.

113. See Kallen, "Democracy versus the Melting-Pot."

114. Kohn's writings on Zionism and nationalism from the period before he moved to Palestine do not mention liberalism or British political theory in a positive light. However, his attitude toward British liberalism begins to change in the mid-1920s and continues to play a central role in his subsequent thought. Kohn's most sustained exploration of British nationalism can be found in Hans Kohn, "The Genesis and Character of English Nationalism."

115. Kohn, *Living in a World Revolution*, 143.

116. Like Zimmern and Kallen, Kohn also used Switzerland in the 1920s as a model for describing the ideal type of national federation. Kohn assures his readers that the question of majority population in Palestine "will cease to be an issue, its importance will decline, like Switzerland." Kohn, *History of the Arab National Movement*, 34.

117. Kohn leaves this possibility open in his definition of the American idea of liberty as the "recognition of diversity in origins and religious background," which has "proved a stronger national cement and a more secure basis for ordered liberty and economic prosperity than bonds of common blood or religion." Kohn, *American Nationalism*, 149.

118. Ibid., 233.

119. *The Age of Nationalism*, published five years after *American Nationalism*, provides an additional example of Kohn's commitment to the vision of states of many

nations. He advocates for "pluralistic federalism," precisely the idea he challenged in *American Nationalism,* which reappears as the form of government that "may overcome many tensions" of integrating diverse ethnic groups. See Hans Kohn, *The Age of Nationalism: The First Era of Global History* (New York: Harper & Brothers, 1962), 155.

120. Ahad Ha'am and Kohn, *Nationalism and the Jewish Ethic,* 16.

121. Absent from Kohn's introduction is any reference to his earlier critiques of Ahad Ha'am as too focused on the specific cultural content of Judaism and not giving enough emphasis to the messianic, and universalistic, core of Judaism.

122. Kohn was not the only Jewish intellectual active in mainstream scholarship who shaped the contours of the American Jewish synthesis during the 1950s. In 1952, the historian Oscar Handlin published *The Uprooted* (Boston: Little, Brown, 1973), which transformed U.S. history from one concerning a small number of native elites to a story that involved millions of immigrants coming to America. In 1955, Will Herberg, a sociologist of religion, published *Protestant-Catholic-Jew.* The book helped place Judaism, the religion of a tiny minority of Americans at the time, as one of three foundational faiths in the country. For a recent exploration on the role of American Jewish thinkers in the shaping of American concepts of psychology during this period, see Andrew Heinze, *Jews and the American Soul: Human Nature in the Twentieth Century* (Princeton, N.J.: Princeton University Press, 2006).

123. For example, Kohn, "Ahad Ha'am: Nationalist with a Difference"; and his "The Jewish National Idea."

124. Kohn, *Martin Buber: Sein Werk und Seine Zeit,* 5.

125. Kohn, "Ahad Ha'am: Nationalist with a Difference," 566.

126. Kohn, *Nationalismus,* 19.

127. Kohn, "Jewish National Idea," 45.

128. Ahad Ha'am and Kohn, *Nationalism and the Jewish Ethic,* 33.

129. Ibid.

130. Letter in File AR 259, Hans Kohn Collection, Box 3, Folder 1, Reel 7, Leo Baeck Archive, New York.

131. Kohn, "Jewish National Idea," 40.

132. Aschheim, *Beyond the Border.*

133. See Arendt, *The Origins of Totalitarianism.*

134. Aschheim, *Beyond the Border,* 167.

135. See Hutchinson, *Dynamics of Cultural Nationalism.*

136. Taras Kuzio has written that Kohn's work "did not reflect historical reality and is out of step with contemporary theories of nationalism." See Kuzio, "Myth of the Civic State," 1.

6. Zionism, Jewish Peoplehood, and the Dilemmas of Nationality in a Global Era

1. Mordecai Kaplan, *A New Zionism,* 25.

2. Ibid., 108.

3. See, for example, ibid., 22, 25, 99, and 108.

4. The emphasis that Ben Gurion placed on this concept reflects, as Kedar points out, his own recognition of the "asymmetry between Jewish nation and the state." See Kedar, "Ben Gurion's Mamlachtiyut," 125.

5. See ibid.; see also Cohen, *Zion and the State,* 201. As Cohen has pointed out,

Ben Gurion's definition of statism far surpasses the definition common in the 1930s. The term "statism" was defined in the late 1930s as "the sum of organizations and institutions by which the political aspects of life common are made possible" (from Cohen, *Zion and the State,* 201). He quotes from a 1939 report on nationalism by the Study Group of the Royal Institute of Internal Affairs.

6. The historian Matthew Frye Jacobson has examined the process by which ethnic groups Americanized through their attachments to their homelands. See Matthew Frye Jacobson, *Special Sorrows.*

7. Takaki reminds readers of "the unique history of Jewish immigrants, especially the initial advantages of many of them as literate and skilled," and notes that including the Jewish case "minimizes the virulence of racial prejudice rooted in American slavery" (Takaki, *A Different Mirror,* 10). Whether or not historical claims about Jews' whiteness and economic training are accurate is certainly worth debating—Takaki's short disclaimer about his decision to distinguish Jews from other groups ignores the contested racial position and limited economic experience of many of the immigrants. Moreover, it is anachronistic to view Jews as economically and racially integrated from the start of their immigration until the middle of the twentieth century. For more on the contested racial position of American Jews, see Goldstein, *The Price of Whiteness.*

8. See Kymlicka, *Multicultural Citizenship.* Similar expressions of the temporary and voluntary nature of immigrant and ethnic group associations, as well as the state's minimal responsibilities for recognizing specific group rights, can be found in such works as Hollinger, *Postethnic America;* and Cohen, "Rooted Cosmopolitanism."

9. See Clifford, "Diasporas"; Hall, "Cultural Identity and Diaspora"; Boyarin and Boyarin, "Diaspora: Generation and the Ground of Jewish Identity"; Tölölyan, "Rethinking Diaspora(s): Stateless Power in the Transnational Moment."

10. Anderson's notion of "imagined communities" acknowledges this limitation to a certain degree. But, Anderson describes relatively rigid parameters (the state) and the modern historical factors that engender such categories. Nor does it mean that a strong sense of collective cohesion did not predate the specific connotations of modern nationalism. A few scholars, such as Aviel Roshwald and Avishai Margalit, have written of the need to expand the study of nationalism to include a greater appreciation for the psychology of national ties. Their approach has helped me identify the importance of Kaplan's, Kohn's, and Rawidowicz's formulations for a larger audience of scholars interested in understanding the ties that bind members of national groups. See Roshwald, *Endurance of Nationalism,* and Margalit, "The Moral Psychology of Nationalism."

11. Benedict Anderson's reference to Kohn at the start of his now classic study of nationality, *Imagined Communities,* indicates his awareness that Kohn's most significant contribution to the study of nationalism was his attack on the notion that each national group has a particular "essence" or "spirit." See Anderson, *Imagined Communities,* 4.

12. Liberal multiculturalists, such as Canadian theorist Will Kymlicka, have downplayed the role of religion in considering various categories of multicultural citizenship. Although Kymlicka has argued for religious toleration, he groups religious groups with ethnic communities as immigrants who have decided to leave their national community to enter another society. Thus, religious ties are secondary to the

national bonds formed through such criteria as language and territory. See Kymlicka, *Multicultural Citizenship*. Unlike most political theorists, scholars of religious studies, such as Talal Asad, have contributed to blurring the bounds between religion and legal/political communities by describing how a Protestant definition of religion colors perceptions of Western thinking about religious categories that do not apply to such legalistic religions as Islam. See Talal Asad, *Genealogies of Religion: Discipline and Reasons of Power in Christianity and Islam* (Baltimore, Md.: Johns Hopkins University Press, 1995).

13. The ongoing prevalence of this concept of religion appears, for instance, in David Miller's *On Nationality*, when he explains religion as a passive, static, and private belief as opposed to a public or political identity. He writes that active identity, such as nationality, "does mark out nations from other kinds of grouping, for instance churches or religious sects, whose identity is essentially a passive one in so far as the church is seen as responding to the promptings of god." See Miller, *On Nationality*, 24. When religious communities demand primary allegiance or coercion, they are often categorized as fundamentalist.

14. See Miller, *On Nationality*.

15. A number of recent works have attempted to argue that national allegiance is fully compatible with liberal principles and universal morality. See McKim and McMahan, *Morality of Nationalism*, and Tamir, *Liberal Nationalism*.

16. "Interview with Michael Walzer," *AJS Perspectives* (2006): 10.

17. My argument about Jewish intellectuals' efforts to make space for Jews mirrors the phenomenon that the theorist Paul Gilroy has described for black intellectuals. Gilroy has argued: "Successive phases of struggle by blacks in, but not completely of, the West have pushed at the very limits of what Euro-American modernity has delineated as the approved space for politics within its social formations." See Gilroy, *The Black Atlantic*, 114.

18. See R. Laurence Moore, *Religious Outsiders and the Making of Americans* (New York: Oxford University Press, 1986).

19. Walzer et al., *The Jewish Political Tradition*. Walzer edited another volume on the Jewish political tradition that is also intended for a general scholarly audience. The book appears as part of a series in comparative ethics. See Michael Walzer, ed., *Law, Politics, and Morality in Judaism* (Princeton, N.J.: Princeton University Press, 2006). A new journal, *Hebraic Political Studies*, aims to "evaluate the place of the Jewish textual tradition, alongside the traditions of Greece and Rome, in political history and history of political thought" (see *Hebraic Political Studies* 1, no. 2 [2006]).

20. See Tamir, *Liberal Nationalism*; Gans, *The Limits of Nationalism*; Roshwald, *The Endurance of Nationalism*; David Novak, *The Jewish Social Contract: An Essay in Political Theology* (Princeton, N.J.: Princeton University Press, 2005).

21. See Michael Walzer, *What Does It Mean to Be an American?* and Roshwald, *The Endurance of Nationalism*.

22. See Gans, *The Limits of Nationalism*, and Walzer et al., eds., *Law, Politics, and Morality in Judaism*.

23. A few non-Jewish intellectuals have also focused on the Jewish case as a group. For instance, David Hollinger, John Higham, and Paul Gilroy have noted the importance of considering Jewish history and thought in understanding the development of categories of difference. See David Hollinger, "Jewish Identity, Assimilation, and

Multiculturalism," in *Creating America's Jews*, ed. Karen Mittleman (Hanover, N.H.: University Press of New England, 1998). See also Gilroy, *The Black Atlantic*.

24. The distinction Walzer introduces between interest and identity demonstrates his own effort to propose a politics of difference that shifts the grounds of solidarity from race and victimization to voluntary attachment. See Walzer, "Multiculturalism and the Politics of Difference."

25. See Cohen and Wertheimer, "Whatever Happened to the Jewish People?"

26. A declaration, signed during the meeting of the General Assembly of North American Jews in 1998, reiterated decades of public rhetoric among American Jewish and Israeli leadership expressing the sentiment that "we are one." See Julia Goldman, "Israelis, North Americans Sign Covenant on Unity, Shared Values," *Jewish Telegraph Agency*, November 20, 1998.

27. Until quite recently, the identity cards of Jewish Israelis listed "Jewish" as the individual's nationality.

28. The historian Jonathan Sarna has detailed the rise and fall of such secular movements. See Jonathan Sarna, "The Rise, Fall, and Rebirth of Secular Judaism," *Contemplate: The International Journal of Cultural Jewish Thought*, no. 4 (2007): 6–13.

29. A number of scholars have discussed the diverging paths of American and Israeli Jewry. See Deborah Dash Moore and Ilan Troen, *Divergent Jewish Cultures*, and Zvi Ganin, *An Uneasy Relationship: American Jewish Leadership and Israel, 1948–1957* (Syracuse, N.Y.: Syracuse University Press, 2005).

30. This bias also endures in Israeli scholarship. Historian Yosef Gorny has evaluated the implications of the split between Israel and Diaspora Jews as follows: "The success of Israel as a collective has transformed the existence of a unique Jewish entity into a natural phenomenon, whereas individual Jewish success in the United States is endangering the continued existence of the same Jewish entity and calls for extraordinary effort for the preservation of its distinctiveness." See Yosef Gorny, *The State of Israel in Jewish Public Thought*, 3.

31. In reviewing his own thoughts about Jewish nationalism during his stay in Palestine from 1936 to 1938, Kaplan acknowledged how closely his own work on Jewish nationalism was influenced by Ahad Ha'am's formulation. On June 14, 1939, Kaplan wrote in his diary, "As I am now reading Achad Haam's essays again for the lecture on Jewish nationalism, I see how little I realized what an Achad Ha'amist I was when I wrote Judaism as a Civilization." ("Mordecai Menahem Kaplan, 1881," box 3, vol. 9, File ARC 65, Kaplan Diaries and Papers, Jewish Theological Seminary, New York.)

32. Caryn Aviv and David Shneer advocate for a decentered model of Jewish national life in their *New Jews: The End of the Jewish Diaspora*.

33. See Charles S. Liebman and Elihu Katz, eds., *The Jewishness of Israelis* (SUNY Press, N.Y., 1997).

34. New venues for Jewish culture, art, and music in the United States have begun to attract a significant following of the younger generation of Jews looking to express Judaism outside of synagogues and federations. See Ari Y. Kelman and Steven M. Cohen, "Cultural Events and Jewish Identities" (New York: National Foundation for Jewish Culture, 2006). A number of Israelis, many trained in the United States and/ or funded by U.S. philanthropies, have created opportunities for secular Israelis to engage with aspects of Judaism. These opportunities include text study at institutions

like Almah, Elul, and Beit Avi Chai as well as other explorations of Jewish liturgy, such as the *piyyut* project.

35. For a study of the intimate link between nationalism and cosmopolitanism within the Zionist movement, see Stanislawski, *Zionism and the Fin de Siècle.* Anita Shapira has discussed the tension within the Zionist movement over the decision to resort to force. See Shapira, *Land and Power* (Stanford, Calif., Stanford University Press, 2000).

36. In Kaplan's case, see for example, Kaplan, *Communings of the Spirit,* 464. Rawidowicz asked: "Where are the commandments of the 'ethical nation' in whose name Zionism waved its flag? Isn't the first command of all chosen people: Thou shalt not uproot man from his land, whether a member of your people or not?" (Rawidowicz, *Babylon and Jerusalem,* 21).

SELECTED BIBLIOGRAPHY

Archives and Manuscript Collections

"Brit Shalom, Jerusalem." File A187. Central Zionist Archives, Jerusalem.

Hans Kohn Collection. File AR 259. Leo Baeck Archive, New York City.

Hans Kohn–Robert Weltsch Correspondence. Weltsch Collection. AR 6908. Leo Baeck Archive, New York City.

Horace Kallen Collection. Manuscript collection #1. Box 32. American Jewish Archives, Cincinnati, Ohio.

Hugo Bergman Archives. File ARC 40. Jewish National and University Library, Jerusalem.

Martin Buber Archives. File ARC 350. Jewish National and University Library, Jerusalem.

Mordecai Menahem Kaplan, 1881. File ARC 65. Kaplan Diaries and Papers. Jewish Theological Seminary, New York City.

"Palestine Foundation Fund (Keren Hayesod) Head Office, London." File KH1. Central Zionist Archives, Jerusalem.

Sir Alfred Zimmern Papers. MS Zimmern 177. Bodleian Library. Oxford University, Oxford.

"Robert Weltsch." File A167. Central Zionist Archives, Jerusalem.

Simon Rawidowicz Archive. Newton, Massachusetts.

Primary Sources

Ahad Ha'am. *Selected Essays of Ahad Ha'am.* Edited by Leon Simon. Philadelphia: Jewish Publication Society, 1912.

Ahad Ha'am, and Hans Kohn, eds. *Nationalism and the Jewish Ethic: Basic Writings of Ahad Ha-am.* New York: Schocken Books, 1962.

Arendt, Hannah. *The Jewish Writings.* Edited by Jerome Kohn and Ron H. Feldman. New York: Schocken, 2007.

Bourne, Randolph. "The Jew and Trans-National America." *Menorah Journal* 2, no. 5 (1916): 277–84.

Brandeis, Louis. "Call to the Educated Jew." *Menorah Journal* 1, no. 1 (1915): 13–19.
Buber, Martin. *A Land of Two Peoples*. Edited by Paul R. Mendes-Flohr. Oxford:
   Oxford University Press, 1983.
———. *On Judaism*. Edited by Nahum Glatzer. New York: Schocken Books, 1967.
Dewey, John. "The Principle of Nationality." *Menorah Journal* 3, no. 4 (1917): 203–208.
Dubnow, Shimon. *Nationalism and History: Essays on Old and New Judaism*. Edited
   by Koppel S. Pinson. Philadelphia: Jewish Publication Society of America, 1958.
Friedlaender, Israel. *Past and Present: A Collection of Essays*. Cincinnati, Ohio: Ark
   Publishing, 1919.
Kallen, Horace M. "Constitutional Foundations of the New Zion." *The Maccabean* 31
   (1918): 22.
———. *Culture and Democracy in the United States*. New York: Boni and Liveright,
   1924.
———. "Democracy versus the Melting-Pot: A Study of American Nationality." *The
   Nation* 100, nos. 2590 and 2591 (1915): 190–94 and 217–20.
———. *Judaism at Bay: Essays toward the Adjustment of Judaism to Modernity*. New
   York: Arno Press, 1972.
———. "Nationality and the Hyphenated American." *Menorah Journal* 1, no. 2 (1915):
   79–86.
———. *The Structure of Lasting Peace*. Boston: Marshall Jones Co., 1918.
———. "Zionism and the Struggle towards Democracy." *The Nation* 101 (September
   23, 1915): 379–80.
———. *Zionism and World Politics: A Study in History and Social Psychology*. Garden
   City, N.Y.: Doubleday, Page, & Co., 1921.
———. "Zionism: Democracy or Prussianism." *New Republic* (April 6, 1919): 311–13.
Kaplan, Mordecai M. *Communings of the Spirit: The Journals of Mordecai M. Kaplan*.
   Edited by Mel Scult. Detroit: Wayne State University Press and the Reconstruc-
   tionist Press, 2001.
———. "The Future of Judaism." *Menorah Journal* 2, no. 3 (1916): 160–72.
———. *The Future of the American Jew*. New York: Macmillan, 1948.
———. "How May Judaism Be Saved?" *Menorah Journal* 2, no. 1 (1916): 34–44.
———. "Judaism and Christianity." *Menorah Journal* 2, no. 2 (1916): 105–15.
———. "Judaism and Nationality." *The Maccabean* (August 1909): 61–63.
———. *Judaism as a Civilization: Toward a Reconstruction of American-Jewish Life*.
   New York: Macmillan, 1934.
———. *Judaism as a Civilization*. Reprint, Philadelphia: Jewish Publication Society, 1994.
———. *A New Zionism*. New York: Herzl Press, 1955.
———. *The Religion of Ethical Nationhood: Judaism's Contribution to World Peace*.
   New York: Macmillan, 1970.
———. "Toward a Reconstruction of Judaism." *Menorah Journal* 13, no. 2 (1927): 113–30.
———. "What Is Judaism." *Menorah Journal* 1, no. 5 (1915): 309–18.
———. "What Judaism Is Not." *Menorah Journal* 1, no. 4 (1915): 208–16.
Klatzkin, Yaakov. *Tehumim*. Jerusalem: Dvir, 1928.
Kohn, Hans. "Ahad Ha'am: Nationalist with a Difference." *Commentary* 2 (June 1951):
   558–66.
———. *American Nationalism: An Interpretative Essay*. New York: Macmillan, 1957.
   Reprint, New York: Collier Books, 1961.
———. "Das kulturelle Problem des modernen Westjuden." *Der Jude* 5 (1920): 281–97.

————. *Die Politische Idee des Judentums* (The political idea of Judaism). Munich: Meyer and Jessen, 1924.

————. "The Genesis and Character of English Nationalism." *Journal of the History of Ideas* 1, no. 1 (1940): 69–94.

————. *The Idea of Nationalism: A Study in Its Origins and Background.* New York: Macmillan, 1944.

————. "The Jewish National Idea." *Menorah Journal* 45, no. 1 (1958): 25–47.

————. *Living in a World Revolution: My Encounters with History.* New York: Trident Press, 1964.

————. *Martin Buber: Sein Werk und Seine Zeit, Ein Versuch über Religion und Politik* (Martin Buber: His work and his time, an essay on religion and politics). Hellerau, Germany: Jakob Hener, 1930. Reprint, with an epilogue by Robert Weltsch, Cologne, Germany: Melzer, 1961.

————. "Nationalism." In *The Jew: Essays from Martin Buber's Journal, Der Jude, 1916–1928.* Edited by Arthur A. Cohen, 19–30. Tuscaloosa: University of Alabama Press, 1980.

————. *Nationalism: Its Meaning and History.* Princeton, N.J.: Van Nostrand, 1955.

————. "Nationalismus." *Der Jude* 6 (1921): 746–64.

————. *Nationalismus: Über die Bedeutung des Nationalismus im Judentum und in der Gegenwart* (Nationalism: Concerning the meaning of nationalism in Judaism and in the present). Vienna: R. Löwit Verlag, 1922.

————. *Perakim letoldot hara'ayon hatzioni* (A history of Zionist thought). 2 vols. Warsaw: Biblioteka Jesodoth, 1929–1930.

————. *Reflections on Modern History: The Historian and Human Responsibility.* Princeton, N.J.: D. Van Nostrand, 1963.

————. *Toldot hatenu'ah hale'umit ha'aravit* (A History of the Arab National Movement). Tel Aviv: Hotza'at po'el hatza'ir, 1926.

————. "Zur Araberfrage." *Der Jude* 4 (1919): 567–69.

Kohn, Hans, and Jüdischer Hochschüler Bar Kochba Verein. *Vom Judentum: Ein Sammelbuch* (On Judaism: a collection of essays). Prague: K. Wolff, 1914.

Rawidowicz, Simon. *Bavel veyerushalayim* (Babylon and Jerusalem). 2 vols. Waltham, Mass.: Ararat Publishing Society, 1957.

————. "Bein ever ve'arav" (Between Jew and Arab). 1951–1955. Rawidowicz Archives. Newton, Mass

————. *Im lo kan hekhan?* (If not here, where?) Lvov: Brit Ivrit Olamit, 1933.

————. *Israel, the Ever-Dying People, and Other Essays.* Edited by Benjamin Ravid. Rutherford, N.J.: Fairleigh Dickinson University Press, 1986.

————. *Iyunim bemahshevet yisrael* (Hebrew Studies in Jewish thought). 2 vols. Edited by Benjamin C. I. Ravid. Jerusalem: Rubin Mass, 1969.

————. "Kiyum hatefutzah" (Endurance of the diaspora). *Moznayim* 3, no. 2 (1934): 125–39, 265–76, 581–609.

————. "Kiyum lelo tenai (Unconditional endurance)." *Metzuda* 3–4 (1945): 5–20.

————. "Leshem hidush sifruteinu" (Toward the renewal of our literature). *Ha'olam* 18 (1930): 971–72, 994–95, 1014–15.

————. *Ludwig Feuerbachs Philosophie: Ursprung und Schicksal* (The philosophy of Ludwig Feuerbach: Origins and fate). Berlin: de Gruyter, 1964.

————. "On Interpretation." *Proceedings of the American Academy for Jewish Research* 26 (1957): 83–126.

———. *Sihotai in Bialik* (Conversations with Bialik). Jerusalem: Dvir, 1983.

———. *State of Israel, Diaspora and Jewish Continuity.* Hanover, N.H.: Brandeis University Press, 1998.

———. *Studies in Jewish Thought.* 1st ed. Philadelphia: Jewish Publication Society of America, 1974.

———, ed. *Sefer Shimon Dubnow* (Simon Dubnow in memoriam: essays and letters). London: Ararat Publishing Society, 1954.

Zimmern, Alfred E. "The Aliens Act: A Challenge." *Economic Review* 21, no. 2 (1911): 195–97.

———. "Einige Eindrücke von Jüdisch-Palästina" (An impression from Jewish Palestine). *Der Jude* 4 (1919): 394–407.

———. "Nationalism and Internationalism." *Foreign Affairs* 1, no. 4 (1923): 115–26.

———. *Nationality and Government, with Other Wartime Essays.* London: Chatto and Windus, 1918.

———. "Nationality in the Modern World." *Menorah Journal* 4, no. 3 (1918): 205–213, 211–15.

———. "Theodor Herzl and the Jewish Renaissance." *The Outlook* (September 23, 1905): 395–96.

Books and Articles

Anderson, Benedict R. O. G. *Imagined Communities: Reflections on the Origin and Spread of Nationalism.* London: Verso, 1991.

Appadurai, Arjun. *Modernity at Large: Cultural Dimensions of Globalization.* Minneapolis: University of Minnesota Press, 1996.

Appiah, K. A. *The Ethics of Identity.* Princeton, N.J.: Princeton University Press, 2005.

———. *In My Father's House: Africa in the Philosophy of Culture.* London: Oxford University Press, 1992.

Arendt, Hannah. *The Origins of Totalitarianism.* New York: Harcourt, Brace, 1951.

Armstrong, John Alexander. *Nations before Nationalism.* Chapel Hill: University of North Carolina Press, 1982.

Aschheim, Steven E. *Beyond the Border: The German-Jewish Legacy Abroad.* Princeton, N.J.: Princeton University Press, 2007.

Avineri, Shlomo, and Avner De-Shalit, eds. *Communitarianism and Individualism.* Oxford: Oxford University Press, 1992.

Avishai, Margalit. "The Moral Psychology of Nationalism." In *The Morality of Nationalism,* ed. Robert McKim and Jeff McMahan, 74–87. New York: Oxford University Press, 1997.

Aviv, Caryn, and David Shneer. *New Jews: The End of the Jewish Diaspora.* New York: New York University Press, 2005.

Bederman, Gail. *Manliness and Civilization: A Cultural History of Gender and Race in the United States, 1880–1917.* Chicago: University of Chicago Press, 1995.

Beiner, Ronald. *Theorizing Nationalism.* SUNY Series in Political Theory. Contemporary Issues. Albany: State University of New York Press, 1999.

Benhabib, Seyla. *The Claims of Culture: Equality and Diversity in the Global Era.* Princeton, N.J.: Princeton University Press, 2002.

Biale, David. "Louis Finkelstein, Mordecai Kaplan, and American 'Jewish

Contributions to Civilization.'" In *The Jewish Contribution to Civilization*, ed. Jeremy Cohen and Richard Cohen, 185–97. London: Littman, 2008.

Biale, David, Michael Galchinsky, and Susannah Heschel, eds. *Insider/Outsider: American Jews and Multiculturalism*. Berkeley: University of California Press, 1998.

Boyarin, Daniel, and Jonathan Boyarin. "Diaspora: Generation and the Ground of Jewish Identity." *Critical Inquiry* 19, no. 4 (1993): 693–725.

———. *Powers of Diaspora*. Minneapolis: University of Minnesota Press, 2002.

Breckenridge, Carol A., et al., eds. *Cosmopolitanism*. Durham, N.C.: Duke University Press, 2002.

Brenner, Michael. *The Renaissance of Jewish Culture in Weimar Germany*. New Haven, Conn.: Yale University Press, 1996.

Brubaker, Rogers. *Ethnicity without Groups*. Cambridge, Mass.: Harvard University Press, 2004.

Calhoun, Craig J. *Nations Matter*. London: Routledge, 2007.

Carr, Edward. *The Twenty Year Crisis, 1919–1939*. London: Macmillan, 1961.

Chatterjee, Partha. *The Nation and Its Fragments*. Princeton, N.J.: Princeton University Press, 1993.

Clifford, James. "Diasporas." *Cultural Anthropology* 9, no. 3 (1994): 302–38.

Cohen, Mitchell. "A Preface to the Study of Modern Jewish Political Thought." *Jewish Social Studies* 9, no. 2 (2003): 1–27.

———. "Rooted Cosmopolitanism." *Dissent* 39, no. 4 (1992): 478–83.

———. *Zion and the State*. New York: Basil Blackwell, 1987.

Cohen, Naomi. *American Jews and the Zionist Idea*. New York: Ktav, 1975.

———. *The Americanization of Zionism, 1897–1948*. Waltham, Mass.: Brandeis University Press, 2003.

Cohen, Steven M., and Jack Wertheimer. "Whatever Happened to the Jewish People?" *Commentary* June 2006: 33–37.

Connor, Walker. *Ethnonationalism: The Quest for Understanding*. Princeton, N.J.: Princeton University Press, 1994.

Eisen, Arnold M. *The Chosen People in America: A Study in Jewish Religious Ideology*. Bloomington: Indiana University Press, 1983.

———. *Galut: Modern Jewish Reflections on Homelessness and Homecoming*. Bloomington: Indiana University Press, 1986.

Elazar, Daniel. *Kinship and Consent: The Jewish Political Tradition and Its Contemporary Uses*. New Brunswick, N.J.: Transaction Publishers, 1997.

Etzioni, Amitai, ed. *New Communitarian Thinking*. Charlottesville: University Press of Virginia, 1995.

Fiedler, Lutz. "Habsburger Verlängerungen—Imperienkonzepte im Werk Hans Kohns" (Hapsburger renewal—The concept of the imperial in Hans Kohn's work). *Jahrbuch des Simon-Dubnow-Institutes* (Simon Dubnow Institute Yearbook) 6 (2006): 477–508.

Fink, Carole. *Defending the Rights of Others: The Great Powers, the Jews, and International Minority Protection, 1878–1938*. Cambridge: Cambridge University Press, 2004.

Fonrobert, Charlotte E. "From Separatism to Urbanism: The Dead Sea Scrolls and the Origins of the Rabbinic *Eruv*." *Dead Sea Discoveries* 11, no. 1 (2004): 43–71.

Frankel, Jonathan. "An Introductory Essay—the Paradoxical Politics of Marginality:

Thoughts on the Jewish Situation during the Years 1914–21." In *Studies in Contemporary Jewry: The Jews and the European Crisis, 1914–21*, ed. Jonathan Frankel, 3–21. New York: Oxford University Press, 1988.

———. *Prophecy and Politics: Socialism, Nationalism, and the Russian Jews, 1862–1917.* Cambridge: Cambridge University Press, 1981.

Friesel, Evyatar. "The Influence of American Zionism on the American Jewish Community, 1900–1950." *American Jewish History* 75, no. 2 (1985): 130–48.

Funkenstein, Amos. "The Dialectics of Assimilation." *Jewish Social Studies* 1, no. 2 (1995): 1–14.

Gal, Allon, ed. *Beyond Survival and Philanthropy: American Jewry and Israel.* Cincinnati, Ohio: Hebrew Union College Press, 2000.

Gans, Haim. *The Limits of Nationalism.* Cambridge: Cambridge University Press, 2003.

Gellner, Ernest. *Nations and Nationalism.* Ithaca, N.Y.: Cornell University Press, 1983.

Gerstle, Gary. *American Crucible: Race and Nation in the Twentieth Century.* Princeton, N.J.: Princeton University Press, 2002.

Giddens, Anthony. *The Nation-State and Violence.* Cambridge: Polity Press, 1985.

Gilroy, Paul. *The Black Atlantic: Modernity and Double Consciousness.* Cambridge, Mass.: Harvard University Press, 1993.

Gitelman, Zvi Y., ed. *The Emergence of Modern Jewish Politics: Bundism and Zionism in Eastern Europe.* Pittsburgh: University of Pittsburgh Press, 2003.

Gleason, Phillip. "American Identity and Americanization." In *Concepts of Ethnicity,* ed. William Peterson, Michael Novak, and Phillip Gleason, 107. Cambridge, Mass.: Harvard University Press, 1982.

———. *Speaking of Diversity: Language and Ethnicity in Twentieth-Century America.* Baltimore: Johns Hopkins University Press, 1992.

Goldsmith, Emanuel S., Mel Scult, and Robert M. Seltzer. *The American Judaism of Mordecai M. Kaplan.* New York: New York University Press, 1990.

Goldstein, Eric. *The Price of Whiteness: Jews, Race, and American Identity.* Princeton, N.J.: Princeton University Press, 2006.

Gordon, Adi. "New Politics in an Old Key: Arnold Zweig, Hans Kohn and the Central European Jewish Generation of 1914." Ph.D. diss., Hebrew University, 2008.

Goren, Arthur A. *New York Jews and the Quest for Community: The Kehillah Experiment, 1908–1922.* New York: Columbia University Press, 1970.

———. *The Politics and Public Culture of American Jews.* Bloomington: Indiana University Press, 1999.

Gorny, Yosef. *The State of Israel in Jewish Public Thought: The Quest for Collective Identity.* New York: New York University Press, 1994.

Greene, Daniel. "A Chosen People in a Pluralist Nation: Horace Kallen and the Jewish-American Experience." *Religion and American Culture* 16, no. 2 (2006): 161–94.

Greenbaum, Avraham. *A History of the Ararat Publishing Society.* Jerusalem: Rubin Mass, 1998.

Gurock, Jeffrey S., and Jacob J. Schacter. *A Modern Heretic and a Traditional Community: Mordecai M. Kaplan, Orthodoxy, and American Judaism.* New York: Columbia University Press, 1997.

Hacohen, Malachi. "Dilemmas of Cosmopolitanism: Karl Popper, Jewish Identity, and 'Central European Culture.'" *Journal of Modern History* 71, no. 1 (1999): 136–39.

———. "The Limits of the National Paradigm in the Study of Political Thought: The

Case of Karl Popper and Central European Cosmopolitanism." In *The History of Political Thought in National Context,* ed. Dario Castiglione and Iain Hampsher-Monk, 247–80. Cambridge: Cambridge University Press, 2001.

Hall, Stuart. "Cultural Identity and Diaspora." In *Identity: Community, Culture, Difference,* ed. J. Rutherford, 222–37. London: Lawrence & Wishart, 1990.

Halpern, Ben. "The Americanization of Zionism, 1880–1930." In *Essential Papers on Zionism,* ed. Jehuda Reinharz and Anita Shapira, 318–36. London: Cassell, 1979.

Handy, Robert T. *The Social Gospel in America, 1870–1920.* New York: Oxford University Press, 1966.

Hansen, Jonathan M. *The Lost Promise of Patriotism.* Chicago: University of Chicago, 2003.

Harris, Jay. *Nachman Krochmal: Guiding the Perplexed of the Modern Age.* New York: New York University Press, 1991.

Harshav, Benjamin. *Language in the Time of Revolution.* Berkeley: University of California Press, 1993.

Higham, John. *Send These to Me: Immigrants in Urban America.* Baltimore: Johns Hopkins University Press, 1984.

———. *Strangers in the Land: Patterns of American Nativism, 1860–1925.* New York: Atheneum, 1963.

Hobsbawm, E. J. *Nations and Nationalism since 1780: Program, Myth, Reality.* Cambridge: Cambridge University Press, 1992.

Hobsbawm, E. J., and T. O. Ranger. *The Invention of Tradition.* Cambridge: Cambridge University Press, 1993.

Hollinger, David. *Cosmopolitanism and Solidarity: Studies in Ethnoracial, Religious, and Professional Affiliation in the U.S.* Madison: University of Wisconsin Press, 2006.

———. "Jewish Identity, Assimilation, and Multiculturalism." In *Creating America's Jews,* ed. Karen Mittleman, 51–59. Hanover, N.H.: University Press of New England, 1998.

———. *Postethnic America: Beyond Multiculturalism.* New York: Basic Books, 1995.

Hutchinson, John. *The Dynamics of Cultural Nationalism.* London: Allen and Unwin, 1987.

Hutchinson, William W. *Religious Pluralism in America: The Contentious History of a Founding Ideal.* New Haven, Conn.: Yale University Press, 2003.

Hyman, Paula. *Gender and Assimilation in Modern Jewish History.* Seattle: University of Washington Press, 1995.

Ignatieff, Michael. *Blood and Belonging: Journeys into the New Nationalism.* New York: Noonday Press, 1993.

Jacobson, Matthew Frye. "More 'Trans-,' Less 'National.'" *Journal of American Ethnic History* (Summer 2006): 74–84.

———. *Special Sorrows: The Diasporic Imagination of Irish, Polish, and Jewish Immigrants in the United States.* Cambridge, Mass.: Harvard University Press, 1995.

———. *Whiteness of a Different Color: European Immigrants and the Alchemy of Race.* Cambridge, Mass.: Harvard University Press, 1998.

Janowsky, Oscar I. *Jews and Minority Rights (1898–1919).* New York: Columbia University Press, 1933.

Judt, Tony. "Israel: The Alternative." *New York Review of Books,* vol. 50, no. 16, October 23, 2003.

Kedar, Nir. "Ben Gurion's Mamlachtiyut: Etymological and Theoretical Roots." *Israel Studies* 7, no. 3 (2003): 117–33.

Kedourie, Elie. *Nationalism*. Oxford: Blackwell, 1994.

King, Desmond S. *The Liberty of Strangers: Making the American Nation*. New York: Oxford University Press, 2005.

Kobrin, Rebecca. "When a Jew Was a 'Landsman': Rethinking American Jewish Regional Identity in the Age of Mass Migration." *Modern Jewish Studies* 7, no. 3 (2008): 357–76.

Kuzio, Taras. "The Myth of the Civic State: A Critical Survey of Hans Kohn's Framework for Understanding Nationalism." *Ethnic and Racial Studies* 25, no. 1 (2002): 20–39.

Kymlicka, Will. *Multicultural Citizenship*. Oxford: Oxford University Press, 1995.

Lavsky, Hagit. "German Zionists and the Emergence of *Brit Shalom*." In *Essential Papers on Zionism*, ed. Anita Shapira and Jehuda Reinharz, 648–70. London: Cassell, 1996.

———. "Hans Kohn: Nationalism between Theory and Practice." *Zion* 67, no. 1 (2002): 189–212.

Liebich, Andre. "Searching for the Perfect Nation: The Itinerary of Hans Kohn (1891–1971)." *Nations and Nationalism* 12, no. 4 (2006): 579–96.

Maor, Zohar. "Mysticism, Regeneration, and Jewish Rebirth: The 'Prague Circle' in the Beginning of the Twentieth Century." Ph.D. diss., Tel Aviv University, 2005.

Markwell, D. J. "Sir Alfred Zimmern Revisited: Fifty Years On." *Review of International Studies* 12 (1986): 279–92.

McKim, Robert, and Jeff McMahan, eds. *The Morality of Nationalism*. New York: Oxford University Press, 1997.

Mendelsohn, Ezra. *On Modern Jewish Politics*. New York: Oxford University Press, 1993.

Mendes-Flohr, Paul. *Land of Two Peoples: Martin Buber on Jews and Arabs*. New York: Oxford University Press, 1983.

Michels, Tony. *A Fire in Their Hearts*. Cambridge, Mass.: Harvard University Press, 2005.

Miller, David. *On Nationality*. Oxford: Oxford University Press, 1995.

Moore, Deborah Dash. *At Home in America: Second Generation New York Jews*. New York: Columbia University Press, 1981.

Moore, Deborah Dash, and Andrew Bush. "Kaplan's Key." In *Key Texts in American Jewish Culture*, ed. Jack Kugelmas, 244–57. New Brunswick, N.J.: Rutgers University Press, 2003.

Moore, Deborah Dash, and Ilan Troen, eds. *Divergent Jewish Cultures: Israel and America*. New Haven, Conn.: Yale University Press, 2001.

Moore, R. Laurence. *Religious Outsiders and the Making of Americans*. New York: Oxford University Press, 1986.

Morefield, Jeanne. *Covenants without Swords: Idealist Liberalism and the Spirit of Empire*. Princeton, N.J.: Princeton University Press, 2005.

———. "A Liberal in a Muddle: Alfred Zimmern on Nationality, Internationality, and Commonwealth." In *Imperialism and Internationalism in the Discipline of International Relations*, ed. Brian Schmidt and David Long, 93–115. Albany: State University of New York Press, 2005.

Mosse, George. "Central European Intellectuals in Palestine." *Judaism* 45, no. 2 (1996): 134–43.

Myers, David. *Between Jew and Arab*. Waltham, Mass.: Brandeis University Press, 2008.

———. "Can There Be a Principled Anti-Zionism? On the Nexus between Anti-Historicism and Anti-Zionism in Modern Jewish Thought." *Journal of Israeli History* 25, no. 1 (2006): 33–50.

———. "Discourses of Civilization: The Shifting Course of a Modern Jewish Motif." In *The Jewish Contribution to Civilization: Reassessing an Idea,* ed. Jeremy Cohen and Richard Cohen, 24–35. Oxford: Littman Library, 2008.

———. *Re-Inventing the Jewish Past: European Jewish Intellectuals and the Zionist Return to History.* New York: Oxford University Press, 1995.

———. *Resisting History: Historicism and Its Discontents in German-Jewish Thought.* Princeton, N.J.: Princeton University Press, 2003.

———. "Simon Rawidowicz, 'Hashpaitis,' and the Perils of Influence." *Transversal 7* (2006): 13–26.

———. "A Third Guide for the Perplexed?" In *History and Literature: New Readings of Jewish Texts in Honor of Arnold J. Band.* Brown Judaic Studies. Edited by William Cutter and David C. Jacobson, 75–87. Providence, R.I.: Brown Judaism Studies, 2001.

Nimni, Ephraim, ed. *National Cultural Autonomy and Its Contemporary Critics.* London: Routledge, 2005.

Penslar, Derek. *Israel in History.* London: Routledge, 2007.

———. "Narratives of Nation Building: Major Themes in Zionist Historiography." In *The Jewish Past Revisited,* ed. David Myers and David Ruderman, 104–27. New Haven, Conn.: Yale University Press, 1998.

Pianko, Noam. "Diaspora Jewish Nationalism and Identity in America, 1914–1967." Ph.D. diss., Yale University, 2004.

———. "Reconstructing Judaism, Reconstructing America: The Sources and Functions of Kaplan's 'Civilization.'" *Jewish Social Studies* 12, no. 2 (2006): 39–55.

Pollock, Sheldon. *The Language of the Gods in the World of Men: Sanskrit, Culture, and Power in Premodern India.* Berkeley: University of California Press, 2006.

Raider, Mark A. *The Emergence of American Zionism.* New York: New York University Press, 1998.

Ratzabi, Shalom. *Between Zionism and Judaism: The Radical Circle in Brit Shalom, 1925–1933.* Leiden, Netherlands: Brill, 2002.

Ravid, A. "From the Letters of Simon Rawidowicz." In *Genazim 1,* ed. G. Kressel, 290–307. Tel Aviv, 1961.

Ravid, Benjamin. "The Human Dimension of Wissenschaft des Judentums: Letters from the Rawidowicz Archives." Festschrift in honor of Raymond P. Scheindlin. Edited by J. Decter and M. Rand, 87–128. Piscataway, N.J.: Gorgias Press, 2007.

———. "Simon Rawidowicz and the 'Brit Ivrit Olamit': A Study in the Relationship between Hebrew Culture in the Diaspora and Zionist Ideology (Hebrew)." *Studies and Essays in Hebrew Language and Literature* (2004): 119–54.

Rich, Paul. "Alfred Zimmern's Cautious Idealism: The League of Nations, International Education, and the Commonwealth." In *Thinkers of the Twenty Years' Crisis: Inter-War Idealism Reassessed,* ed. David Long and Peter Wilson, 79–99. Oxford: Oxford University Press, 1995.

Roshwald, Aviel. *The Endurance of Nationalism.* Cambridge: Cambridge University Press, 2004.

Rosman, Moshe. *How Jewish Is Jewish History.* Oxford: Littman, 2008.

Rozenblit, Marsha. *Reconstructing a National Identity: The Jews of Hapsburg Austria during World War I.* Oxford: Oxford University Press, 2001.

Sandel, Michael. *Liberalism and Its Critics.* Oxford: Blackwell, 1984.

Sarna, Jonathan. *American Judaism: A History.* New Haven, Conn.: Yale University Press, 2004.

Schiller, Nina Glick, and Georges Eugene Fouron. *Georges Woke Up Laughing: Long-Distance Nationalism and the Search for Home.* Durham, N.C.: Duke University Press, 2001.

Schmidt, Sarah. *Horace M. Kallen: Prophet of American Zionism.* Brooklyn, N.Y.: Carlson, 1995.

Scult, Mel. *Judaism Faces the Twentieth Century: A Biography of Mordecai M. Kaplan, American Jewish Civilization Series.* Detroit: Wayne State University Press, 1993.

Seton-Watson, H. *Nations and States.* London: Methuen, 1977.

Shimoni, Gideon. *The Zionist Ideology.* Hanover, N.H.: University Press of New England, 1995.

Shumsky, Dimitry. "On Ethno-Centrism and Its Limits: Czecho-German Jewry in Fin-de-Siècle Prague and the Origins of Zionist Bi-Nationalism." *Jahrbuch des Simon-Dubnow-Instituts* 5 (2006): 173–88.

Skinner, E. P. "The Dialectic between Diasporas and Homelands." In *Global Dimensions of the African Diaspora,* ed. J. E. Harris, 11–40. Washington, D.C.: Howard University Press, 1982.

Smith, Anthony D. *National Identity: Ethnonationalism in Comparative Perspective.* Reno: University of Nevada Press, 1991.

———. *Nationalism and Modernism: A Critical Survey of Recent Theories of Nations and Nationalism.* London: Routledge, 1998.

———. *Nationalism in the Twentieth Century.* New York: New York University Press, 1979.

———. *Theories of Nationalism.* New York: Holmes & Meier, 1983.

Smith, Rogers M. "Beyond Tocqueville, Myrdal, and Hartz: The Multiple Traditions in America." *American Political Science Review* 87, no. 3 (1993): 549–66.

———. *Civic Ideals: Conflicting Visions of Citizenship in U.S. History.* New Haven, Conn.: Yale University Press, 1997.

———, ed. *Stories of Peoplehood.* New York: Cambridge University Press, 2003.

Smith, Steven. *The Ethnic Origins of Nations.* Oxford: Blackwell, 1987.

———. *The Nation in History: Historiographical Debates about Ethnicity and Nationalism.* Hanover, N.H.: University Press of New England, 2000.

———. *Spinoza, Liberalism, and the Question of Jewish Identity.* New Haven, Conn.: Yale University Press, 1997.

Sollors, Werner. *Beyond Ethnicity: Consent and Descent in American Culture.* New York: Oxford University Press, 1986.

———. *The Invention of Ethnicity.* New York: Oxford University Press, 1989.

Stanislawski, Michael. *Zionism and the Fin de Siècle.* Berkeley: University of California Press, 2001.

Takaki, Ronald T. *A Different Mirror: A History of Multicultural America.* Boston: Little, Brown, and Co., 1993.

Tamir, Yael. *Liberal Nationalism.* Princeton, N.J.: Princeton University Press, 1993.

Taylor, Charles. *Multiculturalism and the Politics of Recognition.* Edited by Amy Gutmann. Princeton, N.J.: Princeton University Press, 1994.

———. "Nationalism and Modernity." In *The Morality of Nationalism,* ed. Robert McKim and Jeff McMahan, 66–74. New York: Oxford University Press, 1997.

Toll, William. "Horace M. Kallen: Pluralism and American Jewish Identity." *American Jewish History* 85, no. 1 (1997): 57–74.

Tölölyan, Khachig. "Rethinking Diaspora(s): Stateless Power in the Transnational Moment." *Diaspora* 5, no. 1 (1996): 3–36.

Urofsky, Melvin I. *American Zionism from Herzl to the Holocaust.* Garden City, N.Y.: Anchor Press, 1975.

Walzer, Michael. "The Communitarian Critique of Liberalism." *Political Theory* 18, no. 1 (1990): 6–23.

———. "Liberalism and the Art of Separation." *Political Theory* 12, no. 3 (1984): 315–29.

———. "Multiculturalism and the Politics of Difference." In *Insider/Outsider: American Jews and Multiculturalism,* ed. David Biale, 88–100. Berkeley: University of California Press, 1998.

———. *What Does It Mean to Be an American?* New York: Marsilio, 1992.

Walzer, Michael, Menachem Lorberbaum, and Noam J. Zohar, eds. *The Jewish Political Tradition.* Vol. 1. New Haven, Conn.: Yale University Press, 2000.

Warner, R. Stephen, and Judith G. Wittner. *Gatherings in Diaspora: Religious Communities and the New Immigration.* Philadelphia: Temple University Press, 1998.

Weeks, Theodore. *Nations and State in Late Imperial Russia.* DeKalb: Northern Illinois University Press, 1996.

Weinberg, David H. *Between Tradition and Modernity: Haim Zhitlowski, Simon Dubnow, Ahad Ha-Am, and the Shaping of Modern Jewish Identity.* New York: Holmes & Meier, 1996.

Weiss, Yfaat. "Central European Ethnonationalism and Zionist Binationalism." *Jewish Social Studies* 11, no. 1 (2004): 93–117.

Wieseltier, Leon. "Israel, Palestine, and the Return of the Bi-National Fantasy: What Is Not to Be Done." *New Republic,* October 27, 2003.

Wolf, Ken. "Hans Kohn's Nationalism." *Journal of the History of Ideas* 37, no. 4 (1976): 651–72.

———. "The Idea of Nationalism: The Intellectual Development and Historiographical Contribution of Hans Kohn." Ph.D. diss., University of Notre Dame, 1972.

Yack, Bernard. "The Myth of Civic Nationalism." In *Theorizing Nationalism.* Ronald Beiner, ed. Albany: State University of New York Press, 1999.

Zipperstein, Steven J. "Ahad Ha'am and the Politics of Assimilation." In *Assimilation and Community: The Jews in Nineteenth-Century Europe,* ed. Jonathan Frankel, 344–65. Cambridge: Cambridge University Press, 1992.

———. *Elusive Prophet: Ahad Ha'am and the Origins of Zionism.* Berkeley: University of California Press, 1993.

———. "On Reading Ahad Ha'am as Mordecai Kaplan Read Him." *Jewish Social Studies* 12, no. 2 (2006): 30–38.

INDEX

Balfour Declaration, 26, 29, 128, 142–43
Bar Kochba society, 138–40
Bauer, Otto, 223n94
Beard, Charles, and Mary Beard, 232n6
Bederman, Gail, 109
beinartzit (interland) concept, 72, 74–75, 227n37
Beller, Steven, 218n6
Ben Gurion, David: Blaustein Zionism disagreement, 200; in classroom Zionism exercise, 201–202; Jewish peoplehood and, 198; as Jewish political philosopher, 66; messianic views of, 86–87; on the name "Israel," 61–62, 180–81; statist ideology of, 1, 61–62, 180–81, 198–99, 245n5; status quo agreement, 206
Benderly, Samson, 212n12
Bergmann, Hugo, 139, 143, 157
Bialik, Haim Nahman, 7, 68–69, 225nn14,18
Birnbaum, Nathan, 151
Birthright Israel, 202–203
Blaustein, Jacob, 200
Bourne, Randolph, 105–106, 108, 110, 168–69, 242n74
Boyarin, Jonathan, 236n91
Brandeis, Louis, 129, 157, 201, 220n45
Brit Shalom, 7–8, 175
British internationalism: Ahad Ha'am as model for, 46; Arab Palestinian minority rights and, 54–55; imperialist oversight of multinationalist experiments, 155–56; Kohn on, 140–41, 155–56, 169; liberalism principles of, 52–53; Round Table, 40–41; sovereignty advocated in, 40
Brubaker, Rogers, 14, 17
Buber, Martin: biographical sketch, 241n49; critique of sovereignty, 39–40; cultural Zionism theory and, 16–17; as *Der Jude* editor, 140; influence on Kohn, 7, 133, 135–36, 139, 143, 149–52, 153–54, 156, 159, 162–63, 165, 170, 172–74, 240n45; Jewish nationalism theory of, 149–50; Orientalism influences on, 242n64; as post-WWI intellectual influence, 156–57; on

premodern narrative, 87; "renewal of Judaism" initiative of, 139, 150; Tönnies influence on, 146
Bundism, 214n29
Bush, Andrew, 232n6

Calhoun, Craig, 238n6
center-periphery paradigm, 57–58, 72–74, 173–74, 201–204
Chatterjee, Partha, 215n37
chosenness, 122–24, 220n53
Christianity: American social gospel Protestantism, 35–36, 116; humanism principle in, 160; inclination toward religious nationalism, 106–107; messianic principle in, 149
citizenship: cultural and religious demands on citizens, 35–36; minority citizenship in nation-states, 31–32; participatory citizenship as essence of religious identity, 1; "territorial principle" of citizenship, 39. *See also* civic-versus-ethnic contrast
civic nationalism: absence of historical solidarity in, 137; American Judaism and, 33, 182; intolerance fostered by, 32; melting-pot discourse and, 34–36, 41–43. *See also* civic-versus-ethnic contrast; ethnic nationalism; Kohn, Hans
civic-versus-ethnic contrast, 11; Brubaker critique of, 17–18; cosmopolitanism and, 244n95; Jewish political experience and, 52–53; Kohn presentation of, 161–62, 167, 169–71; legacy of, 176–77, 191; theories of nationalism and, 31–32, 120; Western vs. non-Western culture and, 136–37, 213n23, 238n6, 242n64; Zimmern approach to, 50–53. *See also* civic nationalism; ethnic nationalism; Kohn, Hans
civilization. *See* national civilization
Cohen, Gerson, 230n67
Cohen, Mitchell, 228n50
Cohen, Naomi, 21, 221n59
Cohen, Steven, 197–98
Colin, Paul (Hans Kohn pseudonym), 140–41, 171

collective solidarity: as basis for individual freedom, 121; as basis for Jewish nationalism, 18, 215n35; communitarianism and, 222n76; in cultural humanism, 11; deferred messianism and, 82–83; descent-based identity and, 47–48, 146–47, 162, 184; equality/tolerance as component of, 50; false dichotomies of Jewish identity, 44, 56, 93; folkways as basis for, 112–13; homeland discourse and, 204–205; inadequacy of sovereignty for, 23–24, 185–87; in Kohn theory of American nationalism, 145–48, 161–62, 166–69, 171–72; Kohn transnational solidarity, 159–60; language as source of, 10, 76–81, 112, 190, 204; in national civilization, 111–12; organic vs. political ties (*Gemeinschaft* vs. *Gesellschaft*), 139, 146–47; post-1948 "Jewish corporate entity," 178–80, 183–84; religion as source for, 96, 111–12, 113–16, 127, 131–32, 187; spatiality relationship with, 75; statehood effect on, 92, 201; victimization discourses and, 184, 246n7; "We Are One" campaign, 201, 248n26. *See also Am Yisrael* (people of Israel); peoplehood; Romantic nationalism; spiritual Zionism

colonialism: center-periphery paradigm and, 57; European Orientalism and, 153–54, 162; Jewish leaders in colonial governments, 40, 219n41; liberalism as deflection of anticolonial initiatives, 52–53; as model of stateless community, 40; nationalism as anticolonial resistance, 215n37

communism, 117, 234n60

communitarianism, 222n76

community. *See* collective solidarity

Connor, Walker, 212n19

corporate groups, 35–37, 113–14, 119–22, 216n38

cosmopolitan languages, 77, 80–81

cosmopolitanism, 48–50, 120–21, 167–69, 244n95

counterstate nationalism, 14–16, 26–27, 212nn12,19, 213n25; American Jewish

nationalism as, 108–109; Babylonian Talmud as symbol for, 63; both/and vs. either/or paradigm and, 93; contemporary counterstate trends, 193–95, 207–208, 248n34; dialectics of assimilation, 215n36; Dubnow theory of diaspora nationalism and, 38–39, 73, 214n29, 219n28; ethical nationalism and, 48–50; Kallen nation-of-nationalities approach, 26–27, 41–43, 168; Kohn approach to, 39–40, 147–57, 165–71, 176–77, 179; Meinecke critique of the "power state," 39, 146; post-1948 counterstate approaches, 178–79; postnationalism and, 38–39, 57, 108, 217n48; Renner critique of the "territorial principle," 39; Romantic nationalism and, 44–45; statist resistance to, 212n8; Swiss nationalist model, 169, 244n116; symbiotic national-collective loyalties, 48–49. *See also* cultural humanism; global Hebraism; Jewish nationalism; national civilization; stateless nationalism

Croly, Walter, 35–36

cultural humanism, 4, 138; civic-versus-ethnic contrast and, 176; collective tolerance and, 50; counterstate nationalism and, 180, 185–86; Greek political philosophy and, 160, 243n90; intellectual influences on, 11, 27, 148–49, 151–52, 238n10; Jewish humanism as basis for, 148–52, 160–63, 189–90; Jewish nationalism and, 191–93; Kohn pacifism and, 140–44; political dichotomies and, 15; sources of universal principles, 158–60, 164–67, 171–72; universal human rights, 52. *See also* individualism; Kohn, Hans

cultural nationalism, 137, 167, 176

cultural pluralism: American Jewish nationalism and, 108–109; Americanization campaign and, 105, 107, 125; Arab Palestinians and, 57–58; chosenness incompatible with, 220n53; *eruvin* as preservation of cultural space, 78–80, 89, 227n32; homeland discourse and, 223n99; immigration

restrictions in the U.S., 34, 112, 165; Kallen principle of, 41–43, 50–51, 105, 156–57, 220n53, 221n66, 223n89; Kohn critique of, 166–71; Zimmern "congeries of nations" approach, 168. *See also* ethnicity; minority national groups
cultural Zionism. *See* spiritual Zionism

deferred messianism, 10, 81–89, 149–52, 163–64, 229nn54,63, 230nn64,66
democracy: individual rights in Palestine and, 54; insufficiency of individual liberty, 54, 89–91; Kallen theory of civilization nationalism and, 41–43, 46–47, 51–52, 54; Kaplan theory of national civilization and, 10–11, 104, 110–11; patriotism and, 35–36. *See also* Enlightenment; freedom; liberal nationalism
Dewey, John, 105, 232n6
diaspora nationalism (autonomism), 38–39, 73, 214n29, 219n28, 234n48
diaspora paradigm: anti-sovereignty reaction to Yehoshua, 2, 23–24; center-periphery paradigm, 57–58, 72–74, 201–204; deferred messianism and, 82–87; diaspora communities in global Hebraism, 71, 75; diaspora studies and, 185, 188; diaspora vs. statehood advocacy polarization, 212n8; emancipated national culture and, 72–74, 155, 204; European diaspora nationalism, 21–22; integrationist assumption in, 5–6; Jews as normative post-nation-state model, 38–39, 41; political solidarity of diaspora communities, 24–25; Russian experiments with, 37–38; uniqueness of Jews as diaspora population, 71; vulnerability of post-WWI stateless Jews, 29; Zionist negation of the diaspora and, 201–203, 206, 212n8, 223n96, 248n30. *See also* counterstate nationalism; multinational state paradigm
dissimilation, 46
Dubnow, Simon: on diaspora nationalism, 38–39, 73, 214n29, 219n28, 234n48; on ethical nationalism, 38, 48–50, 52, 222n71; as post-WWI

intellectual influence, 8, 59; Rawidowicz relationship with, 67; Romantic nationalism and, 44–45
Dubois, W. E. B., 109

Eisen, Arnold, 198, 216n45, 234n49
Ely, Richard, 116
Enlightenment, 83–84, 87, 132, 164–67, 188, 193–94. *See also* democracy
Eretz Yisrael, 61–62
eruvin (extended permitted movement during the Sabbath), 64, 72–73, 75, 77–80, 89, 227n32, 228nn44–46
ethical nationalism: as alternative to nation-state model, 38; British and Swiss models, 169; cultural uniformity and, 190–91; Dubnow concept of, 38, 48–50, 52, 222n71; Kaplan national civilization and, 96–97, 110, 118–24; symbiotic national-collective loyalties, 48–49. *See also* liberal nationalism
ethnic nationalism: descent-based identity and, 47–48, 146–47, 162, 184; Jewish political advocacy of, 52–53; minority rights and, 31–32; national civilization as counter to, 98, 111–12; Romantic nationalism and, 44–46, 52; Russification initiative, 38; totalitarianism and, 175; universalism and, 189–90, 216n38. *See also* civic nationalism; civic-versus-ethnic contrast; Romantic nationalism
ethnicity: ethnic studies and, 184–85; "ethnopolitical entrepreneurism" as nationalist counterdiscourse, 18–20; in Kohn theory of American nationalism, 161–62; melting-pot discourse and, 34–36; multiculturalism and, 95–96, 246n12; polycentric vs. ethnocentric nationality, 121–22; self-governing vs. polyethnic rights, 126–27; theory of cultural pluralism and, 41–43. *See also* cultural pluralism; minority national groups; race
Etzioni, Amitai, 194
Europe: Babylon as symbol for European Jewish settlements, 63; ethnic nationalism as model in, 21–22, 33; European

Orientalism, 153–54, 162; Jewish communal life in, 33
Exodus, 200–201
Ezrahi, Sidra, 229n62

Feiwal, Berthold, 141
Feuerbach, Ludwig, 69, 76
Fichte, Johann Gottlieb, 32, 45
Fink, Carole, 30, 218n5
Folkspartei political party, 38
folkways, 112–13
Fonrobert, Charlotte, 228n46
France, 162
Frankel, Jonathan, 28–30
freedom: collective attachment as fundamental to, 50, 121; insufficiency of individual liberty, 54, 89–91; right-to-differ principle, 50, 89–91, 189–90. *See also* democracy; Enlightenment; minority national groups
Friedlaender, Israel, 8, 37–39, 113, 214n33
Friesel, Evyatar, 214n33, 216n45
Funkenstein, Amos, 215n36

Gans, Chaim, 14, 194, 213n25, 217n49
Gellner, Ernst, 13, 213n25
geography. *See* territoriality
German Romanticism. *See* Romantic nationalism
Germany: absolute national sovereignty in, 119, 162; anti-Jewish initiatives, 116–17; German Zionism as intellectual source, 11, 32, 137, 158, 163, 171, 174–75; Hebrew literary renaissance in, 68; philosophical idealism in, 229nn54,55; Rawidowicz history of German fascism, 85. *See also* Nazism
Gerstle, Gary, 33
Gilroy, Paul, 217n49, 247n17
Gladden, Washington, 116
Gleason, Philip, 104
global Hebraism, 4, 64, 203–204; counterstate nationalism and, 9–10, 138, 167, 180, 185–86, 188–89; diaspora communities in, 71, 75; intellectual influences on, 27; Jewish nationalism and, 191–93; legacy of, 182, 204–205; Palestine settlement effect on, 68,

225n14; political dichotomies compared with, 15; religious symbolism in, 71–73; role of myth in, 81–89; Romantic nationalism and, 46; spiritual Zionism compared with, 46–47. *See also* Rawidowicz, Simon; stateless nationalism
globalization, 24–25
Goebbels, Joseph, 116
Goldman, Nachum, 212n12
Gordon, A. D., 151–52, 160, 164
Goren, Arthur, 214n33, 236n98
Gorny, Yosef, 248n30
Goyim shemedabrim ivrit (non-Jews who speak Hebrew), 75–76, 227n38
Greene, Daniel, 220n53
Greenfield, Leah, 194
Gutmann, Amy, 194

Hacohen, Malachi, 216n40
Hall, Stuart, 211n7
Halpern, Ben, 237n107
Handlin, Oscar, 245n122
Harshav, Benjamin, 75–76, 226n27, 228n39
Hartman, David, 201–202
Hayes, Carleton, 161–62, 244n95
Hebrew language and literature: in *Babylon and Jerusalem,* 70, 88, 90; in global Hebraism, 9–10, 64; *Goyim shemedabrim ivrit* (non-Jews who speak Hebrew), 75–76, 227n38; Hebrew literature, 68, 76–81; homeland discourse in, 229n62; language wars, 228n40; linguistic nationalism and, 46–47, 67–68, 76–81; national civilization and, 112; "Second House" symbol and, 82–84, 229n55; as source of solidarity, 10, 76–81, 112, 190, 204
Hebrew Renaissance (1920s Weimar Germany), 9, 68
Hegel, Georg Wilhelm Friedrich, 32, 229n55
Herberg, Will, 113, 245n122
Herder, Johann Gottfried von, 32
Hermann, Leo, 140
Hertzberg, Arthur, 96, 231n3
Herzl, Theodor, 29

Hess, Moses, 151, 216n45
Higham, John, 36
Hitler, Adolf, 69
Hollinger, David, 36, 47, 121, 184, 221n66
Holocaust, 29, 91. *See also* Nazism
homeland discourse: American Jewish homeland discourse, 181–82; assimilation and, 181–82, 246n6; center-periphery paradigm, 57–58, 72–74, 201–204; cultural pluralism and, 223n99; deferred messianism and, 82–87; desacralization of Hebrew language and, 81; diaspora studies and, 185; effect on diaspora identity, 204–205; in Hebrew literature, 229n62; pilgrimage trips and, 202–203; Rawidowicz global homeland argument, 72, 188–89, 204–205; religious civilization and, 128, 236n100; self-determination and, 56. *See also* statehood
humanistic nationalism. *See* cultural humanism
Huntington, Samuel, 95
Hutchinson, John, 176
hybridity, 80
Hyman, Paula, 214

identity. *See* collective solidarity; ethnicity; individualism; minority national groups; race
Ihud, 175
individualism: as American Zionism component, 21–22; as compassionate elimination, 49; corporate nationalism conflict with, 35–37; individual rights in democracies, 54, 89–91, 106; individual rights under British Internationalism and, 54–55; Jewish identity conflict with, 17–18; in Kohn theory of American nationalism, 171–72; particularism as basis for, 121, 132; political nationalism and, 13–14; Rawidowicz critique of the Enlightenment, 83–84; repressive nationalism and, 117. *See also* assimilation; cultural humanism
integrationism: Ahad Ha'am theory of imitation and, 46, 221n60; American Jewish integration, 22, 33, 165–67,

216n42, 220n52, 236n98; dialectics of assimilation, 215n36; dissimilation compared with, 46; *eruvin* as preservation of Jewish space, 78–80, 89, 227n32; failure of interwar European integration, 29; hybridity as model of, 80; Jewish minority status and, 5–6, 184–85, 196, 214n27; in Kohn theory of American nationalism, 165; melting-pot discourse and, 34–36, 41–43; outsider views of Jewish nationalism and, 43. *See also* assimilation
Iraq, 153
Israel (people of Israel). *See Am Yisrael* (people of Israel)
Israel (State of Israel): *aliyah* (immigration to Israel), 181, 200; American Jewish experience and, 181–82, 200–206; critique in *Babylon and Jerusalem*, 71; founding of, 178–79, 200–201; homeland discourse and, 56–57; Jewish peoplehood and, 173–74, 198–99; naming of, 61–62, 180–81; personal status law, 206; Rawidowicz critique of, 90–91, 229n63, 230nn64,66. *See also* Palestine; self-determination; sovereignty; statehood

Jacobson, Matthew Frye, 216n44, 246n6
Jerusalem (as symbol for the Jewish people), 63, 65, 72, 75, 81–87
Jewish Center, 97
Jewish nationalism: American Jewish nationalism as counterstate paradigm, 108–109; British internationalism and, 54–55, 223nn93,94; collective solidarity as basis for, 18, 215n35; as distinct from racial/religious categories, 183; false dichotomies of Jewish nationalism, 44, 56, 93; as Kohn influence, 160–64, 172–73; as "making space" for Jews, 191–97, 247n17; outsider views of Jewish nationalism, 43; Palestine effect on, 226n27; as political resistance, 215n37; scholarship on, 211n6; statelessness influence on, 194, 196; subterranean strategy for, 180, 193; Zionism as counterstate nationalist

Klatzkin, Yaakov, 69, 216n45, 223n95, 228n45

Klausner, Joseph, 69, 75, 227n38

Kleinman, Moshe, 69

Kohn dichotomy. *See* civic-versus-ethnic contrast; Kohn, Hans

Kohn, Hans: biographical sketch, 7–8, 139–44, 157–58, 172–73, 238n9, 239n11; legacy of, 182; pacifism of, 140–44; photo of, *134*

—*Intellectual influences:* Ahad Ha'am, 17, 165, 170, 173–74; Arendt, 175; Bourne, 242n74; Buber, 133, 135–36, 139, 143, 149–52, 153–54, 156, 159, 162–63, 165, 170, 172–74, 240n45; English political philosophy, 163–67, 168–69, 244n114; European colonialism, 153–56; German *Kultur,* 240n45, 241n49; Jewish nationalism, 160–64, 172–73, 191–93, 243n88; Kallen, 242n74; Swiss nationalism, 169, 244n116; Zimmern, 168, 242n74

—*Nationalism:* on American nationalism, 157–58, 162, 163–69, 244nn100,117, 245n122; collective solidarity and, 145–48, 161, 166–69, 171–72; counterstate approach of, 39–40, 147, 165–71, 176–77, 179, 211n6; good vs. bad nationalism, 162–63, 175–76, 241n49; Greek political philosophy and, 160, 243n90; on Jewish humanism, 148–54, 160–61; on multinational federations, 154–55, 244n119; on Romantic nationalism, 136–37, 161–62, 175–76; sovereignty as evolutionary stage toward, 161; transnational solidarity, 159–60; typology of nationalism, 159–61

—*Works:* "Nationalism" (1921), 144, 149–50, 161; *Nationalismus* (Nationalism; 1922), 156–57; *Die Politische Idee des Judentum* (The Political Idea of Judaism; 1924), 11, 149–50, 159, 160, 243n90; *Hapo'el hatza'ir* series (1926), 154, 166; *Toldot hatenu'ah hale'umit ha'aravit* (A history of the Arab nationalist movement; 1926), 152–53; *Perakim letoldot hara'ayon hatzioni* (A

history of Zionist thought; 1929), 11, 149, 151, 159; *Martin Buber* (1930), 139, 172–73; *The Idea of Nationalism* (1944), 11, 120, 136, 158–61, 162–64, 243n90; "Ahad Ha'am" (1951), 173; *Nationalism* (1955), 243n88; *American Nationalism* (1957), 11, 163–69; *The Age of Nationalism* (1962), 244n119; newspaper and journal writings, 140, 142, 172

—*Zionism:* binational Palestine model, 154–55, 166–67, 169, 241n63, 242nn71,73; German Zionist influences, 11, 32, 137, 158, 163, 171, 174–75, 241n49; on humanist-Zionist incompatibility, 208; transnational Zionism, 173–74; views of Palestine, 117, 135–36, 140, 141–44, 152–54, 165–67

See also civic nationalism; civic-versus-ethnic contrast; cultural humanism; Rawidowicz-Kaplan-Kohn

Kotzkin, Amnon Raz, 175

Krochmal, Nachman, 228n52

Kultur, 50–51, 110, 146–48, 222n81, 240n45

Kymlicka, Will: on minority group rights, 121, 184–85, 190, 235nn65,73; on multicultural citizenship, 126, 217n49, 246n12; on nonstatist nationality, 14; on substatist identity, 213n25

Landauer, Gustav, 139

Lavsky, Hagit, 144, 215n34, 241n63

liberal nationalism: chosenness incompatible with, 122–24; communitarianism and, 222n76; as counterstate nationalism, 25; cultural uniformity and, 190–91, 216n38; ethnocultural belonging and, 30–31; individualism and, 48–50; Jewish nationalism as counterpoint to, 193–94; particularist humanism compared with, 189–90; public vs. private sphere in, 126, 132. *See also* democracy; ethical nationalism; minority national groups

libertas differendi (right to differ), 50, 89–91, 189–90

Liebman, Charles, 234n49

linguistic nationalism: cultural Zionism

and, 46–47; form vs. content in, 75–76, 228n39; global Hebraism and, 67–68, 75–81; interpretation vs. everyday usage as source of solidarity, 79–81; national civilization and, 112. *See also* Hebrew language and literature
lo'az (non-Jewish influence), 9–10
long-distance nationalism, 25. *See also* minority national groups
Lorberbaum, Menachem, 194

Magnes, Judah, 8, 124, 144, 175
Maimonides, Moses, 66, 227n32
Mann, Thomas, 241n49
Margalit, Avishai, 246n10
Marshall, Louis B., 212n12
Marxism, 117
maskilim, 67, 76
Mazzini, Giuseppe, 41
McKim, Robert, 119
McMahan, Jeff, 119
Meinecke, Friedrich, 39, 146
melting-pot discourse: Americanization campaign, 34–36; civic nationalism and, 41–43, 169–71; Kallen critique of, 46–47, 50–51; in Kohn theory of American nationalism, 165–71; national civilization and, 104; Palestine as setting for, 54
Mendelsohn, Ezra, 214nn27,28, 216n45, 226n27
Mendelssohn, Moses, 123
Menorah Journal, 51, 101, 105, 156, 220n46
messianism, 10, 81–89, 149–52, 163–64, 229nn54,63, 230nn64,66
Michels, Tony, 220n52
Mill, John Stuart, 13, 49, 167, 170, 222n73
Miller, David, 119, 121, 190, 217n49, 235n68, 247n13
minority national groups: Ahad Ha'am theory of imitation for, 45–46, 221n60; American Jewish nationalism and, 108–109; anti-essentialist conceptions of, 185–86, 246n10; Arab Palestinian minority, 54–55, 91–92; communitarianism and, 222n76; dissimilation and, 46; ethical nationalism and, 119–24, 190–91; globalization and,

25; immigrant vs. displaced minorities, 184–85, 246n8; interwar minority rights initiatives, 30; Jewish marginalization in ethnicity discourse, 184–85, 196; Kaplan theory of democracy and, 10–11; Kohn critique of cultural pluralism, 166–71; League of Nations stance on, 218n5; minority rights under British Internationalism, 54–55; minority rights under liberal democracy, 30–31, 89–91, 104–106, 190–91; moral value of diversity, 48–50; multicultural citizenship, 25, 190, 234n46, 246n12; multiculturalism, 95–96, 126, 184, 196, 228n50; multinational state paradigm, 37–38; nationalism/sovereignty and, 118–22; nativism and racial nationalism in the U.S., 33–34, 218n14; Nazi anti-Jewish initiatives, 116–17; racial assumptions in civilization nationalism and, 53; religious nationalism and, 107–108, 113–16, 127; right-to-differ principle, 50, 89–91, 189–90; Romantic nationalism and, 44–45; self-governing rights and, 124–27; sovereignty and, 8–9, 118–22, 217n49; symbiotic national-collective loyalties, 48–49; voluntary membership, 33, 35, 119, 122–25, 248n24. *See also* civic-versus-ethnic contrast; cultural pluralism; ethnicity; race
Mizrachi party, 99–100
modernism: colonial power differentials and, 52–53; in Kohn theory of nationalism, 153; Rawidowicz critique of, 83–84; teleology of difference and, 18, 50
Moore, Deborah Dash, 232n6
Morefield, Jeanne, 52–54, 59
Moyn, Samuel, 215n35
multicultural citizenship, 25, 190, 217n49, 234n46, 246n12
multiculturalism, 95–96, 126, 184, 196, 228n50. *See also* minority national groups
multinational state paradigm: Ahad Ha'am theory of imitation and, 46, 221n60; experiments with

multinational federations, 37–38, 155–56; global national identity and, 56; Kallen cultural pluralism and, 41–43, 50–51, 105; Kaplan federation of nationalities, 122–25, 156, 167; Kohn binational Palestine model and, 154–55, 166–67, 169, 241n63, 242nn71,73; Kohn critique of cultural pluralism, 166–71; national civilization and, 118–22; Zimmern theory of internationalism and, 40–41, 50–53. *See also* British internationalism; diaspora paradigm; transnationality

Myers, David, 2, 63, 69, 211n6, 214n30, 215n36, 228n51

Myrdal, Gunnar, 164–65

myth, 64, 81–89, 229n54

Nathans, Ben, 214n27

national civilization, 4, 10–11, 96–97, 203; chosenness incompatible with, 122–23; civilization nationalism and, 50–51; "civilization" term in, 104, 109–10, 131–32, 232n6; counterstate nationalism and, 180, 185–86; function vs. content in, 112; homeland discourse and, 128, 237n100; intellectual influences on, 27; Jewish nationalism and, 96, 111–12, 113–16, 127, 131–32, 191–93; "nationhood" concept and, 103–104, 109–10; political dichotomies compared with, 15; religious collectivity importance in, 10, 187, 190; repressive nationalism and, 116–22; in the U.S. civil rights movement, 109; völkisch nationalism and, 111; voluntary membership, 122–26; as Zionist approach, 128–31, 138

nationhood: cosmopolitan languages and, 77; counterstate vs. state-seeking typologies of, 14–15, 26–27; "ethnopolitical entrepreneurism" as counterdiscourse, 18–20; historical narrative and, 216n40; invented nationhood, 13; Kohn definition of, 159–61; minority national groups and, 118–22; in national civilization approach, 109–10; nation-state analytical distinction, 12–13, 146–47; peoplehood compared

with, 198, 233n17; polycentric vs. ethnocentric nationality, 121–22; statism as popular paradigm for, 2–3, 103; as term in *Judaism as a Civilization*, 103–104. *See also* collective solidarity; nation-state paradigm

nation-state paradigm: as cause of WWI, 30; false dichotomies of Jewish nationalism, 44, 56, 93, 183–84; "First House" symbol and, 82–87, 228n51; German fascism as articulation of, 85; nation-state analytical distinction, 12–13; as normative post-WWII paradigm, 58–59, 103; theoretical benefits of, 183; theories of nationalism and, 30–31; WWI effect on, 8. *See also* "sovereign mold" principle

nativism, 33–34, 98, 218n14

Nazism: absolute national sovereignty in, 119, 122; anti-Jewish initiatives, 116–17; German völkisch nationalism and, 111; Rawidowicz history of German fascism, 85; Zionist negation of the diaspora, 29, 69. *See also* Germany; Holocaust

Netherlands, 162

Neusner, Jacob, 201–202

Niebuhr, Reinhold, 117, 119

otherness: American Zionist philosophy and, 37; in contemporary diversity discourse, 185, 196; *eruvin* as boundary creation, 78–80, 89; European views of Palestinian Arabs, 53–54, 153–54; in Greek vs. Jewish philosophy, 160–61; in Kohn theory of American nationalism, 162; normative citizenship and, 35–37; philosophical critique of, 19; self-as-other as ethical principle, 120

Oz, Amos, 69

Palestine: Arab riots of 1929, 128, 136, 142–43; Balfour Declaration, 26, 29, 128, 142–43; binational plan for, 152–56, 166–67, 169, 241n63, 242nn71,73; Dubnow opposition to Jewish centralization, 38; in global Hebraism, 9–10; as Hebrew language center, 68, 75–81, 225n14; history of Jewish settlement, 57–58, 99–100; Jewish national culture and, 226n27; Kallen bicultural model for, 223nn90,91; Kaplan views of, 118, 128–31, 237n104; Kohn views of, 117, 135–36, 140, 141–44, 152–54, 165–67; national civilization relevance for, 10–11; Rawidowicz family relocation to, 68; world state proposal for, 129–30; Zionist approaches to settlement, 19–20. *See also* Arab Palestinians; Israel

Paris Peace Conference, 26, 29, 30

particularism: Jewish humanism and, 148–52, 160–63, 189–90; Kaplan ethical nationalism and, 119–21, 235nn65,66,68; Kohn pluralism approach and, 167–68, 176–77; national civilization and, 121, 132; universal through the particular (*revah derekh tzimtzum*), 83, 196–97. *See also* universalism

patriotism, 31, 35–36, 190–91

Penslar, Derek, 215n37

peoplehood: global Hebraism and, 92–93; interwar Zionist development of concept, 3, 23–24; Jewish diaspora peoplehood, 56, 173–74, 198–99; Kaplan's use of term, 197–98, 233n17; Kohn's transnational view of, 173–74. See also *Am Yisrael* (people of Israel); collective solidarity

pluralism. *See* cultural pluralism

political Zionism, 16–17, 214n33, 231n3

Pollock, Sheldon, 77

post-nation-state paradigm: Jewish collective as, 38; postnationalism, 38–39, 57, 108, 217n48; Rawidowicz theory of collective solidarity and, 10, 79–80; stateless nationalism as post-nation-state ideal, 57, 194, 196

progressivism, 35–36

Putnam, Hilary, 194

race: civil rights movement, 109, 164; descent-based identity and, 47, 146–47; melting-pot discourse and, 104; nativism and racial nationalism

in the U.S., 33–34, 116, 218n14; in Nazi ideology, 85; parallel between black and Jewish intellectuals, 247n17; racial assumptions in civilization nationalism, 53; Romantic nationalism and, 45; slavery in the U.S., 164; victimization discourses and, 184, 246n7; whiteness (of diaspora Jews), 5–6, 218n14, 246n7. *See also* ethnicity; minority national groups

Rashi, 66

Rauschenbusch, Walter, 116

Ravid, Benjamin, 226nn17,23

Rawidowicz, Chaim Isaac, 100

Rawidowicz, Simon: on Arab Palestinians, 91–92, 181, 231n75, 248n36; biographical sketch, 7, 62–63, 65–70, 172–73, 214n30, 223n99, 226nn17,18,23, 232n9; in classroom Zionism exercise, 201–202; critique of Ahad Ha'am, 72–73, 227nn28,30; on dichotomy in Jewish identity, 56, 93; on emancipated national culture, 72–74, 155, 204–205; Jewish political tradition and, 66, 191–93; Jewish textual tradition and, 66–67, 73–81, 227n38; Kaplan connections and parallels, 93, 99–101; Kohn compared with, 171–72; on minority rights, 89–93, 209; on myth and messianism, 81–89, 229nn54,63, 230nn64,66; on the name "Israel," 61–62; photo of, *60*; rejection of secular terminology, 10; on the "right to be different," 50, 89–91, 189–90; theory of territoriality, 72, 188–89

—*Works:* "Kiyum hatefutzah" (The endurance of the diaspora; 1934), 69, 85, 93; "Libertas Differendi" (1945), 89–90; "Al parashat batim" (Israel's Two Beginnings: The First and Second "Houses"; 1957, from *Babylon and Jerusalem*), 81–87, 228nn51,52, 229n55; *Babylon and Jerusalem* (1957), 65, 70–71, 81–83, 86–89, 173, 181, 227n32; "Bein ever ve'arav" (Between Jew and Arab; 1957, unpublished manuscript chapter from *Babylon and Jerusalem*), 90–91; "On Interpretation" (1957), 78

Noam Pianko is the Samuel and Althea Stroum Assistant Professor of Jewish Studies and International Studies in the Jackson School of International Studies at the University of Washington, where he also serves as the undergraduate program adviser for the Jewish studies program. His research interests include Jewish political thought, modern Jewish intellectual history, Zionism, and American Judaism. He has published in *Jewish Social Studies, American Jewish History, American Studies, The Encyclopedia of Religion in America,* and *Ab Imperio.*

9 780253 221841